# THE MESSIANIC CHARACTER
# OF AMERICAN EDUCATION

# The
# MESSIANIC
# CHARACTER
## of
# AMERICAN
# EDUCATION

STUDIES IN THE HISTORY
OF THE PHILOSOPHY OF EDUCATION

*by*

## ROUSAS JOHN RUSHDOONY

*with*

INTRODUCTION BY IVAN R. BIERLY
APPENDIX BY DAVID L. HOGGAN

Presbyterian and Reformed Publishing Company
Phillpsburg, New Jersey

*To Dorothy, with love*

# THE AUTHOR

Rousas J. Rushdoony, editor of the *Philosophical and Historical Studies* of the International Library of Philosophy and Theology and of the University Series (*Historical Studies*), is an American writer and scholar. An ordained minister in the Orthodox Presbyterian Church, he has been a missionary among Paiute and Shoshone Indians as well as pastor of two churches. Currently engaged in research, he also lectures extensively. A contributor to many theological and philosophical journals, he is the author of *By What Standard?*, *Freud* and *Van Til* (Modern Thinkers Series), *Intellectual Schizophrenia*, *This Independent Republic*, *The Nature of the American System*, *The Mythology of Science,* and *Foundations of Social Order.*

# Contents

# Preface

It is a characteristic common to the various professions that no criticism is so much resented as that coming from outside the fraternity, which, of course, is the usual source of attack. Criticism from within the profession is often discounted because the critic is ostensibly a disgruntled partisan of a rejected cause, and criticism from without is regarded as inadmissible because inexpert. This hostility to criticism is not the peculiar possession of any one profession but a monopoly of man. We should not be surprised, therefore, to find it in educators, nor should we regard their sensitivity to it as their peculiar possession. Whatever their shortcomings, they are also the burden-bearers of all kinds of social expectations and hopes. We should not be surprised then at the intensity of their resentment to criticism. One school superintendent in California recently declared, according to the *Palo Alto Times,* November 14, 1962, that educational critics, "many of them admirals and generals," are "irresponsible" and "have the same effect on American education as subversives have." However much such sensitivity to criticism must be by-passed by the scholar, it must still be remembered that very often this sensitivity is a characteristic of dedicated and hard-working men who are honestly irritated by the facile criticism of outsiders. It is one thing to criticize educators, doctors and lawyers, another to meet concretely and answer the problems indigenous to their professions. Nonetheless, every profession flourishes, not only in terms of its own inner elements of growth, but by its ability to draw on resources beyond its borders, by its readiness to evaluate and utilize criticism, and by its recognition of its interdependence with those whom it serves. Admirals and generals, as well as other critics, have no monopoly on error, nor on truth, for that matter, and the same is true of professional men, including educators.

This writer is neither an admiral nor a general, nor is he a practicing teacher. He is not, let it be added, a "subversive." On the other hand, he does have a life certificate, general secondary, in the State of California, an M.A. in education, and has served as a school board member in another state. He has had the assistance, in this study, of various educators, on the grade, high school, and teacher's college levels. But, whatever the background and assistance, this work, of course, must stand on its own merits.

This study is intended to be not only an historical and analytical study of the philosophies of education in state education in the United States, but also a study in an important aspect of American cultural history. If the writer shows what seems to be an uncommon dissent, let it be noted also that for some of the more recent, and controversial, educational thinkers he holds at the same time a marked respect.

This writer is grateful to Dr. Ivan R. Bierly, who made this work possible, for his encouragement to the writing of this study (begun in 1957), to Dr. David L. Hoggan, who prepared the appendix, and to Mrs. Frances M. Braun, for many, many kindnesses. The Index was prepared by Miss Vernelia Crawford.

Rousas John Rushdoony

*October 15, 1963*

# Introduction

At no time in the history of any nation has so much money and so many hours been devoted to the process of education. Participation is almost universal on the part of America's youth, and much thought is being devoted to putting a college degree within the reach of all.

But, somehow, the equation of purpose and accomplishment still does not seem to balance. Wherever parents gather, concern is expressed about the education of their children, questions are raised—and altogether too often confusion reigns. Most of today's parents are past products of the current process.

At a time when philosophical questions are usually bypassed —even by Doctors of Philosophy—this volume is unique as a systematic presentation and critique of the philosophical issues in education today. A vital new perspective is shed on some aspects of the process, and the presuppositions that are often ignored are clearly presented for public review. For the most part, the professionals speak for themselves in these pages; these are dedicated men, honestly and sincerely using their chosen means to the good society with all the vigor they can command.

That their own presuppositions seriously becloud the defining of a "good society" within their own terms is a little-understood fact of major proportions and is cogently summed up at the end of this volume. Absorbed almost entirely in the process of education, as a rule, it never occurs to these good men that the concepts that they took for granted of a good society were purloined from the Christian heritage that they have studiously ignored or denied.

"Man does not live by bread alone"; this language may be excluded from the public classrooms by court order, but the problem which is here involved for education cannot be avoided. The nature and the character of society, and thus of education, hinges on the accepted concept of man; and, whatever this concept is in a given society, it can be based only on an article of faith.

The prevailing faith about the nature of man in educational circles is that he is the highest form of animal life. Consistently, education is that function which is concerned with conditioning man for his role in life. And what is his role? Obviously, the conditioning cannot be done without a goal in view—and yet it eludes us as we read. There was once no such uncertainty in the classroom, the pulpit, or for the most part in the minds of those who actually lived the events of the writing of the Declaration of Independence and the Constitution. That this was a new charter under God—since recognized in the pledge to the flag—was the assurance of its rightness and of its success. Statutory law, even the Constitution, should reflect God's laws insofar as humanly possible; good laws should be obeyed, and bad laws that flouted the Creator's intent should be ignored.

Either man evolved by chance out of the void and has no meaning or purpose other than what he can command, or he is the product of a Creator and subject therefore to the laws of his Creator. The transition from one of these concepts to the other is illustrated by the three meanings that have been attached, over the years, to "Veritas" on the shield of Harvard University. Initially in John Harvard's own words when he wrote the charter, it referred to the communication of divine truth; later this was transposed to mean the communication of human truth in the Greek sense, and finally to the search for truth in the sense that divine knowledge is only mystical, times are different so we can apply little from the past, and so all things are relative to him who searches today.

Meaning is possible, in more than an ephemeral and transitory sense only as correct knowledge and insights lead to predictability. This presupposes a world of order and law, both in the fields of science and in human relations. Obviously, it would be a violation of the law of contradiction to presuppose that such a world originated and is maintained by the caprice of chance!

The search for truth—the interrelationships of cause and consequence—can have meaning only in a world of predictable relationships. Loyalty and even patriotism can and did arise under these circumstances. Education has a genuine mission to fulfill. It was consciousness of the need for understanding in a new nation under God that men should understand their nature and their nation and their own responsibilities that prompted Jefferson to plead the case for public education in Virginia. But even he expressed the view on one occasion that he would as soon see the farms and the factories managed by the state as to see local public education subsidized by the state.

As the prevailing concept of man has changed from God-centered to man-centered, in part as the general acceptance of Darwin's theory of evolution has appeared to permit the putting of God in mothballs, the problems incident to this presupposition have multiplied. The transfer of man's allegiance from God to self has placed an impossible burden on the individual; if the source of meaning and the conceptions of right and wrong are no longer God's responsibility, then *each man* has some fearful decisions to make. In fact, he must either delegate his decisions to others or himself play God.

But when each man must make ultimate decisions, the consequence can be only one thing—anarchy, or war. Even if it is generally accepted that all things are relative, coincident action and or acquiescence must be attained for some matters by some means, and by this time it is clear that only the State is in a position to exercise the force necessary to do this job.

Just as loyalty is adherence to a trust, so treason is failure to abide by the terms of a trust. If all things are relative, and each is entitled to his own views with equal significance given to all views, then there can be *neither loyalty nor treason*. But when the State makes decisions to bring order out of chaos, whether there is loyalty in a moral sense or not, failure to conform is failure in a trust as a member of the society and thus is treason.

The educators of today are aware of the fearsome responsibilities they have undertaken in these times. Whether or not they are fully aware of the road they have followed in the acceptance of these responsibilities, challenges of what they do are, within the "lodge," looked on as obstructionist and a violation of public responsibility. Given the premises, the consequence in this case is predictable, even though most educators might agree that "all is relative."

This book will be bitter medicine, indeed, to those who see the answer to today's problem in more education, unless the question "for what?" is confronted and resolved. Most of modern education is devoted, consciously or unconsciously, to the perpetuation and the extension of the underlying fallacy which has presented the whole effort with its dilemma.

What the educationists have forgotten is that the sense of meaning and purpose in life which they take for granted was bought with the blood of saints from the time of the prophets and Jesus until this day. And the end is not yet in sight. By taking for granted that which can only be acquired by faith, the rationalist tradition of American education has severed itself from its roots, and indeed is paying the penalty for trying to "live by bread alone."

Ivan R. Bierly

Woodside, California

# 1. A Liberal Education

Historically, the orientation of school and university in Western culture has been in terms of concepts of *liberal* education. The differences of opinion have been with reference to what is truly *liberal*. The terms "liberal" and "liberty" are cognate words, alike derived from the Latin *liber, free*. From the days of the Greek city-state, through Roman culture, and to the present, a liberal education has been ostensibly education for freedom and the mark of a free man. But what constitutes a *free* man? And what is the *ground* of his freedom? The question is thus inevitably a philosophical and a religious question, and all the more religious in Western culture because of the influence of Christianity. A liberal education has thus been, either implicitly or explicitly, a religious (but not necessarily Christian) education in purpose and structure.

The question, what constitutes a free man, is also an historical and cultural question. Thus, the American college before 1860 was ostensibly geared to a Christian concept of life, while following a medieval and celibate pattern, and a classical, Greco-Roman, curriculum, aiming to produce young gentlemen in terms of the Enlightenment concept of man. Its concept of a liberal education was thus not systematic but rather traditional. A radical clarification of issues was only to come much later with

1

the progressivists, whose greatest function perhaps was to challenge and steadily shatter the conglomerate and syncretistic character of preceding educational theory.

The syncretism of the older education was furthered by its increasing irrelevance to modern culture. As Lynn White, Jr., able historian and educator, has commented, "the 'liberal' education which was worked out to meet the needs of the old aristocracy of priests and nobles was essentially contemplative, focused on understanding things rather than doing things." It made "a sharp distinction between 'liberal' and 'vocational' education."[1] To the Greek values of truth, beauty and goodness, the "Middle Ages added holiness, which was thought to be either equal to the others or a summation of them." To this has been added, and in many instances substituted, a new value, *skill*, not a value of ends but of means.[2] The change of values has thus led inevitably to a need for a new concept of *liberal* education. If *skills*, scientific and professional, make men free, then skills constitute a liberal education. But if skills are only a necessary but subordinate part of freedom, then *in themselves* they cannot constitute a liberal education, however *necessary* to it. The question again remains basically a religious question, and, to its credit, progressivism has been essentially a religious movement, as indeed has been the whole of the movement from Horace Mann to the present, to liberate man by means of a universal system of state-supported schools.

There has thus been a radically important development in education as a result of the work of the progressivists and their successors. But, while clarifying the issues by their assault on the older and syncretistic philosophies, these proponents of the new education have heightened some of the fallacies of earlier years. As White has observed, in speaking of the masculine and celibate education of the Latin Church:

Aside from natural science, this clergy was personally concerned with three problems: the individual, the state and the church. As the

[1] Lynn White, Jr.: *Educating our Daughters*, A Challenge to the Colleges, p.9. New York: Harper, 1950.
[2] *Ibid.*, p. 11 f.

centuries passed, the influence of the church dwindled, and higher education, apart from science, became focused primarily on the individual and the state. Today all of our humanistic disciplines are profoundly interested in the polarity between these two. Our colleges try to graduate adequately developed persons infused with an understanding of the values of what we call "citizenship," and they do a fairly good job of it. When the safety of the state is threatened, millions gladly offer to lay down their lives. But when the stability of a family is endangered, our college graduates often will not inconvenience themselves to preserve it. They have not been led to feel that the family is basic to their lives or the well-being of the race. The reason, in large part, is that they have been saturated with an education which unconsciously assumes that the educated person is celibate, and which consequently fails to impress them with a sense of the significance of the family as the primary form of human organization and of the importance of their participation in it.[3]

If statism is freedom, then contemporary education is thoroughly liberal. But if the superimposition of the state (or the church) on every order of life and every sphere of human activity is by no means to be identified as liberty, then education today is definitely illiberal. Liberty is not license, and liberty and law are inseparable, but law is not the prerogative of church or state but rather the condition of man, an inseparable aspect of life and environment, and hence coextensive and coterminous with existence. Thus, while a truly liberal education is in terms of a basic concept of order and law, that order cannot be institutionalized, or reduced to an order such as church and state, without a destruction of the liberty desired. No institution can incarnate in itself that which is a part of the total condition of life and therefore of its own existence. Wherever church or state have claimed a prior, or any, jurisdiction over every other sphere of human activity or institution, there has been, with the realization of their claim, a steady diminution of liberty and the substitution of an institutional bureaucracy for law. The emancipation of education from ecclesiastical control was thus a major advance in liberal education, but a truly liberal or free education must be free also of the state, from its support or control.

[3] *Ibid.*, p. 72.

White is correct in viewing higher education as aristocratic, masculine, celibate and statist, while calling attention to the strongly democratic nature of primary and secondary schools. On all levels, however, the statist emphasis has been predominant. The state is the order of liberty, and the school is the means whereby citizens are prepared for the good life. The state has become the saving institution, and the function of the school has been to proclaim a new gospel of salvation. Education in this era is a messianic and a utopian movement, a facet of the Enlightenment hope of regenerating man in terms of the promises of science and that new social order to be achieved in the state. In the United States, it was very early believed that the new federal union constituted the new order of the ages, and the dollar bill today carries this proud description of that hope, *novus ordo seclorum*. This faith was not limited to the United States but shared everywhere by the sons of the Enlightenment, who held with Shelley, who declared in *Hellas* (1821), that

> The world's great age begins anew,
> The golden years return.

Bredvold has called attention to "some of the doctrines" of the Enlightenment's "approaching Millennium." They were, first, "the rejection of history, of the inheritance from the past . . . Let us wipe the slate clean and begin all over again." The clean slate concept was and is basic to the psychology of the modern era. Second, and in essence one with the first, was a rejection of institutions and customs—other than the state. Third, it held that "Our effort to improve life must therefore be directed, in the first instance, not at any supposed evil within human nature, but at the evil in the environment." Man's viciousness is a social product, since man is basically passive, his activity being essentially responsive rather than inherently determinative. Fourth, it was and is held that "by changing human institutions human nature itself will be born again." Fifth, the new managers of man are "the scientific moralists and law-givers, the educators, the statesman."[4]

[4] Louis I. Bredvold: *The Brave New World of the Enlightenment*, p. 111 f. Ann Arbor: The University of Michigan Press, 1961.

The new philosophy, empiricism, led to a conception of the mind as passive, priority resting with the stimulus. Locke's clean slate concept popularized this faith. The mind receives and tnen acts in response and is in this sense passive and receptive. The area of initiation and creativity is the area of the stimulus, the environment. Thus, delinquency has come to be seen as no more than a response, i.e., to a lack of love, education or control in the environment. Human activity is hence seen as conditional and responsive, and the necessary consequence of this is not only the basic passivity but also the ostensible *malleability* of the mind and of man. This means that not man but the controlling environment is master, and that controlling environment, it is held, must be the state and the state school. The result has naturally been a renewed emphasis on education, but also an increasingly negative attitude towards a consistently liberal education. If man, as the empiricism of Enlightenment culture holds, is basically passive and malleable, then can he be truly free? Is a liberal education possible? However formally adhered to, is it not essentially denied?

An observation by White is pertinent:

Seventeen years ago the sight of new schoolhouses adorned with fasces in the remote villages of Sicily first began to sap my typically American confidence in education-as-such. So long as he remained illiterate, the Sicilian peasant was impervious to fascist indoctrination: to control his mind, Il Duce had to teach him to read. Education is not good in itself, but may be either beneficial or harmful.[5]

Fascist education sought deliberately to indoctrinate the "state's children." Marxist and democratic state educational theories are equally governed by a concept of the passive psychology of man and hence dedicated to an inherently illiberal doctrine of man. Democratic education has none the less dedicated itself to the ideal of liberty and the principle of a universal and liberal education through state controlled and state supported schools. What has been the result of this attempt, and what are its presuppositions?

[5] White, *op. cit.,* p. ix.

# 2. The "Divine Rights" of Education

Education today occupies an equivocal position in contemporary life, functioning both as a scapegoat for every failure and as a catch-all for every hope and expectation of society. The schools and colleges are berated for extending their authority beyond the fundamentals of learning into a program which envelopes the whole child or the whole man, and, at the same time, are given additional responsibilities which can only extend their scope even further. Fundamental to this unhappy and contradictory approach is a messianic expectation of education coupled with a messianic attitude on the part of educators. The attitude of people towards education is that it is a god that has failed and yet a god who can perhaps still be whipped into fulfilling his mission. On all hands, there is a misconception as to the purpose, meaning and function of education in life and society.

Behind this misconception lies a centuries-old conflict between church, state and school. Medieval thought, at times far more imperial than Rome, saw society as an indissoluble unit under the suzerainty of God's visible and manifest authority. According to the ruling ecclesiastical interpretation of the later middle ages, the church was not only the continuation and ex

tension of Christ's authority upon earth, but the bearer of His
authority and kingship over all things in the universe. According
to the familiar words of Boniface's Bull "Unam Sanctam," 1302:

. . we learn from the words of the Gospel that in this Church and
in her power are two swords, the spiritual and the temporal. For
when the apostles said, 'Behold, here' (That is, in the Church since
it was the apostles who spoke) 'are two swords'—the Lord did not
reply, 'It is too much,' but 'It is enough.' Truly he who denies that
the temporal sword is in the power of Peter, misunderstands the
words of the Lord, 'Put up thy sword into the sheath' (Lk. 22:38).
Both are in the power of the Church, the spiritual sword and the
material. But the latter is to be used for the Church, the former by
her; the former by the priest, the latter by kings and captains but at
the will and by the permission of the priest. The one sword, then,
should be under the other, and temporal authority subject to spiritual. For when the apostle says 'there is no power but of God, and
the powers that be are ordained of God' (Jn. 18:11) they would not
be so ordained were not one sword made subject to the other . .
  Thus, concerning the Church and her power, is the prophecy of
Jeremiah fulfilled, 'See, I have this day set thee over the nations and
over the kingdoms,' etc. (Jer. 1:19). If, therefore, the earthly power
err, it shall be judged by the spiritual power; and if a lesser power
err, it shall be judged by a greater. But if the supreme power err, it
can only be judged by God, not by man; for the testimony of the
apostle is 'The spiritual man judgeth all things, yet he himself is
judged of no man' (I Cor. 2:15). For this authority, although given
to a man and exercised by a man, is not human, but rather divine,
given at God's mouth to Peter and established on a rock for him and
his successors in Him whom he confessed, the Lord saying to Peter
himself, 'Whatsoever thou shalt bind,' etc. (Matt. 16:19). Whoever
therefore resists this power thus ordained of God, resists the ordinance of God . . . Furthermore we declare, state, define and pro-
nounce that it is altogether necessary to salvation for every human
creature to be subject to the Roman pontiff.[1]

Historians have unwittingly misinterpreted history by calling

---

[1] Henry Bettenson, ed.: *Documents of the Christian Church*, Oxford: Oxford
University Press, 1943, p. 159 ff.

attention to the fact that Boniface VIII, in making these claims, met bitter hostility, Philip IV of France going so far as to summon the States-General to formulate a charge of heresy and magic against the pope and appeal to a general council for judgment. The insulting abuse of Boniface by French and Italian troops and his subsequent death as a defeated and broken man seem to indicate the failure of a grand idea, too audacious and extreme for his age to accept.

In actuality, however, "Unam Sanctam" voiced only the commonplaces of the age, there being nothing new or novel in the presuppositions and doctrines expressed. The intensity of opposition was precisely because the fundamental validity of the claims were recognized as true but misappropriated. All were agreed that a supreme power, responsible only to God, existed. The question was, who constituted that power? *Sacerdotium, imperium,* and *studium* were the three basic powers or virtues of medieval society whose harmonious functioning was basic to the life and health of Christendom. These three were not conflicting powers but properly cooperating powers, whose harmonious and interlocking functionings were imperative to true society. Church, empire, and university believed in Christendom; they believed that unity was essential; their conflicts were a result of differing opinions as to their respective functions and divinely given rights. As Rosenstock-Huessy has pointed out, the Church, for centuries previously, had never been called *Una Sancta* for the emperor and empire were the symbols of unity and source of authority. The Roman Church was only *prima sedes,* the first among many sees. "On earth the duty of maintaining visible Uniqueness and Unity belonged to the emperor. The popes of the first millennium refused steadfastly to be addressed as 'universal.' "[2] Behind Dante's conception of the Holy Roman Emperor as true vicar lay a long record of historical actuality, of church reform accomplished by imperial power. Otto III exercised apostolic authority using St. Paul's formula in his letters,

[2] Eugen Rosenstock-Huessy: *Out of Revolution,* Autobiography of Western Man. New York: William Morrow and Co., 1938. p. 489f.

calling himself "servus Jesus Christi." The motto of the empire was "Jerusalum visio pacis."[8]

Against this, what Rosenstock-Huessy aptly calls the Papal Revolution asserted at first no new categories of thought but advanced a new claim as to the source of unity and authority, the papacy, with a new source of law resulting. "The popes now called their canon laws by a new term, Ius Poli, the law of the firmament."[4] The Roman Pontiff came to be known as "Most Blessed Lord, Holy Father of Fathers, Pontiff of Christians, Pontiff of all Presidents, by autonomasia Ruler of the Church, Universal Archbishop, Universal Patriarch."[5] His authority was not merely international but rather universal.

Thus empire and papacy, church and state, were at one with regard to the fundamental presuppositions of Unam Sanctam. The Kingdom of God on earth had an earthly and visible authority in which the sovereignty and manifestation of God and His Kingdom were revealed. Both the authentic authority and interpretation of that Kingdom came from that one "supreme power" which could "only be judged by God, not by man." The point of argument was, who is that supreme power? The Roman Church's answer has found developed formulation in the Vatican Council and the dogma of papal infallibility. The imperial answer led to the doctrine of the divine right of kings, the democratic concept of *vox populi, vox dei,* and the Hegelian and Marxist concepts of the historical process and the state.

Society was unitary, authority was central, and was where the Kingdom manifested itself, responsible only to God, and with all other authorities responsible to it and under it. The concept, one Lord, one faith, one baptism, underlies all modern thought; the difference lies in the interpretation of Lord, faith and baptism. Again, authority is in every instance ultimately beyond judgment, whether manifested in the church, the king, the state, democracy, the people, or the proletariat and the historical proc-

---

[8] *Ibid.,* pp. 485-515.
[4] *Ibid.,* p. 518.
[5] Alexius Aurelius Pelliccia: *The Polity of the Christian Church,* J. C. Bellett trans., London, 1883. p. 115.

ess. It asserts itself to be beyond human accounting and sufficient unto itself as far as its responsibility to other human agencies is concerned. Thus it has a high concept of its own freedom and a strict concept of the limitations of other spheres of society. Lenin's words are accordingly understandable when he commented, "It is true that liberty is precious—so precious that it must be rationed." Whether they be philosopher-kings, pontiffs, or leaders of the proletariat, true liberty can be given only to those having true authority. Freedom becomes both the privilege and responsibility of authority, and a necessary condition to its operation. Freedom and authority have thus been closely linked, and the increase of authority in any one realm means a corresponding decline of freedom in another.

The medieval church and state were thus deeply concerned with limiting one another. In the first millennium of the church's history, since no great threat existed to the state's manifest authority as the visible sovereignty of the Kingdom of God, her attitude to the Church could be more liberal because it was paternalistic. The conflict came with the church's claim to that same visible sovereignty.

But an important and unduly neglected claim arose from another direction, the university. There were thus three areas claiming to be ministers of God and authentic priests and prophets, mediating and interpreting the Kingdom of God. Priestly robes became not only the garb of the ecclesiastical hierarchy but of the state, lawyers and judges declaring their priesthood in their black robes. The universities also, in their academic hoods and gowns, revealed their priestly role and origin as mediators and interpreters of the mysteries of the Kingdom, their graduates "bachelors," the young gentry or apprentices in the arts. Students at universities who were foreigners had originally no legal rights, lacking local citizenship, and, as a result, came to be organized as guilds or nations, each having their rector, who served as a consul or bishop to protect the rights of citizens in an alien land. The recognition of student rights began as an outgrowth of certain conceptions of personal law and influenced by the contemporary guild movement, but it developed ultimately into a concept of independence of the university and its men as such from other authorities. Wherever a student or scholar was involved as plaintiff or defendant, the universities claimed for the rectors an exclusive jurisdiction in all cases, a claim comparable to the church's right to try priests in her own courts. The long political history of this claim is not our concern, but rather its relationship to the modern doctrine of academic freedom. Although, over a period of centuries, the immunity from civil law was gradually eliminated, the universities asserted increasingly in the areas of thought a concept of the same immunity. The world of the university was a priesthood and a brotherhood, a privileged realm, so that in some Spanish universities, the new doctors were invested with the sword; "in all universities the ring formed one of the insignia of the doctorate, and at Vienna the preliminary bath of the candidate for knighthood appears to have been imitated by candidates for degrees."[6] Scholars were thus a brotherhood, a priesthood, a knighthood, whose importance was not lost on church or state, both of whom sought to control this third power, either by limiting the study of secular law, or by emphasizing it, in order to have an ally in the university. Beginning with Charles V, for example, the University of Paris was called "The eldest daughter of the King." The university had a privileged place both in the state, in the States General in France, for example, and in the church by virtue of the priestly status of scholars.

For some time, the University of Paris exercised a "theological dictatorship" in the church; "again and again Paris led the way and Rome followed."[7] Pope Alexander IV was compelled to condemn the Franciscan "Everlasting Gospel." Later, Pope John XXII, in another controversy involving the Franciscans, was reprimanded by Paris and brought to a humble apology for daring to offer a pronouncement on matters of faith. The Coun-

[6] *The Universities of Europe in the Middle Ages,* Vol. I, Salerno-Bologna-Paris. Hastings Rashdall. 3 vol. ed. ed. by F. M. Powicke and A. B. Emden. Oxford University Press, 1936, p. 287.

[7] *Ibid.,* p. 549.

cil of Constance (1414-1418) was an instance of the power of the University of Paris, but "When no council was sitting, the University of Paris was able to act as a sort of standing committee of the French, or even of the Universal Church." Paris became " 'the first School of the Church'—the theological arbiter of Europe" and exercised a "theological dictatorship."[8] At Constance, not only was Pope John XXIII deposed, but the superiority of the Council over the pope asserted. In its fourth session, on March 30, with the Emperor Sigismund present, the direct authority of the council from Jesus Christ was asserted, an authority which every person, including the pope himself, must obey in all matters pertaining to the faith, the extirpation of schism, and in the reformation of the Church in its head and in all its members. In 1682, this session and its decrees, together with the fifth session, was approved in full and received by the clergy of France. On May 14, Pope John XXIII, in submitting to the council, recognized it as holy and infallible, although against his will. Between the 42nd and 43rd sessions, the new pope, Martin V, confirmed the acts of the Council. The Council of Basle in 1431 reaffirmed these principles, and, when Pope Eugene resisted, the Council named Amadeus pope under the name of Felix V, and he was so recognized by various monarchs and princes, and the universities of Germany, Paris, and Cracow.[9] A century earlier, the power of the University of Paris was officially recognized by Pope Benedict XII, himself a D.D. of the Cisterian College of Paris, when he "began the custom of officially notifying his election to the university, which was thus recognized as one of the great powers of Europe."[10] The failure of the councils was the failure of the universities as well; they represented a professionalism concerned mainly with reforming the workings of the church, rather than the church itself, of ending scandal rather than the source of scandal. The councils did nothing to further reform; they functioned to destroy it at Con-

[8] *Ibid.*, p. 547f.
[9] See Edward H. Landon: *A Manual of Councils of the Holy Catholic Church,* vol. I, Edinburgh: Grant, 1909, pp. 69-90, 173-184.
[10] Rashdall, *op. cit.*, p. 554.

stance. They did not challenge the concept of authority; they questioned its current location.

The result was the failure, not only of the conciliar movement, but of the universities, and their consequent decline. In recent years, scholars have endeavored to show that the universities of the later middle ages were neither as devoid of students or of competent studies as sometimes assumed. But this is not the point. What happened was that, while functioning as a necessary part of professional machinery of the age, the universities became increasingly irrelevant to the temper of the age, a relevancy restored by Luther. The Reformation was born in a university and it gave renewed status and power to the university throughout Europe.

Why were the universities so powerful? Arab scholarship was meaningless in terms of Muslim culture, the scholars merely court favorites without standing. Scholarship was suppressed, and books burned without leaving a ripple of influence except on Christendom. Thus, while Arab scholarship was at times freer and bolder, it was Christian scholarship which had a vital relationship to its society and an authority accordingly. The university was more than a mere creature of the church or state, although both hoped to limit it to the role of an adjunct. In both realms, the scholar had a recognized authority. In Bologna, for example, the rector was formally recognized as ranking above all cardinals and archbishops.[11] Students themselves were able to assert and gain extensive powers. Moreover, universities sought independence, securing benefit of clergy for their members, jails in Germany for their own courts and members, and, as in England, their own representatives in Parliament.

Both church and state could claim authority from Scripture, Romans 13 and other passages asserting the ministerial status of magistrates as well as pastors. What the university came to possess was in effect a third ministry, that of reason. Although by 1300 the lawyers tried to theorize that no university could be

[11] Herbert B. Workman: *The Church of the West in the Middle Ages*, vol. II, London: Kelly, 1900, p. 263.

founded except by a pope or monarch, they had to admit that in actuality valid creation could have its source in long custom, *ex consuetudine*. Of the fourteen universities of 1300, nine had their origin *ex consuetudine,* three had been founded by princes, and only two by popes. Yet the university spoke with an authority that at times made the papacy defer to it.

The reason for this independence is two-fold. Its origin was in the biblical concept of the divine ministry, and the Greek conception of the ideas, forms, types, and reason. Status in medieval society required authority, divine authority. Although professionalism prevailed, and church office was no place for a saint or reformer, still the management and control of the machinery required divine authority. In democratic nations, ballot boxes have been stuffed by politicians already in control, not because they could not seize or retain control without benefit of vote, but because the concept of authority they shared required the formal approval of the ballot box, however secured, to ensure legitimacy. The middle ages were no different; however cynical the purely professional clergy might be, they could only conceive of power as founded on divine authority. God had ordained two powers, church and state, each culminating in a head, pope and emperor. To resist them was to resist God, and the question of legitimate rebellion against divine authority was one requiring divine justification or authority, which indeed political theorists and conciliar advocates earnestly sought. The scholar, historically, had a relationship to both domains.

Greek thought regarded the universe, not with the principle of discontinuity held to by biblical thought, but in terms of continuity. There was no radical distinction between Creator and creature, God and man, but rather a scale of being, with differing degrees of participation in being. Man's autonomous reason was capable both of understanding and participating in this scale of being. There was no conception of God as self-sufficient and absolutely independent, nor was there a true concept of creation; neither was it necessary to know God in order to interpret creation. The human mind, freely and independently, was regarded as capable of knowing reality and understanding all facts without reference to God. The Greek conception of reason was closely related to its conception of the soul. Plato sometimes spoke of the soul as having three parts or functions: reason, will and sensuous appetites, with reason being its rational nature, and will the noble part of its irrational nature, and the sensuous appetites the ignoble. At times, he spoke of all three parts, and at other times of the soul only, as immortal. Aristotle's concept of the soul was closely related to his concept of entelechy, and man's real self his rational rather than vegetative and appetitive souls. Man's rational soul guided him in his development and made it possible to consider the mind as actualized body, and the body as potential mind, in this impulse upward to realize perfect Form. Plotinus tied the soul and reason more closely to the Godhead.

Because Greek thought had no conception of an independent and self-sufficient God who is the source of all true authority, it could not develop the authority of this God-related reason. For the Greeks, authority came from the *polis,* not from God. Its deity when manifest as authority was immanent and not transcendent, and lacking in more than local scope, usually in terms of the city-state. Now two concepts were brought together with great potentialities. For the Greeks, the soul was an intimate relation with the world of Ideas, but not itself an Idea, having a vision of reality, the Ideas, and being immortal. Medieval Christianity developed a concept of authority in terms of a transcendent and self-sufficient God. Aquinas maintained that the end of the universe must be the good of the intellect, which is truth. This intellect, independent and autonomous in its functions, had, by its nature, an independence of human authority implicit within it and in addition was linked with God in the scale of being. Revealed truth came from God; reason constituted a separate realm of interpretation which could be shown to be in agreement with the Christian religion. Man ascended by means of the creatures to the contemplation of God, rising step by step in the contemplation of being to the divine truth, with other truths perfecting and preparing the intellect for the divine truth. The principle of interpretation thus comes from man and is applied to God, rather than derived from God and applied to creation, and the superimposition of revelation cannot eliminate this important role of reason. For the consistent Calvinist, by way of contrast, one common principle prevails in regard to reason, revelation, science, all knowledge, namely, that God, as Creator, is also the only interpreter of creation. But, for Scholasticism, reason, while *guided* and *controlled* by revelation, had nevertheless an independence and autonomy. It *confirmed* revelation on independent grounds; it had an independent voice and an independent power, one which had to be controlled because its independence and move to autonomy were recognized. The church thus both expressed its doubts of Aristotle as well as its approval of him within a few years. Reason, in terms of the medieval use of Aristotle, had a tremendous power because of its relationship to God and the soul; it had an authority not possible in non-Christian thought. It could constitute a threat to the church, and also a great bulwark to its authority. Both church and state needed this support. The three great authorities of the middle ages came to be church, state, and reason, and none was above suspicion. Herein was and is the ground of the university's power. The church was the authoritative institution representing revelation, and the state sought its authority not only from revelation but in natural law. The university could rely on the authority of reason, as recognized by church and state and utilized for their own ends. If reason was often in bonds, and the university with it, it was because it was recognized as being a veritable Samson; if often distrusted, it was because it was seen as a Daniel, possessing great power and authority directly from the throne and yet, somehow, alien to it.

The power of the Christian scholar and university was strongly asserted by Luther, as Rosenstock-Huessy has pointed out. This was done in the new biblical confidence in the authority of God and the power of true faith. When, in March, 1552, Luther left his hiding place in the Wartburg near Eisenach, he attempted to reassure the troubled and distressed Prince-Elector by offering him his protection. Frederick had only his secular power, but Luther had the authority of God. "The voice of the prophet speaking to the Kings of Israel, the voice of Paul speaking before the governors of Rome, was made a public institution of the German nation when Luther offered Frederick his protection."[12] As a result, "the universities became the heirs of the bishops' chair, the cathedra. These Katheders became a church-like institution, like the Commons in England."[13] "The chairs of the universities derived all their authority from the fact that they were Christian chairs of the German nation . . . The universities represented the life of the Holy Ghost in the German nation."[14] Teaching was a public trust, and "The public in Germany thought of the universities as *keepers of the nation's conscience* . . . This salvation-character of scholarship, utterly foreign to the rest of the world, is the religious key to the political building erected by the Reformation."[15] This situation ended only in 1918-1933, but was dying in its Christian significance for some time previously.

The salvation-character of scholarship and education was not limited to Germany, however, although best defined there and most systematically Christian. Elsewhere, on the basis of the medieval concept of reason, without Luther's emphasis, the university gradually developed its concept of academic freedom, that is, an independent authority for reason and scholarship which made it responsible to none other, and its concept of the redemptive, authoritative and power-endowing nature of knowledge, of reason, of university and school.

[12] Rosenstock-Huessy, *op. cit.*, p. 389.
[13] *Ibid.*, p. 390.
[14] *Ibid.*, p. 395.
[15] *Ibid.*, p. 399.

# 3. Horace Mann and the Messianic Character of American Education

The messianic character of American education received its direction from Horace Mann (1796-1858), aptly called the "Father of the Common Schools." It would be easy to point out that European educators have surpassed Mann in maintaining that the schools are the means, instruments, vehicles, and true church by which salvation is given to society. The marked difference between continental and American educational theory has been that continental Europe often developed its schools with either a specifically anti-Christian impetus or a post-Christian concept of society, whereas in America, for some time, both because of inherent developments and as a result of Mann's work, education presented its aims as the fulfillment of Christianity. In the controversies with the churches, Mann's stand was basically this, that true religion would best be served by the schools, and that the churches were in error in their interpretation of their faith and its realm. Mann himself was an active and earnest churchman. In Europe, the parochial school was identified with the Christian religion, the public school in many areas with organized and militant secularism, atheism and anti-clericalism. In either extreme, however, education remained messianic in purpose and character. But no understanding of the American school situation is possible without a recognition of the devout and ostensibly Christian intent in its origins.

Mann was a faithful church-goer and a man who spoke religiously of education. His sympathy and theology were Unitarian, but to understand this fact it is necessary to recognize that in the early 19th century Unitarianism had not yet, as it was to do subsequently, separated itself from Christianity. Rather, it presented itself as the true version of Christianity and the fulfillment of Protestantism. It was not yet sufficiently divergent from other groups to be beyond the pale, and Mann's election to the presidency of Antioch College in later years is not too surprising. That college, begun as a denominational school of the Christian Church, could call a known Unitarian without any surprise on either side. Indeed, Mann considered Antioch's establishment as a great forward step in that it was free from Calvinist orthodoxy and could thus constitute "breaking a hole in the wall and letting in the light of religious civilization where it had never shone before."[1] For him, Calvinism was sectarianism, and anything else in varying degrees catholic and libertarian. This was a common opinion in his day, when not infrequently an equal hatred was reserved for Calvinism and atheism, both constituting blasphemy to many ostensible Christians.

The orthodox Calvinism of the day had provided Mann his home church training, his childhood pastor being the beloved Nathaniel Emmons, a kindly and genial man. Yet Mann later described "the inward joy of my youth blighted" by Emmons' teaching and doctrine.[2] That the Calvinism of the age was defective is clear-cut, but had it not been so, Mann's antagonism would have remained. Mann was, as Williams points out, "a thorough believer in the doctrine of the 'perfectibility of man.' "[3] In contrast to all Puritan and Calvinist thought, for

[1] p. 314, E.I.F. Williams: *Horace Mann, Educational Statesman*, New York: Macmillan, 1937.
[2] *Ibid.*, p. 11.
[3] *Ibid.*, p. 205.

him religion was essentially moralism rather than piety.[4] And yet Mann could hark back to the Puritan fathers of New England and consider himself their truer descendant than the current Calvinists. This is a point of no small significance. Both the contemporary Calvinists and the Unitarians felt themselves to be legitimate heirs of the Puritans in religious faith. How was this construed to be true? The Calvinists claimed a theological affinity; they were both committed to the Westminster standards and a common body of divinity or doctrine. Mann, however, and other Unitarians felt they had no less a claim. The difference lay in their respective interpretations of Christianity; for the Calvinists, it was essentially a *salvation* religion; for the Unitarians, it was essentially a *Libertarian* religion. So interpreted by the Unitarians, the Puritans broke with the past and its bondage to create a new and freer society, and America represented the great forward step of Puritan Protestant Christianity. This spirit of freedom was the essence of Christianity, and Christianity so construed rendered the current Calvinists retrogressive, reactionary, and unchristian. The Calvinist approach to Christianity was *theological,* the Unitarian and Mann's was *anthropological.* Thus, a *product* of Christian faith and society was absolutized and made the essence of that faith, thereby destroying it. The disintegrating character of Unitarianism was inevitable because of this confusion.

Mann in his "Prospectus of the Common-School Journal," (November 1838), identified Protestant Christianity with freedom. It has "always tended towards free institutions," and hence needs public schools to survive. Political equality requires an equality of education and character, and hence public schools are a necessity.[5] The Pilgrim Fathers very early required the education of every child, the General Court in 1642 declaring that parents failing to obey would be fined, the purpose of the

[4] For an important study of this distinction, see Joseph Haroutunian: *Piety Versus Moralism, The Passing of the New England Theology.* New York: Henry Holt, 1932. Emmons himself contributed to the change while trying to stem it.

[5] *Life and Works of Horace Mann,* Vol. II. Boston: Lee and Shepard, 1891, pp. 1-32.

act being "to see first that none of them shall suffer so much barbarism in any of their families." Commented Mann, "Such was the idea of 'barbarism' entertained by the colonists of Massachusetts Bay more than two centuries ago."[6] The Pilgrims, Puritans and Unitarians were thus at one in their libertarian impetus, and America was to prosper and become a heaven on earth only as this essential Christianity prospered and freedom found greater sway through education.

Since this implicit interpretation of Christianity was anthropological, the natural realm was of more immediate interest as an arena of revelation than the supernatural. Accordingly, natural law looms large in Mann's thinking.

I believe in the existence of a great, immortal, immutable principle of natural law, or natural ethics,—a principle antecedent to all human institutions, and incapable of being abrogated by any ordinance of man,—a principle of divine origin, clearly legible in the ways of Providence as those ways are clearly manifested in the order of Nature and in the history of the race, which proves the *absolute right* to an education of every human being that comes into the world; and which, of course, proves the correlative duty of every government to see that the means of that education are provided for all . . . the minimum of this education can never be less than such as is sufficient to qualify each citizen for the civil and social duties he will be called to discharge . . The will of God, as conspicuously manifested in the order of Nature, and in the relations which he has established among men, founds the *right* of every child that is born into the world, to see a degree of education as will enable him, and, as far as possible, will predispose him, to perform all domestic, social, civil, and moral duties, upon the same clear ground of natural law and equity as it founds a child's *right*, upon his first coming into the world, to distend his lungs with a portion of the common air, or to open his eyes to the common light, or to receive that shelter, protection, and nourishment, which are necessary to the continuance of his bodily existence . . . No one man, nor any one generation of men, has any such title to or ownership in these ingredients and substantials of all wealth, that his right is invaded when a portion of them is taken for the benefit of posterity. This great principle of natural law may be illustrated by a reference to some of the unstable elements, in regard to which each individual's right of *property* is strongly qualified in relation to his contemporaries, even while he has the acknowledged right of *possession* . . . While a stream is passing through my lands, I may not corrupt it . . nor divert it to any other direction . .[7]

Part and parcel of this thinking was Mann's assumption, "If God is our *Father*, all men must be our brethren."[8] His ideology is so thoroughly the reigning thought of the 20th century, and so axiomatic to the contemporary mind, that it seems almost too familiar to describe. This all-powerful natural law implants "a powerful, all-mastering instinct of love . . . in the parental, and especially in the maternal breast, to anticipate the idea of duty, and to make duty delightful."[9] Thus, not original sin, but natural law and its implanted sense of duty and joy in duty reigns in men. Why then crimes? Failure to educate, failure to utilize this natural law, lead to the social diseases known as ignorance, crime, and poverty. These things are frustrations of natural law and hence alien to man's nature. Education works *with* natural law and in *harmony* with man's basic nature, rather than against his nature as Calvinism asserts with its doctrine of total depravity. In education, therefore, "motives are everything, MOTIVES ARE EVERYTHING." Since duty and a delight in duty is native to man, and goodness also, an appeal to rewards and punishment frustrates true education and is rarely to be resorted to, except in the most extreme cases. Teachers and parents, by rewarding good behavior, pervert their children.

They hire them to go to school and learn, to go to church and remember the text, and to behave well before company, by a promise of dainties. Every repetition of this enfeebles the sentiment of duty, through its inaction, while it increases the desire for delicacies, by its exercise; and as they successively come into competition afterwards,

[7] *Ibid.*, 115f., 118f.
[8] *Ibid.*, p. 218, Eleventh Annual Report, 1847.
[9] *Ibid.*, p. 126, Tenth Annual Report, 1846.

the virtue will be found to have become weaker, and the appetite stronger. Such parents touch the wrong pair of nerves,—the sensual instead of the moral, the bestial instead of the divine. These springs of action lie at the very extremes of human nature,—one class down among the brutes, the other up among the seraphim. When a child, so educated, becomes a man, and circumstances make him the trustee or fiduciary of the friendless and unprotected, and he robs the widow and orphan to obtain the means of luxury or voluptuousness, we exclaim, 'Poor human nature!' and are ready to appoint a Fast; When the truth is, he was educated to be a knave under that very temptation. Were a surgeon to operate upon a human body, with as little knowledge of his subject as this, and whip round his double-edged knife where the vital parts lie thickest, he would be tried for manslaughter at the next court, and deserve conviction.[10]

It was upon these principles that the professional training of public school teachers was established, and modern educational theory is the direct outcome of these ideas. As against the Calvinist conception of man as sinner, man is good; as against the doctrine of man's responsibility and accountability to God, of life as a stewardship, the non-biblical conception of natural rights is introduced into education. *The pupil is therefore a person with rights rather than responsibilities. Instead of being accountable to God, parents, teachers, and society, the pupil can assert that God, parents, teachers and society are responsible to him.* In this conception, nurtured by normal school principles and germinating in the 19th century, lie the essentials of Dewey's educational philosophy and progressive education. The doctrine of the natural rights of man involve a democratization of rights which destroys all other standards save the will of man, thus ultimately destroying man's freedom in subservience to the common will.

The opposition to rewards and punishment is significant. For Mann, punishment excited fear, "and fear is a most debasing, dementalizing passion." When Scripture declares "The fear of the Lord is the beginning of wisdom," Mann notes that while

[10] *Life and Works*, Vol. II, p. 129f., Lecture II, 1838, "Special Preparation a Prerequisite to Teaching."

such fear sometimes indeed checks the growth of vice, "it has, at the same time, a direct tendency to check the growth of every virtue."[11] "The fear of bodily pain is a degrading motive; but we have authority for saying, that where there is perfect love, every known law will be fulfilled."[12] It has been seen that Mann regards this concept of education as an appeal to the divine rather than the bestial in man. Here again an important aspect of Mann's anthropology appears, the divinity in men. God, being divine, needs no motive outside of Himself; He is self-contained and self-sufficient. He is responsible to none, accountable to none, and has no value or standard other than Himself. Every doctrine of man which asserts or implies his divinity, strives to give man this same divine autonomy. Rewards and punishments are tokens of external authority and of accountability. If man is responsible to God, then his sense of duty and his sense of satisfaction are dependent on his relation to God, on his rewards and punishments received from the sovereign God who is arbiter of all his life. If man is a creature of the state, then his sense of duty and satisfaction are dependent on his relation to the state, as Marxist theory asserts, and rewards and punishments must be forthcoming; men must be sent to slave camps, or be proclaimed people's heroes. When man asserts his divinity and his natural rights, then he must either be an anarchist or assert a community of rights and a socializing of man in order to direct and coalesce his common body of divinity and rights. The result is a sovereign and deified state which punishes citizens who fail to understand their rights, and rewards those who exalt the common divinity, the common will. The parenthood of the State was a familiar idiom in Mann's thinking, even as much earlier the motherhood of the Church had been used to assert the nursing rights of that institution over men. "Society, in its collective capacity, is a real, not a nominal sponsor and godfather for all its children."[13] It is a common assumption that the

---

[11] *Ibid., p.* 341f., Lecture VII, 1840, "On School Punishments."

[12] *Ibid.,* p. 74, Lecture I, "Means and Objects of Common-School Education."

[13] *Ibid., p.* 96, Lecture II, 1838, "Special Preparation a Prerequisite to Teaching."

progressive educational concept of educating the whole child rather than giving the fundamentals, or "the 3 Rs," dates from Dewey. Rather, it dates from Mann, and from every attempt to claim the child for the state. "In the education of a human being, all his powers are to be regarded. When the perfection of a work depends upon the proportion and harmony of its parts, the absence of any part defeats the whole."[14] It was only a question of time before the state's claim to the child and the doctrine of natural rights led to progressive education. Indeed, Mann believed "The fundamental maxim of true education is, not so much to inculcate opinions, and beliefs, as to impart the means of their formation."[15]

For Mann, any democratic concept of education rested on three principles of "natural ethics."

The successive generations of men, taken collectively, constitute one great commonwealth.

The property of this commonwealth is pledged for the education of all its youth, up to such a point as will save them from poverty and vice, and perhaps to prepare them for the adequate performance of their social and civil duties.

The successive holders of this property are trustees, bound to the faithful execution of their trust by the most sacred obligations; and embezzlement and pillage from children and descendants have not less of criminality, and have more of meanness, than the same offences when perpetrated against contemporaries.[16]

These principles Mann saw in progress in Massachusetts. "Massachusetts is *parental* in her government. More and more, as year after year rolls by, she seeks to substitute prevention for remedy, and rewards for penalties."[17] Here we see again two basic principles. *First,* the state can reward, because the state as collective man is not an alien principle as is God, for whom

[14] *Ibid.,* p. 19, "Prospectus of the Common-School Journal," Nov. 1838.
[15] Williams, *op. cit.,* p. 38, Annual oration at Brown University to the United Brothers Society, 1825.
[16] *Life and Works,* IV p. 131f., Tenth Annual Report, 1846.
[17] *Ibid.,* p. 132f.

such principles mean an appeal to fear. Mann, while opposing parental, scholastic, and religious rewards and punishment ethics, was ready to condone it and indeed insist on it in the state. For him, compulsory education, which involved coercion and fear of punishment for failing to educate one's children, was beyond question. Rewards and punishment ethics were basic to establishing the state's power and school law. When "the successive generations of men" are "one great commonwealth," the internal affairs of that organism do not constitute an external application of fear and compulsion. It is a matter of internal and natural necessity. *Second,* natural law gives property ultimately to this body, the commonwealth or state, and the state thus exercises the natural rights of the individual by its sovereign actions. Much of the drift to socialism in Western culture, ascribed so exclusively to Marxist influence, is clearly and definitely to be traced to the natural rights and natural law doctrines.

The state thus is the basic institution and therefore the basic educational institution. Not only that, but moral education is also its basic concern, and "the Sabbath school, the pulpit, and so forth" are "cooperative or auxiliary institutions."[18] Certainly the schools had as part of their curriculum in those days moral instruction, and Bible reading. Mann had more than this in mind; education would result in such moral improvement that vice and crime would be eradicated. Education led to self-reformation. Knowledge is not only power but moral virtue. For him, "education is not only a moral renovator, and a multiplier of intellectual power, but . . . the most prolific parent of material riches."[19] The millennium of Christian hope is to be obtained by means of education, "which—so far as human agency is concerned—must be looked to for the establishment of peace and righteousness upon earth, and for the enjoyment of glory and happiness in heaven."[20] Education can become "the most effective and benignant of all the forces of civilization" for two rea-

---

[18] *Ibid.,* p. 159, Report for 1847, 11th Report.
[19] *Life and Works* VII, p. 109, Fifth Annual Report, 1841.
[20] *Ibid.,* p. 128.

sons. First, it has "a universality of operation," and, second "the materials upon which it operates are so pliant and ductile." "As 'the child is father to the man,' so may the training of the schoolroom expand into the institutions and fortunes of the State."[21] "What Paley so justly said of a parent, that 'to send an uneducated child into the world is little better than to turn out a mad dog or a wild beast into the streets,' is just as true when applied to parliament and hierarchy, as when applied to an individual." "For, in the name of the living God, it must be proclaimed, that licentiousness shall be the liberty; and violence and chicanery shall be the law; and superstition and craft shall be the religion; and the self-destructive indulgence of all sensual and unhallowed passions shall be the only happiness of that people who neglect the education of their children."[22] To read Mann, the issue was ostensibly education, or no education. Actually, the issue was between state-controlled education and community-controlled education, and this was the basic issue. Mann's work was two-fold, *first* to secularize education, and, *second,* to make it the province of the state rather than the community and parents. An educational historian has aptly summarized his work. According to Cubberley, *first,* Mann changed the function of education from "mere learning" or religiously oriented education, to "social efficiency, civic virtue, and character." *Second,* he transferred control of community schools into state hands.[23] That "mere learning" as an object of education persisted as long as it did, almost 80 years beyond Mann's day, was due to the fact that rural America made difficult the purposes envisioned by Mann's presuppositions. The urbanization of America destroyed the isolation of American communities and supplanted "mere learning" with "social efficiency" and "civic virtue." Character by this time ceased to be a concern.

[21] *Life and Works,* IV, p. 232f., Twelfth Annual Report, 1848.
[22] *Ibid.,* pp. 380, 403, Boston, 4th of July Oration, 1842.
[23] Ellwood P. Cubberley: *The History of Education,* p. 690. Boston: Houghton Mifflin, 1920.

Education had not been neglected previously; it had been more limited in time, but more intensive in nature. As Mann himself noted, so seriously was responsibility to educate regarded that "In both the Old Colonies of Plymouth, and of Massachusetts Bay, if a child, over sixteen, and under twenty-one years of age, committed a certain capital offense against father or mother, he was allowed to arrest judgment of death upon himself, by showing that his parents, in the language of the law, 'had been very unchristianly negligent in his education.' "[24] All this Mann admired in his forbears, but progress now required secularization and state control.

For Mann, a republic's security rested in morality and intelligence, both the products of education.[25] Education is the cure-all for sin and for the weaknesses of nature.[26] Defective education or the lack of any education are the causes of mob violence and such irresponsible revolutions as that in France. "The mobs, the riots, the burnings, the lynchings, perpetrated by the *men* of the present day, are perpetrated, because of their vicious or defective education, when children."[27] "Education is to inspire the love of truth, as the supremest good, and to clarify the vision of the intellect to discern it." "A love of truth,—*a love of truth;* this is the pool of a moral Bethesda, whose waters have miraculous healing."[28] To make this true education possible, "Two grand qualifications are equally necessary in the education of children —Love and Knowledge. Without love, every child would be regarded as a nuisance, and cast away as soon as born. Without knowledge, love will ruin every child."[29] He spoke of teaching as "an actual predestination of what the rising generation shall

[24] *Life and Works* II, p. 46 Lecture I "Means and Objects of Common School Education."

[25] *Ibid.*, p. 151, Lecture III, 1838 "The Necessity of Education in a Republican Government."

[26] *Ibid.*, pp. 191 ff., Lecture IV, "What God does, and What He Leaves for Man to Do, In the Work of Education."

[27] *Ibid.*, p. 41, Lecture I, "Means and Objects of Common School Education."

[28] *Ibid.*, pp. 80, 82.

[29] *Ibid.*, p. 212, Lecture IV 1840, "What God Does, and What He Leaves for Man to do in the Work of Education."

be."[30] What it would predestine is a new earth, paradise restored to a large measure.

*The Common School is the greatest discovery ever made by man ...* Other social organizations are curative and remedial; this is a preventive and an antidote; they come to heal diseases and wounds; this to make the physical and moral frame invulnerable to them. Let the Common School be expanded to its capabilities, let it be worked with the efficiency of which it is susceptible, and nine-tenths of the crimes in the penal code would become obsolete; the long catalogue of human ills would be abridged; men would walk more safely by day; every pillow would be more inviolable by night; property, life and character held by a stronger tenure; all rational hopes respecting the future brightened.[31]

Here we have two basic claims of professional educators, now long familiar. *First,* we are the agency which can change society and create a true Utopia, paradise on earth, and, *second,* "let it be worked with efficiency," that is, give us the money and we can do it; our failure thus far is your fault in that we have received insufficient funds.[32]

The common schools were thus the cure-all for sin and crime. Education meant moral reformation, moral virtue, knowledge cured sin. Teach physiology, Mann asserted, and youth will be less tempted by "Gin, Swearing and Tobacco."[33] Mann's liberal doctrine of man appeared again in his conflict with the Boston schoolmasters, who, faithful to their Puritan tradition and academic approach, declared that "duty should come first, and pleasure should grow out of it." Involved in this concept is the Calvinist doctrine of man as sinner and accountable to God. For

[30] Williams, *op. cit.,* p. 53.

[31] *Ibid.,* p. 248f., cited from *The Common School Journal,* Vol. III, p. 15, January 1, 1841, introduction.

[32] Yet, according to Mann, who complained of insufficient funds for schools, in one year approximately the same sum was spent for the established churches of Massachusetts as for the common schools, one million dollars of tax funds to both, no small sum in that day. See *Life and Works,* III, p. 134, Tenth Annual Report, 1846.

[33] *Ibid.,* p. 128, 1838 Lecture III "Special Preparation a Prerequisite to Teaching."

Mann, the "pleasure promoting principle" was paramount, "affection first, and then duty."[34] Methods were more important than subject matter, because the person, not the subject matter, was paramount, and the person was one endowed with rights and thus destined to *receive* rather than to *produce*. Riesman, Glazer and Denney, in their analysis of *The Lonely Crowd* (1950), have emphasized the shift from production-centered and morality-centered character to consumer-centered and group-oriented character. This antithesis was present in the conflict between Mann and the school-masters. Mann's concept of education was clearly messianic as well, and his language self-consciously echoes biblical salvationist phraseology. Education is the Messiah. "The question for us is, has not the fulness of time NOW come?"[35] In 1823, at Dedham, in his Fourth of July address, he declared, "Intelligence, like the blood sprinkled upon the doorposts of the Hebrew houses, will prevent the destroying angel of despotism from entering."[36]

The State Board of Education, newly organized and with Mann its first secretary, in approving library books, made, not truth but common consent, the criterion. Its principles of operation were thus in harmony with the Mann creed. On March 7, 1840, in another context, the Committee on Education of the house of representatives reported that the operations of the Board were "incompatible with the principles on which the common schools are founded and maintained." Nothing could have been truer, or more emphatically denied. They found Mann looking to foreign schools, including those of Prussian statism, as his patterns, these schools being alien to the American situation, having been devised, "more for the purpose of modifying the sentiments and opinions of the rising generation, according to a certain government standard, than as a mere means of diffusing elementary knowledge."[37] Mann, however, won the day, and his victory has been so complete that even his

---

[34] *Ibid.*, p. 258.
[35] *Life and Works,* III, p. 466, Eighth Annual Report, 1844.
[36] Williams, *op. cit.*, p. 37.
[37] *Ibid.*, p. 215f.

biographer Williams, professor of education at Heidelberg College, Tiffin, Ohio, a church-related institution, sings the praises of Mann. The Christians are in Mann's camp now. His alien standards have become the American educational creed, and his concept of state education has supplanted the community education of his day; the common school has become the state school, maintaining only the facade of a local board, with increasing pressure at present to abolish this last bulwark of the community against the state.

It should be noted that Mann strongly insisted on the need for more Bible in the schools than existed in his day. He was ready to defend its value and *necessity* with documented testimonies of its effect on the lives of students. But it should be noted that Mann was not interested in the Bible as a means toward promoting *godliness* but rather *social efficiency*. Religion should be used because it is productive of civic virtue; social orientation was everything. Mann's basic principle was the pragmatic use of religion. The basic reference in religion is therefore not to God but to society.

The messianic character of education has not changed; it has only expanded its scope, and, accordingly, its claims to support, financial and intellectual. Sex education, counselling, psychological testing, psychiatric aid, all these things are added in the abiding conviction that knowledge is not only power but moral virtue. Given these things and more, it is asserted the new society will be created. Meanwhile, social disintegration grows more rapidly, for the doctrine of universal human rights ends in the mutual cancellation of rights in either social anarchy or the surrender of rights to the mass man, to the state. Democracy always perishes from an overdose of democracy. Standards perish before majority rule; the group morale outweighs morality; the insistence on rights nullifies the doctrine of responsibility.

Mann was pious, and believed himself to be a true Christian; but *by interpreting Christianity as freedom, and education as salvation,* he undercut both Christianity and the republic. Since his day, Unitarianism has repudiated Christianity and become generally religious, seeing good in all religions; in terms of its basic convictions, this is an honest step. And in terms of Mann's presuppositions, what he envisioned was a new religion, with the state as its true church, and education as its Messiah. Mann's heirs were to make this implicit faith explicit.

# 4. James G. Carter:
## An Engine to Sway the People

James G. Carter (1795-1849) shared with Mann the leader
ship in Massachusetts of the movement for state control and support of the common schools. Carter was influential in securing
passage of enabling legislation, and established, at Lancaster,
Massachusetts, in 1827, one of the earliest normal schools, a private institution.

An earnest and dedicated man, Carter was concerned not only
with state support and control of schools, but also with improved methods of instruction in the various subjects. His specific ideas in this regard are not our immediate concern except
that they indicate not a mere enthusiast (of whom there were
many at this period) but a practical educator.

The Constitution of Massachusetts of 1780 had expressed that
state's interest in education:

Wisdom and knowledge, as well as virtue, diffused generally among
the body of the people, become necessary for the preservation of
their rights and liberties; and as these depend on spreading the
opportunities and advantages of education in the various parts of
the country, it shall be the duty of Legislatures and Magistrates, in
all future periods of this Commonwealth, to cherish the interests of

literature and the sciences, and all seminaries of them; especially the University at Cambridge, public schools, and *grammar schools* in the towns.[1]

The development of this interest into "legislative provisions" was Carter's work, together with Mann's.

The Congressional provision of land for school use was seen by Carter as an important step towards the self-preservation of the union, and he saw education itself as the basic and perhaps only means of preserving the state.

As the first object in the formation of every government is to provide for its own preservation; and as the general diffusion of knowledge and virtue is the most effectual, if not the only means of insuring stability to republican institutions, the policy of the liberal appropriations made by Congress for education, in every new state they incorporate, is undoubtedly an enlightened policy, and worthy of an enlightened and free government.[2]

Education meant an enlightened people, without which free institutions cannot survive. "The only question as to the permanency of free institutions" is the educational one: can "the *whole* population" be kept "so well educated as the existence of such institutions suppose and require?"[3] An educated electorate was, for Carter, a preventative against revolution and a dictatorship. While the burden of taxation for state-supported schools would fall upon the rich, they too would reap a benefit through an educated lower class, which would now no longer be "impatient of the influence and authority, which property naturally confers." The rich would profit from "the improved condition of society, and the increased security of their property."[4] This argument was not infrequently invoked in favor of state education. It would be a mistake, although not an uncommon one, to

[1] James G. Carter: *Letters to the Hon. William Prescott on the Free Schools of New England, with Remarks upon the Principles of Instruction*, p. 23. Boston: Cummings, Hilliard & Co., 1824.

[2] *Ibid.*, p. 18f.

[3] James G. Carter: *Essays upon Popular Education*, Containing a Particular Examination of the Schools of Massachusetts, and An Outline of the Institution for the Education of Teachers, p. 48. Boston: Bowles and Dearborn, 1826.

[4] Carter: *Letters to Prescott*, p. 51.

see this as a capitalistic device of exploitation. *First,* it was coupled with a sincere desire to advance the general welfare, and the proponents were earnest humanists. *Second,* although it was never associated with the name of welfare economy, it was nonetheless essentially identical with it. Whether it be agriculture, labor, or business, whenever and wherever a government exists to serve as the instrument of class welfare, or general welfare, rather than impartial justice, it is not a free economy, and it is a welfare state. Through tariffs, special legislation, subsidies and other means, from very early years, both business and agriculture were recipients of extensive welfare legislation. The New Deal increased, rather than introduced, this welfare legislation and gave a new primacy to labor.

The Tenth Point of Karl Marx's *Communist Manifesto* was a demand for state schools:

10. Free education for all children in public schools. Abolition of children's factory labor in its present form. Combination of education with industrial production, etc., etc.

Marx, no less than Carter, saw education as a means whereby the managers of the state could control society. For Marx, factory labor was to be abolished only "in its present form," and a state-controlled relationship of education and industry effected. For Carter, no less, the school was an instrument of social control, and he quoted with approval Webster's statement, "We regard it as a wise and liberal system of police, by which property, and life, and the peace of society are secured."[5] Early socialists and latter-day mercantilists and interventionists were united in the battle for state-controlled education as a means of social control. The uncontrolled mind was a dangerous mind. Marx, in the *Communist Manifesto,* praised the bourgeoisie for creating "enormous cities" and thus having "rescued a considerable part of the population from the idiocy of rural life." He was not alone in his contempt of the isolated and hence uncontrolled farmer. Marx further declared, in that same document, "The Communists have not invented the intervention of society

[5] *Ibid.,* p. 48.

in education; they do but seek to alter the character of that intervention, and to rescue education from the influence of the ruling class."

For Carter, this intervention, while a great "police" power, had as its noble goal the reformation of the body politic. The "free schools . . . are the foundation not only of our whole system of public instruction, but of all our free institutions. Let our rulers take care, then, that this basis be not allowed to crumble away on any pretense. If it do so, there will be a wrenching in the political fabric . . . and impending ruin."[6] Moreover, Carter believed that he had a democratic concept of 'control'; "But who shall reform the theory and the practice of our discipline for the young, so as to make its influence the greatest and the best upon individuals and upon the public? All. Every member of the community."[7] By this, however, he meant social influences rather than actual government of education, so that the direct control of education by the parents was exchanged for a broader and general education by "influence" and "example." This surrender of education to the state would result in the great benefit of *levelling* classes regularly, and a removal of the fear "that a monopoly of talent, of industry and consequently of acquirements would follow a monopoly of property." This principle, never likely to be fully in operation, would nevertheless further the continual development of a new and natural aristocracy of distinction.

Its tendency, however, is not to level by debasing the exalted; but by exalting the debased. And it is a more effectual check against an aristocracy of wealth, and consequently of political influence, than would be a national jubilee and the equal distribution of property once in fifty-years, without such a principle at the foundation of our system of public instruction. "Knowledge is power," says Lord Bacon; and so is property power, because it will procure knowledge. If we suppose society divided into two classes, the rich and the poor, the property of the former class, if there were no such institution as the free schools, would procure such immense advantages of educa-

[6] Carter: *Essays Upon Popular Education*, p. 33f.
[7] *Ibid.*, p. 8.

tion, as to bring second, third, and any rate talents, into successful competition with those of the first order, without such advantages.[8]

Thus, while Carter saw state schools as a police power and a means to social control, it was not merely to perpetuate class control but to create a constantly new aristocracy and controlling power, with free opportunity provided to the poor for advancement. Ability was to be given priority over property and men of ability given an opportunity thereby to gain property. The *U. S. Review* quoted the foregoing passage and two other paragraphs with approval and urged the support of state schools on the rich: "It is a tax, however, which they ought, and which they are generally willing to pay, because, like every other judicious tax, it strengthens good government, and thus secures to them the enjoyment of their property, which otherwise might be in danger of violation or encroachment."[9] Two facts appear clearly, among others, 1) the rich were "generally willing to pay," i.e., in favor of state education, 2) and they saw it as conducive to social order. The sympathies of merchants were predominantly anti-Calvinist and pro-Unitarian, and hence by no means conservative. They were often not of the colonial aristocracy and hence were ready to see the old order challenged. Without their readiness to tax themselves, the state support of education would have failed.

A third factor was, however, the basic influence in the adoption of state support. The Utopian hopes engendered by the new thought of the day found their focus in education as the means to paradise regained. There were hints of that glorious future. "Bacon has thrown forward an anchor, with which the world has not yet come up."[10] Bacon's philosophical and scientific method was thus already an anchor in that future world, and the ship of state, by means of state education, must be pulled forward into that future, when locks and bars will be unnecessary, and in Webster's phrase, man will have "a security, beyond

[8] *Ibid.*, p. 20.

[9] *U. S. Review:* "Remarks Upon Mr. Carter's Outline of an Institution for the Education of Teachers," p. 8. Boston: University Press, 1827.

[10] Carter: *Letters to Prescott*, p. 122.

the law, and above the law, in the prevalence of enlightened and well principled moral sentiment."[11] The results as Carter saw them were glorious: "The whole earth will then constitute but one beautiful temple, in which may dwell in peace, all mankind; and their lives form but one consistent and perpetual worship."[12] Carter did not say whether it was God or education which was to be so worshiped.

Before this could be done, the state must also train the teachers. Teachers training he saw as the great "engine" of social control:

An institution for the education of teachers, as has been before intimated, would form a part, and a very important part of the free school system. It would be, moreover, precisely that portion of the system, which should be under the direction of the State whether the others are or not. Because we should thus secure at once, an uniform, intelligent and independent tribunal for decisions on the qualifications of teachers. Because we should thus relieve the clergy of an invidious task, and ensure to the public competent teachers, if such could be found or prepared. An institution for this purpose would become by its influence on society, and particularly on the young, an engine to sway the public sentiment, the public morals, and the public religion, more powerful than any other in the possession of government. It should, therefore, be responsible immediately to them. And they should, carefully, overlook it; and prevent its being perverted to other purposes, directly or indirectly, than those for which it is designed. It should be emphatically the State's institution. And its results would soon make it the State's favourite and pride among other literary and scientific institutions. The Legislature of the State should, therefore, establish and build it up, without waiting for individuals at great private sacrifices to accomplish the work. Such would be the influence of an institution for the education of teachers; and such is the growing conviction of the strength of early associations and habits, that it cannot be long before the work will be begun in some form. If it be not undertaken by the public and for public purposes, it will be undertaken by individuals for private purposes.[13]

[11] *Ibid.*, p. 49.
[12] *Ibid.*, p. 123.
[13] Carter: *Essays Upon Popular Education*, p. 49f.

In this amazing statement, it is clear that Carter at one and the same time saw the potential power of *total social control* through controlled teachers and yet believed that this "engine," if controlled by the State, would be both "intelligent and independent"! Carter was ready to see the schools remain private, if necessary, if only teachers could be controlled, and yet he could believe that such a control could produce an independent-spirited education. How did he reconcile total control and freedom? The answer was simplicity itself. The State, like God, was beyond suspicion. It was the vehicle of social salvation and the order of that redeemed life, and the state school was its handmaiden. True order and true liberty were synonymous with the triumph of the American states and the federal union, the destined vessels of redemption. The church was viewed with suspicion, but not the State.

This refusal to be suspicious of the state in America led to a readiness to examine and adopt practices of European state-controlled education while frankly acknowledging their use by despots. The Ohio Legislature actually requested Calvin E. Stowe (husband of Harriet Beecher Stowe, author of *Uncle Tom's Cabin*) to study European state schools as a guide to education in Ohio.[14] *The colonies had rebelled against the omnipotence of parliament. A new doctrine, the omnipotent rights of man, had arisen. Those rights were now identified increasingly with the state, popular sovereignty conferring an omnipotence upon the state and making it thereby the true realm of right and of human fulfillment.* James Carter was instrumental in creating a mighty "engine" to sway the people; it was not to go unused, and, a century later, the implications of its potentialities became a major issue as men began to use that engine to recreate society with dedication and with zeal.

[14] See Calvin E. Stowe: *Report on Elementary Public Instruction in Europe,* made to the Thirty-Sixth General Assembly of the State of Ohio, December 19, 1837. Boston: Dutton and Wentworth, 1838. See also Edgar W. Knight, ed.: *Reports on European Education by John Griscom, Victor Cousin, Calvin E. Stowe.* New York: McGraw-Hill, 1930.

# 5.  Edward A. Sheldon:
# Oswego and the Secular School

Edward Austin Sheldon (1823-1897) best illustrates why state support of education triumphed in the United States. Many of the early champions of secular education were Protestant clergymen, very often of unorthodox tendencies, and Unitarians were notable in their zeal for all kinds of statist activities, with education gaining particular emphasis. But Sheldon, who had planned to enter the ministry, came from a home dedicated to Calvinism "of the New England type." His father gave a set of Emmons' sermons to each child, had daily prayer with the family, and left a lasting mark on his son in Sabbatarian observances. Referring to the 'Calvinistic' doctrines of his father's faith, Sheldon observed, "Rightly interpreted and understood, I doubt whether there is any escape from the conclusions to which these doctrines led. At any rate, such was our faith, and having been so trained, it never ceases to influence our minds and our lives."[1] Sheldon, moreover, married the daughter of Dr. Ezra Stiles, again reinforcing his roots in New England conservatism. And yet this man, whose background and faith should have predisposed him

[1] Mary Sheldon Barnes, ed.: *Autobiography of Edward Austin Sheldon*, p. 36. New York: Ives-Butler, 1911.

to be an outstanding opponent of the new education, was one of its greatest champions. Although the Oswego, New York, Normal School (1861) was preceded by several much earlier normal schools in this country, its influence was such that it came to be regarded as the "Mother of Normal Schools," and its graduates played an important part in the histories of many subsequent state normal schools.[2] William Torrey Harris, on the occasion of Oswego's twenty-fifth anniversary, spoke of his visit to the school as "a pilgrimage to the shrine at Oswego."[3] Hollis spoke of the work of Oswego as "the dawn of childhood's day in America."[4] The contemporary neglect of Oswego is in part due to the fact that the school's contribution to education did not include the currently central emphasis on "social democracy."

But Sheldon is important for an understanding of American education. His *Autobiography*, it can be added, is one of the most readable of all educational documents and is an invaluable document, better knowledge of which would correct many misconceptions concerning life and thought in conservative circles in western New York.

Sheldon through Oswego popularized Pestalozzi's educational philosophy in America and naturalized it. Although this was not without criticism both in Oswego and in educational circles, his work was eminently successful. From 1861-1886, until Francis W. Parker appeared on the educational scene, Oswego dominated American education.[5] Thus, for twenty-five years, Sheldon and his school were the major influence in American education. For Parker's work, Sheldon felt only "enthusiasm" and regarded Parker as "a *great* man."[6] The criticisms of Oswego's principles were directed locally against its deviation from basic education,

[2] Andrew Phillip Hollis: *The Contribution of the Oswego Normal School to Educational Progress in the United States*, pp. 15, 39-75. Boston: Heath, 1898. See also Ned Harland Dearborn: *The Oswego Movement in American Education*, pp. 94-108. New York: Columbia Teachers College, 1925.

[3] Hollis, p. 23.

[4] *Ibid.*, p. 27.

[5] Dearborn, *op. cit.*, p. 1.

[6] Sheldon, *op. cit.*, pp. 181, 246; italics are Sheldon's.

its "frills," its increased cost, and its adherence to Pestalozzi.[7] In 1872, the schools of Oswego rejected the Oswego Normal School's principles to return "to the old three R's."[8] In educational circles, H. B. Wilbur attacked the Pestalozzi principles as a mixture of truisms and vague generalizations.[9]

In methodology, Sheldon sought to follow Pestalozzi faithfully.[10] His union of evangelical piety with this methodology is often apparent. For example, in the lesson on parchment, he concluded,

> I took the sacred Book of God,
>   To keep, to fear, to read it free;
> But holy martyrs shed their blood
>   To win this word of life for me.[11]

The "application" of the "lesson on the bat" stressed at length "God's goodness:"[12]

Lead the children to trace the hand of God in all this. If we see anything beautifully fitted for some purpose, we conclude it was made for that purpose. God's wisdom, benevolence, and power to be shown in the adaptation of all the parts of the animal to its habits.[13]

Sheldon was not a convert to state-supported and oriented education because of Pestalozzi but rather turned to Pestalozzi's principles as the ready-made philosophy for a position he had already come to champion. Sheldon stated quite candidly:

Other men had thought and planned everything before me. Pestalozzi covered the whole field of educational reform long before my day, but I had never heard of Pestalozzi. I had read very little and knew nothing of educational theories and principles. My knowl-

---

[7] *Ibid.*, pp. 222ff.

[8] Dearborn, *op. cit.*, p. 81.

[9] H. B. Wilbur: *Object System of Instruction as Pursued in the Schools of Oswego, N.Y.* Republished from Barnard's *American Journal of Education* for March, 1864.

[10] See Sheldon: *A Manual of Elementary Instruction, . . . Containing a Graduated Course of Object Lessons*, pp. 14f. New York: Scribner, Armstrong, 1872.

[11] *Ibid.*, p. 24.

[12] *Ibid.*, p. 31f.

[13] *Ibid.*, p. 27.

edge of educational principles was largely intuitive. I do not speak this in a boastful way, but rather in the spirit of humility. What little of educational knowledge I may have possessed was given to me.[14]

It was thus clearly not Pestalozzi who supplied Sheldon with his zeal for state-supported education; Sheldon, moreover, felt that he had come intuitively to the same position previously, and then found in Pestalozzi the mature formulation of his feelings and desires. What, then, was the origin of Sheldon's activity and of his concern? It is described by Sheldon in a letter from Oswego to his sister, November 23, 1848. Sheldon, on attending a "mission Sabbath school" soon after his arrival to Oswego, was surprised (indicative of the fact that it had not previously been a normal condition) at the "large number" of "children eight and ten years old, who could not read their A, B, C!" He and his "chum," making both plans and estimates for a school, then "got upon our knees and implored the blessing of God to give it success. We first introduced the subject in a public manner at a prayer meeting; there appointed Committees to make further investigations." The result was further "meetings of the citizens generally." "Christians are praying for it in private and public; our ministers are all urging it from the pulpit; several discourses have been based entirely on this subject."[15] The popular support as the school began, and as it became part of a state-supported school system later, and as the normal school came into being, was very great. The break with the people came only as the ideas of Pestalozzi introduced what the citizenry felt were alien and useless concepts of education into the schools. The method of pedagogy at first was missionary zeal and a love of children, and the like temper in Pestalozzi commended his philosophy later to Sheldon.

To understand the origins of state-supported education in the United States, it is necessary to recognize its close relationship to the breakdown of Puritanism. On the one hand, many of the

[14] Sheldon: *Autobiography,* p. 124.
[15] *Ibid.,* p. 75.

enemies of Puritanism saw in the public schools a new religion and a new established church whereby the commonwealths could be regenerated and sanctified. On the other hand, despite some opposition within its ranks, much of Puritan latter-day 'orthodoxy' saw the schools as a new means for reviving the holy Commonwealth as now interpreted. American thought had begun its return to the thoroughly English premise of one undivided realm, church and state being opposite sides of a common coin. Calvinism was in part disliked because of the growing rejection of the divided realm which Calvinistic polity created. The emphasis in the new thought, whether in its 'orthodox' or Unitarian formulation, was less on piety, a product of supernatural grace, and more on moralism, works, human activity. The natural order thus gained increasing priority.[16] As the New England theology itself changed from *piety* to *moralism*,[17] it became progressively easier for the holy Commonwealth to be seen as primarily manifest in the state as the truly catholic realm because it was the ethical or moral realm. The weakening of the church covenant was hastened by the Sheldon family's spiritual guide, Nathaniel Emmons, who reduced the church to a "voluntary society, formed by a voluntary compact."[18] The church thus ceased to exist as a necessary body created by Christ and became a body created by men, so that a new institution, one more in keeping with the primarily *moral* needs of the holy Commonwealth, was urgently needed. Chard Powers Smith quite rightly identifies the successful crusade for state-supported education as the accomplishment of a transformed and renascent Puritanism, one rapidly making its influence felt throughout the United States.[19] The extensive emphasis on moralism and patriotism in the state-supported schools was in fulfilment of this purpose in

16 See Joseph Haroutunian: *Piety Versus Moralism*, The Passing of the New England Theology.

17 See Peter Y. De Jong: *The Covenant Idea in New England Theology, 1620-1877.* Grand Rapids, Eerdmans, 1945.

18 De Jong, p. 175, quoting from Emmons: *A Dissertation on the Scripture Qualifications for Admission and Access to the Christian Sacraments*, p. 119.

19 Chard Powers Smith: *Yankees and God*, p. 367. New York: Hermitage House, 1954.

their creation, to become the "catholic" church of the people of America and the moral identity of the body politic. This aspect of educational history is in abundant evidence; it has been neglected only because, while latter-day Puritans helped powerfully to make state support a reality, the schools fell steadily into the hands of the anti-Puritans. As a result, the school continues today as the true established church of these United States, dedicated to a catholic faith which is no longer semi-Christian moralism but social morality and social democracy.

When Sheldon began his "ragged school," he continued, during the summer months, such Sunday missionary activity as "distributing religious papers and tracts to sailors and boatmen." He also visited the jail "for a similar purpose and for religious conversation and instruction."[20] His primary mission, however, became increasingly education. It is no wonder that, when state supported schools were subsequently introduced into Oswego, taking over such missions as Sheldon's "ragged school," many adherents of the Church of Rome opposed it, in Sheldon's words, "as a Protestant movement to build up Protestant institutions, to be paid for by the Catholics."[21] This objection was raised very widely, and with justice. Careful as the Protestants usually were to keep the church out of the schools, the whole conception of the schools was that of the Protestant moral establishment in the new holy Commonwealth, the United States. State unification was thus very quickly championed in the various states, and by Sheldon in New York.[22] Local support was not enough. A state-wide unification was needed to provide the state with a single system: one state, and one unified school system. Federal support and control very early had its champions. To this day, the developed idea of the holy Commonwealth is so strong in popular thinking that power, distrusted, and rightly so, in the hands of the church, is freely and *religiously* granted to the state.

[20] *Autobiography*, p. 89.
[21] *Ibid.*, p. 90.
[22] *Ibid.*, pp. 229 ff.

Educators have had no doubts, unhappily, of the ability of the state to use unlimited powers beneficiently. Ellwood P. Cubberley, for example, approvingly titled a major chapter of his influential *History of Education* (1920) "Education Becomes a National Tool."

In terms of this, much of the contemporary criticism of the schools by conservatives becomes understandable. This "established church" has been captured, and they seek a restoration of an older order and doctrine. By holding to the same statist doctrine of the established school, they are unable to attack effectively concepts which are the logical developments of that establishment.

The order of society, as seen in the United States from the colonial era to the present, has taken three main forms. In the first form, best exemplified among the Puritans, although, in varying degrees or manifestations, common to the English colonies, the pattern can be summarized thus:

> The Triune God
> The Bible
> The Covenant of Grace
>
> The Holy Commonwealth:
> limited, separate powers.

| Church: the religious covenant. Grace, as the source of liberty | The Personal covenant of Grace | State: the social covenant. Law, as the condition of liberty. |
|---|---|---|

With the breakdown of Puritanism, the Unitarian Church came forth with a variation of this concept, one which many like Sheldon followed as the best version of the old faith. By its very enthusiasm for statist education, Unitarianism also helped materially to make the school the new established church of the realm, the mother-teacher-savior of the flock. The second pattern, to which most elements in society made some contribution, al-

though Calvinistic critics like Charles Hodge were sharply critical of statist education, was as follows:

> God
> The Higher Law Concept
> Constitutionalism

| The Established School | The State |
|---|---|
| Learning as power and freedom | Natural law as man's charter of liberty. |

The steady decline of religious faith, of the higher law concept,
and of constitutionalism, and their progressive replacement by
faith in democracy, gave rise to a further interpretation of the
holy Commonwealth:

> The Higher Law of Equality
> Democracy

| School. | State. |
|---|---|
| Social living as the new covenant and means of grace. | Social legislation as the road to Societal salvation, to paradise on earth. |

All three are interpretations of the holy Commonwealth. The
first, as trinitarian, had a multiplicity of powers; the unitarian
version had a unity of powers, a return to the unitary concept of
ancient society, but with the Puritan zeal for the establishment
of God's Kingdom on earth. Herman Melville, at the age of
thirty, declared:

> We are the heirs of all time, and with all nations we divide our
> inheritance. On this Western Hemisphere all tribes and peoples are
> forming into one federated whole; and there is a future which shall
> see the estranged children of Adam restored as to the old hearthstone
> in Eden.[23]

This religious purpose, the creation of a new Eden, was the pur-

[23] Cited in Eugen Rosenstock-Huessy: *Out of Revolution,* Autobiography of
Western Man, p. 678. New York: William Morrow, 1938.

pose and calling of the holy Commonwealth. The new version was however an ancient heresy, one often challenged by Roman Catholic thought of the Gelasian tradition, and by Calvinism, but too often accepted by churches from early times to the present. Moreover, vast segments of Protestantism, accentuated in its vagaries by means of Arminianism and Pietism, have steadily surrendered to the state areas that biblically belonged to Christian man (and had in the middle ages been claimed by the church) : " (1) marriage laws and regulations; (2) the control of wealth; and (3) the control of education."[24] As theology declined in most churches, and sociology became the major 'Christian' concern, the churches became steadily more irrelevant, in that school and state were now the truly effective institutions, and the role of a harmless club became progressively the function of the church. Meanwhile men, hoping in happy unity to move forward to Eden, found themselves drifting closer to Babel and confusion.[25]

[24] Conrad Henry Moehlman: *School and Church: The American Way*, An Historical Approach to the Problem of Religious Instruction in Public Schools, p. 13. New York: Harper, 1944. Moehlman favored these surrenders.

[25] For an analysis of the unitary as against the pluralistic conception of society, see R. J. Rushdoony: *Intellectual Schizophrenia*, Culture, Crisis and Education. Philadelphia: Presbyterian and Reformed, 1961.

# 6. Henry Barnard:
## The Wheeling of the Spheres

Horace Mann, as against some contemporary opinion "that a difference in education is the sole cause of all the differences existing among men," held to the saner belief that "There are certain substructures of temperament and disposition, which education finds, at the beginning of its work, and which it can never wholly annul."[1] It is significant that Mann felt it necessary to correct this opinion; it was widely held and symptomatic of the current messianic expectations of education. Many persons, including some educators, were ready to assert this extreme claim, and, while Mann himself differed with it, he had given acceptable and influential focus to the concept of educators as the new priesthood, and the school as the true church and chosen ark. In his "Remarks" at the dedication of the Massachusetts State Normal School-House at Bridgewater, August 19, 1846 Mann declared,

There is oppression in the world which almost crushes the life out of humanity. There is deceit, which not only ensnares the unwary,

[1] Horace Mann, "A Lecture, on Special Preparation, a Prerequisite to Teaching, 1838" in Henry Barnard, *American Educational Biography*, p. 379. Syracuse, N. Y.: C. W. Bordeen, 1859.

but almost abolishes the security, and confidence, and delight, which rational and social beings ought to enjoy in their intercourse with each other. There are wars, and the question whether they are right or wrong tortures the good man a thousand times more than any successes or defeats of either belligerent. But the feeling which springs up spontaneously in my mind, and which I hope springs up spontaneously in your minds, my friends, in view of the errors, and calamities, and inequities of the race, is, *not* to flee from the world, but to remain in it; *not* to hie away to forest solitudes or hermit cells, but to confront selfishness, and wickedness, and ignorance, at whatever personal peril, and to subdue and extirpate them, or to die in the attempt. Had it not been for a feeling like this among your friends, and the friends of the sacred cause of education in which you have enlisted, you well know that the Normal Schools of Massachusetts would have been put down, and that this day would never have shone to gladden our hearts and to reward our toils and sacrifices. Let no man who knows not what has been suffered, what has been borne and forborne, to bring to pass the present event, accuse me of an extravagance of joy . . .

I believe Normal Schools to be a new instrumentality in the advancement of the race. I believe that, without them, Free Schools' themselves would be shorn of their strength and their healing power, and would at length become mere charity schools, and thus die out in fact and in form. Neither the art of printing, nor the trial by jury, nor a free press, nor free suffrage, can long exist, to any beneficial and salutary purpose, without schools for the training of teachers; for, if the character and qualifications of teachers be allowed to degenerate, the Free Schools will become pauper schools, and the pauper schools will produce pauper souls, and the free press will become a false and licentious press, and ignorant voters will become venal voters, and through the medium and guise of republican forms, an oligarchy of profligate and flagitous men will govern the land; nay, the universal diffusion and ultimate triumph of all-glorious Christianity itself must await the time when knowledge shall be diffused among men through the instrumentality of good schools. Coiled up in this institution, as in a spring, there is a vigor whose uncoiling may wheel the spheres . . .

(Referring to the gift of Edmund Dwight, pending an equal sum by the legislature, for normal school establishment, Mann declared)

The time, the spot, the words of that conversation can never be erased from my soul. This day, triumphant over the past, auspicious for the future, then rose to my sight. By the auroral light of hope, I saw company after company go forth from the bosom of these institutions, like angel ministers, to spread abroad, over waste spiritual realms, the power of knowledge and the delights of virtue. Thank God, the enemies who have since risen up to oppose and malign us, did not cast their hideous shadows across that beautiful scene . . .

The truth is, though it may seem a paradox to say so, the Normal Schools had to come to prepare a way for themselves, and to show, by practical demonstration, what they were able to accomplish. Like Christianity itself, had they waited till the world at large called for them, or was ready to receive them, they would never have come.[2]

This speech, in spirit like so many others dealing with normal schools, sets forth a neglected aspect of the 19th Century educational philosophy, namely, its identification of the educational movement with teacher training and educational administration. Education indeed will accomplish great miracles, it was held, and reform the nation, but, without the development of an educational hierarchy and cultus, these miracles could not occur. It should be noted that Mann (who enjoyed these things before the state schools and normal schools existed) believed that free schools, a free press, free suffrage, a free government, and indeed Christianity itself, required for their existence not merely the public or state school but a state-trained corps of teachers, administrators and teacher training schools. The teachers, as the new priesthood, must have their particular training which is more than academic competence or a way with children. It is educational theory and experience. This is the power "whose uncoiling may wheel the spheres." A more dedicated and ambitious program for the new priesthood was hardly conceivable. The cause of education was not so much learning as indoctrination into a new way of life by state-trained teachers.

In Connecticut, Henry Barnard's Second Annual Report, 1839-40, showed this condition among the common schools of

[2] *Ibid.*, pp. 393-395.

that state: "The studies pursued are spelling, reading, writing, and arithmetic, in all of the schools, and the rudiments of geography, history and grammar, in nearly all. Book-keeping, natural philosophy, astronomy, chemistry, algebra, geometry, surveying, and other branches, are pursued to some extent."[8] The main purpose of the educators was not mere learning but taxation, teacher training, legal requirements for days of schooling, state supervision, and guidance or supervision in matters of school architecture, textbooks, and the like. Much later, John Dewey was to insist that religion, to flourish and be true, must be a free and unforced 'flower' of man's spirit. This concept neither he nor his predecessors ever found tolerable in relation to education. It had to be the forced and controlled 'flower' of state-trained educators.

The great early leader in educational circles was Henry Barnard, born on January 24, 1811, dying at 89 at his birthplace, Hartford, on July 5, 1900. Henry Barnard was the dedicated, self-sacrificing and crusading father of educational bureaucrats. Barnard, a central figure in 19th century education in the United States because of his extensive services and varied offices, is something of an embarrassment also. Whereas Mann in his day was accused of socialist ideas, Barnard was an ardent champion of capitalism and prepared a school catechism designed to demonstrate the social value of great profits by capitalists. Moreover, Barnard showed no committment to any developed current philosophy of education but was primarily, as a writer, a transmitter and mediator of contemporary educational theory, and as an educator, an administrator rather than a thinker. What philosophy he held to is often better revealed in his practice than in his writings. Furthermore, Barnard held mildly to orthodox Christianity, being a faithful Episcopalian. His faith permitted him to marry a Roman Catholic, and he allowed his children to be reared in that faith (and on neither point was he

---

[8] Henry Barnard: *Second Annual Report of the Board of Commissioners of Common Schools in Connecticut, Together with the Second Annual Report of the Secretary of the Board, May, 1840*, p. 28. Hartford: Case, Tiffany and Burham, 1840.

ever criticized, indicative of the radical divorce of Christianity and the political life which was then in process). Thus, no great religious zeal can be ascribed to him, nor did Christian doctrine dominate his thinking. It did, however, preserve him from the utopianism of many of his contemporaries. Horace Mann had shown marked tendencies in that direction, and only Mann's thorough acceptance of phrenology, in common for a time at least with William Ellery Channing, Ralph Waldo Emerson, Walt Whitman, Charles Sumner and Henry Ward Beecher, prevented him from believing that all men were equal in intellect and ability and hence could be educated into equal capabilities. Men who had deserted biblical faith now substituted science, in the form of phrenology, for God, as the source of unique differences in the potentialities of individuals. From this and other opinions of the day, Barnard was preserved by his earnest if easygoing adherence to traditional Christianity. Finally, this absence of utopianism preserved Barnard from the radical adherence to various crusades of the day which characterized others of the new school of educators. Neither phrenology, abolition, temperance, or any other crusade, could deflect him from his central concern, education. Without being pro-slavery, Barnard kept strictly to his task and was thus equally respected in slave states and in the north. Barnard believed in creating a priesthood of teachers, and to this calling he gave his full allegiance. No other cause, however worthy, could command his attention or be allowed centrality in educational thinking. This fact, together with his religious and political conservatism, has made him somewhat less appealing than Mann to such historians as Merle Curti.[4]

Barnard began his educational career as a teacher in Wellsboro, Pennsylvania, 1830-1831, and then, after studying law, served as a member of the Connecticut legislature, 1837-1840, where he championed the cause of "free schools." He became the first Secretary of the Board of Commissioners of Common

[4] Merle Curti: *The Social Ideas of American Educators*, pp. 139-168. Paterson, N. J.: Littlefield, Adams, 1959.

Schools in Connecticut, 1838-1842. The resistance to taxation for schools was widespread in the country, and taxation was introduced only with difficulty and sometimes political maneuvering. In Connecticut, the situation was somewhat different; not only was education required, as elsewhere, for the purposes of godly instruction, but a general property tax contributed to the support of schools. These schools, however, were in a sense a branch of the establishment, and the separation of church and state in 1818 detached the schools from parochial supervision and left them without supervision until the state assumed responsibility. This assumption was the consecrated responsibility of Henry Barnard. During the period of the church's establishment, the school had been religious in orientation. Barnard's purpose was to make its orientation statist. Thus, while no small amount of religion remained within the curriculum, the atmosphere and motive power of education was no longer Christian faith and life. It was instead life within the state and in the service of society. Summarizing Barnard's purpose, Curti has observed, "Education, in short, was to serve the actual needs of the community."[5] The chief end of man shortly before this had been defined as glorifying God and enjoying Him forever. Now it was to glorify the community and enjoy life therein. A little earlier, James Madison, John Adams and others had been sharp in their condemnation of democracy and emphatic in asserting that the Constitution established not a democracy but a republic. Now the advocates of state-supported schools hailed the Connecticut state supervision as a major advance for democracy. Both friend and foe recognized its meaning: "Democracy is on the advance."[6] Barnard himself opposed the private school, not, as Mann unwisely did, on its educational merits, but because "it classifies society at the root" and thereby such schools "open a real chasm between members of the same society, broad and deep, which

[5] *Ibid.*, p. 159.
[6] James Wadsworth, 1840, in a letter to Henry Barnard. Cited in Anna Lou Blair: *Henry Barnard, School Administrator*, p. 38. Minneapolis: Educational Publishers, 1938.

equal laws and political theories cannot close."[7] Not all the economic and religious conservatism of Barnard's thinking could
overcome the radical implications of his educational theory. The
central purpose of the schools was not learning as such but
learning in terms of living a common life in an unclassified
society. Curti is unhappy because so much of Barnard's humani-
tarian efforts and educational goals "were in large part designed
to remove the menace of a 'populace.' "[8] But Barnard was a
realist and saw the inadequacies of men. His goal was nonetheless a unified society. Reformed Christian faith had once been
the bond between rich and poor, making them alike brothers in
Christ and fellow priests in the Commonwealth of God. This
aspect of New England society was more or less gone, and its
counterpart in other areas also disappearing. Barnard realized
that a society without a common creed would become a battle-
ground. The school must therefore supply the social cement for
society by opposing stratification and classification and creating
a common life. Not a socialistic common life was Barnard's ideal,
but a common life as fellow members of a society, and, whether
capitalist or laborer, each man recognizing his common cause
with others. Accordingly, Barnard favored the legal and required
use of the Bible in schools and pointed "to the noble effects produced even by . . . imperfect observance" of such laws.[9] Christianity was not to be eliminated; it was to be used for the welfare
of society and the control of the populace, not in any sinister
sense, but to bring them faith, dignity and moral stature. Man's
life was religious, but not primarily religious but rather societal,
lived essentially within the State. Barnard was most appreciative
of the role of the clergy, of Sunday Schools, their teachers, and
their libraries; "From no portion of the community have we re-

[7] Cited in Curti, p. 148, from the *Journal of R. I. Institute of Instruction*, Vol.
I, Dec., 1845, p. 38; *Report of the Superintendent of Common Schools in Connecticut*, 1850, pp. 33-34.
[8] Curti, p. 168.
[9] From the *Connecticut Common School Journal*, Vol. I, p. 15, Sept., 1838, cited
in John S. Brubacher: *Henry Barnard on Education*, pp. 136-138. New York:
McGraw-Hill, 1931.

ceived more cordial cooperation or more personal kindness in visiting different sections of the State."[10] The church was no longer the unifying force in society; the state had taken its place, and in vast areas the church was glad to be recognized as essential to the new society rather than an outsider to it. Like Mann, Barnard saw Protestantism as the source of freedom and liberty, but, unlike Mann, he was more cordial to it and more broadly appreciative of its social necessity. For Barnard, the school was the true church in the new society, and every institution should nurture and promote that temple of society.

> Every school-house should be a temple, consecrated in prayer to the physical, intellectual, and moral culture of every child in the community, and be associated in every heart with the earliest and strongest impressions of truth, justice, patriotism, and religion.
> The school-house should be constructed throughout in a workmanlike manner. No public edifice more deserves, or will better repay, the skill, labor, and expense, which may be necessary to attain this object, for here the health, tastes, manners, minds, and morals of each successive generation of children will be, in a great measure, determined for time and for eternity.[11]

As Brubacher has pointed out, for Barnard, "schools were agencies of social rejuvenation."[12] Thus, education in the public school necessarily involved far more than mere book-learning or subject matter mastery. Such things were "mere knowledge" and far short of the full scope of the school's purpose:

> If education was properly understood—if all the influences which go to mould and modify the physical, moral and intellectual habits of a child, were felt to be that child's education—parents and the public would not tolerate such school-houses, with all their bad influences, indoors and out of doors, such imperfect and illiberal school arrangements, in almost every particular, as are now found

[10] From the *Connecticut Common School Journal*, Vol. II, p. 101, January, 1840, in Brubacher, p. 63-65.

[11] Henry Barnard: *Fourth Annual Report of the Board of Commissioners of the Common Schools in Connecticut, Together with the Fourth Annual Report of the Secretary of the Board*, May, 1842, Appendix, "School-house Architecture," p. 3. Hartford: Case, Tiffany & Burnham, 1842.

[12] Brubacher, *op. cit.*, p. 69.

in a large majority of the school districts of the State. If they had a proper estimate of the influence of teachers, for good or for evil, for time and eternity, on the character and destiny of their pupils, they would employ, if within the reach of their means, those best qualified to give strength and grace to the body, clearness, vigor, and richness to the mind, and the highest and purest feelings to the moral nature of every child entrusted to their care.

If the *ends* of education were regarded, something more would be aimed at than to enable a child to read, write, and cypher, or to attain to any degree of mere knowledge. As far as the individual is concerned, it would be to secure the highest degree of health, powers of accurate observation, and clear reflection, and noble feelings; as far as the public is concerned, the prevention of vice and crime, and the keeping pure of the peace, order, and progress of society.

Parents and society must be made to regard education in this light, as their first concern; the common school, as the chief instrumentality for accomplishing it; and the teacher, as determining the character of the school. If this can be effected, the work of improvement will be begun in earnest, and will not cease, until each district school shall witness the triumphs of education.[13]

We should aim at something, in common school education, which is very apt to be missed in the college course, and perhaps no less frequently in private schools and academies. We mean a proper preparation for the real business of life.[14]

Barnard is thus quite plain-spoken. The school, rather than church or home, is "the chief instrumentality" in the nurture of man's body, mind and spirit. Indeed, the family should guide its table and fireside talk along lines intended to implement and further the school's teaching, according to Barnard. Education for living was the great task to which he summoned church, home, school and society, with the school as its central institution and temple, and teachers as the new priesthood. Teachers, as has often been observed by scholars, were to Barnard the needed and true priesthood of man.[15] Although Barnard's own faith was Christian immediately, the implications of his position

---

[13] Henry Barnard, *Second Annual Report*, May, 1840, Connecticut, p. 52.

[14] Barnard, in the *Connecticut Common School Journal*, Vol. I, p. 113, May, 1839, cited in Brubacher, p. 70.

[15] Curti, p. 142, Blair, p. 261.

were ultimately pragmatic and utilitarian, in that education was both "for living" and essentially functional in character. "Education, in its enlarged sense, is the disciplining, cultivating, and furnishing of the man, as a man, and for the particular position which he is to hold."[16]

Barnard's next position was in Rhode Island, as state superintendent of schools, 1843-1849, where he agreed to "make history." Because Rhode Island had, unlike Connecticut, been established on the principle of religious liberty, it had been bitterly hostile to the establishment of church or school alike. State control of the schools was thus resisted. Barnard had, in his *Second Annual Report* (1840) in Connecticut repeatedly asserted the prior right of the state to educate, as against the church and parents. He was thus the ideal man to institute a program of State Control, which he successfully did. He then returned to Connecticut to become principal of New Britain Normal School, 1850-1854.

Following this, he edited the American Journal of Education, giving it his major attention from 1855-1860, but publishing from 1855-1881, at no small expense to himself. The Journal exercised a decisive role in publicizing the new education and in transmitting foreign educational theory, and Barnard was not only a leader in his own right but the great transmitter of his day. Many of the articles were subsequently reprinted in book form, as witness *American Educational Biography, American Pedagogy, English Pedagogy,* and others.[17] Rev. Charles Brooks expressed his appreciation of the Journal's work in a letter to Barnard, January 28, 1860, "I think you should be canonized, as the 'American Education Saint'—or perhaps 'Martyr.'"[18]

[16] Henry Barnard, "Education and Educational Institutions" in J. T. Hodge, etc., *First Century of National Existence; the United States as They Were and Are,* p. 384. Hartford: L. Stebbins, 1872.

[17] The first, in its original appearance, in 1859, was titled *Memoirs of Teachers, Educators, and Promoters and Benefactors of Education, Literature and Science, Part I.* Of this volume alone, 1,650 copies were purchased by the Ohio Commissioner of Education. For other topical volumes from the Journal, see Richard Emmons Thursfield: *Henry Barnard's American Journal of Education,* p. 309. Baltimore: Johns Hopkins, 1945.

[18] Thursfield, p. 32.

Brooks was not alone among clergymen in sharing his enthusiasm for statist education; the liberal clergy were solidly in favor of the new concept. For example, William Ellery Channing, outdid the educators. Jesus had spoken (John 4:10; 7:38) of himself as the water of life and believers by union with him as fountains of living water. Channing deliberately spoke of normal schools in the same language: "An institution for training men to train the young, would be a fountain of living waters, sending forth streams to refresh present and future ages. As yet, our legislators have denied to the poor and laboring classes this principal means of their elevation. We trust they will not always prove blind to the highest interest of the state."[19] Many clergymen, having forsaken orthodoxy and the historic concept of the church, had made state and school the new instruments of salvation and outdid educators in their assertions.

From 1858-1860, Barnard served as chancellor of the University of Wisconsin and agent of the Wisconsin Normal School Regents. The radical "mismanagement" of public school finances in that state did not disturb Barnard's faith in statist control. Then as now, the proponents of the state are ready to blame "outside" forces for every corruption on the part of the state. Among other things, Barnard urged more work in agricultural training on the part of the University as a means of enlisting farm support as well as a step towards functionalism in education.

Barnard's next position was in Maryland, as president of St. John's College, 1866-1867, where his functional concept was again promoted.

From 1867-1870, Barnard served as the first U. S. Commissioner of Education, where, despite hindrances, he quickly established a statistical survey of education in the states. Almost all the basic elements of modern school survey and supervision were foreshadowed or set forth in some aspect of Barnard's work. The office of Commissioner had been established with vague or little scope as a sop to educators lobbying for the nationalization of schools and the assumption of federal responsibility for them.

[19] In an address, Feb. 28, 1837, Boston, in Henry Barnard, *American Pedagogy: Education, the School, and the Teacher,* p. 275. Hartford: Brown and Gross, 1876.

Mann had declared the messianic character of education, and had seen the hope of society in educational theory and experience so formulated. Therein was the power "whose uncoiling may wheel the spheres." To this task, Barnard, who in a letter addressed Mann as "my guide, my hope, my friend, my fellow-laborer and fellow-sufferer in 'the cause,'" dedicated himself.[20] For them, their work was a holy crusade, and they willing martyrs in its cause. The sense of martyrdom in the face of any challenge or opposition has been characteristic of educators then and now and is suggestive of the neurotic tendency that has often characterized religious ascetics and masochists. Mann, for example, never hesitated to provoke people, but his response to criticism, as in the case of the Boston schoolmasters, was one of intense suffering. Mann, upset by their criticism, asked Dr. Jarvis, "Can you do anything for a man's brain that has not slept for three weeks? I can feel the flame in the center of my cranium flaring and flaring around just as you see that of a pile of brush burning on a distant heath in the wind. What can be done to extinguish it?"[21] Barnard's attitude as U. S. Commissioner had often been provocative and presumptuous, in that he assumed that Congress was only an obstructionist agency and the work of the government less pressing or central than his own. Thus, very early the typical educational neurosis and syndrome was established. Their "enemies" are vile opponents of progress and light and "cast . . . hideous shadows." Whether well paid or not, whether commanding popularity or not, whether gaining unlimited funds or not, the educational administrator and bureaucrat has masochistically seen himself as the misunderstood, unloved, unappreciated, unrewarded and by-passed prophet. As a class, they are in their own eyes, The Great Misunderstood. Their real tragedy, however, usually occurs when they are all too well understood and their nature recognized and identified.

---

[20] From a letter to Mann, Feb. 13, 1843, cited in Curti, p. 139.
[21] Cited by Curti, p. 110, as an instance of Mann's heroic and sensitive devotion to the cause.

# 7. William Torrey Harris:
# The State and the True Self of Man

William Torrey Harris (1835-1908), whose administative work in St. Louis from 1857-1880, and whose term of office as U. S. Commissioner of Education from 1889-1906, placed him in strategic positions of influence, added to those positions his own intellectual abilities to exercise a long and decisive influence on education in the United States. Merle Curti, in his assessment of the life and work of Harris, named him "The Conservator," and, in a sense, this title has merit to it. Harris stemmed the tide of much radicalism in education, i.e., political and economic radicalism, and prevented the early and more extensive triumph of progressive education through the work of Colonel Parker, whose influence Harris, as the decisive philosophic thinker of the day in education, helped stem and reshape. The influence of Harris was extensive, in both education and philosophy, and his imprint large on such diverse persons as Nicholas Murray Butler and John Dewey. Leidecker reports that, when St. Louis was once mentioned to Henri Bergson, that philosopher immediately responded, "Oh, that is the city Dr. Harris made famous by his great insight into philosophy!"[1] Both

[1] Kurt F. Leidecker: *Yankee Teacher: The Life of William Torrey Harris,* p. viii. New York: Philosophical Library, 1946.

through the *Journal of Speculative Philosophy*, which he founded when only thirty-two and edited through twenty-two volumes, and through educational media, Harris made a profound impact on the thinking of his day. When his death was noted at the National Educational Association meetings of July 2-8, 1910, in Boston, James M. Greenwood in his memorial address, declared, "His rank is among the world's greatest men."[2] From such an eminence, the name of William Torrey Harris has passed into obscurity in other than educational circles, and even there, his work has been superseded by that of Dewey and others, and his outlook to a large degree by-passed.

In spite of this fact, the importance of Harris is very real, and his temporary eclipse is in part due to his conservatism in certain areas, aspects of his work which go against the grain with men who are in other respects his followers. The key to both the neglect of Harris and to his continuing influence is in his Hegelian philosophy. Let us examine first a common evaluation of Harris' Hegelianism as expressed by Curti:

> The Hegelian philosophy which Harris made the basis of all his social and educational thinking possessed the virtue of being thoroughly optimistic and idealistic in character. It infused the world with a divine purpose and endowed the individual with a noble and immortal destiny. At the same time it justified the existing order and authorities by declaring that whatever is, is an inevitable stage in the unfolding of objective reason or the world spirit, and is therefore right.[3]

The decisive influence of Hegel on Harris must be recognized immediately, and its continuing influence noted. As numerous writers have observed, shortly before his death, Harris said (1908), "I have now commenced the reading of Hegel's *Philosophy of History* for the seventeenth time, and I shall get more out of it at this reading than at any previous one."[4]

[2] *N.E.A., Journal and Proceedings*, p. 99, 1910.
[3] M. Curti, *op. cit.*, p. 312f.
[4] See *N.E.A. Journal and Proceedings*, 1910, p. 92; John S. Roberts: *William T. Harris, A Critical Study of his Educational and Related Philosophical Views,*

But this Hegelian influence was not quite the conservative influence Curti believed it to be, and Harris' conservatism was more apparent than real. Harris as a philosopher refused to permit the over-evaluation of schools and of education. As Mc-Cluskey has noted, "He rejected Spencer's idea that each child should be brought to school to learn the art of complete living."[5] While on occasion Harris slipped into the contemporary and continuing belief in education as a panacea, he usually spoke sharply against such a temper. As he observed at the 1885 N.E.A. meeting at Saratoga Springs, New York:

It is a serious error to confine the definition of education in such a way as to make it include the province of the school only, and not the various educative influences of the four cardinal institutions of civilization—family, civil society, state, and church. . . . The school is not one of the cardinal institutions of civilization, but is a supplementary special institution, designed to reenforce one or more of the cardinal institutions in their educative functions.[6]

The institution to be re-enforced depended on the particular culture. It was this element in Harris which has been the real offense to many educators since. Harris made himself even more clear at Chicago in 1887, stating forcefully, "There are many items in which the school must be on its guard, lest it be an *aggressor,* or even a *transgressor.*"[7]

Since the school was not to be a determining agency, but a "supplementary special institution" to re-enforce the cultural agencies, it had to reflect that culture rather than attempt to

p. 6. Washington, D.C.: N.E.A., 1924; see also Walton C. John: *William Torrey Harris, The Commemoration of the One Hundredth Anniversary of his Birth, 1835-1935,* p. 18. U.S. Dept. of the Interior, Bulletin 1936, No. 17. In this bulletin, Payson Smith also noted Harris' statement, "I endeavor to read Goethe's *Wilhelm Meister* every year."

[5] Neil Gerard McCluskey, S.J.: *Public Schools and Moral Education, The Influences of Horace Mann, William Torrey Harris and John Dewey,* p. 132. N.Y.: Columbia University Press, 1958.

[6] William T. Harris: "Methods of Pedagogical Inquiry", p. 492f., in *N.E.A. Journal,* 1885.

[7] William T. Harris: "The Function of the American Public School," p. 267, in *N.E.A. Journal,* 1887.

mold it. Thus, Harris, while he was personally opposed to religion in 'public' schools and clearly for the separation of religious instruction from 'public' schools,[8] could also affirm, in conformity to his principle, "Were the community homogeneous in its profession of faith, dogmatic religious instruction could still properly remain in the school."[9]

There were times indeed when Harris fell into the messianic language of educators, as two utterances give particular evidence. In 1892, in speaking to the N.E.A. on "Twenty Years' Progress in Education," he saw its meaning in thoroughly religious terms:

> In these lines of progress we see the development of the missionary spirit of Christianity, which goes out into the highways and by-ways and seeks out the maimed, the halt, and the spiritually blind, and brings them into the house of the Father.[10]

Again, in 1893, at the World's Columbian Exposition in Chicago, July 25-28, in the "Report of the Committee of Arrangements" for the International Congress of Education, Harris spoke of the fact that "the central place of school education among the great regenerating movements of modern civilization is obvious."[11]

> In our system of government, we must never cut loose from the people. The object of the school manager should be two-fold: to improve the schools, and to educate public opinion in favor of improvement.[12]

It would be wrong to attach any importance to these remarks, however. Harris was successful in part because he reflected both intelligently, philosophically and fairly the culture of his day, and did so as his duty and privilege. The key to this amenability

---

[8] See W. T. Harris: "The Separation of the Church from the School Supported by Public Taxes," p. 351-360, in *N.E.A. Journal*, 1902.

[9] W. T. Harris: "School Statistics and Morals," p. 11, in *N.E.A. Journal*, 1893.

[10] *N.E.A. Journal*, 1892, p. 61.

[11] *Proceedings of the International Congress of Education*, 1893, under the charge of the N.E.A. of the U. S., p. 26.

[12] W. T. Harris: "City School Systems," p. 438, in *N.E.A. Journal*, 1889.

to diverse opinions, an amenability which made Harris so popular and powerful a figure in his day, was his Hegelian philosophy. Rather than being productive of *conservatism*, as Curti
believed, it was productive of a thorough-going *pragmatism*, and
an idealistic pragmatism at that. The Hegelianism of Hegel led
to the *absolutization* of a particular social order. The Hegelianism of Harris led to the *relativization* of every social order and
philosophy in terms of a continuous process and was thus the
fountainhead of pragmatism. Harris was in a very real sense a
more consistent Hegelian than Hegel, and, as a brilliant mediator between systems, was capable of abstracting a synthesis out
of ostensibly contrary systems without making his synthesis more
than a step towards the next manifestation of process in time.
Whereas Hegel and Marx arbitrarily crystalized the process into
a final order, Harris consistently held to the process. In terms
of their finality, Hegel and Marx could turn intolerantly on the
process with the perspective of a 'final truth.' For Harris, the
goal was "ethical freedom," the triumph of man's freedom as
man, a sufficiently general ideal to make possible its continuous
development in a continuous process.[13] There being no absolute
order for Harris, and a continuous process and development
always manifesting progress, Harris could face the future both
with optimism and also with a certain detachment from the entire process. All things manifested a partial truth and none a
final truth, so that the wise man saw the relative nature of each
particular and approached it pragmatically. The Hegelian
idealism of Harris was thus the basis of his pragmatism. The
Hegelian foundation of the pragmatism of James and Dewey has
been studied.[14] The relationship is even more pronounced in
Harris.

What was the educational significance of this pragmatic
Hegelianism of Harris? Because Harris believed in progress, he

[13] See W. T. Harris: *Psychologic Foundations of Education*. N.Y., Appleton,
1898.
[14] See Burleigh Taylor Wilkins: "James, Dewey, and Hegelian Idealism" in the
*Journal of the History of Ideas*, June, 1956, vol. XVII, No. 3, pp. 332-346.

fought against the primitivism and return-to-nature tendencies common to many educators under the influence of Rousseau and Pestalozzi. Such a movement, which he was ready to appreciate as a corrective to "cramped formalism," was nevertheless in error in reducing man to the level of nature. Harris drew a distinction between "nature in general" and "human nature," human nature being something which "only exists as a product of culture." All Pestalozzian stress on "spontaneous activity" is destructive. of the cultural activity which alone makes for civilization. It puts a premium on "caprice," which "destroys the work of one moment by that of the next. It is only *self-consistent* activity that can be free. . . . What is done through caprice will be controlled by accident." The state of nature and the state of culture, however, must not be falsely separated, for they are antitheses, "and all true systems of education must mediate between" them. The ideal of "free men in a free state" cannot be realized by the reduction of men to a lower state of nature. Accordingly, textbook education is no blind traditionalism but a respect for the highest attainment of human nature and a resolve to begin with the best of the past in order to advance to still higher culture and civilization. The textbook thus serves to liberate man from the past, from tradition, from himself, and is the true basis of all truly progressive education which is not a product of that confusion sometimes characterizing Rousseau, whereby nature is elevated over culture.[15] That this position was no empty verbiage with Harris was apparent in his sharp remarks, during the course of a discussion, on all false confidence in contemporary knowledge, learning or science.

. . . We forget that all education, and all knowledge and all we gain of knowledge is going from the known to the unknown. The danger is that we leave the factor, the unknown, out of the question and wander around among the known, on the hither side; and the greatest point is to keep the unknown as far out of the way as pos-

15 W. T. Harris: "The Theory of American Education," pp. 177-191, in *Addresses and Journal of Proceedings of the American Normal School, and the National Teachers' Associations,* 1871.

sible, and when the child approaches it throw him off; put in soft things, words, and smuggle the knowledge into the scholar. This is a way of teaching him that the unknown is really something familiar and that it is not any work for him to know it. If he will just repeat over a few of the terms he already knows, he will find himself in possession of the knowledge of the unknown. In that way we make education seem a simple thing. I think it is too simple and too easy. It seems to me that error is committed in the direction in which most of the discussion went this morning.[16]

For Harris, education has as its purpose "the preservation of civilization—not of its evolution, growth, or decay, for the causes of these lie far deeper than in a system of education." Education is hindered by "the would-be social reformer" and by all men who "refer to education things entirely beyond its scope." Education as conceived has a two-fold purpose: first, "initiation in the practice of what belongs to civilized man," and, second, "an invitation into the ideas that lie at the basis of that practice." The first is moral education, and the second intellectual education.[17]

Because education cannot be a return to nature, and because it is an initiation into the past in terms of the future, it cannot be conceived of in terms of the individual in isolation from past and present society. Man is not man in isolation from man and in terms of nature in general but rather in terms of society, in terms of culture and civilization. To negate that societal aspect of man in preference to an anarchistic concept of man in nature is to destroy education.

Now it is evidently a great mistake—a heresy in education—to suppose that the unaided individual can develop into a rational being except through participation in the labors of the human race. It is a heresy in education to suppose that education is anything else than this initiation of the individual into the wisdom which mankind has accumulated.[18]

[16] *Ibid.*, p. 171.
[17] W. T. Harris: "The Early Withdrawal of Pupils from Schools: Its Cause and its Remedies," in *N.E.A. Journal*, 1873, pp. 260-271.
[18] Harris: "Text-Books and Their Uses," *N.E.A. Journal*, 1880, p. 106.

In looking to that past into which man is to be initiated, Harris' orientation was classical rather than Christian, and "the embryology of modern civilization" is to be found in "these wonderful peoples" of ancient Greece and Rome. Since "the immature mind of youth" is not capable of making a wise choice, "the wisdom of his instructors" must be his guide, for they "know the wants of the pupil and the best mode of supplying them."[19] Harris, personally not a Christian in any accepted sense, strove always to be fair and honest in reflecting the prevailing culture and strove to avoid any "leading" in such matters. Nevertheless, he was unable, in choosing the process into which the pupil was initiated, to avoid a basically religious choice and to create a religious framework for education which was other than Christian.

Education viewed thus as an initiation or baptism into a process (and initiation is like baptism a basically religious concept), meant initiation into a culture and society whose supplementary instrument the school was. This society is an organism and has a self even as does man. Man's individual self or ego is "hemmed in by limitations qualitative and quantitative." In his institutional lives, man organically becomes "a series of giant selves, each one formed in the general image of man and having its heads, its hands—its deliberative power, its will power to execute with." In his giant self, man, himself "finite," becomes "infinite." The individual "limitations are cancelled or annulled through participation, each man participating in the life of all men."[20] Thus, while man's goal is "infinitely reflected self-activity," and education seeks to further the independence, freedom and "self-help" of the individual,[21] this goal can only be attained as man joins his finite self to organisms which make

[19] Harris: "Equivalents in a Liberal Course of Study," *N.E.A. Journal,* 1880, p. 174f.

[20] Harris: "The Tenth Census from an Educational Point of View," *Circular of Information of the Bureau of Education,* No. 2, 1880, p. 61.

[21] Harris: "Psychological Inquiry," in *N.E.A. Journal,* 1885, p. 101, and Harris: "Pedagogics as a Science," in *The National Council of Education, Proceedings of Fourth Annual Meeting,* 1884, p. 54.

him in effect infinite. This is therefore an individualism which exalts the collective whole.

Participation in the whole is an essentially religious experience and is characterized as "vicarious suffering." Young girls ought to read the daily newspapers, because they can therein enter into this mystical experience of participation.

Mounted, as it were, on a high throne, each man can behold his greater self—the self of humanity in the aggregate—with all its nations and peoples, under all climes, and in every stage of development; he can behold this stupendous revelation of human nature moving onward toward its goal. . . .

The divinest fact in society is that of vicarious suffering. Each human being participates in the wisdom of the race and learns through the successes and failures of others. What one does in this world is not alone for himself, but likewise for his fellowmen . . . Participation is the greatest fact of human spiritual life, and our religion makes vicarious suffering the supreme condition of salvation. It is not, we see, alone the fact that the good suffer for the wicked, but in this world Providence has decreed that the wicked vicariously help their good fellowmen by the spectacle of their own disaster. The broader the view the truer the vision.[22]

The answer is thus very clear-cut: young girls ought to read the daily newspapers as a religious experience. Thus, while the school was not divinized by Harris, the processes of history and participation therein were divinized. The process of history is Allah, and the newspaper is Mohammed his prophet! Certainly modern man, by virtue of all his immersion in evil and disaster, should consider himself greatly blessed, if Harris is right. The antinomians of Paul's day said, let us sin, that grace may abound (Rom. 6:1). In Harris' version, let us behold sin, that grace may abound. It is not surprising therefore that Harris saw "the three characteristic instruments of modern civilization" as "the railroad, the daily newspaper, and the common school," and rejoiced in that fact.[23] All three were instruments of participation

[22] Harris: "Ought Young Girls to Read the Daily Newspapers?" in *N.E.A. Journal*, 1888, p. 87f.

[23] Harris: "Twenty Years' Progress in Education," *N.E.A. Journal*, 1892, p. 56.

in the great mass of humanity and furthered the binding of the finite self to society, the state, and other institutional and infinite selves of man. Man is truly man not so much under God as *in humanity*, and in organic relationship thereto. Thus Hegelianism leads to mass man, whether in the dictatorship of the proletariat in Marx's version, or in the democratic society of John Dewey, in this respect an apt follower of Harris.

It should be noted that Harris, by *his faith in the inevitability of progress through process,* his confidence that time and flux moved steadily forward, associated that triumph of mass man with the triumph of freedom, intelligence and virtue. For him, the progress of democracy meant also the inevitable progress also of liberty, good character and intellectual and cultural advance. Thus he could say without hesitation, in his "Response" at the 1890 N.E.A. meeting in St. Paul, Minnesota, "The nation that proclaims itself a government of all the people by all the people, a government of universal freedom, is necessarily founded on virtue and intelligence."[24] There is no understanding the vast areas of presupposition underlying subsequent pragmatism apart from this basic faith. *All the benefits of past cultural attainment accrue to the present without loss.* Christianity may disappear or be superseded, but all its advantages will remain without diminution as the inheritance of man. Such were the implications and assumptions of this Hegelian concept of society.

Since the constant tendency of the Hegelian process is to effect a synthesis, it follows therefore that synthesis is the continued goal of societal relationships, and order and unity are emphasized above all else in such systems. This note was not lacking in Harris, as his idea of morals very clearly shows:

I have heard the protest that we are neglecting moral education in the schools. I think there is a confusion here between moral philosophy and moral education. We pretend to try to teach the intellect and endeavor to secure good behavior, and not moral education. We hear a good deal about morals not being taught in the

[24] Harris: "Response," p. 87, *N.E.A. Journal,* 1890.

schools. Is there a school that does not teach good behavior? This is considered the basis of all things. Order is Heaven's first law. Now every teacher teaches exercise, punctuality, self-restraint, regularity, and industry, in order that the whole may produce something . . . There is an additional restraint—the pupil is met with the arm of the teacher.[25]

These certainly are commendable virtues, but a man limited to these is hardly a moral man in any Christian sense. Order may be heaven's first law in a Hegelian heaven, but the Shorter Catechism teaches that man's chief end is to glorify God and to enjoy Him forever, a very different and more inclusive standard.

Harris most certainly believed in individualism, a common emphasis in his day, but his was not the individualism of others, in that it called for vicarious participation as the goal of individualism. As he declared at Charleston, South Carolina, in 1900:

I close with my thesis, assumed at the beginning, namely, that our movement toward individualism is possible only in connection with a reverse movement from the individual toward what is universal, and the attainment of this by means of culture—by means of the increase of education of all kinds, especially of higher education.[26]

This universalism means in part vicarious experience, and vicarious experience has as its purpose the furtherance of individualism. Higher education in particular furthers this kind of individualism.[27] It was natural, therefore, for Harris to see this goal best fulfilled in the state school with its democratic nature and experiences, and Harris declared himself to be in hearty agreement with Horace Mann and James G. Carter concerning "the right of the state to educate at public expense."[28] His definition of slavery and freedom is also revealing. "If the individual exists for the social whole alone, and is not endowed with the beneficence of the whole, we have slavery. When we look at the

[25] Harris: "Remarks," p. 356, *N.E.A. Journal,* 1890.
[26] Harris: "Education at Close of Century," p. 203, *N.E.A. Journal,* 1900.
[27] Harris: "University and School Extension," p. 245, *N. E. A. Journal,* 1890.
[28] Harris: "Horace Mann," p. 62, *N.E.A. Journal,* 1896.

individual as receiving the gift of the whole, and the whole handing to it what all has produced, we have freedom."[29] This indeed is freedom after the manner of Soviet Russia; it is freedom only in terms of production and consumption. Certainly, Harris would have included, in "the gift of the whole," cultural factors and personal liberties, but if such liberties are gifts of society or of the state, then man has no true liberty and only sufferance. For Harris, without any qualifications, "whatever gives to the mind a larger view increases individuality."[30] For Harris the state exercises "directive power upon the individual" and assumes "the functions of a will-power like him. But the state always assumes the control of the individual for the benefit of the social unit. Against this social unit he has no substantial existence." Civil society, the most important phase of which is the organization of man's industry in the form of division of labor, is the area of individuality, not the state.

Civil society seems to be an organization of the social unit for the use of the individual, while the state is the social unit in which the individual exists not for himself, but for the use of that unit, the state. In civil society the whole exists for each; in the state each exists for the whole.[31]

Harris earnestly believed that "the self-determination of the individual is the object of all government," but his conception of this, in his own words, was that "the great end of all government is the elevation of mere individuals to the dignity of self-directive *persons*: the concentration of the realized products of *all* in *each*."[32] This in itself was a commonly affirmed ideal, but Harris joined to it his divinized process, a state which was a mystical entity and an organism, without any fear that statism could over-rule the victories and liberties of the past and present. How startling his conception was is apparent in his discussion of

[29] Harris: "Remarks," p. 196, *N.E.A. Journal*, 1896.
[30] Harris: "How the School Strengthens the Individuality of the Pupils," p. 125, *N.E.A. Journal*, 1902.
[31] Harris: *Psychologic Foundations of Education*, p. 260.
[32] Leidecker, *op. cit.*, p. 286.

the French Revolution, that mainspring of modern statism. For Harris, the French Revolution and the Reign of Terror taught emphatically that "mere individualism" is no guarantee of freedom. "There came to be an insight into the necessity of the government, the institution of the state, as the guarantee of the life and liberty of the citizen . . . The ideal nature of man gets realized in his institutions." *Man's fulfilment is thus institutional rather than God-centered, social rather than individual.* "The relation of the individual to this larger self incarnated in institutions is that of obedience to authority. The institution, which is a social whole is one of its forms, prescribes to the individual, and he obeys." For the child who leaves the circle of the family for the larger circle of the democratic school, it does mean an estrangement and an isolation, but this must be seen as an "emancipation" "from the immediate sway" to the distant, larger, and more important. "It is a process of correcting the judgment of the individual as to what his true self is, and as to what is of permanent value in human endeavor."[33] Clearly, the implication is very obviously that the family is a lesser order, the larger institutions having a more mature and emancipating influence.

The various economic and political opinions of Harris, together with his readiness to accept the outcome of the Spanish-American War and empire as a forward step, are now unpopular with educators, but they are far from basic to his position. Instead of being "The Conservator," Harris was in many respects a great transmitter, giving to educators a concept of the state as an organism in terms of which man must find his true self and fulfilment. R. Freeman Butts, in a passing comment on Harris' influence as a philosopher, has been most aware of his significance. The Hegelian and idealistic "emphasis upon the organic relationship between society and the individual"[34] which was

[33] Harris: "Isolation in the School—How it Hinders and How it Helps," pp. 357-363, *N.E.A. Journal*, 1901.
[34] R. Freeman Butts: *A Cultural History of Western Education*, p. 475. New York: McGraw-Hill, 1955.

promulgated through the *Journal of Speculative Philosophy* by Harris and others, and in Harris' numerous addresses, led, together with the doctrines of evolution and pragmatism, to the educational philosophy of John Dewey. Others had prepared the way with their concepts of education; Harris gave to philosophers and educators the doctrine of society and the state as the true self of man.

# 8. John Swett:

# The Self-Preservation of the State

The study of educational history and theory in the United States is usually confined to the eastern states, and to the key thinkers and educators thereof. In a sense, this emphasis is justified, in that the decisive conflicts, decisions and developments were made there. In another sense, the emphasis is misleading, in that the absence of major conflict in other areas, especially the west, is more significant and led to the freer development of the same premises. The eastern states began with a background of an established church, long-standing popular education without state control, a highly literate culture in certain areas and intellectual and religious traditions of major proportions. Indeed, a strong case can be made for the superiority of colonial culture as contrasted to the post-revolutionary mind. It was inevitable, therefore, that conflict ensue. There was opposition to the secularization and vulgarization in the new culture, as well as to its provincial and national outlook as contrasted to the older universality. The men who made the Constitution soon lost the nation. Classical education, Christian culture, the supremacy of law over popular demands, the insistence on the need in society for an aristocracy, the insistence that only a landed people were a responsible people, these and other causes had their champions in various areas, waging a steady if losing battle throughout the 19th century. Steadily, as the people moved westward, this background grew thinner, and its battle-lines less relevant. New Englanders migrated westward in great numbers, but had themselves less and less of the old standards to carry with them, and progressively less interest in doing so. Indeed, many were more ardent champions of the new gods, as witness John Swett. Swett sailed from Boston Harbor, September 15, 1852, in the merchantman *Revere,* bound for San Francisco by way of Cape Horn, arriving there on the last day of January, 1853. Here was a man whose background included, among other things, the old Calvinism, the age of homespun and its independence, and the memories of the Revolution, sailing on a ship named *Revere.* But, rather than a new Revere to cry alarm at the new redcoats of statism and taxation, Swett landed to seek gold first, and, failing that, to teach and to espouse state power in the schools. His life's motto came, not from the Catechism, but from Horace Mann: "Be ashamed to die until you have won some victory for humanity."[1] Humanity is a vague unshapen mass, hard to serve unless organized, and hence such service and victory must have reference to organized humanity, the state. Evolutionary, Hegelian and nationalist thinking had served to re-enforce the growing idea that *the true society of man is the state.*

In California, Swett found a vast territory filled with willingly displaced men like himself, men whose California politics were determined in terms of pro-Union or pro-Southern interests. The local issues were rarely as pressing for some years to come. Churches, schools, and clergymen existed, but their roots were not deep; they had not *created* the California culture, if such existed, but had only been *added* to it, a radically different picture from much of the Atlantic seaboard.

[1] William G. Carr: *John Swett, The Biography of an Educational Pioneer,* p. 1, Santa Ana, Calif.: Fine Arts Press, 1933. See also John Swett: *Public Education in California . . . with Personal Reminiscences,* p. 148. New York: American Book Company, 1911. Swett again emphasizes this same motto in his *Methods of Teaching,* p. 19. New York: American Book Company, 1880.

Only one group in California had any roots, the Church of Rome. Its original adherents, however, were Spanish and Mexican, people who were now aliens in their own territory, and aliens as well to many of the American Roman Catholics. The fact that the incoming Americans were increasingly divided in terms of Northern and Southern allegiances further complicated the picture. All shared, however, in a common pride in California and its wealth.

California became a state in 1850, without the usual preliminary stage of territorial government, without indeed the development of a common public opinion or heritage and yet with a tremendous common pride and ambition. A state superintendent of public instruction was called for in the state constitution adopted in 1849 before a system of schools had even been created. Except for San Francisco's school committee and school, very few other public schools existed in the state, "and the history of these is known only by tradition."[2] Private schools existed, but were new and had not developed strength in tradition and roots. This fact separates California and other states from the eastern areas, where long-standing systems were gradually taken over by the state, usually with great controversy. In California, it was presupposed that such was the proper procedure, and that the various church and private schools were but preliminary stages in the development of the school system. Swett was the fourth man to serve as state superintendent, and the decisive man, framing the basic legislation of the state system. The following were the state superintendents during the first thirty years:

| | |
|---|---|
| John G. Marvin | 1851-1854 |
| Paul K. Hubbs | 1854-1857 |
| Andrew J. Moulder | 1857-1863 |
| John Swett | 1863-1868 |
| Rev. O. P. Fitzgerald | 1868-1872 |
| Henry N. Bolander | 1872-1876 |
| Ezra S. Carr | 1876-1880 |

[2] John Swett: *American Public Schools, History and Pedagogics,* p. 103. New York: American Book Company, 1900.

This list is of interest in its variety. Marvin and Hubbs were Democrats, as was Moulder. Swett was elected on the Union ticket, re-elected on the Republican ticket. Fitzgerald was both a Democrat and a clergyman. Bolander and Carr were Republicans. Of these men, Swett was the decisive figure, but all showed in varying degrees the same statist concept of education. Indeed, Swett was far from being an extremist in the matter.

According to William G. Carr, Swett "saw more clearly than any of his predecessors the relationship between the State and education."[3] Swett himself expressed the fundamental principles of all his educational legislation and work in terms of two fundamental axioms in speaking to the State Teachers' Institute in 1863:

> . . . early in the history of our country these two fundamental principles were enunciated and adopted: *That it is the duty of a Republican Government, as an act of self-preservation, to educate all classes of the people, and that the property of the State should be taxed to pay for that education.*[4]

Swett was accurate in seeing these as fundamental principles in American educational history. They are indeed so familiar that their implications are not readily seen. Why is the state school necessary for the self-preservation of the state? States, after all, have existed for countless centuries with even greater stability than republics have manifested, yet without state education. Swett answered in part that the franchise required educated voters. But to this it could be objected that the United States was established, its Constitution written and its basic character established without the existence of a single state school. "Ignorance and prejudice" have been abolished or neutralized by other forms of education. "This general education of the citizens of the State can only be secured by Public Schools." So Swett believed and acted. Moreover, he held that such schooling should include rich and poor to "prevent the formation of castes and classes in society. The only aristocracy which they recognize

[3] Carr, *op. cit.*, p. 102.
[4] John Swett: *History of the Public School System of California*, p. 113. San Francisco: Bancroft, 1876.

is that of talent—an aristocracy which always commands respect and wields power." Swett did not foresee the day when, in the name of democracy, report cards would be dropped from some California schools to prevent the recognition of such an aristocracy. What did such "common school" education do for man? Here Swett turned to the ardent rhetoric of Horace Bushnell to point out that, great men who had even a slight "common school" education, were "yet all *educated men,* because they were MADE ALIVE."[5] Somehow, reading, writing and arithmetic, when learned under democratic circumstances, have a mystical capacity of making man truly man and truly alive. In other words, even as men are made "alive in Christ," so they are ostensibly made alive in democracy. To this mystical nation‑ alism, Protestant liberals and modernists in each era gave ardent support, and even the Church of Rome was not without its "American heresy." Thus, *statist education is essential to the self-preservation of the state only if the state is seen as the total society of man and the only area in which man can be truly man and truly alive. Inevitably, such a state cannot be a free state, because it cannot permit man to transcend the state, his one and only true society. The function of religion accordingly becomes the duty of providing social cement.*

The second axiom supported the first. "The property of the State should be taxed to educate the children of the State." Notice Swett's language, very often repeated, "the property of the State," not the property *in* the State, and, "the children of the State," not children residing *in* the territory of the State. In‑ deed, Swett plainly justified his language, affirming, "children arrived at the age of maturity belong, not to the parents, but to the State, to society, to the country."[6] This ostensibly gives the state the right to reach back into the home and claim the right

---

[5] *Ibid.,* pp. 113ff. While Swett did not foresee the abolition of the report card in certain grades, he did report, without any criticism, the legal prohibition in his day of homework for children under fifteen years, and the limitation of the school day to four hours for eight year olds and younger. John Swett: *The Ele‑ mentary Schools of California,* p. 13. San Francisco: Dept. of Education, California Louisiana Purchase Exposition Commission, 1904.

[6] *Ibid.,* p. 115.

of jurisdiction over its property, the children. In 1864, in his Biennial Report, Swett affirmed, and quoted judicial decisions of some eastern states to maintain, the following propositions:

1. *The schoolmaster and the king.* —In school, where the mind is first placed under care to be fitted for the grand purposes of life, the child should be taught to consider his instructor, in many respects, superior to the parent in point of authority. The infant mind early apprehends and distinguishes with a surprising sagacity, and is always more influenced by example than precept. When a parent, therefore, enters the school, and by respectful deportment acknowledges the teacher's authority, the pupil's obedience and love for the master are strengthened; and the principle of subordination is naturally engrafted in the child, and in the most agreeable and effectual matter possible—that is, by the influence of example. It is by this happy conspiracy between the teacher and parent that a new power—a genial influence over the infant mind—is acquired, which is of infinite importance to the welfare and happiness of society. To aim a blow at this power would be to strike at the very basis of *magisterial authority.* It was to support this important element of good government that the learned and judicious schoolmaster said to Charles II, in the plenitude of his power: 'Sire, pull off thy hat in my school; for if my scholars discover that the king is above me in authority here, they will soon cease to respect me.' . . .

2. *Every man's house is his castle.* —This old maxim of English law . . is as applicable to the schoolmaster as to any other person who is in the lawful possession of a house. It is true that the school officers, as such, have certain rights in the schoolhouse; but the law will not allow even them to interfere with the teacher while he keeps strictly within the line of his duty. Having been legally put in possession, he can hold it for the purposes and the time agreed upon; and no parent, not even the Governor of the State, nor the President of the United States, has any right to enter it and disturb him in the lawful performance of his duties. If persons do so enter, he should order them out . . he may use force . . .

3. *The vulgar impression that parents have a legal right to dictate to teachers is entirely erroneous.* As it would be manifestly improper for the teacher to undertake to dictate to the parents in their own house, so it would be improper for the parents to dictate to him in

his, the schoolhouse . . . In private schools the case is somewhat different; for the parents there, in legal effect, are the employers of the teacher, and consequently his masters; but in the common and public schools they are neither his employers nor his masters, and it is entirely out of place for them to attempt to give him orders; for 'there is no privity of contract between the parents of pupils to be sent to school and the schoolmaster. The latter is employed and paid by the town, and to them only is he responsible on his contract' (Spear v. Cummings, 23 Pick., 224).

4. *The statutory law as to disturbing schools.* —. . . there is no clause in it favoring parents; consequently, if they disturb or disquiet the school, they are subject to the same penalty as others. It is the policy of the States generally to encourage education; and many of them having established free schools, have thought proper to make provisions to protect their schools from indiscreet interference. Consequently, all well conducted schools may now, in a certain sense, be regarded as the wards of the State. . . .

' 5. *Parents have no remedy as against the teacher.* —As a general thing, the only persons who have a legal right to give orders to the teacher, are his employers—namely, the committee in some States, and in others the Directors or Trustees. If his conduct is approved of by his employers, the parents have no remedy as against him or them. . . . .[7]

Schools are thus not extensions of parental authority but "wards of the State," extensions of state sovereignty, and so to be respected. Children accordingly become wards of the school on entry therein, and parental rights are forfeited, except, as Swett noted, in private schools. In recognition of this fact, an antipathy to and assault on private schools was not lacking or long in developing.

On March 28, 1874, during Bolander's term of office, the California Legislature made it a penal offense for parents to send their children to private schools without the consent of the local state school trustees:

SECTION I. Every parent, guardian, or other person in the State of

[7] John Swett: *First Biennial Report of the Superintendent of Public Instruction of the State of California,* for the school years 1864 and 1865, pp. 164-6.

California, having control and charge of any child or children between the ages of 8 and 14 years, shall be required to send any such
child or children to a public school for a period of at least two-
thirds of the time during which a public school shall be taught in
each city and county, or school district, in each school year, com-
mencing on the first day of July, in the year of our Lord one thousand eight hundred and seventy-four, at least twelve weeks of which
shall be consecutive, unless such child or children are excused from
such attendance by the Board of Education of the city, or and
county, or of the trustees of the school district in which such parents,
guardians, or other persons reside, upon its being shown to their
satisfaction that his or her bodily or mental condition has been such
as to prevent attendance at school, or application to study for the
period required, or that the parents or guardians are extremely poor
or sick, or that such child or children are taught in a private school
or at home in such branches as are usually taught in the primary
schools of this State, or have already acquired a good knowledge of
such branches; Provided, In case a public school shall not be taught
for three months during the year, within one mile by the nearest
travelled road of any person within the school district, he shall not
be liable to the provisions of this act.

SECTION 3. In case any parent, guardian, or other person shall fail
to comply with the provisions of this act, said parent, guardian, or
other person shall be deemed guilty of a misdemeanor, and shall be
liable to a fine of not more than twenty dollars; and for the second
and each subsequent offense, the fine shall not be less than twenty
dollars nor more than fifty dollars, and the parent, guardian, or
other person so convicted shall pay all costs. Each such fine shall be
paid to the clerk of the proper Board of Education or of the district
trustees.[8]

The self-preservation of the state thus involved enforced state
education, and its goal was democracy and a democratic culture.
Ezra S. Carr, one of Swett's successors, was vocal on this point,
with Swett's earnest agreement. In September, 1875, Carr spoke
on "Child Culture" before the State Agricultural Society. His
concern was "how to grow a crop of sound bodied, right-
minded, clean-hearted children, who will 'take to work' as na-

---

[8] Zach. Montgomery: *The School Question*, p. 19f. Washington: Gibson, 1886.

turally and kindly as a duck takes to water." "Culture realized, culture put to work" was the need of the State, Carr believed, in agreement with many of his day. Agricultural and industrial education were thus needed. The schools must be rescued from the pedants, for Broderick's words, Carr warned, "are fast coming to be true, that—'WORKING-MEN WILL RULE THIS NATION.'" As with many other educators, Carr (and Swett) approved of the Prussian enforcement of these principles. The schools must meet the needs of modern civilization. "I am not one of those who think a thing must be good because it is bald-headed with antiquity." The natural conservatism of education must be disturbed. Activity, manual and physical activity, are essential. A hoodlum is "a boy gone to waste, rotten before he is ripe, because society does not know enough to preserve and economize him." The fault is thus society's, not man's, and action must be social, not personal. The monastic background of education makes it impractical. The European centrality and dominance can be broken, Carr urged, now that California is the supplier of gold to all nations, with an education that will be practical and designed to give California the desired world supremacy, and "industrial supremacy is the prize of industrial education." Practical, universal intelligence must be fostered, and "That universal intelligence is the only guarantee of universal liberty, is one of the fundamental ideas of the American's political faith; but the right and duty of the State to educate has been better stated in monarchical Germany than in republican America." To separate the schools from the state would not only destroy the schools, "it would be the destruction of the State." The choice was between "educated helplessness" or "educated power." "A good time" is coming, in terms of the advance in state and school, and "the reign of words" ("dogmas, religious or political"), and of literature, as well as the existence of war ("no longer necessary"), "is almost over." The workers' paradise was near.

. . . between the standing armies of soldiers, which tell how imperfect still is human government, and the sitting armies of sophists, whose mission is to perpetuate existing evils, another great army is being drilled—the army of labor—in which we shall find the most practical philosophy, the broadest intelligence, and the most Christian patriotism . . . With conscious pride, the farmers and laboring men of America are building a commonwealth whose spirit shall be peace on earth and good will to man; whose weapon, suffrage; whose conservatism, education; whose objects are freedom, order, and economy within our own boundaries, and an eternal brotherhood with those who are our wider neighbors.[9]

Swett himself had secured his 1862 nomination for state superintendent after a fighting speech that carried an otherwise committed convention. It was, of course, war-time, and Swett urged, "You will never make California union to the backbone until you have a school system so thorough that all the people shall be brought into the schools and thoroughly Americanized." Such education was a necessary preparation for future crises. Swett's goal was, whether as teacher or superintendent, the "Americanizing the children of this State and inspiring them with a love of liberty and a regard for the rights of man."[10] Teachers, Swett believed, "mould character," and were thus the necessary "master-masons to hew the cornerstones" for "the foundations of the State for all future times." The employment of trained and "skilled master-masons" was thus urgent.[11] Swett was earnest in believing state schools to be "essential to the existence of a free people, and to the permanence of a republican government."[12] The very fact that California had a population of so diverse origins made state education and indoctrination all the more urgent.[13] The system of state education Swett and Cali-

[9] John Swett: *History of the Public School System in California,* pp. 237-246. In including Carr's address in his book, Swett called it "What We Need" and saw it as an outline of "a want to be supplied during the next century," p. 237. In December, 1862, Swett had called working-men "the real wealth of California" and declared that "intelligent free laborers are working out the problem of civilization from ocean to ocean" and the "common schools, free as air, vital as electricity, vivifying as the sunlight, are silently molding the life of the nation." This address was delivered before the San Francisco City Teachers' Association.
[10] William G. Carr, *op. cit.,* p. 71. See also Swett: *Public Education in California,* p. 143f.
[11] Carr, *op. cit.,* p. 104.
[12] Swett: *Public Education in California,* p. 157.
[13] *Ibid.,* p. 165f.

fornia developed to accomplish the goal became the object of admiration by educators everywhere.[14]

As a teacher, and a very capable one, Swett wrote verses at times for school programs, giving earnest expression to his faith in state education.

> Great God protect the Common School,
> The surest stronghold of the free,
> The guardian of the people's rule
> Palladium of Liberty!
>
> At the shrine of Learning kneeling,
>    Sisters, brothers, hand in hand;
> *One* in heart and *one* in feeling,
>    *Brotherhood* of *Schools* we stand!
> *On*ward, in our high endeavor,
>    *On*ward, in the strength of youth,
> For *progressive* action ever
>    Brings us nearer *God* and *Truth!*
>
> Earth is rousing from her slumbers
>    On the shore of every sea;—
> Toiling millions without number
>    Marshalling for Liberty.
> Raise the shout of exultation
>    Let the banners be unfurled.
> Education
>    For each nation,
> Common schools for all the world![15]

As these verses indicate, for Swett, Yankee, Unitarian, able schoolman and zealous crusader, the state schools were a marching faith. His work was at all times that of a dedicated man, conscientious and without compromise where his prinicples were involved. He fought valiantly and ably against political interference in schools, and, when the vicious Boss Christopher T. Buckley came to San Francisco in 1880 and soon established

[14] *Ibid.,* p. 180.
[15] Carr, *op. cit.,* p. 65f.

himself as one of the worst blights in the history of that city, Swett refused to compromise, and, as a result, had to resign on June 10, 1890, from the San Francisco school system he had served so remarkably well. Public indignation secured his election to the higher office of city school superintendent, a major vindication, and he took office on January 1, 1891. Swett failed to see that state education inevitably means political control. He had hoped that his vindication meant that the people would support him in asserting the independence of the schools, but found instead that it was simply "a vote of confidence in him as a person and a rebuke to his enemies."[16] No change could be made with regard to politics and the schools.

In July, 1864, Swett had threatened recalcitrant school trustees who refused to use the state text-books with loss of state funds. In 1888, however, in addressing the National Educational Association, he had grave doubts about the textbook situation in California.

California is the only state that has entered into the business of publishing school-books . . . some of us have grave doubts about it . . . in large and populous states the power of adopting books is too great to be entrusted to any one board.[17]

In his address to the N.E.A., meeting in Los Angeles in July, 1899, he expressed even stronger fears: "There is a growing tendency in California towards uniformity and state centralization of power, which, if continued, might lead us into a kind of Chinese civilization. I have no love for Chinese uniformity in education."[18] But Swett failed to see that the very democracy he demanded, together with state control, meant an inevitable "Chinese uniformity." He had asserted, in apparent reference to Montgomery's *School Question,*

[16] *Ibid.,* p. 159. For a summary account, see also Peter Thomas Conmy, "John Swett," in *CTA Journal* (California Teachers Association) , vol. 54, No. 7, October 1958, pp. 16-19.

[17] John Swett, "The General Function of the State in Relation to School Books and Appliances," p. 200, *Journal of Proceedings,* N.E.A., 1888.

[18] Swett: *Public Education in California,* p. 318.

No prophets of evil can convince the American people that vice, crime, idleness, poverty, and social discontent are the results of free public schools. On the contrary, there is an abiding conviction that it is only by means of general education brought within the reach of all classes that a people can permanently maintain free institutions. The idea of universal education has fairly entered into the minds of men.[19]

What Swett failed to see was that state control and its uniform indoctrination destroyed the freedom of differences, of cultural independence and integrity. The group, democracy, would inevitably be exalted above the individual and his freedom, and the independence of free institutions wiped out by the overall power and control of the monolithic state. The school *can* be the helper of democracy, but it *cannot* create independent men at the same time that it shapes them into a democratic mass. The urge to conform, group-directed and mob-controlled thinking, these become the order of the day whenever democracy is the goal. *Classes cannot be levelled without levelling man also.* An aristocracy of talent and intelligence cannot prevail in a culture which is hostile to aristocracy in any form, and to any and all independence by man of mass man. Swett and his many dedicated fellow-workers believed earnestly in both state schools and independence. In the end, the state schools won, and Swett himself could see signs of a dreaded "Chinese uniformity." But Swett, as an eminently practical man, saw more than most of his contemporaries.

However, other educators soon saw the impossibility of the earlier ideal of democracy. One of these, a noted and not sufficiently appreciated Californian, was Ellwood P. Cubberley of Stanford University, whose extensive writings influenced two generations of teachers. Writing in 1909, Cubberley observed, "Our city schools will soon be forced to give up the exceedingly democratic idea that all are equal, and that our society is devoid of classes, as a few cities have already in large part done, and

[19] Swett: *American Public Schools*, p. 168.

begin a specialization of educational effort . . ." Moreover, Cubberley insisted, "The evils and shortcomings of democracy are many and call loudly for remedies and improvement." The way out is "to awaken a social consciousness as opposed to class consciousness," to emphasize, in effect, the group as against the individual and his equality or inequality, and to this end, "our teachers must become more effective social workers."[20]

The development here is very significant. If the schools are agencies of the state, they must inevitably serve the purposes of the state rather than God, man, the family, or any institution. Furthermore, if democracy in its total sense be abandoned, then this mass society must become a state governed by philosopher-kings or Platonic guardians for the welfare of the state and its citizens, and state schools are to be used to that end. The free state gives way to the welfare state, and pure democracy is sacrificed to total control. Briefly outlined, this is the development:

First step: The self-preservation of the state as the total society of man is seen as necessitating state schools. The goal is the independence of man in a democracy.

Second step: Earnestly as both man's freedom and democracy are maintained, gradually the levelling demands of democracy call for the surrender of liberties to democracy, and "rugged individualism" becomes anathema, and independence anti-social, as democracy gains sway.

Third step: As the state grows in power, society becomes less free and also less democratic. Democracy now begins to give way to a more "realistic" appraisal of society, whereby total control is necessary to further the welfare of the masses. Thus democracy is sacrificed to total control in the name of social or state welfare.

This third step was in plain-spoken evidence after World War I, and more vocal after World War II. According to one high

[20] Ellwood P. Cubberley: *Changing Conceptions of Education*, pp. 56f., 64-66. Boston: Houghton Mifflin, 1909.

school principal, one-third of the youth cannot be taught to read and must be classified as a "nonverbal" type "who for the life of them cannot master the mechanics of pronouncing and writing words."[21] Of the remaining two-thirds, it must be assumed that only a minority, those perhaps congenial to the hierarchy, can qualify for the ranks of the Platonic guardians of society!

In terms of this growing contempt of liberty and insistence on welfare control, students must be protected from such disturbing things as religion. Recently, as Russell Kirk has pointed out, a division of the University of California prohibited membership in the local Inter-Varsity Fellowship, an evangelical Christian study group, because religious discussion ostensibly made students neurotic. The dean of women was ready to grant the girls permission for a Marxist Discussion Group, but not a Christian group. The ban against any student group discriminating against any "race, color, or creed" could be used at any university branch against Roman Catholic Newman Clubs, Armenian Students' Club, or any society having such a restricted basis or membership. Again, as Kirk has stated, the State of California has taken action, through its Department of Social Welfare, against Mrs. Lila Joralemon of Berkeley, who conducts a Melody Workshop for children of three and a half to five years of age. The state insists that a nursery school must be licensed and must have certain required equipment, including hammers, nails, live ducks and rabbits, a punching bag, a stripped old car, and the like, and to restrict children to their desired musical training is "regimentation of children"![22] Freedom is thus called regimentation, and regimentation freedom. To have determined principles is to be discriminatory and hence evil. Ultimately, the self-preservation of the state becomes the obliteration of all things, including man, that dare set themselves apart from the state, and requires the creation of an ant-hill society. Towards the creation of that ant-hill society great strides have been made.

[21] George H. Henry, "Can Your Child Really Read?," p. 75, *Harper's Magazine*, CXCII, January, 1946. For critical comment, see Sibyl Terman and Charles Child Walcutt: *Reading: Chaos and Cure*, p. 29f.

[22] Russell Kirk, "Californian Follies," *National Review*, p. 280. November 5, 1960, IX, 18.

# 9. Charles De Garmo:
## Morality as Social Adjustment

Charles De Garmo (1849-1934), president of Swarthmore and then professor of education at Cornell, was important in American education for his part in introducing Herbartian pedagogy to the United States. Its overpowering influence over American teachers and students in the nineties has been likened to a "tidal wave" by educational historians.[1] C. C. Van Liew, Charles McMurry and Frank McMurry were among those also important in the Herbartian movement in the United States, whose major influence was between 1889 and 1901. Subsequently, the National Herbartian Society changed its name to the National Society for the Scientific Study of Education, and men like G. Stanley Hall and John Dewey developed new concepts in education often in Herbartian categories of thought.

Johann Friedrich Herbart (1776-1841), a successor (1809) to Kant's chair of philosophy at the University of Konigsburg, made a major impact on western education, particularly in Germany and the United States. Basic to his educational philosophy was the insistence that education be *moral* in outlook, morality,

[1] Frederick Eby and Charles Flinn Arrowood: *The Development of Modern Education*, In Theory, Organization and Practice, p. 786. New York: Prentice-Hall, 947.

however, being not primarily religious in nature but *social,* "a matter of adjustment of the individual to society."[2] This was not the negative concept it was later to become; for Herbart it meant more, in terms of the ideals of his day: "The term *virtue* expresses the whole purpose of education. Virtue is the idea of inner freedom which has developed into an abiding actuality in an individual."[3] His "fundamental postulate" in approaching this concept, was "the plasticity, or educability, of the pupil," but "unlimited plasticity" was an "inadmissible" concept.[4]

The first and foremost idea in Herbart was thus moral education in this non-religious and educational sense. The second idea was apperception, or the mental assimilative powers of the child as the means to this education, involving the important doctrine of *interest* as basic to education.[5] The five ethical ideas in Herbartian thought reflect Kant: (1) The law-giving will, or inner freedom, an idea related to Kant's dictum, "So act that through your own will the maxims of your conduct might become universal laws." (2) The idea of perfection, or efficiency of will, in terms of this inner freedom, i.e., the "coincidence of volition with judgment." (3) The idea of benevolence, sympathy, or good will, unselfishness. (4) The idea of rights, thus defined by Herbart: "Rights (legal) is the concordance of several wills, regarded as a rule for the prevention of strife." The idea of rights is thus legal rather than supernatural or natural rights. (5) The idea of justice, or equity. While "the ideas of Inner Freedom and of Perfection are merely formal," the ideas of benevolence, of right, and of justice are "substantial." The three universal virtues are these, love, right, and justice. These are, let it be noted, "substantial" and not *objective* virtues. For Herbart, while religious law is very significant for "the germination and

---

[2] R. Freeman Butts: *op. cit.,* p. 404.

[3] J. F. Herbart: *Outlines of Educational Doctrine,* p. 7. Trans. by A. F. Lange, annotated by C. De Garmo. New York: Macmillan, 1901. Italics are in English trans.

[4] *Ibid.,* pp. 1, 4.

[5] *Ibid.,* p. 44. De Garmo in Chr. Ufer: *Introduction to the Pedagogy of Herbart,* p. v. Trans. by J. C. Zinser. Boston: Heath, 1896.

growth of moral character," yet "he who does right only from a consideration of God and the future life, is still very remote from true morality." The regard for religion is based on the fact that "with occasional exceptions the way to morality passes only through legality."[6] It is immediately apparent that Herbart's morality is Kantian and well on the way to existentialism and pragmatic relativism. As the religious coloration of the times began to wane, the purely social aspect of Herbartian educational theory grew more vocal.

The Herbartian psychology furthered this socialization of man. One of the best definitions of Herbartian apperception came from Karl Lange:

Apperception is therefore that psychical activity by which individual perceptions, ideas, or idea-complexes are brought into relation to our previous intellectual and emotional life, assimilated with it, and thus raised to greater clearness, activity and significance.[7]

At first glance, it would appear that this concept is in disagreement with the Enlightenment's concept of the passivity of the mind, and its malleable character. This is definitely not so. As De Garmo pointed out,

The Herbartian psychology rejects as pure myth the idea that there is in the human mind any independent, or transcendental, faculty whose function is to will, and which is free in the sense that it can originate actions that are independent of all ideas or of thought processes. On the contrary, with Herbart's system, volition is strictly dependent upon ideas,—a product of them either as they originally appeared in the mind, or as they have come to be through repeated returns to consciousness.[8]

It is in terms of this essentially passive concept of the mind that Herbartians denied the transfer of training or the efficacy of the

---

[6] Ufer, pp. 34-53.

[7] Karl Lange: *Apperception*, A Monograph on Psychology and Pedagogy, p. 41. Edited by C. De Garmo. Boston: Heath, 1896. See also De Garmo: *The Essentials of Method*, p. 43. Revised edition. Boston: Heath, 1893. The original edition was published in 1890; and the additions in the revised edition deal with apperception.

[8] De Garmo: *Herbart and the Herbartians*, p. 57. New York: Scribner, 1896.

doctrine of mental discipline, the formal culture of the mind.[9] Because of this passivity, De Garmo could say, with Herbart, "Children have at first no real moral character."[10] Herbart, long before Freud, whom he influenced greatly, introduced the doctrine of man's determination by the unconscious into educational thought. For Herbart, the overwhelming aspect of man's mind was the unconscious, in contrast to which the range of consciousness and the threshold of consciousness are relatively small. Even the content of the conscious mind is guided by the ever active content of the unconscious.[11]

The culture-epoch, or recapitulation concept, was also basic to Herbart's thinking.[12] *Thus, man's mind is not only governed by racial history and the unconscious, but must be conformed to society to be moral.* It is not surprising that Herbartian thinking, instead of creating the free man of many-sided interests desired by Herbart, led to a socialized man. Indeed, the goal was, in De Garmo's words, "a socialized individual in an individualized society."[13] Thus, De Garmo found himself in agreement with E. A. Ross, who in *Sin and Society* distinguished between the old and new conceptions of sin and vice:

1. Old—Sin is violation of the laws of God,
   Crime is violation of the laws of man.
2. New—Sin is conduct that injured others.
   Vice is conduct that injures self.[14]

In terms of this anthropocentric view, De Garmo did not believe that justice required retribution in terms of God's righteousness and the protection of society, but that justice should concern itself more with the reformation of the criminal than with God's

---

[9] *Ibid.,* p. 25.
[10] *Ibid.,* p. 94.
[11] See Eby and Arrowood, pp. 766-770; Lancelot Law Whyte: *The Unconscious Before Freud,* pp. 142-144. New York: Basic Books, 1960.
[12] Eby and Arrowood, p. 778.
[13] De Garmo: *Principles of Secondary Education, Basic Ideals,* Vol. I, p. 125. New and enlarged edition. New York: Macmillan, 1913.
[14] De Garmo: *Principles of Secondary Education,* Vol. III, *Ethical Training,* pp. 9, 52. New York: Macmillan, 1910.

law and man's society.[15] Accordingly, all things must be read in terms of a society without God, and that society must dedicate itself to the adjustment of its members. "Not only must education be adjusted in ends and means to the society in which we live, but it must also be adjusted to the individual to be educated."[16] In this education, interest is essential.

A more adequate conception of the group of psychical states known as impulse, desire, interest, volition, is that the self is seeking through its own activity to express or realize itself. . . .
We may say in general that interest is a feeling that accompanies the idea of self-expression.[17]

Man's "salvation" depends on interest which enables him to discover his "deepest self."[18]

Not only interest but *play* was important to De Garmo. To him athletics and athletic training represented "the new asceticism" of his day.[19]

Art, however, had central importance. De Garmo was an early and able champion of the functional concept of beauty. As he stated it, "There is an actual, possibly, a necessary, correlation between mechanical efficiency and aesthetic proportion. In other words, as a tool or a machine increased in all-around efficiency there is a corresponding increase in the aesthetic quality of its proportions."[20] For De Garmo, after Schiller, art "is the bridge we must cross in going from animality to rationality."[21]

The elimination of religion thus is complete, and the excision of any absolute law from ethics a radical one. It is aesthetic ex-

[15] *Ibid.,* p. 78.
[16] De Garmo: *Principles of Secondary Education,* Vol. I, *The Studies,* p. 15. New York: Macmillan, 1907.
[17] De Garmo: *Interest and Education,* The Doctrine of Interest and its Concrete Application, pp. 12, 18. New York: Macmillan, 1903. It is not surprising that De Garmo "respectfully" dedicated this book to John Dewey.
[18] *Ibid.,* p. 17.
[19] De Garmo: *Principles of Secondary Education,* Vol. I, *Basic Ideals,* p. 26f., 1913 ed.
[20] De Garmo: *Aesthetic Education,* p. 75. Syracuse: Bardeen, 1913.
[21] Ibid., p. 2. See also *Principles of Secondary Education.,* Vol. III, *Ethical Training,* p. 160: "Art is truly the bridge between animality and rationality"

pression, a purely personal activity and a subjective response, which makes man truly human. It is not character, intelligence, godliness or scientific inventiveness. Man's morality, moreover, is social adjustment. The results of such education have not been, however, new achievements culturally and advances ethically, but the rise of the holy barbarians, men who have invested their ancient lusts and violence with a modern sanctity.

# 10. Col. Francis Wayland Parker:
# The Divine Child in the Divine State

At the July 8-12, 1901 meeting of the National Educational Association at Detroit, Michigan, a brief exchange of opinion between Col. Francis Wayland Parker (1837-1902) and William Torrey Harris brought to focus their divergent theories concerning the child and his education. Col. Parker stated, "In the first four years of school life the child must learn about all the great industries, and learn by doing. ' Harris responded, "That idea is all wrong. The child learns thru inhibition."[1] Both men were statists. Harris, however, had none of Parker's rosy illusions about the nature of man, whatever his illusions concerning the state. But for Parker, romanticist and sentimentalist par excellence, the child was a bundle of happy divinity whose trailing clouds of glory only inept adults marred. Parker, with no small enthusiasm, was much given to declaring that he had never met a naturally lazy child, or a child who did not enjoy work, or a boy who did not delight in manual training, or whatever at the moment concerned this zealous Yankee teacher and Civil War veteran.

Parker is perhaps best known as "the father of the progressive

[1] *N.E.A. Journal,* 1901, "Discussion," p. 588.

educational movement," a title given to him by none other than John Dewey in an article in the July 9, 1930 *New Republic*. The progressive education of Parker, however, differed markedly from that of contemporary theorists and practitioners, in that Parker sought goals which in part are more congenial to basic education. Riesman, Glazer and Denney, in *The Lonely Crowd,* have distinguished between the older inner-directed, production (or work) centered character and the contemporary group-directed and consumption centered person. Modern progressive education is very clearly group-directed, and it can with justice look to Parker for much of its leadership in this area. In spite of all that he contributed to the creation of such an orientation, Parker himself saw the purpose of education as definitely inner-directed and work-centered in his early years and never fully overcame that emphasis. Such a conception of education is especially marked in his talks at the Martha's Vineyard Summer Institute, July 17 to August 19, 1882, published as *Notes of Talks on Teaching*. His definitions of education were especially revealing:

*Education is the generation of power;* and the generation of power, in the right way, is the very highest economy of which man can conceive. We learn to do by doing, to hear by hearing, and to think by thinking.

. . . the end and aim of school education, is to train a child to work, to work systematically, to love work, and to put his brains into work . . . I wish to make a sharp distinction here, between *real work,* and *drudgery*. Real work is done on real things, producing tangible results, results that are seen and felt. Real work is adapted at every step to the child's power to do . . .[2]

While emphasizing play in the progressive school, Parker did it in terms of this context of work, declaring, "Play is God's elementary method of training the child to work."[3] The familiar phraseology of progressive education is heard in Parker with

---

[2] F. W. Parker: *Notes of Talks on Teaching*, reported by Lelia E. Patridge, pp. 117, 179f. New York: Kellogg, 1883.
[3] *Ibid.*, p. 158.

morning vigor: "The rule is *begin where you find the child*" But the orientation is different. "The study of *man at work* should have a prominent place in the school-room. . . . The history of labor is the history of man."[4] At the N.E.A. meeting of 1880, Parker defended his Quincy method as old common sense, and declared that, instead of throwing out the text-books as charged, "We use more books than under any other system. We claim the teacher should be as useless, the child as useful as possible."[5] Parker's 1894 *Talks on Pedagogics* reflects the influence of Dewey and others, but the emphasis on inner-direction and work is still strong. *"Self-activity is the fundamental principle of education. . . . Education depends upon the use the being makes of the conditions in which he finds himself the center."*[6] Spontaneity, self-activity and concentration were closely correlated. Although the group loomed large in Parker's thought, the relation of the individual to the group was one of activity, doing good, so that he could declare, "Education consists wholly and entirely in the cultivation of the altruistic motive; the motive without which religion is a delusion; the motive presented in the life and words of Christ; the motive of making one's own life and character of the greatest possible benefit to mankind."[7] The New England Primer had observed that "The Idle Fool is whipt at School." Parker hated punishment, but, like his Yankee forbears, of whom five were ministers,[8] he hated idleness and believed it to be an alien, demonic importation into the universe, unnatural to the child. Activity and work were man's life and nature. In these presuppositions, a central fallacy in Parker's thinking becomes apparent: he assumed the character of his day to be inherent in man for all time. Certain results were inevitable, in terms of progressive education, when children of inner-

[4] F. W. Parker: *How to Study Geography*, pp. 85, 351. Englewood, Illinois: Parker, 1888.

[5] *N.E.A. Journal*, 1880, "Discussion," p. 50.

[6] F. W. Parker: *Talks on Pedagogics*, An Outline of the Theory of Concentration, p. 87f. New York: John Day, 1937.

[7] *Ibid.*, p. 261.

[8] Ida Cassa Heffron: *Francis Wayland Parker*, An Interpretive Biography, p. 19. Los Angeles: Deach, 1934.

directed and work-centered lives were given leadership and freedom for self-development which can by no means follow with
group-directed and play-centered children. This possibility,
however, never occurred to Parker, and hence the radical difference in perspective and goal between his concept of progressive
education and that of more recent theorists. Like many another
thinker, *Parker assumed the historical past, a cultural and religious heritage, to be the biological reality concerning man.* This
*confusion of culture and biology,* however, was virtually made
law by evolutionary thinking and so accepted by Parker. The
past could not be annulled, because biology, the new queen of
all sciences, absorbed all else into her maws more thoroughly
than theology had ever done. Parker himself affirmed this cul-
tural-biological amalgamation in a lecture on "The Child,"
wherein he outlined the "natural" stages and pointed by way of
conclusion to the great messianic goal, the state of glory:

First . . . *the little child is born a savage;* . . it has a savage instinct
. . I am a firm believer in children living out their lives in the
mythical stage . . The child is a born savage, but he rapidly ascends
step by step, by love and works of love, up through all the rays of
blessed sunshine! up and up, to eternal light, and the everlasting
truth, and the eternal God . . .

*The child is born a naturalist . . .*

*Every child is a born worker. . . .* There never was a lazy child born
in God's busy world . . .

*The child is a lover of humanity . . .* There never was such a thing
as a selfish child born—they grow selfish later. Train the child up to
pure love. Love is a sacrifice . . .

Feed the lambs of God, and the gates of glory shall be lifted up, and
the King of Glory shall enter in.[9]

In this romanticist scheme of things, only the stupid and restricting adult (in particular, the teacher) could halt the march of
this divine child to the creation of the divine society. In this

[9] *N.E.A. Journal,* 1889, "The Child," pp. 479-482.

child-centered aspect of his thinking, Parker, for all his work-centered and inner-directed emphasis, was clearly the father of all progressive educators. Again, while claiming to use textbooks more than other educators, Parker, by stressing the primacy in learning of the unconscious in his *Talks on Pedagogics,* undercut the importance of both text-books and reasoning in favor of life-situations and conditioning.

Parker's stress on the centrality and divinity of the child was strong and insistent. "The child is the climax and culmination of all God's creations, and to answer the question, 'What is the child?' is to approach nearer the still greater question, What is the Creator and Giver of Life?"[10] In other words, to ask 'what is the child?' is virtually to ask, 'What is God?'! At one N.E.A. meeting, Parker misquoted Scripture to assert, "A little child shall lead us into truth."[11] This natural divinity of the child is best seen in unrestricted and free activity, for "The spontaneous tendencies of the child are the records of inborn divinity."[12] For this reason, both the freedom of the subconscious and the stress on spontaneous self-activity were of utmost importance to Parker.[13] Although he believed myths have a kernel of truth, it was not the truth that concerned Parker in his emphasis on the importance of myths, but the freedom of the child, for "who knows the whole truth? Shall the child be robbed of that which delights his soul and lays the foundation of true religious life? No greater mistake can be made in regard to the spontaneous activities of the child, for the myth is the true fire-mist of character, it contains symbols which point upward to God and to heaven."[14] Parker held that "God made the child His highest creation, He put into that child His divinity, and that this divinity manifests itself in the seeking for truth through the visible and tangible."[15] But, since Parker was vague on the meaning

[10] *Talks on Pedagogics*, p. 1.
[11] *N.E.A. Journal*, 1891, "Discussion," p. 101f.
[12] *Talks on Pedagogics*, p. 18.
[13] *Ibid.*, pp. 87f, 101, 104, 173, etc.
[14] *Ibid.*, p. 5.
[15] *Ibid.*, p. 7.

of truth, and stressed, for example, a purely subjective concept of numbers,[16] and vague also on the nature of God, it was clear that he was a forerunner of the existentialist emphasis on the anarchic freedom of man as the essence of truth. Education for him therefore was never a matter of objective knowledge; rather, "The working out of the design of a human being into character is education."[17] While he also defined education as "the development of the attitude of the soul toward truth," and, after Pestalozzi, "Education is the generation of power," this truth and this power were democracy, and "the responsibility of each for all, and all for each." Democracy is freedom, and "The means of acquiring freedom may be summed up in one word—education. True education is the presentation of the conditions necessary for the evolution of personality into freedom."[18] The goal is freedom, and the "conditions necessary" are again freedom, since the child is naturally good (although outwardly savage in his first stage) and also divine. The child "inevitably gravitates toward good." The child also gravitates towards truth and its best welfare. "That which is best for the unspoiled child gives it the greatest pleasure."[19]

It follows therefore that interference with the self-education of the child is a cardinal sin. "Discipline" was an ugly word for Parker; it constituted outside force, the death of spontaneity; it meant that "pupils have no opportunity to exercise their own wills." "So-called order" meant "the immediate will of the teacher; the children are wrenched into line; they are forced into habits of quietness." All this is evil; it is the radical freedom of choice by the pupil which is educative. Parker therefore hated that complement of discipline, punishment, and even more, that corollary of incentive, reward.

Bad as corporal punishment has been and is, the substitute of a system of rewards is infinitely worse. Fear of punishment is bad

---

[16] *Ibid.*, p. 53.
[17] *Ibid.*, p. 21.
[18] *Ibid.*, pp. 116, 312, 316ff.
[19] *Ibid.*, pp. 265, 271.

enough, indeed, but the systematic development of selfishness is damnable. The infliction of corporal punishment is degrading to the mind, but the hope of extraneous reward for study destroys the highest motive and sedulously develops its opposite, selfishness. I would place corporal punishment and reward-giving as in the highest degree criminal; as criminal as lying, stealing or swearing. I know it is not generally understood in this way; but I ask of you, my fellow teachers, to look at it with the greatest care. Why is it that the sordid nature of man is so highly developed in our country? Why is it that man looks upon his fellow man as a means to his own selfish ends? Why is it that we doubt almost every man who seeks for office—doubt whether he loves his country more than he does himself? To-day, one of the most prominent products of our schools is the systematic cultivation of selfishness—want of an interest in public welfare, public interests, the best needs of the commonwealth? Do you question this? Study the situation with that courage which dares to doubt![20]

Thus for Parker selfishness was the result of imposition of authority on the child, whereas altruism was the natural result of uninhibited egoism! What Parker did not dare openly say was that Christianity, with its heaven and hell, was in terms of his thinking the epitome of perverted teaching.

Implied also in this attack on rewards and punishment was not only a rebellion against report cards and promotion, but, even more, *against the whole concept of human responsibility*. Parker attacked prize-giving on this basis: "Prize-giving is the rewarding of an ancestor; rewarding a child for the virtues and mental power of his great-great grandfather."[21] Here we have the nemesis of all such anarchic concepts of man: *the child is made divine and absolutely free, only to have this freedom result in the denial of freedom in the name of inheritance!* Thus, the divine and free child is not really free, an empty divinity. What then must control this child who is merely the product of his ancestors and cannot be punished and rewarded for their vices or virtues? The way is thus prepared for man's subjection to the state.

[20] *Ibid.*, pp. 271f., 274, 275f.
[21] *Ibid.*, p. 276.

Parker did believe in conformity rather than anarchy, but his conception of conformity was at odds with Christianity and also with classical culture. It was a new law and new standard that he established as the principle of conformity:

The center of all movement in education is the child. We must grant that human beings are absolutely governed by immutable, ever-acting, all-efficient laws of growth and development, and that all development means conformity to the laws of being; non-conformity is decay, degradation, and death. Ideally the process of education consists in the presentation of conditions, and all the conditions, for the most complete action of the laws of the being. The central law of education is self-effort, that action of the ego, which, when normal, either consciously or unconsciously conforms to law. The constant adjustment and fulfillment of the laws of being ever condition the action of higher laws and form the ever-moving path of educative action.[22]

For Parker, the law of being meant also man's fulfilment in democracy. The state school is the great means to that "divine inspiration," "the mingling, blending, and freeing of all classes of society" in democracy. "The salvation of all children" is possible through democracy and democratic education.

Parker believed that man was as amenable to training and conditioning as animals. A Kentucky farmer, he pointed out, expected each of his hundred colts to become a useful horse. Why should it be different with children under proper "education"? "We must know that we can save every child. The citizen should say in his heart: 'I await the regeneration of the world from the teaching of the common schools of America.' "[23] Parker could not believe sufficiently in the integrity of man's personality to believe that, in a hundred children, many would, for good or bad reasons, resist his program of conditioning, or that others would accept it with equally mixed motives. Like every statist, he saw in animal husbandry an "unanswerable" logic for his position.

[22] *Ibid.*, p. 289.
[23] *Ibid.*, p. 328f.

For Parker, the school was thus the true home of the child, even as the democratic state was the true home of man. "A school should be a model home, a complete community of embryonic democracy."[24] "Every school in the land should be a home and heaven for children."[25]

The ideal school is an ideal community—an embryonic democracy. We should introduce into the school what we must have in the state, and this is democracy in its pure sense. The child is not in the school to learn, not in there for mere knowledge; but he is in there to live, to learn to live—not a preparation for life so much as real living. The pupil should in school learn to live. He should there learn to put himself into life. The teacher is the leader in this community life. Self-government is the only true government. A child should be taught to live for others. We are too apt to ignore the divinity of a child.[26]

At the 1895 N.E.A. meeting in Denver, Parker again emphasized "the evolution of pure democracy" as the goal of education. "The child is not in school for knowledge. He is there to live, and to put his life, nurtured in the school, into the community."[27] Radical integration was thus an absolute necessity, and private schools must be wiped out so that every child can have his "inalienable right" to total democracy.[28] *The schools, accordingly, are not for knowledge or education in any historical sense but are religious and political instruments for the total reshaping of man and his society and the conditioning of the child in terms of that way of life.* This concept was "true" Christianity for Parker, who declaimed, "The day will come when ministers will preach the gospel of common education from the pulpit; yea, when it will be the grandest part of the great gospel of Jesus Christ."[29] He spoke with glowing and rhapsodic joy of the New York bill requiring compulsory teachers' training after 1897, de-

---

24 *Ibid.*, p. 340.
25 Heffron, *op. cit.*, p. 41f.
26 *N.E.A. Journal*, 1895, "Discussion," p. 408.
27 *Ibid.*, "Response," p. 62.
28 *Talks on Pedagogics*, pp. 332, 341.
29 *N.E.A. Journal*, 1895, "The Training of Teachers," p. 972.

claring, "Mine eyes have seen the glory of the coming of the Lord."[30]

In 1891, at the Toronto, Ontario, Canada meeting of the NEA, Parker portrayed true learning and education as beginning after Darwin and after the development of democratic state schools (as against non-democratic state schools, as in Prussia, criticized in *Talks on Pedagogics*), and saw it as "rooted and grounded upon the people—'vox populi, vox dei.' " This meant, in the fullest sense, majority rule, and "the spirit and nourishment of the common school system has always depended, and depends to-day, entirely upon the will of the majority." The state school "is the newest of all the great human institutions that make for righteousness" and must absorb or eliminate all other schools. "The republic says to its citizens, 'You cannot be educated outside of the common school, for the common school is the infant republic.' " To oppose the growth of the state school, which is the child's true community and home, and to seek to maintain private schools is "bigotry," and "Hate is the devil, and should be remanded to the infernal regions, else there is a hell on earth." It is the state school which alone can shape the child for his democratic destiny, and to oppose such a course and maintain private education is thus demonic bigotry. The teacher has the key role in this future in shaping the child and creating that pure democracy in the classroom. "Here lies the way of the future school. Exalt the common school by the exaltation of the teacher. . . . Make them capable of undertaking the problem of man and the destinies of humanity."[31]

In the discussion that followed this address, A. P. Marble of Worcester, Massachusetts, observed that the ancient doctrine of the divine right of kings had been succeeded by "the divine right of the people." Marble saw that, in the name of this divine mass organized as state, the integrity and life of the family were being destroyed by Parker, and he sharply challenged this direction in education:

[30] *Ibid.*, p. 191f.
[31] *N.E.A. Journal*, 1891, "The School of the Future," pp. 82-89.

If the school of the future is to take the place of the parent, and attend to the entire training of children—to be responsible for bodily health, intellectual training, and moral culture; if the duty of parents is to cease when once the child is old enough to enter the kindergarten, and the school is to turn him out fully equipped for the battle of life, and for entrance into bliss hereafter,—then we must have a good deal more time and more funds. It would seem as if so broad an aim would need to include dormitories, clothing-stores, and refectories. Such was the Spartan scheme of education. It is not likely to be repeated. It is not desirable. Nothing of a public and institutional nature can supply the place of parents. They were ordained of God; and no incubator of modern science or education should ever supplant them. The duty of rearing and disciplining their children ought to be thrown back upon them to the largest possible extent; any institution or any school which tends to beget in the parental mind a feeling of irresponsibility is evil, and only evil, and that continually. The school of the future will not usurp the functions of the parent.[32]

This perceptive criticism by Dr. Marble, himself a life member of the N.E.A., Parker failed to answer, for he was immune to reason and a complete enthusiast. As was typical of him, he merely denied the charge and launched into a new rhapsody concerning the glories of the divine child and that divine state, pure democracy:

I believe, of course, that the home is the centre of the world, and the time is coming when mothers are to study the subject of education . . . obliged . . to study . . . The heavenly light that fell on the hills of Bethlehem teaches us of the divinity of the little child . . . 'Feed my lambs, feed my lambs;' and the gates of glory shall be lifted up and the King of glory shall enter in.[33]

The school, which began as an adjunct of the home, was now, in Parker's vision, to make the home its adjunct and require a pre-scribed course of study for mothers!

The success of progressive education in influencing schools far

[32] *Ibid.*, p. 93.
[33] *Ibid.*, p. 101f.

beyond its frontiers has been clear-cut and beyond a doubt, but this success has not been due to the abilities of its leaders, many of whom like Parker were pitifully inadequate thinkers, but to the logic of its position. Progressive education, by making explicit the logic of democratic state-controlled education, has had the power of an inevitable logic at its command, for *the educational socialization of the child means the socialization of all life.* If the spring, the home, is socialized, then the stream is inevitably socialized also, and every other agency steadily destroyed. The welfare state is a stage on the way, in that the independent agencies of society cannot survive when independent man and his society are supplanted by socialized man and the state. The home and its members no longer become the mainstay of life but rather that new home of the child, the school, and the adult's home, the state, become the sources of guidance, leadership, relief, sustenance and faith.

All this is done in the name of altruism and the love of humanity, and is ostensibly a transcending of personal egoism. But this love of humanity is only and always an extension of a diseased self-love which masquerades as righteousness. Man does not widen his horizon or transcend himself by multiplying his ego or substituting humanity for himself, but only by transcending himself in the obedience to, and glorifying and enjoying of God, the transcendent and ontological trinity.

Let us examine the implications of democratic education as conservatively developed by Southern educators in *Schools for a Growing Democracy*, 1936, by James S. Tippett in collaboration with the Committee of the Parker School District, Greenville, South Carolina. There is no evasion of the issues, and in Chapter I, "The Demands of a Democratic State," the first paragraph sets them forth as self-evident truths which even a district believing in "old-fashioned" virtues and report cards must affirm:

A democratic state must demand of its servants allegiance to and active maintenance of the fundamental principles upon which it has been founded. Teachers in the public schools are particularly important to the state. They deal with its future citizens at the most formative stage of growth. Upon them depends largely the success of the venture in human living upon which their government has set forth. Democracy requires supporters to insure its permanent existence, exactly as any other form of government requires them. Teachers in the public schools of democratic states, who must consider themselves servants of those states, should be active in spreading the understanding of all that a democracy means.[34]

There is no mistaking the implications of these forthright and honest words. Teachers must be considered servants of the state, not of parents, and the ends of the state, not the home, must be served. This is the socialization of the home and of the child. The perpetuation of democracy is the goal of the state schools, and "Schools for all the people are publicly supported for no other purpose." The school is a failure if pupils are given "no experience with democratic principles in action." Everyone must experience democracy and must be required to cooperate. "A democratic state demands co-operation among all its members." Moreover, "A democratic state demands leaders and followers," and the school is the training ground for both. The goal of education is "to meet the demands of the democratic state."[35]

In terms of these principles, it would follow that Southerners are clearly wrong in resisting integration of white and Negro pupils, since the attainment of pure democracy requires total social integration.[36] Likewise, it would follow that fraternities are an evil, in that they are based on a principle of social discrimination. Similarly, we would have to affirm that churches cannot be permitted their divisive and creedal differences, in that such principles of faith are anti-democratic, and a faith for all peoples and one more or less effortlessly credible to all is needed. *If democracy be the goal and the supreme virtue, then every other standard, virtue and faith must be levelled and elimi-*

[34] James S. Tippett, etc., *Schools for a Growing Democracy*, p. 3. Boston: Ginn, 1936.
[35] *Ibid.*, pp. 4-10.
[36] As a matter of record, this writer would like to make clear his opposition to both legal segregation and integration, believing that both involve an infringement on the individual's freedom of association.

*nated as hostile to democratic living. No more exclusive "good" than democracy exists in that its nature requires the destruction of all other standards.*

Again, the socialization of the school and child by the state is basically the same in principle, whether done by Nazi Germany, Soviet Russia, Roman Catholic and fascist Italy, or the democratic United States. In each and every instance, it involves a usurpation of home and school by the state. It is socialism in every instance, whether Roman Catholic or Protestant, national, international or democratic. There is no escaping this dilemma of socialization, with its subversion of learning to the goals of the state, *except by the radical disestablishment of the schools, the separation of school and state.* The state ownership of children is the implicit or explicit fact of all statist education: "German youth belongs to the Fuehrer," and all statist youth belong to the state. Whether stated by Hitler, Parker or Conant, it involves a view of life in which the nature and destiny of man is to be fulfilled in and through the state.

The triumph of statist education in a democracy means the triumph of radical integration of all life into the statist mold, *the triumph of social objectives over education.* The introduction of religion into the schools, or the inclusion of parochial schools into state and federal financial aid, will only intensify the triumph of statism over education.

Men like Marble could point to the deadly fallacies in Parker's thinking, but Parker's statist thinking is shared by those today who oppose progressive education, because, *given the principle of state schools, the primacy of statist purposes becomes the inevitable corollary.* Despite all his absurdities, therefore, the logic of Parker was wiser than the wisdom of his enemies.

# 11. William James:
## Education and Conditioning

William James (1842-1910) was not only influential in education through his influence on such men as J. Stanley Hall and John Dewey, but also through his *Talks to Teachers* (1899), for a time very popular in educational circles. This little book, first delivered as lectures in 1892, served, with his *Psychology*, as a major factor in hastening the introduction of scientific and experimental psychology into the theory and practice of education. Although *Talks to Teachers* showed extensive traces of the older educational thinking, both James' enthusiasm and direction were in terms of the new education.[1]

In essence, James' educational thinking was simply a reflection and extension of his psychology. Central to his psychology was his concept of habit.[2] For James, habit was basic to man and society:

[1] See the comments on this by John Dewey and William H. Kilpatrick in their introduction to William James: *Talks to Teachers on Psychology*, new edition, 1939. New York: Holt. This edition omits chapters from the original.

[2] The chapter on "Habit" in his *Psychology* has been extensively quoted and reprinted in part, as witness the Houghton Mifflin volume of 1901, *Two College Essays by L. B. R. Briggs; Habit by William James*. The influence of this chapter is almost beyond assessment.

Habit is thus the enormous fly-wheel of society, its most precious conservative agent. It alone is what keeps us all within the bounds of ordinance, and saves the children of fortune from the envious up-risings of the poor. It alone prevents the hardest and most repulsive walks of life from being deserted by those brought up to tread therein. It keeps the fisherman and the deckhand at sea through the winter; it holds the miner in his darkness, and nails the countryman to his log-cabin and his lonely farm through all the months of snow; it protects us from invasion by the natives of the desert and the frozen zone. It dooms us all to fight out the battle of life upon the lines of our nurture or our early choice, and to make the best of a pursuit that disagrees, because there is no other for which we are fitted, and it is too late to begin again. It keeps different social strata from mixing. Already at the age of twenty-five you see the profes-sional mannerism settling down on the young commercial traveller, on the young doctor, on the young minister, on the young counsel-lor-at-law. You see the little lines of cleavage running through the character, the tricks of thought, the prejudices, the ways of the 'shop,' in a word, from which the man can by-and-by no more escape than his coat-sleeve can suddenly fall into a new set of folds. On the whole, it is best he should not escape. It is well for the world that in most of us, by the age of thirty, the character has set like plaster, and will never soften again.[3]

This passage is typical of James. Curti, after Lippmann, has observed of him that "He gave a respectful hearing to all, even to ghosts."[4] It should be added that, in the process, he made ghosts seem perfectly natural and respectable, if true, although not necessarily so. The same persuasiveness is true with respect to habit. Pavlov's conditioning of dogs has always had an unpleas-ant ring to most men, and hence has often been rejected in its theoretical application to man. William James, however, said the same thing in winsome words and was applauded for it. Be-hind his conventional truisms on habit stands an iron-clad theory of conditioning. *Habit,* not family, education, Christian-

---

[3] William James: *Psychology*, p. 143f. New York: Henry Holt, 1910. American Science Series, Briefer Course, edition.
[4] Curti, *op. cit.*, p. 440.

ity, morality or any other force, is society's "most precious conservative agent." Habit, therefore, must be given priority over
all these other factors, and must become basic in education,
religion and morality, or else society is in peril. It is thus not
God, principle, reason, loyalty, or any other factor that is central but simply *habit.* James' *habit* is thus not a *product* of conviction and an expression of a way of life but the *creator* of it.
In view of this, James' view of religion, and every area of life,
becomes explicable. His well-known observation on faith is set
in this context: "*Act* faithfully, and you really have faith, no
matter how cold and even how dubious you may feel."[5] Habit is
not thus the outcome of faith but the creator of it; instead of
philosophy creating a way of life and the habits thereof, *the
habits create the philosophy.* In terms of this, if true, the potentiality of conditioning is almost beyond imagination. By molding the habits of mind and activity, the state can ensure that the
philosophy and way of life of the adult will be exactly that which
the state desires. William James himself was politically conservative, but his psychology had some very revolutionary implications.

James believed thus, that "The renovation of nations begins
always at the top, among the reflective members of the State, and
spreads slowly outward and downward. The teachers of this
country, one may say, have its future in their hands."[6] Inevitably, a theory of such radical conditioning requires that power,
however used, always emanate from the top down. Thus, James
called the schools, not common or public schools, but, realistically, "the State school system."[7]

In view of his "stream of consciousness" theory of thinking and
his conception of habit, James naturally stressed the non-rational

[5] William James: *Talks to Teachers* on Psychology: And to Students on Some
of Life's Ideals, p. 202. New York: Henry Holt, 1907. This observation was made
in the context of the approbation of Hannah Whitall Smith's *The Christian's
Secret of a Happy Life.* For Mrs. Smith, see B. B. Warfield: *Perfectionism,* Presbyterian and Reformed Publishing Co., Philadelphia.
[6] *Ibid.,* p. 3.
[7] *Ibid.,* p. 4.

in education, and saw substantiation for this shift of emphasis from the mind to the practical, emotional and habitual in the theory of evolution.[8] Animal psychology was thus brought into relevance as man and animals were made "less discontinuous."[9] "Education, in short, cannot be better described than by calling it *the organization of acquired habits of conduct and tendencies to behavior.*"[10] "Education is for behavior, and habits are the stuff of which behavior consists."[11] James' *habit* is comparable to the Hindu *Karma*: "We are spinning our own fates, good or evil, and never to be undone. Every smallest stroke of virtue or of vice leaves its never-so-little scar.... Nothing we ever do is, in strict scientific literalness, wiped out."[12] Christianity's liberation of man from relentless fate, Karma, and from necessity is wiped out by James, conversion and regeneration eliminated, and man again reduced to the working out of his past or *Karma*. Although James at times expressed himself in terms of the older education, or defined "the process of education . . . as nothing but the process of acquiring ideas or conceptions,"[13] and wrote of habit as the means of freeing the "higher powers of mind . . . for their own proper work,"[14] in essence his position was a reduction of education to *habit* or conditioning. As a result, educational psychology came into rapid prominence, and, together with it, a devaluation of the mind and its role in education characterized the new education.

The controlled mind became for many the goal of education. In the hands of Nazis, Fascists, dictators, Communists and others, this was seen as reprehensible. In the hands of democracy, this controlled mind was a great social goal of unlimited beneficence. Many years after James, S. L. Pressey, professor of Educational Psychology at The Ohio State University, stated, in

---

[8] *Ibid.*, p. 23f; cf. p. 36.
[9] *Ibid.*, p. 25.
[10] *Ibid.*, p. 28; italics are James'.
[11] *Ibid.*, p. 66.
[12] *Ibid.*, p. 77f.
[13] *Ibid.*, p. 145.
[14] *Psychology*, p. 145.

a book of widespread influence and popularity, his "central theme" in these words:

Modern psychological investigations tend to indicate that, to an extent hardly dreamed of even a decade ago, people are what the world has made them. In character, in personality, in usefulness, in happiness, they are the product of forces which can be controlled. And the chief agency for such control must be education. Further, the effectiveness of education can be increased manyfold. It is hoped that the treatment (of this subject by Pressey) may give a new sense for both the responsibilities and the potentialities of educational behavior.[15]

A new doctrine of man, radically at odds with Christian faith, and also Western culture of recent centuries, undergirds all such educational theories. It was thus truly a "new education" into a new concept of life and faith. Unfortunately, the new destiny of man bore a strong resemblance to old tyrannies "writ large."

[15] S. L. Pressey: *Psychology and the New Education*, p. 6. New York: Harper, 1933.

# 12. Nicholas Murray Butler:
## Education for the State

Nicholas Murray Butler (1862-1947), long president of Columbia University, and often mentioned as a possible candidate for the presidency of the United States on the Republican ticket, played, in his earlier years, an important role in the development of American education. But was Butler an educational conservative? Politically, despite certain contradictions in his thinking, Butler represented a conservative Republicanism. In 1924, when the income tax was as yet relatively new and mild, Butler stated bluntly that "the Sixteenth, or Income Tax, Amendment . . . levels to the ground all immunities that hitherto existed to protect private property. Private property is now wholly at the disposal of the Congress of the United States." Every constitutional protection was in effect undercut by the radical nature of that amendment, and the historian of the next century would, Butler believed, see it in that light.[1]

At that same time, in 1924, Butler opposed any attempt, such as the Oregon law, to make "elementary education a government monopoly."[2] The purpose of education he defined as "de-

[1] Nicholas Murray Butler: *The Faith of a Liberal*, Essays and Addresses on Political Principles and Public Policies, p. 244f. New York: Scribners, 1924.
[2] *Ibid.*, p. 257.

veloping human personality to the largest possible comprehension of the many-sided world in which we live, with a view to taking part in the life of that world and in some slight degree aiding it to progress."[3] Butler spoke sharply, no doubt with more than half an eye on Columbia and Columbia Teachers College, of those who

. . are now laying down as a principle that there are no principles, but that each individual, each group, each generation must follow its own instincts and respond to its own emotions, finding out from its own experience what is pleasurable and what painful, what is useful and what harmful. Such teaching reduces man with all his history to the level of an animal, with no past save such as is organized in his bodily reactions and his self-protecting and self-satisfying instincts. The American people were once substantially unanimous in their faith in certain fundamental principles of government and of life. More than once they did battle for those principles, but now their children are told that no such principles exist. Can we wonder that under such circumstances the foundations of government are changing?[4]

Butler stated the issue ably, and, at Columbia Teachers College, Kilpatrick, Rugg and others were well aware of the growing rift between Butler and Teachers College. But this statement by Butler was as much an indictment of himself as anyone else.

The rift was an ironic one, in that Teachers College, originally the New York College for the Training of Teachers, was launched in 1886 under the presidency of Nicholas Murray Butler, changing its name to Teachers College in 1892. The college was established in part by converting an earlier philanthropic association into an educational institution.[5] Shortly prior to its establishment, young Butler, then a Columbia University Fellow in Philosophy, offered a series of lectures in education.

[3] *Ibid.*, p. 260.
[4] *Ibid.*, p. 72.
[5] Different dates, from 1886 to 1888, are given for this change. Butler states that "Teachers College came into existence in the winter of 1886-87." Butler: *Across the Busy Years*, Recollections and Reflections, vol. 1, p. 176. New York: Scribners, 1939.

It was predicted by others that the undertaking was futile, although Butler chose Saturday mornings in order to be available to both teachers and prospective teachers. Not only was the largest room at the university crowded, but fifteen hundred requests for tickets had to be declined. This interest, being refused development at Columbia, led to the formation of the college, with Butler as president. When the College petitioned Columbia for affiliation with the university, the university council, according to Butts, refused, stating, "there is no such subject as education, and, moreover, it would bring into the university women who are not wanted."[6] Butler has given the actual text of the Council report, which reads rather differently. The University Council did not give an outright refusal but suggested an "alliance" rather than "consolidation." Its first reason for rejecting consolidation was the necessity of maintaining a practice teaching school from kindergarten through high school, which was deemed an unwise responsibility. "The second reason is that such a consolidation as is proposed would introduce co-education into Columbia in a most pronounced form." Columbia would thus be committed to matters which were separate administrative decisions apart from consolidation. An "alliance" without "consolidation" was suggested, but rejected by the trustees on both the same grounds which the Council had urged against consolidation.[7] The affiliation without consolidation was achieved, according to Butts, in 1898. Dr. Walter Hervey had succeeded Butler in 1891, serving until 1897. James E. Russell then served as dean from 1897 to 1927, and developed the school rapidly; his son, William F. Russell, then succeeded him. Butler became Dean of the Faculty and Professor of Philosophy and Education in 1890, and then, twelve years later, became president of Columbia University, serving for forty years.

Butler's role was, therefore, a major one, and his disagreement with the Columbia Teachers College he helped create, an ironic one. Why the rift? Harold Rugg stated the case briefly some years later. Butler had begun his career as one of many current

[6] R. Freeman Butts: *op. cit.*, p. 468.
[7] Butler, *op. cit.*, pp. 182-187.

champions of the theory of evolution who sought to apply its significance to all of life. Butler's "Principles of Education" course had, as its stated purpose, according to the *Teachers College Record* for 1900:

... to lay the basis for a scientific theory of education considered as a human institution. The process of education is explained from the standpoint of the doctrine of evolution, and the fundamental principles thus arrived at are applied from the three-fold standpoint of the history of civilization, the developing powers of the child, and the cultivation of individual and social efficiency.[8]

Butler's writings on education give clear-cut witness to this attempt.[9] As Rugg analyzed it, the advocates in education of the theory of evolution were of two points of view, "the Conforming Way and the Creative Path."[10] Those who held, like Butler, to the conforming way were inconsistent evolutionists, in that they were past-bound, adhering to traditions, creeds, social classes, and principles having no justification in evolution. The creative path, held by those who recognized the law of change and flux, saw the rise of the common man as the order of the day, and looked to the future for evolution's highest 'laws' rather than to a lower past; it refused to see any 'law' as final. Thus, when Butler wrote, "The modern world has sat at the feet of the ancient world for a long time, but has not yet learned all that the ancient world has to teach,"[11] his thinking was traditionalist rather than evolutionary. In accepting evolution, he had acknowledged *continuity* and *change* to be the fundamental laws of being, but, by his anti-pragmatism, he was unwilling to accept the logical implications of his position.[12] Butler was thus rejecting the very

---

[8] Harold Rugg: *The Teacher of Teachers*, Frontiers of Theory and Practice in Teacher Education, p. 59. New York: Harper, 1952.

[9] See Butler: *The Meaning of Education, and Other Essays and Addresses*, pp. 4ff., 13f. New York: Macmillan, 1905. See also his *The Meaning of Education, Contributions to a Philosophy of Education*, pp. 312ff. New York: Scribners, 1917. The second volume includes a few chapters from the first but includes fourteen new chapters also.

[10] Rugg, *op. cit.*, p. 43f.

[11] Butler: *Philosophy*, p. 50. New York: Columbia University Press, 1911.

[12] *Ibid.*, p. 42f.

educational philosophy he had helped set in motion. In his disagreement with Teachers College, Butler had the unhappy position of being in radical self-contradiction and hence unable to develop a valid case against Kilpatrick, Dewey, Rugg, or any others of that school of thought.

The problem was simply this: *if all reality is continuous and hence equally ultimate, then there is no ground for preferring good to evil, life to death, and any one thing to another, for all are equally absolute, equally valid, and equally basic reality. All standards and differentiations are therefore invalidated and eroded. Moreover, if change together with continuity is the fundamental law of being, then change is merely change and never growth, and higher and lower, past and present, are equally ultimate, equally meaningful, and equally meaningless.* Because this was Butler's dilemma as well as that of those whom he criticized, he was unable to come to grips with the issue, and the more consistent adherents of *continuity* and *change* carried the day, and *the progressive erosion of all meanings into the great commonality of the ocean of being continued apace.*

The seeds of that commonality were in Butler's educational thinking, not only in his adherence to evolution, but in his insistence that education in a democracy "is a failure" if it "does not relate itself to the duties and opportunities of citizenship."[13] In itself, this statement is harmless, but let us see it in the broader context of Butler's views on "Democracy and Education":

It is easy to cry "Liberty, Equality, and Fraternity," and to carve the words in letters of stone upon public buildings and public monuments. It is not so easy to answer the query whether, in truth, unrestricted liberty and perfect equality are at all compatible. For it has been pointed out that liberty leads directly to inequality, based upon the natural differences of capacity and application among men. Equality, on the other hand, in any economic sense, is attainable only by the suppression in some degree of liberty, in order that, directly or indirectly, the strong arm of the state may be able to hold back the precocious and to push forward the sluggish. Obviously

[13] Butler: *The Meaning of Education, Essays, 1905*, p. vii.

there is food for thought in this,—thought that may serve to check the rhetorical exuberance of the enthusiast, and lead him to ask whether we yet fully grasp what democracy means.[14]

At this point, Butler, as an educator, was thinking clearly and consistently. What many of the critics of education fail to grasp is this, that *educators have simply made explicit the presuppositions of contemporary culture.* In order to have democracy with liberty, Butler held, education was essential. At this point, his inspiration was "Greek Philosophy."

Both Plato and Aristotle had a deep insight into the meaning of man's social and institutional life. To live together with one's fellows in a community involves fitness so to live. This fitness, in turn, implies discipline, instruction, training; that is, education. The highest type of individual life is found in community life. Ethics passes into or includes politics, and the education of the individual is education for the state.[15]

Man is not only a social animal, he is a statist animal. Being continuous with all reality, he has no discontinuity with the mass, and no law to live by in terms beyond that commonality and continuity. Hence, "the education of the individual is education for the state." Man in evolution, unlike man created in the image of God, has no element of transcendence and no law beyond the commonality. He is continuous with his fellow men, and that continuity is best fulfilled in democracy, which is man's "completion."

Failure to understand the political life of a democratic state and failure to participate fully in it, leads directly to false views of the state and its relations to the individual citizen. Instead of being regarded as the sum total of the citizens who compose it, the state is, in thought at least, then regarded as an artificial creation, the plaything of so-called politicians and wire-pullers. This view, that the individual and the state are somehow independent each of the other, is not without support in modern political philosophy, but it is a

14 *Ibid.*, p. 106f.
15 *Ibid.*, p. 109.

crude and superficial view. It gives rise to those fallacies that regard the state either as a tyrant to be resisted or as a benefactor to be courted. No democracy can endure permanently on either basis. The state is the completion of the life of the individual, and without it he would not wholly live. To inculcate that doctrine should be an aim of all education in a democracy. To live up to it should be the ideal of the nation's educated men.[16]

Columbia Teachers College was more faithful to this concept than Butler himself: Man is only man when he is a statist man. Daniel Defoe was thus clearly wrong when his Puritan Robinson Crusoe became, in isolation, himself civilization and culture, and was able to introduce a savage into Western civilization, present in his own person. If the "completion" of man by the state "should be an aim of all education in a democracy," then too the *state* has supplanted *society* as the order of the societal life of man. While Butler was ready to declare, as "fundamental to our American educational system" that, "while all forms of education may be under government control, yet government control of education is not exclusive" nor "exclusively a government function,"[17] it was still true that the government was inseparable from it. Education is "a state function," although "the State claims no monopoly in education." Rather, the state "protects private initiative."[18] Butler, at this point, is inconsistent with himself. If "the state is the completion of the life of the individual," then education must be the exclusive function of the state. If for man there is no salvation outside the institutional church, then it follows that education must be under the jurisdiction of that church, for whatever order claims to *complete* man or to *redeem* him, claims accordingly the right to educate him. If the claims of both church and state to be the order of salvation be disallowed, then the right of both to be the educators must be challenged. Butler, with others of his day, saw the necessity of half of that fact. "Democracy and the conviction

16 *Ibid.*, p. 110f.
17 Butler: *The Meaning of Education, Contributions, 1917*, p. 323f.
18 *Ibid.*, p. 347.

that the support and control of education by the state is a duty, in order that the state and its citizens may be safeguarded, have necessarily forced the secularization of the school."[19] Equally necessarily, the conviction that man is not the creature of the state must force the disestablishment of the schools. Butler never changed his premises; he simply disliked their logical development in the hands of men like Kilpatrick. He was not in any sense an educational hope for conservatism. Moreover, the educational 'conservatives' had fought the statist schools; Butler had not.

True educational conservatism, therefore, was an impossibility for Butler, however much he sought to be a national champion of conservatism. On two grounds, he had rendered such a position untenable for himself: (1) *continuity* and *change* cannot be made absolutes without thereby giving them free rein over all things, and (2) *it is impossible, logically, to begin by socializing the child and then balk at the socializing of the state. If the child educationally belongs to the state and to its care or oversight, it is then a far lesser thing to ask that property be likewise surrendered to the state.* Can a man logically surrender his children to the state and then withhold his property without becoming thereby a contradiction, and a monstrous contradiction at that? In Christian terms, in the Reformed interpretation, the issue is simply this: *is it man, the church, or the state who is created in God's image? If it be man, then it is idolatry and a violation of the first commandment to kneel before or bow down to church or state.* The issue, in Butler's terms, is logically this: there is no issue. Man is an evolving being in an evolving universe which has no law beyond continuity and change, a universe in which all other things, good and evil, life and death, truth and error, are equally ultimate and equally valid and members, together with man, of one continuous, changing abyss of being. Hence, all power to and exaltation of the commonality of being!

[19] *Ibid.*, p. 184.

# 13. G. Stanley Hall:
## The Child-Centered Society

Granville Stanley Hall (1846-1924), a man from Massachu-setts and Mayflower stock, was, like Dewey and others, to give evidence of the radical reversal of all Puritan values that charac-terized the messianic educational theories of latter-day New Englanders. Hall, best known for his recapitulation theory, held in that dogma that the supposed recapitulation of evolution by the embryo was also characteristic of the development of man from birth to maturity. This theory, while now denounced, still leaves its marks on the current curriculi. Hall's influence in other and less publicized areas is more decisive.

Prior to his every particular theory, Hall held to a faith which was the presupposition and governing motive of his entire con-cept of education, namely, that education is a scientific disci-pline which must conform to the biology, anthropology, physi-ology and psychology of man. Moreover, since the governing 'fact' in these various sciences and the life of man is the concept of evolution, this concept must be basic to any valid approach to education. Thus, tests and measurements, psychological studies, biological factors and conditions rather than 'abstract' religious or moral principles must be the basic approach in education.

Two important approaches to this ideal means of education were for Hall the questionnaire method and the recapitulation theory, both now discarded, as are the German psychologists he valued so highly,[1] but the emphasis on the scientific approach has been deepened and broadened. His students alone, however they later differed from him, were in many instances a major factor in developing a scientific and psychological approach to education. They included John Dewey, J. McKeen Cattell, W. H. Burnham, M. W. Swift, Phyllis Blanchard, Florence Mateer, M. H. Small, Howard Odum, E. S. Conklin, E. W. Bohannon, Edward Conradi, H. D. Sheldon, E. B. Huey, G. E. Partridge, L. M. Terman, J. H. Leuba, E. D. Starbuck, H. H. Goddard, and many others.[2] The Gilbreths, pioneers in industrial psychology, a field of interest to Hall, studied under him also. At Johns Hopkins, Woodrow Wilson took minors with Hall.[3] Hall was also the head of a notable attempt, Clark University, to establish a purely graduate institution of higher learning, the project ultimately failing because of Clark's failure to support it adequately.[4]

A brief survey of some central aspects of Hall's thinking will serve to indicate the nature of his influence.

First and foremost in Hall's philosophy of education was the doctrine of evolution, with its then current belief in recapitulation. Hall by no means originated this theory but merely popularized its educational usage. According to Hall, "The child repeats the race. This is a great biological law."[5] Accordingly, Hall insisted that intellectual demands on the child were unwar-

---

[1] See G. Stanley Hall: *Founders of Modern Psychology*. New York: Appleton, 1912. For an influential example of the questionnaire method, see G. S. Hall: *The Contents of Children's Minds on Entering School*. New York: Kellogg, 1893.

[2] Curti, *op. cit.*, p. 426.

[3] G. S. Hall: *Life and Confessions of a Psychologist*, p. 240. New York: Appleton, 1927.

[4] *Ibid.*, pp. 258-353. For Hall's hopes and plans concerning it, see also N. Orwin Rush, ed.: *Letters of G. Stanley Hall to Jonas Gilman Clark*. Worcester, Mass.: Clark University Library, 1948.

[5] G. S. Hall, "Some of the Methods and Results of Child Study Work at Clark University," *N.E.A. Journal*, 1896, p. 862.

ranted, and kindergarten should be continued to the age of eight.[6] In youth, rationality comes to the fore and a highly intellectual discipline of study is then necessary. Prior to that, learning is by play. Much of the radical imbalance between grade schools and academically oriented high schools is due to Hall's recapitulation theory, with its belief that the child is also a primitive man with limited intellectual abilities. For Hall, the line of separation between animals and man was a false one. In his ideal society, Atlantis, the unity of man and animals is affirmed:

Animals are our elder brothers and are far better adapted to their conditions than man has yet learned to be. They have taught him many arts, and the lives of many of them are full of morals for man as the animal epos here, which was very highly developed, abundantly shows. Many species are our direct ancestors and all are our cousins. Man needs their strength, keenness of sense, power of flight, as well as their hides and flesh. Each ascending order was once a lord of creation, till at last man became their leader. Medicine and hygiene were largely the products of experiments upon them. Even now all their wisdom and industry combined could perhaps surpass that of man. They are our totemic ancestors and natural objects of fear and love, and great educators of these sentiments in us.[7]

Such an attitude is not surprising, although Hall's romanticism made him more ready to follow its implications than most. If "every child, from the moment of conception to maturity, recapitulates, very rapidly at first and then more slowly, every stage of development through which the human race from its lowest animal beginnings has passed,"[8] then *man, by virtue of evolution, is closer to his animal past than to the greatness of his human present. This animal past, all men share; the great human achievements are the experience of the few.* Thus, Hall inevitably down-graded reason, however much he sought to promote it. Moreover, he trusted "instinct" far more than reason.

[6] G. S. Hall: *Educational Problems,* v.II, p. 611. New York: Appleton, 1911.
[7] G. S. Hall: *Recreations of a Psychologist,* p. 75f. New York: Appleton, 1920.
[8] Hall: *Life and Confessions,* p. 380.

According to the biblical doctrine of man, long influential in Western history, *man, created in the image of God, is only to be understood in terms of God,* but, for Hall, *the race is to be understood in terms of the child, and the child and race in terms of evolution and the primitive past.* The application of animal psychology and experimental results to education thus quickly developed in later years.

The principle that the child and the early history of the human race are each keys to unlock the nature of the other applies to almost everything in feeling, will, and intellect. To understand either the child or the race we must constantly refer to the other.[9]

This means then that geneticism is the key to knowledge, and to the understanding of man. Hall's recapitulation theory is largely by-passed today, but his insistence on geneticism is not; it has merely taken more sophisticated forms. Hall, with some reservations, welcomed psychoanalysis and the work of Jung and Freud because, like evolution, it was a form of geneticism.[10] The basic law being no longer recognized as God's but nature's, and evolution being that law, geneticism in one form or another is an influential factor in educational premises.

Second, as a result of this new law, the study of the child became central to educators, and child-study continues to be emphasized. In 1893, Hall insisted, "the school of the future must be based on original child-nature," a logical conclusion in view of his premises.[11] Accordingly, innumerable studies of children's thinking, activities and interests, as witness Hall's own "The Story of a Sand Pile" were made and regarded as new wisdom.[12] *The concept of play as education,* by no means original with Hall, received new focus and added impetus when set in the context of his evolutionary faith. Play thus became a central teaching device, as did dancing, pantomime and like activities.[13]

[9] Hall, "The Natural Activities of Children," *N.E.A. Journal,* 1904, p. 443.

[10] Lorine Pruette: *G. Stanley Hall, A Biography of a Mind,* with an intro. by Carl Van Doren, p. 4f. New York: Appleton, 1926.

[11] Hall, "Child Study as a Basis for Psychology and Psychological Teaching," *N.E.A. Proceedings,* 1893, p. 718.

[12] Hall: *Aspects of Child Life and Education.* Boston: Ginn, 1907.

[13] Hall: *Educational Problems,* I, pp. 42-90.

For some time, therefore, the school must teach through play, and then with youth apply discipline, remembering always the late arrival of intellectual skills and their artificiality. As Partridge, with Hall's approval, summarized it:

Both reading and writing are usually taught too early. For countless centuries, in the race, language was all oral, and it should be so for the child during a longer period than is customary. Reading and writing, as processes, are artificial and uneducational in themselves. Therefore the less we appeal to consciousness and effort in acquiring them the better. By delaying them until precisely the time when the mind is best adapted to such drill, and working intensively, trusting much to the child's native powers of assimilation, they are learned much more readily and more perfectly, than when they are attempted earlier. Oral language methods are correct, for they put more work upon the memory, afford a more natural state of attention, and make use of rhythms and cadences which greatly assist the child in learning language. Methods of reading and writing cramp the attention to a narrow focus, take away the interest from the content, and put it upon the details of form.[14]

Third, Hall held to the parallelism of mental and physical life, so that a sound mind *requires* a sound body. Eby and Arrowood have gone so far as to call this "Hall's fundamental theory."[15] Hall here revealed an insistent consistency of theory. If the supernatural be denied, and the unity of mind and body be affirmed, then the sickness of the one *must* be the sickness of the other. Accordingly, then, as Hall held, music to be understood must be danced. "I believe it is not going too far to urge that no music of any kind is or can be fully comprehended without motor accompaniment."[16] As a result of this concept, projects, activities, folk-dancing and other 'motor activities' became the means of learning, and books were relegated to a subordinate

---

[14] G. E. Partridge: *Genetic Philosophy of Education,* An Epitome of the Published Educational Writings of President G. Stanley Hall of Clark University, p. 230. New York: Sturgis and Walton, 1912. The introductory note to Partridge's study is by Hall and gave his approval to the work.
[15] Eby and Arrowood: *The Development of Modern Education,* p. 844.
[16] Hall: *Educational Problems,* I, p. 69.

or coordinate position. Dewey used this same concept extensively without bothering to re-affirm or argue it. As Hall pointed out, Dewey formally by-passed Hall's theory but actually operated on its basis.[17]

Fourth, *the child became the norm,* both for education and for all life. "Love of nature and of children is the glory of manhood and womanhood, and the best of civilization."[18] In his old age, with unquenched faith, Hall repeated his life-long premise: "Childhood is the paradise of the race from which adult life is a fall."[19]

Just as in the Renaissance man remembered again his golden age and a new light came into the world, so we live in an age of the renaissance of child-life, and all teachers who carefully answer a good questionnaire help on the dawning of a new day, whether or not they have ever heard of pedagogy or ephebics.[20]

As Curti has observed, "Like Parker, Hall made a gospel of childhood."[21] Childhood as the norm meant the subservience of all society to the service of the child, a goal largely accomplished in modern society by the educational apostles of this faith.

There is really no clue by which we can thread our way through all the mazes of culture and the distractions of modern life save by knowing the true nature and needs of childhood and adolescence. I urge then that civilizations, religions, all human institutions, and the schools, are judged truly, or from the standpoint of the philosophy of history, by this one criterion: namely, whether they have offended against these little ones or have helped to bring childhood and adolescence to an even higher and completer maturity as generations pass by. Childhood is thus our pillar of cloud by day and fire by night.[22]

---

[17] Hall: *Life and Confessions,* p. 500.
[18] Hall, "Some of the Methods and Results of Child Study Work at Clark University," *N.E.A. Journal,* 1896, p. 864.
[19] Hall: *Recreations of a Psychologist,* p. 314.
[20] Hall, "Unsolved Problems of Child Study and the Method of Their Attack," *N.E.A. Journal,* 1904, p. 787.
[21] Curti, *op. cit.,* p. 411.
[22] Hall, *Forum,* XXIX, August, 1900, p. 700, cited by Curti, p. 416.

Hall knew his Bible well enough, as a one-time divinity student at Union Theological Seminary, to recognize that this last reference was tantamount to saying, childhood is thus our god. As a consequence of this faith, the god-child could not be forced in his learning. His curiosity and interest must be aroused, and the child then gently led into learning.

We must bear in mind that interest is the very Holy Ghost of education and that so-called formal studies and methods of discipline are only, for the most part, a delusion and a snare. They make degenerate mental tissue. It is not culture to learn to speak or write well upon trivial or indefinite subjects but rather to keep up with the great human interests, which will come to expression spontaneously if they are given a fair chance to do so.[23]

Spontaneity, permissiveness, and freedom to educate oneself through the electives system were thus cardinal emphases from this perspective. Hall could speak happily of the results of this educational approach and insistence on child study:

Instead of the child being for the sake of the school, we have had a Copernican revolution, and now the school, including its buildings, all its matter and method, revolve about the child, whose nature and needs supply the norm for everything.[24]

Hall had hoped that Clark University might gradually be changed to "devote all its funds ultimately to the cult of the child."[25] The child and his play became the sources of wisdom and must be studied and understood. "Play at its best, is only a school of ethics."[26] To force a child into book-learning is wrong when his natural activities provide the best means of education. It is by no means surprising, in view of all this, that Hall was hostile to the biblical doctrine of original sin and total depravity.

---

[23] Hall, "Introduction," p. xiv, in Ransom A. Mackie: *Education During Adolescence*, Based Partly on G. Stanley Hall's Psychology of Adolescence. New York: Dutton, 1920.

[24] Hall: *Educational Problems*, I, vi.

[25] Hall: *Life and Confessions*, p. 405.

[26] Hall: *Youth, its Education, Regimen, and Hygiene*, p. 76. New York: Appleton, 1908.

How then to account for sin was a problem he refused to give much attention to, although, like all romantics, he was ready to ascribe it to environment, which environment included other persons. Thus, with regard to sex, wherein he followed the sickly romanticism of the Havelock Ellis type, the sinner was always sinned against by society and hence not culpable. As he described it in his ideal Atlantis,

Each party was made to realize that it was vastly easier to win than to hold affection, and since, as we have seen, failure to do the latter involved separation, the methods and spirit of courtship must be maintained through life, for there was no legal or religious bond to be relied on to perpetuate a loveless union, so that these were almost unknown or impossible in early Atlantis. If, as rarely happened, a husband fell a victim to inebriation, gossip became curious about his home table and the attractiveness of his domestic circle. If he sought other women, gossip suspected that the wife, who had every advantage of position, propinquity, safety, and seclusion, had not surrounded the most sacred part of the marital relation with all the subtle charms of allurement, of very gradual approach and finally the full abandonment of which this relation is capable and without which it is liable to lapse, for what married man, they said, could possibly forsake all this for a few wild hours of surreptitious orgy with purchasable favors? If a wife went astray, the husband was suspected to be at fault, for it was felt she was probably a victim of his neglect, over-absorption in outside affairs, failure to study and adjust to her nature and needs, or at least to her moods and fancies, or that he had become less, not more, a lover, the reverse of which should be the case, with every year of domestic companionship; or perhaps he had been wanting in thoughtful protection or had shown the imperfection of his true paternal feeling by relaxation of tenderness when it was most needed, *viz.,* at the time when from being his mistress his partner's life began to be transfigured by motherhood. If then he had allowed her trust in time, which is so often tried and strained at this season, to falter and becloud her bliss over her newborn, it was well understood that this impaired her true maternal function and handicapped the future of the child.[27]

[27] Hall: *Recreations of a Psychologist*, p. 101f.

Such an attitude, with its radical belief that *character is the product of conditioning,* places a double burden on the parent, who is then assumed to be totally responsible for the life of the child. Hall thus contributed materially to one of the great myths of this dying age, one summed up by more than one pompous judge and "child expert" in proverbial fashion: There are no delinquent children, only delinquent parents. The effect of this myth has been to further this irresponsibility of the child. Coupled also with evolutionary mythology, which has been used to imply, as it tends to, that each generation is or should be superior to the previous one, and therefore needs to break its shackles in every area, it has come practically to mean that *rebellion is youth's destiny,* an assumption characteristic of this present culture and by no means the biological or common cultural fact it is presumed to be. The child is the norm; his greatness is his closeness to the race's primitive past, and his future lies in his affirmation of those primitive roots. The pathway of progress lies through primitivism, backward to Eden.

We must collect states of mind, sentiments, phenomena long since lapsed, psychic facts that appear faintly and perhaps but once in a lifetime, and that in only few and rare individuals, impulses that, it may be, never anywhere arise above the threshold, but manifest themselves only in automatisms, acts, behavior, things neglected, trivial and incidental, such as Darwin says are often most vital. We must go to school to the folk-soul, learn of criminals and defectives, animals, and in some sense go back to Aristotle in rebasing psychology on biology, and realize that we know the soul best when we can best write its history in the world, and that there are no finalities save formulae of development.[28]

For Hall, the doctrine of evolution was the fundamental fact in terms of which all life must be re-organized, and, as a revelation of magnificent law within nature, it required that man turn

[28] Hall: *Adolescence, its Psychology, and its Relations to Physiology, Anthropology, Sociology, Sex, Crime, Religion and Education,* vol. I, p. vii f. New York: Appleton, 1904.

religiously downward to that fountain rather than upward to any God.

It even seemed to me that evolution rightly and broadly interpreted gave a new basis for democracy and government of, for, and by the people because the basal assumption of this political ideal is that the folk-soul can be trusted, and this trust can never be complete until we fully realize that everything great and good in the world, including religion, science, and the social and industrial order, has sprung out of the unfathomable depths of human nature.[29]

Because this "folk-soul can be trusted," it is the business of education, government and religion to work in conformity to the folk-soul rather than some alien standard.

Fifth, *the new agency of evolution is the school,* called into being to bring about the great goal of evolutionary process. The school is thus "sacred," possessing a holier "consecration than the Church." It is doing more "than the Church, for it is gradually uniting all creeds and hastening the grand federation of mankind." In terms of this, "the elevating, moralizing power of school education" (i.e., state school education) is without equal.[30] No institution in history has been as potent as the school, and all evolutionary agencies "culminate in the teacher:"

Evolution has taught the teacher that he or she is to be the chief agent in the march of progress, and if we are to have a higher type of citizenship, of manhood, or of womanhood in the world, it is to be done by conscious agencies, and those agencies culminate in the teacher. In the vision of the super-man, if it is ever to be realized, it will be because the school, the college and university will succeed in bringing childhood to more complete maturity, physically, mentally, and, above all, morally. The physical man will be better developed.[31]

Hall felt the need for a demonstration school, set up with unlimited funds, "to show the world once and in some favored spot what can be done." People could visit this school "almost

[29] Hall: *Life and Confessions,* p. 363.
[30] Hall; "Discussion," *N.E.A. Journal,* 1891, p. 99.
[31] Hall, "Remarks on Rhythm in Education," *N.E.A. Journal,* 1894, p. 84f.

like an educational holy city to be prayed toward, as devoted Mussulmans pray toward Mecca," and this pilot school would be "the center of reconstruction, till the lump was leavened." The school would educate in terms of the gospel of childhood, and the results would be conclusive. "At least half the time, labor, and expense now spent upon the three R's might at once be saved and the rest devoted to other and no less useful acquisitions." The experiment must be native to this country and in terms of its development and needs. "As our republican-democratic government is built upon the rights of man, so the school should be based upon a new interpretation of the rights of childhood."[32] The true university, as the center of scientific research, "is or ought to be the chief and fittest organ for the evolution of the true superman, and without this at the top an educational system is a truncated and arrested thing." Universities are, or should be, "true shrines of the spirit and nurseries of these supermen." Men should think religiously, as the medieval man did of his church, of the university, and "the University Invisible," "the splendid temple of science which is the supreme creation of man," would be man's "new church of science." It will usher in the "new, third dispensation . . . namely, the dispensation of the Spirit."[33]

There was more to Hall's new religion of education. Culminating the whole fabric of his faith was his sixth basic concept, *the state as the capstone of man's evolution*. In and through the state, the process comes to fulfilment and maturity. "All organic education may be regarded as educational," and the "higher stage" of evolution is "social adjustment." This stage is "artificial or telic," and it leads to a general spirit of altruism as the true self-interest.[34] Hall, who cautiously admitted that he "half-accepted" Marx,[35] was strongly inclined to socialism as the true and unselfish order of man and society, although unwilling to

[32] Hall: *Educational Problems*, II, p. 632f.
[33] Hall: *Life and Confessions*, pp. 559f., 540, 546f. This concept was earlier presented by Hall in an article in the *Scientific Monthly*, August, 1921.
[34] Hall: *The Psychology of Adolescence*, II, p. 447.
[35] Hall: *Life and Confessions*, p. 222.

champion it. For him, justice was essentially service, which begat happiness and virtue, whereas selfishness was wickedness.[36] "Civic virtue" is "the prime requisite of a good social order," and the schools should inculcate knowledge of the wickedness of "the grasping private interests that flourish at the expense of the public good." The religion of public welfare culminates in social action.

The vocation of teaching should furnish many true saints for the calendar of this new religion, and would if the schoolroom were indeed a worship of the Holy Ghost and if teaching were done with the abandon and self-abnegation which makes the work an inspiration to both teacher and pupil and which gives some of the spirit of consecration to the race which should be the religion of business of whatever kind. So sacrosanct should be this holy function of teaching that it should indeed be a *calling*, and even boards that control public education should feel it, for they should be recruited from the best citizens, who never refuse but seek to serve, to give instead of to get, realizing that office means only opportunity for usefulness.[37]

Hall was confident that the time would come when every young woman of leisure would consider it her duty "to do something for others," and every young man who can will be a "big brother to a younger boy needing help." Teachers will seek out the problem homes and become "adviser, helper and friend to the families." Hall saw these things beginning to come to pass: "cities are now really getting souls." "The school is the training ship for the ship of state," and civics "must be the new religion of the secular schools."[38] Thus, the state is again the true society of man, and his actual god on earth. There can be no transcendent factor or God. Indeed, "If there be a God, we serve Him best by serving mankind." Theology, he said, must be converted to anthropology. If there be a God, "Perhaps He would now prefer us to neglect or even deny His existence if thereby we became

[36] Hall: *Recreations of a Psychologist*, p. 29.
[37] Hall: *Educational Problems*, II, pp. 668, 671f.
[38] *Ibid.*, pp. 678f., 682.

more serviceable to our brethren." We can even say that "perhaps God and His transcendentalities are dying again for the greater glory of man."[39] "All morality is doing good for others."[40] Such an outlook is inevitable wherever a theocentric position is abandoned. If maturity is not the worship of God, then it is socialism and the service of man. For Hall, mature morality meant the abnegation of self for other men, and the best and surest means of this abnegation is statist action. However much Hall stressed the private means of service, and conformed outwardly to laissez-faire thinking, he saw the civic and state forms as ultimately the surest and best. His socialism, though suppressed as inadvisable for the times, was still real.

Hall was confident of the rightness of his views and ideas, and, in his vision, equal, he believed, to Jesus and Buddha:

> In the views I have attained of man, his place in nature, his origin and destiny, I believe I have become a riper product of the present stage of civilization than most of my contemporaries, have outgrown more superstitions, attained clearer insights, and have a deeper sense of peace with myself. I love but perhaps still more pity mankind, groping and stumbling, often slipping backward along the upward Path, which I believe I see just as clearly as Jesus or Buddha, the two greatest souls that ever walked this earth and whom I supremely revere. If my intellectual interests have been in the past and present, my heart lives in the future and in this sense I am younger than youth itself.[41]

Hall's vision of man's return to Eden involved also one further factor, the glorification of woman in her purely procreative function. The woman is thus not primarily a person, helpmeet or wife, but a mother. Sex also became of central importance to Hall as having a redemptive function. "As a psychologist, penetrated with the growing sense of predominance of the heart over the mere intellect, I believe myself not alone in desiring to make a tender declaration of being more and more passionately in

[39] *Ibid.*, p. 667f.
[40] Hall, "Child Study," *N.E.A. Journal*, 1894, p. 179.
[41] Hall: *Life and Confessions*, p. 596.

love with woman as I conceive she came from the hand of God.
I keenly envy my Catholic friends their Mariolatry." Women,
however, were deserting their femininity for "mannish ways,"
but Hall was confident in the processes of evolution and their
conformity to their true sphere. "Meanwhile, if the eternally
womanly seems somewhat less divine, we can turn with unabated
breath to the eternally child-like, the best of which in each are
so closely related. The oracles of infancy and childhood will
never fail." The "new education" must be "a true workshop of
the Holy Ghost—and what the new psychology, when it rises to
the heights of prophecy, foresees as the true paradise of restored
intuitive human nature."[42] Such was the faith and doctrine of
G. Stanley Hall, philosopher, psychologist and educator, a zealous champion of salvation by means of a particular concept of
education, and "prophet" of "the cult of the child."

[42] Hall: *The Psychology of Adolescence*, II, p. 646f.

# 14. Herman Harrell Horne: Man and the Universal

After Harris, no Hegelian or idealist again dominated the American educational scene, and, with the passing years, their ranks became steadily thinner. One such thinker, however, long exercised an influence, in particular through a single book. Herman Harrell Horne (b. 1874), after teaching modern languages at the University of North Carolina, went to Dartmouth to teach both philosophy and pedagogy (1899-1909), and then to New York University in 1909. His *Philosophy of Education,* first published in 1904, was regularly reprinted and extensively used, appearing in 1927 in a revised edition, with a supplementary chapter on Dewey. Another work of Horne's has also been influential, *The Democratic Philosophy of Education* (1932, 1946), an exposition, with critical comment, of Dewey's *Democracy and Education.*

The balance and thoughtfulness of Horne's studies give evidence of his ability, but his works also give telling reason why his position was always a secondary one. The writings of no other major educational thinker show less relevance to the issues of his day. The essays and writings of Dewey reveal an intense involvement in many forgotten issues, in the day by day affairs of his time, and his educational theories, for better or worse, are *relevant* to these events and the contemporary world. Horne could write through war and depression and scarcely note their existence. This idealistic abstraction did not commend itself to the pragmatic and passionate temper of the age.

The three major emphases of Horne's philosophy, as summed up by Brown, are " (1) ontological idealistic monism, (2) Christian theism, and (3) educational optimism."[1] The perfectability and the perfecting of man in terms of an idealistic philosophy and a liberal Christian faith, was basic to Horne's concept of education. While restricting perfection to eternity, Horne did not thereby adhere to the orthodox Christian doctrine, inasmuch as he rejected its concept of original sin.

At first glance, it would appear that Horne and Dewey were of necessity poles apart in their thinking. In actuality, by virtue of their common debt to Hegel, they were very much in agreement on many things, and Horne was ready to give his approval to much in Dewey's philosophy. As Horne himself stated it, "Pragmatism is the child of idealism."[2] Horne regretted the absence of God from Dewey's philosophy, but the God of Horne was nonetheless present, though nameless. In Idealism, God, however exalted in rhetoric, nevertheless, especially since Hegel, labors mightily merely to bring forth the new universal, man. In Horne, this strange "God" was still on the stage; in Dewey, having brought forth the child of destiny, man, this "God," like a salmon whose life ends with spawning, faded quietly out of the picture.

The absence of the dimension of eternity in Dewey troubled Horne. But there was another major aspect of Dewey's thought that Horne repeatedly criticized: man's loss of his selfhood to

[1] James M. Brown: *Educational Implications of Four Conceptions of Human Nature,* A Comparative Study, p. 42. Washington: The Catholic University of America Press, 1940.

[2] H. H. Horne: *The Philosophy of Education,* Being the Foundations of Education in the Related Natural and Mental Sciences, p. 316. Revised ed., with special reference to the educational philosophy of Dr. John Dewey. New York: Macmillan, 1927.

society. Man is never himself in Dewey unless submerged in a group. Commenting on Dewey's society, Horne wrote:

Philosophy becomes sociology and religion becomes science. This proposed reconstruction of experience enriches the values of living in certain scientific and social ways but impoverishes it in many personal, philosophical, and religious ways. Man has lost his self and his God, but he still has left his own adaptive behavior and that of his fellow organisms.[8]

The diminished man in Dewey was thus a major concern to Horne. As he observed aptly at one point, with reference to Dewey's own classical education, "It would probably be better to have Dr. Dewey's education than to have the education his theory provides."

It is well to note, however, that Horne was not immune to the drift of his day. He did oppose it sharply at points, as witness his insistence that teaching is an art, not a science, although "there may be a science of teaching."[4] On the other hand, he could insist, "We need to socialize art,"[5] meaning thereby that democracy means that every member of society should each in his way become an artist and "joy in the expression" of his creative urge. This was a definite echo of a note common to the progressive education of that era. He echoed at times the shoddy educational jargon of the moment, as witness his statement, *"Education is adjustment . . .* the process of becoming ever better adjusted inwardly and outwardly, that is to say, in our relations with ourselves, with our fellows, with nature, with God."[6]

Horne's faith in education was very great. In his own words,

I believe, in short, that the great secondary causes which make men and women are heredity, environment, and will as they are

---

[3] Horne: *The Democratic Philosophy of Education.* New York: Macmillan, 1946.

[4] Horne: *The Teacher as Artist,* An essay in Education as an Aesthetic Process, p. 7. Boston: Houghton Mifflin, 1917.

[5] Horne: *Story-Telling, Questioning and Studying,* Three School Arts, p. 7. New York: Macmillan, 1916.

[6] Horne: *This New Education,* p. 125f. New York: Abingdon, 1931. Italics are Horne's.

used by the First Cause, and that education is a mighty cooperating agent with each of these secondary forces.[7]

A firm believer in evolution, he held that "evolution is now proceeding along mental instead of physical lines." In this new stage of evolution, education is the central agency, and the teacher "is the prophet and priest of progress."[8] Since evolution has shifted "from the material to the mental plane," according to Horne, it means that "man is now beginning to take a conscious part in his own making. Conscious effort wonderfully abbreviates the slow processes of Nature."[9] Education, moreover, can help religiously since it is capable of eradicating evil.[10] Thus, education, which "is the process of evolution become conscious of itself,"[11] is not only the biological but religious agency for the further development of man.

It is not surprising, in view of Horne's philosophy, that he gave education this function, since, as he asked, "Is not reality mental?"[12] Horne was ready to give the body an important role, however, in education, and at times echoed the progressivists in his emphasis. He cited with approval the fact that Radcliffe College "had a gymnasium before a dormitory."[13] The body is important, not for its own sake, but because of its organic relation to the mind. "The body is the home of the mind, in the forceful New Testament phrase, 'the temple of the Holy Ghost.' "[14] For Horne, "the perfecting of humanity in the image of divinity, is *idealism in educating.*"[15]

The central emphasis, however, was not on the divinity but on

[7] *Ibid.,* p. 51.

[8] Horne: *The Psychological Principles of Education,* A Study in the Science of Education, p. 40. New York: Macmillan, 1906.

[9] Horne: *Idealism in Education,* or First Principles in the Making of Men and Women, p. 163. New York: Macmillan, 1910.

[10] Horne: *The Philosophy of Education,* p. 156. New York: Macmillan, 1908. This is the 1904 edition.

[11] *Ibid.,* p. 261.

[12] *Ibid.,* p. 264.

[13] *Ibid.,* p. 94.

[14] *Ibid.,* p. 64.

[15] Horne, *Idealism in Education,* p. 177. Italics are Horne's.

*humanity*. For Horne, "personality, which is the union of ideas and purposes," is "the ultimate reality."[16] God "is not an ab stract inaccessible being, nor a supernatural anthropomorphic being, but the inclusive personality in whose life all natural and human processes occur. The true immanence is not of God in us, but of us in God."[17] Thus, the centrality belongs to man.

"The goal of social evolution" is "an individualized society and a socialized individual."[18] The goal of religion also is similar: "Religion is the recognition in life of the rights of the Ideal Person."[19] Man, not God, is the center, the goal, and the driving force in the entire process of history, and God himself has been "completely" moralized in man's successful ascent.[20] Man "is the highest manifestation in the temporal process of the true reality." Man's relationship to the Absolute is an integral one.

The self activity of man, conditioning his education, is the clearest expression in the limits of time of the immanent and transcendent self-activity of reality. It is as though in man realizing his destiny through self-activity, the Absolute beheld himself reflected. The Absolute is; the finite becomes.[21]

Lest we be misled into believing that the Absolute has priority for Horne, it is well to note that his concluding words were the approving use of the words of Everett, "who says from the point of view of thought what we have tried to say from the point of view of education:"

*The individual is the universal*. This is the type of every logical proposition. . . . Our fundamental and typical proposition is false. The individual is not the universal. The universal stretches far beyond the individual. A single man does not exhaust the possibilities of humanity . . . The individual is not the universal, but it *will* be.

16 *Ibid.*, p. vii.
17 Horne: *The Psychological Principles of Education*, p. 340.
18 Horne: *Idealism in Education*, p. 116.
19 Horne: *The Philosophy of Education*, 1904, p. 180.
20 Horne: *Idealism in Education*, p. 156.
21 Horne: *The Philosophy of Education*, 1904, p. 268.

. . . Everywhere the universal strives to shape itself in the individual, and everywhere, failing its aim, it breaks to pieces its own work, and presses onward to new forms.[22]

Thus, the movement of the universal is to incarnate itself in man as the true home of the universal and the true nature and destiny of man. For Horne, this process is operative in all historical movements and is their basic impetus. The failures of history are due to the failures of men and movements to make man fully this *realized* universal. For Horne, the process was never fully attainable. For Dewey, as a more intense idealist, the process is realized in democracy, in the "Great Society." Horne's restraint, under the influence of Christian thought, from making the jump into universalizing man, nonetheless did not prevent his thinking from pointing logically to Dewey, whose pragmatism he recognized as idealism without God.

Why did the *self* which Horne so valued disappear into Dewey's *Society*? The answer is an obvious one: man cannot become the universal, or society humanistic, without a destruction of individualism and selfhood. As John S. White has observed, in his study of Castiglione, as long as God was man's universal, *man could be independent of man, because God was the focus of his life, and the source of his law, standard, and status.* But, with man-centered faith, "the individual needs society as a resonance box." *Humanistic man's law is man, which means government by social approval, and hence the socialization of his life, law and living.* "The medieval saint was virtuous in the desert also. The invisible eyes of God hovered above him. Universal Man needs society in order to display his virtues. His realm is only of this world."[23] Horne tried to keep man on a treadmill, ever near but never quite capable of incarnating the universal. Dewey took him off the treadmill. But his apotheosis of man was rather the apotheosis of society and the death of man

[22] *Ibid.*, p. 286f.
[23] John S. White: *Renaissance Cavalier*, p. 8f. New York: *Philosophical Library*, 1959.

as men. Before long, teachers would tell troubled and anxious mothers that their sons, because individualistic, were "isolates," and hence socially retarded. Society, as the new Moloch, demands the sacrifice of the self of man to the "social self."

# 15. John Dewey's New Jerusalem: "The Great Community"

When John Dewey was not yet twenty-eight, in 1887, he expressed this conviction concerning the priority of metaphysical thought:

We believe that the cause of theology and morals is one, and that whatever banishes God from the heart of things, with the same edict excludes the ideal, the ethical, from the life of man. Whatever exiles theology makes ethics an expatriate.[1]

It is generally assumed that Dewey the instrumentalist or pragmatist radically abandoned this position in favor of a "scientific" philosophy which had no room for metaphysics, a priori assumptions, purely religious presuppositions or eternal truths. Lynd, for example, in summarizing the essentials of Dewey's philosophy states as its first premise, "There are no eternal truths."[2] This, of course, is Dewey's avowed belief. In terms of his prag-

---

[1] John Dewey, "Ethics and Physical Science," *Andover Review*, VII, 576, June, 1887, cited by Neil Gerard McCluskey, S.J.: *Public Schools and Moral Education*, The Influence of Horace Mann, William Torrey Harris and John Dewey, p. 203. New York: Columbia University Press, 1958.

[2] Albert Lynd: *Quackery in the Public Schools*, p. 191. New York: Grosset and Dunlap, 1950.

matic or instrumental view of truth, things are good or true only in terms of their consequences; the absurdity of this idea Bertrand Russell has noted, pointing out that the consequences then can be evaluated only in terms of their consequences, so that no judgment becomes possible. But need we believe Dewey? Is he a pragmatist? Is not his demand that he be read as an instrumentalist an attempt to evade the devastating critique of metaphysical theory which Dewey as a Hegelian had known? An avowed metaphysics is an open and vulnerable metaphysics. But a metaphysics can be presupposed and veiled behind a facade of pragmatism, and an implicit metaphysics is no less a metaphysics. Dewey the pragmatist was more firmly wedded to eternal verities than many a metaphysician, and his theory, based on an implicit and unreasoning dogmatism, unleashed a new Islam into American education and philosophy, savagely intolerant, belligerently contemptuous of all previous learning and thought, and dedicated to an educational jargon unfamiliar and irrational to all who were not devotees of this new Mohammed. An unrecognized and uncriticized metaphysics is therefore all the more naive, and it ceases to be a philosophy and becomes an unreasoning and uncritical cult dedicated to its own brand of truth. This is admittedly harsh language, but plain and blunt speaking is required to blast the claim of Deweyism to a philosophy of pragmatism. In spite of himself, Dewey was a preacher of truth, or at least of his conceptions of truth, and by no means a pragmatist. For him there were hard and fast truths that were beyond dissent or discussion, presupposed as the very ground of his thinking. Against all other philosophies and religions, Dewey could unleash a corrosive cynicism and assert his "pragmatic" tests, denying their eternal verity even as he presupposed his own.

What then were these eternal truths of Dewey's system, the presuppositions and axioms of his philosophy?

First of all, Dewey, as a good Hegelian to the last, assumed without question the truth of the *concept of continuity.* Any dualistic system was by definition false; 'science' required a continuous reality and a oneness of being that made for a necessary equalization of all being. As Dewey himself admitted, his whole conception of democracy *"assumes continuity."* Accordingly, mind and body are a false dualism, and continuity requires a democracy of science and play in education, so that book learning and prescribed experiments cannot claim superiority over play. "Progress" is based on a belief in continuity; those who "withstand change" believe in discontinuity.[3] "The principle of continuity" was accordingly Dewey's avowed "criterion of discrimination" with respect to experience and education.[4] As one critic of Dewey, W. T. Feldman, has observed, "the belief that such continuity holds throughout nature is a pure assumption, and it is one of the most perilous of all assumptions for both science and philosophy; for it tends to hasty and dogmatic unifications and to a blindness to the actual diversity of things."[5]

A second presupposition of Dewey's philosophy was *growth*, a substitute concept for that of *progress*, then rapidly coming into disrepute; Dewey's concept is more definitely biological in orientation, but still closely related to the older notions of inevitable progress. "Growth, or growing as developing, not only physically but intellectually and morally, is one exemplification of the principle of continuity."[6] Again we find ourselves on neither a pragmatic or a scientific ground, but are in the realm of hard and fixed "principle," of religious faith and presupposition; the source of the idea of growth is another idea, continuity. Darwin was of major importance to Dewey's thinking in that he saw in Darwin the assertion of the principle of continuity and change, and of animal growth, and the overthrow of "law," but only of

[3] John Dewey: *Democracy and Education,* An Introduction to the Philosophy of Education, pp. 388-401. New York: Macmillan, 1923.
[4] John Dewey: *Experience and Education,* p. 26. New York: Macmillan, 1948.
[5] W. T. Feldman: *The Philosophy of John Dewey, A Critical Analysis,* p. 87f. Baltimore: Johns Hopkins Press, 1934. Feldman, in his first chapter, "The Concept of Organism," speaks of Dewey's Hegelianism; in Chapt. III, "Temporalism," p. 34, he summarizes Dewey thus and notes, "Reality, as it is in itself, exists in a dimension incommensurable with the categories of mind; cognition reshapes reality, it does not mirror it. In short, a pragmatist version of Kant!"
[6] Dewey: *Experience and Education,* p. 28.

law as "a priori intelligent causal force to plan and preordain" natural processes.[7]

Accordingly, Dewey, instead of holding to an ethical relativism, held rather to "inherent moral forces" in terms of this doctrine of continuity:

The one thing needful is that we recognize that moral principles are real in the same sense which other forces are real; that they are inherent in community life, and in the running machinery of the individual. If we can secure a genuine faith in this fact, we shall have secured the only condition which is finally necessary in order to get from our educational system all the effectiveness there is in it. The teacher who operates in this faith will find every subject, every method of instruction, every incident of school life pregnant with ethical life.[8]

Note the religious emphasis on "faith," a common aspect of Dewey's thought. The principle of continuity required that these moral values of course be social The basic moral requirements are met through the "spontaneous instincts and impulses" because they are inherent.[9] By what strange process of reasoning is the belief in original sin called exclusively religious rather than philosophical and experiential as well, and this belief in inherent moral forces called philosophical and pragmatic? Rather, we have a fanatical faith all the less philosophical because of its inability to see its radically religious presuppositions. Dewey rightly used the language of faith at every turn. "The foundation of democracy is faith in the capacities of human nature; faith in human intelligence and in the power of pooled and cooperative experience."[10]

Because of his concept of continuity and growth, and the semi-biological re-interpretation of the doctrine of inevitable

[7] Dewey: *The Influence of Darwin on Philosophy and Other Essays in Contemporary Thought,* p. 11f. New York: Holt, 1910.

[8] Dewey: *Ethical Principles Underlying Education,* p. 33. Chicago: University of Chicago Press, 1903.

[9] Dewey: *Moral Principles in Education,* pp. 47-58. New York: Philosophical Library, 1959.

[10] Dewey: *Problems of Men,* p. 59. New York: Philosophical Library, 1946.

progress, Dewey had a strong faith also in *change,* change at least until the Great Community was born. While rightly challenging beliefs in fixity and other attempts to arrest historical process, Dewey himself was often ready to believe in the value of change as mere change. For him, "to exist is to be in process, in change."[11] But what Dewey believed had to change was every philosophy that he differed with, but not his own. He assumed, as Clark has observed, "that nature speaks unambiguously,"[12] and had implicitly as fixed a doctrine of the inerrancy of nature as any orthodox Christian has of the inerrancy of Scripture. There was in Dewey both a receptivity to change and an amazingly uncritical attitude towards it. His essays on political events thus make embarrassing reading. He was unduly enthusiastic about Soviet Russia and Ataturk's Turkey, although both were dictatorships, because they represented change. Only much later was he disillusioned with the Soviet Union. His principle of approval was *change,* change, however, understood only as rebellion against religion, capitalism and individualism. Any return to such things was not change but retrogression.[13] Because his concept of growth and change were so doctrinaire, he lacked the realism of Burke in assessing movements, and could be clearly utopian in his political and economic thought, as well as in his hopes and efforts to outlaw war.[14] Thus, change involved the levelling of aristocratic and supernatural concepts, and the progressive unification of all men in terms of the concept of continuity. Change is thus process toward the Great Community.

We come closer to the heart of Dewey's faith and religion as we deal with democracy. Dewey spoke of "the experiential continuum" as central to his thinking. This experiential continuum

[11] Dewey in *Living Philosophies,* p. 26. Cleveland: World Publishing Co., 1930.

[12] Gordon H. Clark: *Dewey,* p. 39. Philadelphia: Presbyterian and Reformed Publishing Co., 1960.

[13] See Dewey: *Characters and Events, Popular Essays in Social and Political Philosophy,* 2 v. New York: Holt, 1929.

[14] See Dewey, Joseph Ratner, ed.: *Intelligence in the Modern World,* pp. 511-604. New York: Modern Library, 1939. See also Dewey's "Afterword" in Charles Clayton Morrison: *The Outlawry of War, A Constructive Policy for World Peace,* pp. 301-319. Chicago: Willett, Clark and Colby, 1927.

comes into its own in fully democratic experiences precisely because they are democratic and common. "Can we find any reason that does not ultimately come down to the belief that democratic social arrangements promote a better quality of human experience, one which is more widely accessible and enjoyed, than do non-democratic and anti-democratic forms of social life?"[15] Note again the appeal to faith, a constant emphasis in Dewey. The necessity for democratic experience in fulfilment of the concept of continuity makes mandatory an essential aspect of Dewey's faith, namely, *integration downward*. Democracy requires identification with the continuum, and such identification necessitates a surrender of all exclusive and aristocratic concepts. Thus, Dewey consistently advocated democratic experiences and identification as necessary to true education. At the July 1-7, 1933 N.E.A. meetings in Chicago, Dewey criticized attempts of educators and teachers to exalt themselves into an aristocratic or "professional" group. The great need for teachers was "identification of sympathy and thought," but with labor and the masses rather than with "bankers" or professional and hence limited groups.[16] This integration downward is basic to much contemporary educational practice, and the tendency in many circles to classify the gifted child as "abnormal." It is the background in part of such opinions as that expressed by Dr. William G. Carr and the Educational Policies Commission of the N.E.A. in 1938: "It is at least open to question whether there is anything intrinsically more dramatic and elevating in watching the struggle on a darkening stage between Macbeth and his conscience than in watching under a warm summer sun a good nine-inning pitching duel."[17] Experience is thus "the means and goal of education," and this means democratic and "growing, expanding experience."[18] Teachers must "ally themselves with

[15] *Experience and Education*, pp. 17, 25.

[16] Dewey, "Education and our Present Social Problems," *N.E.A. Proceedings*, 1933, pp. 687-689.

[17] Wm. G. Carr and the Educational Policies Commission, N.E.A.: *The Purposes of Education in American Democracy*, p. 65. Washington, D.C.: N.E.A. 1938.

[18] Dewey: *Experience and Education*, p. 113f.

organized labor" as a step towards the new social order, true democracy. This meant also that teachers must indoctrinate pupils into that socialized order, although Dewey quibbled mildly at the word "indoctrinate." "There is an important difference between education *with respect to a new social order* and indoctrination into settled convictions about that order. The first activity in my judgment is necessary."[19] The only discernible difference, however, is that the one has succeeded in creating the socialist state, whereas the other is in process; educationally, for Dewey education and indoctrination had no intrinsic difference. The choice, indeed, as Dewey saw it, was either to accept his brand of education and be persuaded into socialism, or face socialism by means of dictatorship. "Social planning can be had only by means approaching dictatorship unless education is socially planned."[20] Democracy is the criterion and the true faith, and democracy to be explicit and logical requires socialization:

In conclusion, we may say that the conception of the school as a social center is born of our entire democratic movement. Everywhere we see signs of the growing recognition that the community owes to each one of its members the fullest opportunity for development. Everywhere we see the growing recognition that the community life is defective and distorted excepting as it does thus care for all its constituent parts. This is no longer viewed as a matter of charity, but as a matter of justice—nay of something higher and better than justice—a necessary phase of developing and growing life. Men will long dispute about material socialism, about socialism considered as a matter of distribution of the material resources of the community; but there is a socialism regarding which there can be no such dispute—socialism of the intelligence and of the spirit. To extend the range and the fullness of sharing in the intellectual and spiritual resources of the community is the very meaning of the community. Because the older type of education is not fully adequate to this task under changed conditions, we feel its lack and demand that the school shall become a social center. The school as

[19] Dewey: *Education and the Social Order*, p. 10. New York: League for Industrial Democracy, 1936.
[20] *Ibid.*, p. 13.

a social center means the active and organized promotion of this socialism of the intangible things of art, science, and other modes of social intercourse.[21]

Several things are here immediately apparent. First, Dewey was a champion, as Levi has pointed out, of "the Lost Individual."[22] But the individualism Dewey espoused was one which called for the indulgent subsidy of the individual by the socialist state. He spoke of the *debt* of the community to each and every member, but not of the individual's *responsibility*. Second, the requirements of justice and old-fashioned individualism were transcended by the social requirement "of developing and growing life," which meant *the assumption of character by the state rather than the individual.* Dewey contrasted the "methods of changing the world through action" with "changing the self in emotion and idea."[23] For Dewey, the method of action constituted the true redemption of man, since liberty today "signifies liberation from material insecurity and from the coercions and repressions that prevent multitudes from participation in the vast cultural resources that are at hand. The direct impact of liberty always has to do with some class or group that is suffering in a special way from some form of constraint exercised by the distribution of powers that exist in contemporary society. Should a classless society ever come into being the formal *concept* of liberty would lose its significance, because the *fact* for which it stands would have become an integral part of the established relations of human beings to one another."[24] Liberty is thus only a social relationship and purely an external factor, so that again character is an aspect of the life of the state and a condition of individual life rather than the ground of it. Third, and closely related to the second, there is a belief in the necessity for "socialism of the intelligence and of the spirit," and this in itself

---

[21] Dewey: "The School as Social Center," *N.E.A. Journal*, 1902, p. 382f.

[22] Albert William Levi: *Philosophy and the Modern World*, p. 324. Bloomington, Indiana: Indiana University Press, 1959.

[23] *Intelligence in the Modern World*, p. 275.

[24] *Ibid.*, p. 450f.

constitutes the essence of community life. The older conceptions of community life held to the independent development of each in terms of his calling, and the bond of unity was a common faith. Now, the bond of unity and community is a surrender of individuality in this older sense to a radical socializing not only of man, but of his intelligence and his spirit. Fourth, the school, i.e., the state or socialist school, is the established church of this creed. In the school, the socialized life is lived and experienced, and man refashioned in terms of the democratic state.

How is this democratic state, constantly integrated downward, to be kept from running down? According to Dewey, education is "a process of renewal of the meanings of experience through a process of transmission."[25] What this mystical process means is never quite clear, but that it is mysticism is clearly manifest. How can alien, aristocratic and individualistic experiences of the past be transmitted to the socialist 'future'? And what renewal can they give, except in anti-democratic terms? If only democratic experiences are transmitted, where then is the renewal? Is it not simply filtered continuity? And how can this filtering process be called education?

To return to democracy itself, Dewey saw it as the fulfilment of nature. "Is democracy a comparatively superficial human expedient, a device of petty manipulation, or does nature itself, as that is uncovered and understood by our best contemporaneous knowledge, sustain and support our democratic hopes and aspirations?" Dewey found this and more in nature, including "a metaphysical mathematics of the incommensurable in which each speaks for itself and demands consideration on its own behalf. If democratic equality may be construed as individuality, there is nothing forced in understanding fraternity as continuity, that is to say, as association and interaction without limit."[26] Dewey believed that a thorough-going socialization and organized planning meant the fulfilment of the individual in the

---

[25] *Democracy and Education*, pp. 1-4, 375.
[26] "Philosophy and Democracy," in *Characters and Events*, v. II, pp. 849, 854.

socialist state without communism and its evils, a paradoxical conclusion.[27] But Dewey was able to re-define concepts and thereby preserve them, and not above contradicting himself when necessary.

.. democracy is so often and so naturally associated in our minds with freedom of *action,* forgetting the importance of freed intelligence which is necessary to direct and to warrant freedom of action. Unless freedom of individual action has intelligence and informed conviction back of it, its manifestation is almost sure to result in confusion and disorder. The democratic idea of freedom is not the right of each individual to *do* as he pleases, even if it be qualified by adding "provided he does not interfere with the same freedom on the part of others." While the idea is not always, not often enough, expressed in words, the basic freedom is that of freedom of *mind* and of whatever degree of freedom of action and experience is necessary to produce freedom of intelligence. The modes of freedom guaranteed in the Bill of Rights are all of this nature: Freedom of belief and conscience, of expression of opinion, of assembling for discussion and conference, of the press as an organ of communication. They are guaranteed because without them individuals are not free to develop and society is deprived of what they might contribute.[28]

This statement draws protection to Dewey from the Bill of Rights, and falsely so, because his conception of freedom is radically different. The Constitution guarantees to man certain liberties, i.e., immunities against the State, which are his on the premises of the Christian doctrine of man and the doctrine of the *natural rights* of the individual, not because of the fancied *social results,* i.e., "because without them individuals are not free to develop and society is deprived of what they might contribute." Again, Dewey defined 'democratic freedom' as freedom of mind, because, "unless freedom of individual action has intelligence and informed conviction back of it, its manifestation is almost sure to result in confusion and disorder!" The free mind

[27] Dewey: *Philosophy and Civilization,* p. 328. New York: Minton, Balch, 1931.
[28] Dewey: *Problems of Men,* p. 61.

is the democratic or socialist mind, and hence alone capable of acting without danger of "confusion and disorder." A man apparently has no right to make mistakes in Dewey's democracy, even if he does not interfere with the rights of others. But, since for Dewey the true individual is democratic and socialist man, this strange denial of liberty is ostensibly true liberty for the true man, *demos.*

As we have already seen, another basic faith and presupposition in Dewey's system is *the state school as the new established church,* the new vehicle of social salvation. Dewey very early declared that the result of the new movement in education was a Copernican revolution: "Now the change which is coming into our education is the shifting of the center of gravity. It is a change, a revolution, not unlike that introduced by Copernicus when the astronomical center shifted from the earth to the sun. In this case the child becomes the sun about which the appliances of education revolve; he is the center about which they are organized."[29] This child, however, was Dewey's reshaped child, *the child as creditor,* to whom society owed all things, and *the child as consumer,* demanding happiness and fulfilment by means of social action rather than personal attainment or inner change. It was, moreover, the child as member of the democratic school and as sharer in the democratic experience. As Dewey declared, "I believe that all education proceeds by the participation of the individual in the social consciousness of the race. . . . The only true education comes through the stimulation of the child's powers by the demands of the social situations in which he finds himself."[30] Basic to this faith was Dewey's radical reliance on stimulus-response psychology, so that the child received stimuli and responded, was essentially passive and consumption centered rather than aggressive and capable of himself creating the stimuli and the social situation. The school for

[29] Dewey: *The School and Society,* p. 47. Chicago: The University of Chicago Press, 1899.
[30] Dewey: *My Pedagogic Creed,* p. 13. Washington, D.C., The Progressive Education Association, 1897, 1929.

Dewey was a social institution designed to train the child in "the inherited resources of the race, and to use his own powers for social ends." "Education is the fundamental method of social progress and reform," religion being by-passed.

I BELIEVE THAT
—the teacher is engaged, not simply in the training of individuals, but in the formation of the proper social life.
—every teacher should realize the dignity of his calling; that he is a social servant set apart for the maintenance of proper social order and the securing of the right social growth.
—in this way the teacher always is the prophet of the true God and the usherer in of the true kingdom of God.[31]

The true God has spoken, and Dewey is his prophet! Let none dare to look for the "3 R's" in that new mosque, the school, as it builds this "true kingdom of God" without God and with no God.

The purpose of the schools is to create a faith in the one world of man, "and of membership in a single family."[32] The biblical faith that humanity is divided in terms of faith in, versus rebellion against, God, and that any attempt to set this division aside is sin, is by-passed by Dewey as he seeks to build anew the Tower of Babel, man's ancient symbol of oneness and commonality irrespective of truth. Indeed, for Dewey religion and education are scarcely to be distinguished, for both call for social unification:

... the American people is conscious that its schools serve best the cause of religion in serving the cause of social unification; and that under certain conditions schools are more religious in substance and in promise without any of the conventional badges and machinery of religious instruction than they could be in cultivating these forms at the expense of a state-consciousness.[33]

State-consciousness thus, and social unification, are the hallmarks of true religion rather than God-consciousness and reli-

[31] *Ibid.*, 6, 15, 17.
[32] Dewey: *Problems of Men*, p. 43.
[33] Dewey: *Characters and Events*, II, p. 515.

gious faith. Dewey was *emphatic* about this goal of education: "Apart from the thought of participation in social life the school has no end nor aim."[84] *Mere learning is thus not an end or aim of education.* Moral education cannot be associated with particular habits or virtues; ethics is to be seen entirely in terms of this state-consciousness:

Ultimate moral motives and forces are nothing more or less than social intelligence—the power of observing and comprehending social situations,—and social power—trained capacities of control—at work in the service of social interest and aims. There is no fact which throws light upon the constitution of society, there is no power whose training adds to social resourcefulness that is not moral.[85]

As long as these things are manifested in school life, as long as "the moral trinity of the school" is present, "social intelligence, social power, and social interests," "so far as general principles are concerned, all the basic ethical requirements are met."[86] It must at least be said that Dewey is plain-spoken here: *there is no morality beyond the state and its social interests.*

Since "education is itself a process of discovering what values are worth while and are to be pursued as objectives,"[87] and Dewey was increasingly sure that the "worth while" was the social, it became important to define that society, for "The conception of education as a social process and function has no definite meaning until we define the kind of society we have in mind." This *"particular* social ideal" means "two points selected by which to measure the worth of a form of social life," namely, (1) "the extent in which the interests of a group are shared by all its members," and (2) "the fullness and freedom with which it interacts with other groups."[38]

This ideal social order, being democratic, is anti-supernatural

---

[84] *Ethical Principles Underlying Education,* p. 12.
[85] *Moral Principles in Education,* p. 43.
[86] *Ibid.,* p. 43f.
[87] Dewey: *The Sources of a Science of Education,* p. 74. New York: Liveright, 1929.
[38] Dewey: *Democracy and Education,* pp. 112, 115.

by nature, since supernaturalism is a destruction of the concept of continuity. Religion is not to be identified with the supernatural but is at its best when natural, for the supernatural is divisive and hence anti-democratic. "A clear and intense conception of a union of ideal ends with actual conditions is capable of arousing steady emotion," and such a union can be named "God."[39] A truly religious man must of necessity be anti-supernaturalistic, for "depending upon an external power is the counterpart of surrender of human endeavor," which ostensible surrender is for Dewey not a religiously acceptable attitude.[40] More than that, supernatural Christianity is basically and radically anti-democratic because it holds to a God and an ultimate and unchanging law in terms of which men shall be saved or lost. Christianity, by separating "the saved and the lost" is committed to a "spiritual aristocracy" and is thus an alien creed. "I cannot understand how any realization of the democratic ideal as a vital moral and spiritual ideal in human affairs is possible without surrender of the conception of the basic division to which supernatural Christianity is committed."[41] *If God is not permitted to distinguish between saints and sinners, need we wonder that Dewey's progressive education forbade school failures and report cards?* Need we wonder that labor unions through featherbedding protect the misfits and the discarded? After all, what is required of 'God,' i.e., total indulgence, must be required of teachers, of labor unions, and of courts as well. Thus, away with any hint of crime, failure, or shortcomings! Democracy must prevail, and this means integration downward. As Eby and Arrowood have stated it, "An individual cannot be regarded, according to Dr. Dewey, as a being apart from society."[42] We can add that society must accordingly, in this view, do nothing to man which will set him apart from the group, whether by way of promotion or retention. Dewey's society and its ethics are not distinguish-

[39] Dewey: *A Common Faith*, p. 51f. New Haven: Yale University Press, 1934.
[40] *Ibid.*, p. 46.
[41] *Ibid.*, p. 84.
[42] Eby and Arrowood: *op. cit.*, p. 869.

able from the pack and the law of the pack. His religious attitude outlaws both failure and success in order to equalize man and avoid an anti-democratic aristocracy. For Dewey, a common faith is thus not only one on which all men can agree, but one which condemns no man to failure or judgment, and which is not "confined to sect, class, or race"[43] because it will ultimately tolerate the existence of no group save the Great Society. *Since man in the mass is his universal rather than God, a judgment on or a fracturing of his universal is intolerable.* The true community will thus strive to achieve this democratic unity by eliminating the higher law concept of that alien universal, God, in the liberation of man by that "one method for ascertaining fact and truth —that conveyed by the word 'scientific' in its most general and generous sense. . . . I should describe this faith as the unification of the self through allegiance to inclusive ideal ends, which imagination presents to us and to which the human will responds as worthy of controlling our desires and choices."[44] But these "ideal ends" cannot have any truth in themselves other than our response and approval to our own will.

Dewey, indeed, spoke of "the necessity for the participation of every mature being in formation of the values that regulate the living of men together: which is necessary from the standpoint of both the general social welfare and the full development of human beings as individuals," and called this "the keynote of democracy as a way of life." Thus, men must play gods to become truly human. But for Dewey democracy is "the truly human way of living," and "the foundation of democracy is faith in the capacities of human nature."[45] "Man is a social animal," and education is into sociality, and "the heart of the sociality of man is in education."[46] To move forward in this faith will produce "a fuller and deeper religion," possibly manifest already in the decay of the older forms, and "the spiritual import of science

---

[43] Dewey, *op. cit.*, p. 87.
[44] *Ibid.*, p. 33.
[45] *Intelligence in the Modern World*, p. 400-402.
[46] *Ibid.*, p. 629.

and of democracy" will lead to "that type of religion which will be the fine flower of the modern spirit's achievement."[47]

From continuity through democracy and its established church, the state school, we arrive at Dewey's governing presupposition, *The Great Community,* the secular version of the New Jerusalem. Clark has observed, of Dewey's concept of ethics and the state, "The state can do no wrong, for right is determined by what the state does."[48] Steam and electricity have created the Great Society, which must now be transformed into the Great Community. Dewey's language, always flavored with biblical allusions, becomes even more so in this context. "The old Adam, the unregenerate element in human nature, persists" to block the method of obtaining results by "communication" and relies instead on "force."[49] "Communication" means self-determination, not as an individual, but as a community, with every member participating in the social decisions, activities and achievements. It assumes also the desire of every individual to share in these things, so that not only a deliberative action is involved but religious and mystical participation therein. Even as the religious mystic "finds" himself by losing himself in God, in absorption in Him, so the social mystic finds himself by willing absorption into the Great Community.

We have the physical tools of communication as never before. The thoughts and aspirations congruous with them are not communicated, and hence are not common. Without such communication the public will remain shadowy and formless, seeking spasmodically for itself, but seizing and holding its show rather than its substance. Till the Great Society is converted into a Great Community, the Public will remain in eclipse. Communication can alone create a great community. Our Babel is not one of tongues but of the signs and symbols without which shared experience is impossible.[50]

[47] *Ibid.,* p. 715.
[48] Clark, *op. cit.,* p. 33.
[49] *Intelligence in the Modern World,* p. 389f.
[50] Dewey: *The Public and Its Problems,* p. 142. New York: Minton, Balch, 1930.

Hegel had held that the State is the actuality of the ethical Idea, in and by itself the ethical whole, the actualization of freedom, mind on earth, "the march of God in the world," the "actual God" and the manifestation of history. For Hegel, these things came to focus in the Prussian State. Dewey, holding the same faith, more modestly than Hegel and Marx, saw this "actual God" as yet in the future but drawing near in his Great Community. At present, because it is unborn or at best shadowy, "the Public will remain in eclipse." Man will not be truly man until this "actual God," the Great Community, is born. Man is not created in the image of God but of society, and therefore as yet not fully man.[51] It is no wonder that even a non-Christian such as Bertrand Russell has seen in Dewey's philosophy a "cosmic impiety" which increases "the danger of vast social disaster."[52]

For Dewey, "the seer" of the Great Community was Walt Whitman, and "democracy is a name for a life of free and enriching communion."[53]

Dewey's conception of the Great Community is anti-pluralistic, monistic, and medieval, requiring as it does the total unification of society under a common goal rather than permitting a pluralism of faiths, goals, and cultures. The state school is his established church, and the Great Community his New Jerusalem, the kingdom of man realized and present. But a healthy society requires diversity and pluralism precisely because man is man, diverse in capacity, potentiality, faith and culture. The growth of man's epistemological self-consciousness will develop rather than limit this pluralism. Hence, the Great Community can only be a great graveyard, a Tower of Babel leading to vaster confusion, a new Holy Roman Empire and a new inquisition.

[51] "Human nature is not a reflection of the image of God but of society" for Dewey. John H. Hallowell: *Main Currents in Modern Political Thought*, p. 548. New York: Henry Holt, 1959.

[52] *Ibid.*, p. 549, from Russell's *A History of Western Philosophy*, p. 827f. New York: Simon and Schuster, 1945.

[53] Dewey: *The Public and its Problems*, p. 184; *Intelligence in the Modern World*, p. 399f.

The quest for certainty is more present in Dewey than in those whom he criticizes, but his quest is shifted from eternity to time. For this reason, it is all the more dangerous a claim to certitude, and a more deadly tyranny.

The major influence of so minor a thinker is the triumph, certainly, of banality, but it is also a manifestation of a radical demand for certainty in time, for a certainty in the form of that "actual God" the State, the Great Community, a merciless god whose wheels of juggernaut have always had their willing devotees of death. This demand for certainty in time is intensified wherever there is a denial of any certainty in God and it leads to the deification of a human order and of the human will, with its consequence being social disaster.

Dewey's influence on contemporary life and thought has been extensive in religion, philosophy and other areas, but chiefly in education and jurisprudence. The Supreme Court in particular has long reflected his influence with a devastating cynicism of all categories of faith and life other than the omnipotent state, which has been exalted and furthered with unrelenting force. It is questionable whether liberty can long survive under a continued onslaught of Deweyism. Indications of its possibly waning power are thus hopeful signs of another spring.

# 16. J. B. Watson:
## Science and Utopia

John Broadus Watson (1878-1958), through his psychology of behaviorism, made a major impact on modern science, sociology and industry, and had an influence in psychology so pervasive as to be described by Thorne Shipley thus: "It is hard to overestimate the influence which Watson has had on the subsequent development of psychology in America."[1] Watson's influence outside of psychology was equally important in that he met a common temper in science and politics and made it vocal by means of his psychology. Today, his ideas are more than ever the axioms of contemporary thought. But they succeeded only because they made more explicit the implicit faith of Enlightenment culture.

Watson studied under John Dewey at the University of Chicago, where he immediately became, after receiving his Ph.D., Assistant in Experimental Psychology. He soon went to Johns Hopkins University, in 1904, remaining until 1919. He lectured subsequently at the New School for Social Research and then devoted his time to industry. His work very early made a major

[1] Thorne Shipley: *Classics in Psychology*, p. 820. New York: Philosophical Library, 1961.

impact on intellectual and popular thought. The *New York Times* said of Watson's *Behaviorism* that "it marks an epoch in the intellectual history of mankind," and the *New York Tribune* wrote, "Perhaps this is the most important book ever written. One stands for an instant blinded with a great hope."[2] What was this blinding "great hope?"

The Enlightenment culture began and continues on the premise of the perfectibility of man by man. Essential to this fact of perfectibility is the passive nature of man, who is born without innate ideas or tendencies, or any original and sinful nature, and is hence at worst only neutral and therefore perfectly malleable. In the name of science and of empiricism, all influences in the life of man were ruled to be *external*, i.e., sense impressions, environmental factors, and socially applied controls being the essence of man's development and personality. By means of this "scientific" concept, the horrors of Christianity, of Calvinism in particular, with its doctrine of total depravity, man's inner apostasy against God and hence inner determination, his responsibility to God, and his irreducibility to social control, were to be met and overcome. Man *could* be educated; man is like a blank sheet of white paper, ready for science and society to use, and society is thus free to use him to build its true city of man as against the alien and hostile city of God. History can thus be wiped out by revolution, educational, social, political, economic and above all scientific revolution, and man and society made anew. Education in this sense is empirical education and is hence *total conditioning*. Education in the true sense of the word, meaning leading out or developing the native abilities of the person, presupposes either innate ideas or an original nature which is resistant to and non-malleable by the scientific educator, and it is hence highly objectionable and invalid to the consistent Enlightenment man.[3] Thus, predestination by God, coupled with the doctrine of human responsibility, must be

---

[2] Shipley, *loc. cit.*

[3] See R. J. Rushdoony: *Intellectual Schizophrenia,* pp. 1-11. Philadelphia: Presbyterian and Reformed, 1961.

ruled out in favor of *predestination by society,* i.e., total social control by scientific man. Science was at first associated with "the social speculations of the encyclopaedists" and was "discredited by the failures of the Revolution."[4] The French Revolution however discredited only one version of the Enlightenment hope, which came to exuberant revival in 1859 with Darwin's *Origin of Species,* which despite myths concerning opposition to it, sold out its first edition on the day of publication and immediately stimulated a revival of the Enlightenment hope in science, religion, politics, education and every other area of thought.

It is in this tradition that Watson stands as a militant champion of the Enlightenment faith. Its "self-evident" truths he confirmed by declaring them to be fully scientific. In order to arrive at empirical man, man totally controllable and totally subject to empirical influences, Watson denied the validity and usefulness of the 'concept' of consciousness, which for him was hopelessly religious and led directly to the 'soul' and hence to 'God.'

Behaviorism, on the contrary, holds that the subject matter of human psychology is the *behavior or activities of the human being.* Behaviorism claims that "consciousness" is neither a definable nor a usable concept; that it is merely another word for the "soul" of more ancient times. The old psychology is thus dominated by a kind of subtle religious philosophy.[5]

The fact that consciousness leads to religion, being inexplicable otherwise, is enough to rule it out of court. A question immediately arises, however: if consciousness can be thus casually outlawed, why not man? Why stop with consciousness? Watson was here consistent. For him, man "is a whole animal."[6] "The behaviorist, in his effort to get a unitary scheme of animal re-

---

[4] Lord Percy of Newcastle: *The Heresy of Democracy,* A Study in the History of Government, p. 211. Chicago: Regnery, 1955.

[5] John B. Watson: *Behaviorism,* p. 3. New York: The People's Institute, 1924. Italics here and throughout are Watson's.

[6] *Ibid.,* p. 75.

sponse, recognizes no dividing line between man and brute."[7] Accordingly, Watson was an unabashed and proud defender of the validity of and application to man of animal experimentation, and the psychology of rats, dogs, etc. If other psychologists continued to look down on this kind of experiment, Watson declared, "the behaviorists will be driven to using human beings as subjects and to employ methods of investigation which are exactly comparable to those now employed in the animal work."[8] And, to his fellow functionalists, Watson rightly observed, "I feel that *behaviorism* is the only consistent and logical functionalism."[9]

The starting point of behaviorism, it needs to be borne in mind, is the oft-repeated rejection of consciousness.

In one sweeping assumption after another, the behaviorist threw out the concepts both of mind and of consciousness, calling them carryovers from the church dogma of the Middle Ages. The behaviorist told the introspectionists that consciousness was just a masquerade for the soul.[10]

The behaviorist finds no mind in his laboratory, sees it nowhere in his subjects . . . If the behaviorists are right in their contention that there is no observable mind-body problem and no observable separate entity called mind, then there can be no such thing as consciousness or its substratum, the unconscious.[11]

The result is a concept of man as essentially passive and subject at all points to conditioning. Man will be what the behaviorist chooses to make of him, and he can be conditioned into the desired shapes in terms of this scientific concept of control. Watson spoke freely of the possibilities:

In short, the cry of the behaviorist is, "Give me the baby and my world to bring it up in and I'll make it crawl and walk; I'll make it

<hr/>

[7] Watson, "Psychology as the Behaviorist Views It," in Shipley, *op. cit.*, p. 798, and in *Psychological Review*, 1913, 20:158.

[8] In Shipley, p. 799f.

[9] *Ibid.*, p. 807.

[10] Watson: *The Ways of Behaviorism*, p. 7. New York: Harper, 1928.

[11] *Ibid.*, p. 96.

climb and use its hands in constructing buildings of stone or wood; I'll make it a thief, a gunman, or a dope fiend. The possibility of shaping in any direction is almost endless. Even gross differences in anatomical structure limit us far less than you may think. Take away man's hands and I will make him write, use a typewriter, drive an automobile, paint, and draw with his toes. Cut off his legs and paralyze his trunk muscles so that he will be bedridden, but give me only his hands and arms, and I'll have him playing the violin, writing, and doing a thousand other things. Make him blind and he can still play ice hockey, shoot with some degree of skill, read and write, model, and earn his living in a hundred different ways. Rob him of his ear at birth and I can teach him to carry on a conversation with you by watching you speak. Make him a deaf mute and I will still build you a Helen Keller."[12]

Thus, *prediction and control* are the essence of behaviorism's creed. Given the stimulus, the response can be predicted; given the response, the stimulus can be named.[13] "Personality is man made—is not a divine gift."[14] *"My personality is but the totality or sum of my habit systems, my conditionings."*[15] Even adults, if total control were possible, could be reconditioned radically.[16] Watson saw no wrong in the ideal of controlling the individual to "have him behave as society specifies"; for him, the problem was to get the knowledge necessary to do the job properly.[17]

For Watson, social control of man's behavior means control of his actions, for *thoughts* are not the primary source of influence in this empirical theory but actions, which are external.

Behavior is thus the central problem. Thought can be safely left to take care of itself when safe methods of regulating behavior can be obtained. What a man thinks is only a reflection of what he does.[18]

[12] *Ibid.*, p. 35f.
[13] *Ibid.*, p. 2.
[14] *Ibid.*, p. 116.
[15] *Ibid.*, p. 120.
[16] *Ibid.*, p. 138.
[17] *Ibid.*, p. 19.
[18] Watson, "Practical and Theoretical Problems in Instinct and Habits," in H. S. Jennings, J. B. Watson, A. Meyer, W. I. Thomas: *Suggestions of Modern Science Concerning Education*, p. 54. New York: Macmillan, 1917.

The "goal of the psychologist" is (1) to *predict* human behavior by its knowledge of stimulus and response, and (2) to control human behavior "if it is demanded by society that a given line of conduct is desirable."[19]

Watson's theories of talking and thinking were closely related, and a stimulus, to much modern quackery in semantics, in that his empiricism required him to hold that faulty conditioning by misused words is basically identical with faulty behavior.[20] Behaviorism was thus credited with the ability to correct thinking as well as behavior by proper conditioning.

Behaviorism would also replace "religion" with "experimental ethics,"[21] which means ethics as determined by science and society. Given free rein, behaviorism "will gradually change the universe." Moreover, men and women should desire this conditioning.

It ought to make men and women eager to rearrange their own lives, and especially eager to prepare themselves to bring up their own children in a healthy way. I wish I had time more fully to describe this, to picture to you the kind of rich and wonderful individual we should make of every healthy child if only we could let it shape itself properly and then provide for it a universe in which it could exercise that organization—a universe unshackled by legendary folk lore of happenings thousands of years ago; unhampered by disgraceful political history; free of foolish customs and conventions which have no significance in themselves, yet which hem the individual in like taut steel bands. I am not asking here for revolution; I am not asking people to go out to some God-forsaken place, form a colony, go naked and live a communal life, nor am I asking for a change to a diet of roots and herbs. I am not asking for "free love." I am trying to dangle a stimulus in front of you, a verbal stimulus which, if acted upon, will gradually change this universe. For the universe will change if you bring up your children, not in the freedom of the libertine, but in behavioristic freedom—a freedom which we cannot even picture in words, so little do we know of it. Will not these chil-

---

[19] *Ibid.*, p. 54f.
[20] See Watson: *Behaviorism*, pp. 180ff., *The Ways of Behaviorism*, pp. 78ff.
[21] Watson: *Behaviorism*, p. 18.

dren in turn, with their better ways of living and thinking, replace us as society and in turn bring up their children in a still more scientific way, until the world finally becomes a place fit for human habitation?[22]

It could be observed that the fitness of the world "for human habitation" is not the question, but the moral fitness of man. The experimental ethics of Watson is, in terms of his pragmatism and functionalism, radically relativistic. It is the ethics of meeting the requirements of the social will. This society and its social will are to be geared to the fulfilment of man in terms of Satan's temptation of Jesus in the wilderness: *give the people bread and miracles; provide them with social conditions which will make it unnecessary for men to be good.* Let the Good Society replace the good man, and social ethics supplant personal ethics. In this society, man can be free only to be what society wishes him to be.

I am not arguing for free anything—least of all free speech. I have always been very much amused by the advocates of free speech. In this harum-scarum world of ours, brought up as we are, the only person who ought to be allowed free speech is the parrot, because the parrot's words are not tied up with his bodily acts and do not stand as substitutes for bodily acts. All true speech stands substitutable for bodily acts, hence organized society has just as little right to allow free speech as it has to allow free action, which nobody advocates. When the agitator raises the roof because he hasn't free speech, he does it because he knows that he will be restrained if he attempts free action. He wants by his free speech to get someone else to do free acting—to do something he himself is afraid to do. The behaviorist, on the other hand, would like to develop his world of people from birth on, so that their speech and their bodily behavior could equally well be exhibited freely everywhere without running afoul of group standards.[23]

Two things are here clearly apparent: (1) When mind and body are made one, mind being resolved into body, thought and

22 *Ibid.,* p. 248.
23 *Loc. cit.*

action are also made indistinguishable, and any priority of thought destroyed. (2) Man's only freedom is to be conditioned to act in conformity to "group standards."

Watson's goals, now less naively stated, are the goals of science today. Science now aims at (1) the creation of life itself through biochemistry, (2) the creation of minds through machinery, (3) the reconditioning of minds by medication and drugs capable of controlling and remaking man, and (4) total social engineering and control through the state. It has even been proposed that man be wired at birth for permanent control through electrical impulses! Watson's particular dream is now far exceeded by contemporary scientists, one of whom has candidly stated, "Theologians will protest, but it is certainty itself that man will play God."[24] And educators, having become scientific, and themselves products of the Enlightenment, will also continue to play God. But every Enlightenment attempt to create Utopia has only brought man a step closer to the borderlands of a totalitarian hell. Its expectant followers are indeed being "blinded," but not by "a great hope."

[24] Biochemist Philip Siekewitz in *The Nation*, September 3, 1958, cited by Edmund A. Opitz: *Despotism by Consent*, p. 8. A mimeographed study. Irvington-on-Hudson, New York: Foundation for Economic Education, 1961.

# 17. Carleton Washburne:
## Education to Save Democracy

The usual confidence of educators in democracy is not always to be found in the writings of Carleton Washburne (b. 1889), whose educational experiments in the Winnetka, Illinois, schools were a highly prized specimen of progressive education. Washburne did not attempt to transcend his day, but sought to work in terms of it as effectively as possible. He was not hostile to democracy, and was indeed more than ready to be congenial to it. He showed not even the slightest tendency to indulge in the backward look. On the other hand, he was thoroughly alive to the perils of democracy and its instability, and his concern was to educate the citizens of democracy to use their power wisely.

Commenting at some length on H. G. F. Spurrell's *Modern Man and His Forerunners,* Washburne noted in 1928 that "the downfall of each civilization has been due either to invasion from the outside or to the rise of the masses within."[1] This

[1] Carleton Washburne and Myron M. Stearns: *Better Schools,* A Survey of Progressive Education in American Public Schools, p. 11. New York: John Day, 1928. Spurrell held a basically skeptical view of democracy. See H. G. F. Spurrell: *Modern Man and His Forerunners,* A Short Study of the Human Species, Living and Extinct, pp. 146-160; London: Bell, 1917. This was not, however, because he held to any other form of government with any real faith. Rather, he saw de-

downfall has usually been preceded by the decay of civilization and the internal collapse of the ruling power.

Such decay of civilization from within confronts us to-day. From the few, power has passed to the many. The franchise has been gradually extended until every adult votes, women as well as men. In no previous civilization, Spurrell points out, has there arisen within a democracy, in its later stages, any centralizing or unifying force sufficient to give the weakened body politic new power. With the removal of dangers from without, with the rise of individual opportunity and power within, the units of civilization pull apart. Selfish ends replace service. City competes against city, class against class, interest against interest, individual against individual. There comes the time when to each member of the community, of the nation, of the civilization, his own immediate needs and desires transcend those of his group, of his class, of his nation, of his race. For every leader strong enough effectively to coordinate the efforts of unselfish individuals, there are self-seeking interests to set up counter movements able collectively to overcome and destroy the effectiveness of that leadership. Like an individual suffering from senile decay, the body politic becomes once more merely a number of members, unable to coordinate. Dissolution is the result.

That is the history of every civilization of which we have record which, overcoming outside dangers, has perished from within. That is the danger our civilization is facing to-day. That is the danger

mocracy as the most obvious in its hostility to intelligence and independence. He believed it "hardly possible for a man with intelligence and integrity to rule in an advanced democracy." Moreover, he observed "that nations in decay continue producing men of ability after they fail to produce men of character," and these able but unscrupulous men hasten the decay (p. 150f). Spurrell, writing early in World War I, doubted that the war would make for greater democracy in any ideal sense but would more likely lead to "a revival of concentration of power on a military basis," together with such an "equilibrium between population and the resources of the world" as possibly to "lead to a reconsideration throughout the world of the rights and duties of the individual" (p. 160). Spurrell held it possible, in view of some present trends, that man might "remain after civilization has gone." Apart from that, and from the biological perspective so important to Spurrell, "The ultimate extinction of man is, of course, as inevitable as was that of the innumerable species with whose remains the geological strata are packed" (p. 188). Spurrell's point of view points up a fact most American educators have not been willing to face up to, namely, that the scientific perspective is not necessarily the democratic perspective and is often quite hostile to it.

which education, through developing people more capable of co-operation, must help us avoid.

It is no longer possible to prevent the masses from gaining control in our civilization to-day as they have done in the past. Even if it could have been prevented, it is doubtful if such prevention would have been desirable. Our hope lies in training continually greater numbers to use power wisely, when they have it.[2]

In other words, education alone can save democracy from itself. This task was Washburne's concern.

It can be argued that this unhappy view of democracy represented the opinion of Myron M. Stearns, his collaborator. On the other hand, Washburne and Stearns were in sufficient agreement to have collaborated also on a series of articles for *Collier's Weekly,* and on an earlier book, *New Schools in the Old World* (1926), a study of the progressive schools of Europe. Washburne did not hesitate, on his own, to state opinions, which, while sometimes reflecting common educational practice, were not readily owned up to by other educators. In Winnetka, candidates for the Board of Education were hand-picked by a caucus and had little trouble in gaining election.[3] Washburne believed in a strong superintendent always, and he associated progressive education with authority and responsibility in the person of "the superintendent of schools;" he believed in "one-man control."[4] He was hostile to the undermining of authority and responsibility in the name of democracy. On the other hand, he opposed any dictatorial hold on that office.

While the superintendent and his administrative and advisory staff should be the experts to determine the value of a teacher to her children and to the school organization, the teachers themselves are the experts as to whether the superintendent and members of his staff are giving them the help, the stimulus, the understanding, and the freedom necessary for them to do their best work. Therefore I would propose—and have actually inaugurated it in my own

2 *Ibid.,* pp. 11-13.
3 Washburne: *A Living Philosophy of Education,* p. 487. New York: John Day, 1940.
4 Washburne and Stearns: *Better Schools,* p. 103.

schools—the right of the teachers to recall the superintendent or any other person in an administrative or advisory position.[5]

However, the Winnetka Board of Education adopted a much milder policy in this matter than Washburne's radical proposal.[6]

Another unusual aspect of the Winnetka experiment begun in 1919, was that it began, in the planning stages, with the desire of well-to-do parents to "start a private school that would fit their children for Eastern colleges." One parent objected to the plan and suggested rather that the 'public' schools be "made good enough for our own children to go to."[7] This then was the beginning of the Winnetka experiment, and, with all its zeal in progressive education, it never lost this orientation towards "Eastern colleges." It was to be a thoroughly modern system, embodying the latest ideas in education, and democratic since 'public,' but still with an orientation upwards. It was progressive, and half the school day was formally devoted to master factual information, and the other half given to "creative and socializing activities,"[8] but there was no fixed commitment with regard to any "progressive" practice. In practice, books were important, and, unlike some progressive educators, Washburne did not try to devaluate books, and gave attention to children's reading.[9] A strikingly different aspect of Washburne's approach to the problem was the fact that, while clearly a strong adherent of the new movement, he did not despise or take time to criticize the older education. Washburne was more concerned with doing the properly fitting thing for his particular day and age, and in terms of particular and changing circumstances. In terms of this, he was a faithful progressive educator and perhaps the most consistent pragmatist of them all.

The Winnetka experiment had two goals in mind, among

[5] Washburne: *A Living Philosophy of Education*, p. 511.

[6] *Ibid.*, p. 517f.

[7] Washburne and Stearns: *Better Schools*, p. 50.

[8] Washburne: *Adjusting the School to the Child*, Practical First Steps, p. xv. Yonkers-on-Hudson, N. Y.: World Book Co., 1932.

[9] See Washburne and Mabel Vogel: *What Children Like to Read*, Winnetka Graded Book List. New York: Rand McNally, 1926.

other things: (1) "to make much greater adaptation to individual differences than is customary in public schools," and (2) "to provide more time for socialized and self-expressive activities."[10]

Washburne had no desire to diminish the educational content but rather to heighten it by means of "interest replacing discipline."[11] Like other educators, he believed in guiding and developing the child's interests, but he did not decry discipline in the process. He failed, however, to reckon with the decline of discipline that would follow such an emphasis on the child's interests, because, however much the child's interests are guided, he is aware very quickly that his interests rather than guidance or discipline is the principle of legitimacy.

"The ends of education" as seen in "the aims of better schools," Washburne cited as:

1. Soundness of body.
2. Skill of muscle-coordination of hand and mind.
3. Efficiency in a vocation to which one is naturally adapted.
4. Hobbies for wise use of leisure time.
5. Mastery of the tools of learning.
6. Knowledge of essential facts, as determined by research.
7. An inquiring mind, interested and alert.
8. Ability to pursue knowledge independently.
9. Contact with life.
10. The habit of settling social problems thoughtfully and in the light of knowledge.
11. Large-group consciousness, or a REALIZATION of the interdependence of mankind.
12. Emotional control and development, with freedom from harmful inhibitions.[12]

The eleventh aim became steadily more important to Washburne, and, in 1928, it was still central:

[10] C. Washburne, Mabel Vogel, William S. Gray: *Results of Practical Experiments in Fitting Schools to Individuals, A Survey of the Winnetka Public Schools,* Under a Subvention from the Commonwealth Fund, p. 9. Bloomington, Illinois: Public Schools Publishing Co., 1926.

[11] Washburne and Stearns: *Better Schools,* pp. 230ff.

[12] *Ibid.,* pp. 329-337.

In Babylon there was universal education. All people knew how to read and write and figure. The fact provided no safeguard against the obliteration of that great civilization. Our one safeguard consists in developing what Franklin Bobbitt of the University of Chicago calls "the large-group consciousness."[13]

Washburne failed to explain how the family, tribe or nation-conscious man who still destroyed the unit he made central would be preserved from destroying a world order, despite his allegiance thereto.

Moreover, despite a certain detachment that marked much of his thinking, Washburne did share many of the presuppositions of progressive education.

Every child is a person, a living, growing human being, with the right to physical and mental health, with the right to happiness. Our schools must be organized and conducted to help every child who enters their walls to live wholesomely and in a way that is fundamentally and lastingly satisfying.[14]

He thus held to the child-centered emphasis, and at the same time, the society-centered emphasis, and believed that "the two movements are complementary."[15] But the two can be complementary only if society assumes more and more responsibility and leaves the individual more and more 'free' to be an irresponsible child who concerns himself with 'rights' rather than responsibilities. It means some degree of socialism, and Washburne, refusing to see socialism as "an all-or-nothing idea," for 'public' schools are socialistic institutions, approved of the spread of government control in 'necessary' areas as 'need' arises.[16] Washburne had confidence in the outcome of the child-centered approach. Experiments conducted with children who were given at weaning age a free choice of foods indicated some self-regulation of diet in terms of instinctive or physiological

[13] *Ibid.*, p. 156f.
[14] Washburne: *A Living Philosophy of Education*, p. 3.
[15] Washburne and Stearns: *Better Schools*, p. 338.
[16] Washburne: *The World's Good*, Education for World-Mindedness, pp. 88ff. New York: John Day, 1954.

needs. The environment was controlled, as Washburne indicated, and candy in-between meals barred. But he believed that with similar controls and similar freedom a degree of natural self-regulation in the child would lead to a healthy education.[17]

As a practical (rather than theoretical) pragmatist, Washburne tried to avoid preconceived standards, and hence his statistical norm was the average person. Why he should be in any sense normative, and why statistics should have any weight, we are not told. At any rate, in terms of this, "All the rest of us are deviates. All education is therefore education of deviates."[18] From this concept of norm stems the common classification of the gifted child as abnormal because a deviate from the norm.

Since external norms are barred (although why internal norms are more valid, we are not told), three major needs appear in children which education must minister to in order to fulfil the needs of the child and his self-regulating nature. "The first major need of every child is self-expression."[19] By this Washburne did not mean undisciplined self-expression, and he was critical of some progressive schools for so interpreting it, but rather self-expression related to social living.

A sense of security is the second of the child's rights and fundamental needs. Security, however, must not be confused with overprotection or overindulgence, or even absence of risk. It means, rather, a fundamental at-homeness in one's environment, a sense of certainty that one is loved and wanted, a feeling of confidence in oneself and a recognition that others have confidence in one. The sense of security is the feeling of a firm foundation under one's feet. One may leap off it, but he knows that when he comes down the solid ground is there to rest on.[20]

The third essential need and "drive" is "social integration." Man finds his security only as part of a social group. Social integration "means the identification of oneself with a group of one's

---

[17] Washburne: *A Living Philosophy of Education*, pp. 113-115.
[18] *Ibid.*, p. 23.
[19] *Ibid.*, p. 37.
[20] *Ibid.*, p. 38.

fellows, an identification of one's happiness and well-being with those of the group to which one belongs and with more and more inclusive groups."[21] It is not necessary to challenge the necessity of these three things to differ with Washburne. Important as these things may be, are they the responsibility of the schools? Indeed, is there not a danger of destroying the child by attempting to accomplish these things institutionally? Does the school *cure* in cases where these needs are lacking, or does it often *aggravate* an existing ailment? Furthermore, what about the basic *educational* needs of the child? The mind of the child seems to be forgotten in this scheme of things.

But, states Washburne, children are constantly rendered maladjusted by inadequate or faulty homes and parents. The teacher must thus be trained "in the principles of mental hygiene" to aid these maladjusted children. From teacher to nurse to psychiatrist, a chain of reference must be established. "Psychiatric service should be available to all schools for the more serious cases of maladjustment." Mental hygiene as well as sex education must be taught in the schools and is their "responsibility." It should be required, and, in Winnetka, unless the parents by interview "assured me that they would give their children complete, frank sex education at home," it was required. As Washburne observed, few parents wanted the embarrassment of such interviews. By conferences, parents should be educated into the philosophy and practice of the schools.[22] Washburne does not mention another logical step: if the state through the school has so vast a right to the child, why not require the couples to request permission, and gain instruction, *before* having a child? *If the state has a right to the child after birth, it logically has a right to the child before birth. The socialization of the child means also the socialization of the parent.* Sooner or later, states develop their every claim.

And yet, in spite of his radical demands for the school's control over the child, Washburne tried to hold to individualism.

[21] *Ibid.,* p. 42.
[22] *Ibid.,* pp. 45-106.

"It is not the well-rounded individual we want, but the fully de-veloped individual—developed along his own lines."[23] This in-dividualism, however, is set in the context of an organic concept of the unity of society. Even as, "in biological evolution, cells are first independent, then grouped but unspecialized, then more and more highly specialized and interdependent until they are incapable of separate existence," so man has developed from "first independent individuals, then grouped for mutual protec-tion, but with little specialization, then more and more spe-cialized and interdependent. Now few would be capable of sus-tained independent existence."[24] This means that man no longer can call his life his own; he is merely a cell in a body, and his "individuality" is merely his particular function to the body. Thus Washburne ends up with mass man in spite of his desire to transcend him. For Washburne, the social sciences must teach "that, in the long run, his good is the world's and the world's good is his own."[25] Such a view is the triumph of the state over man, who is totally absorbed into the group. Lacking a higher law than the group or "world," he cannot in the name of his insignificant cell-like particularity challenge the right of the whole. The life is in the organism as a whole, and right and wholeness go hand in hand. Washburne, however, trusted that the individual would still find self-realization in the group. His definition of democracy returned to this theme. "Fundamentally, *democracy is a way of life that gives every individual the utmost possible opportunity for self-fulfillment as a member of an inter-dependent society.*"[26] This involves freedom, social responsi-bility (i.e., "realization of one's identification with the society of which one is a member, the subordination of temporary to permanent values and of individual and small-group action to large-group purposes; and the ability to co-operate with others in work and in thought, and to play an active part in determin-

23 *Ibid.*, p. 112.
24 *Ibid.*, p. 373f.
25 *Ibid.*, p. 423.
26 *Ibid.*, p. 448. Italics are Washburne's.

ing the social, political, and economic life of society") and understanding.[27] It should be noted that democracy is seen primarily as *a way of life* rather than *a form of government,* and the role of governing is given minor attention as a form of social responsibility. Indeed, Washburne believed in the prior right of experts in matters of government. Thus, he held that student courts were "a misapplication of democracy," in that students are incompetent to judge. This is true also of civil judges, whose role is "one of the worst features in our present political democracy." True democracy is not necessarily political democracy. "Expert psychiatrists and criminologists should have the sole right to decide what is to be done with the violator, in order to rehabilitate him and make him into a good and useful citizen, and in the meantime how society can best be protected from his possible depradations."[28] Washburne's democracy thus shares the fate of all democracies; it begins as the ostensible triumph and freedom of the people and ends with them ruled by a new oligarchy whom they must obey as true democratic authority more intensively than any previous power demanded. The masses must do their work as faithful cells of the new leviathan, be fed, content, silent and obedient.

Washburne's confidence in this society grew rather than diminished, and his earlier doubts grew fainter, and his confidence that evolution would be stepped up by democratic interdependence became marked. He appealed for "faith in man's potentialities for mutual helpfulness and ever-increasing wisdom,"[29] warning that, if man failed to learn "swiftly to adapt to his fellow man," he "will destroy the interdependent civilization he has built." However critical the situation, still "human evolution has been accelerating more and more as man's interdependence has increased."[30] Interaction and interdependence must lead to, and social integration "consists of the identification

[27] Washburne, *loc. cit.*
[28] *Ibid.,* p. 475f.
[29] Washburne: *The World's Good,* p. xiii.
[30] *Ibid.,* p. 60.

of oneself with one's fellows."[31] The Bible defines "Love thy
neighbor as thyself" as meaning obedience to the second table
of the law, i.e., respect for the life, home, property, and reputation of others in word, thought and deed (Rom. 13: 9, 10). For
Washburne, however, love of neighbor means social integration,
a radically different thing.[32] Democratic living is not majority
rule, therefore, but "a way of life."[33] Differences in people are
necessary in a true democracy, because "every organism consists
of different cells performing their functions differently, and co-
ordinating these functions. This differentiation is essential to
the life of the organism."[34] It is to be expected that Washburne
would be strongly in favor of the United Nations, a great organism in the making. His view of the Russian Revolution was not
sympathetic, and he insisted on the right to wage war, being
definitely not a pacifist, but his view of the constituency of the
United Nations was far from pessimistic. He saw its differences
not so much as a basic cleavage but as potentially reconcilable
points of view.[35]

This then was Washburne's cure for "the rise of the masses."
As in other instances, it remains questionable whether the
"cure" is any improvement over the "disease."

[31] *Ibid.*, p. 5.
[32] *Ibid.*, p. 16.
[33] *Ibid.*, p. 43.
[34] *Ibid.*, p. 73.
[35] *Ibid.*, pp. 107-291.

# 18. Edward Lee Thorndike: Education as a Science

The contributions of Edward Lee Thorndike (1874-1949) to education have lately been somewhat obscured by the influence of Curti's appraisal of them. According to Curti, Thorndike, who sought to be the impartial scientist, was actually guided by very conservative economic and ethical motives which undercut the validity of his work. "One must question to what extent his social opinions are truly related, scientifically, to his experimental work, and to what extent they are determined by his own unconscious participation in the prejudices of our own time."[1] Some of Thorndike's ideas were hostile to the notion of unlimited educational opportunity for all, and his concepts of original nature gave "little support to democracy."[2] Thorndike, however, as professor of educational psychology in Teachers College, Columbia University, did not see himself at odds with Dewey and other colleagues in any radical sense. Indeed, at even a cursory glance, his contributions to progressive education and to the breakdown of the older basic and classical curriculum were notable. First of all, Thorndike's approach was hostile in

[1] Curti, *op. cit.*, p. 498.
[2] *Ibid.*, pp. 474, 485.

essence, if oblivious in practice, to the older concepts of education as a philosophy grounded on metaphysics. Experimental psychology was largely advanced in educational circles as a result of Thorndike's influence. Influenced by Wundt, Thorndike also shared with Dewey a thorough-going assumption of evolution, and a functional concept of mind as a functioning of the organism in its adaptation to the total environment. Thus, in his functionalism, Thorndike was at one with Dewey and the progressive educators. Second, and as a consequence of the first, Thorndike's work was a major factor in overthrowing the older curriculum, with its emphasis on religious and classical ideas, and its belief in the transfer of training. Subjects were previously taught not only for their own sakes but as valuable mental disciplines. Thorndike's experiments, while indecisive, were still widely influential in breaking the older education in most schools.[8] So successful was Thorndike in overthrowing the transfer of training and mental discipline concepts, that subsequent experiments which indicated some merit in the concepts fell on deaf ears. Thorndike had provided a much-needed lever to overthrow the old, and nothing could restore it, least of all facts. Third, Thorndike, through his new stimulus-response psychology provided another valuable weapon for the progressive educator's approach. The older "faculty" psychology, with its introspective aspects, was rapidly discarded in favor of Thorndike's stimulus-response (S-R) concept, which not only provided a scientific concept of educational psychology but made possible a science of education. Fourth, scientific educational theory meant testing and measurement as its necessary corollary, and involved a faith in science. Butts, describing the prevalence of this "faith" in the 1920's and 1930's, described it aptly: "Whatever exists at all

[8] For criticisms of Thorndike, with especial reference to this concept, see Rev. Walter T. Pax: *A Critical Study of Thorndike's Theory and Laws of Learning,* The Catholic University of America, Educational Research Monographs, XI, 1, January 15, 1938, The Catholic Education Press, Washington, D. C., and Pedro Tamesis Orata: *The Theory of Identical Elements,* Being a Critique of Thorndike's Theory of Identical Elements and a Re-interpretation of the Problem of Transfer of Training, Columbus, The Ohio State University Press, 1928.

exists in some amount; anything that exists in amount can be measured; and measurement in education is, in general, the same as measurement in the physical sciences."[4] Thorndike, whose work made him influential in this movement, was accordingly strongly concerned with tests and measurements.[5] The premise and conclusion of this faith was simplicity exemplified. As stated by Thorndike himself, "Experience has sufficiently shown that the facts of human nature can be made the material for quantitative science."[6]

The point of offense in Thorndike was his strong emphasis on heredity: "The one thing that educational theorists of to-day seem to place as the foremost duty of the schools—the development of powers and capacities—is the one thing that the schools or any other educational forces can do least."[7] The influence of environment he saw very much "over-estimated," and very much misunderstood, in that environment "includes a practical infinitude of different causes" which "act differently upon different types of original nature and at different ages and with different cooperating circumstances."[8] As a result, environment is not constant, nor, in the same time and place, the same for two people. "All theories of human life must accept as a first principle the fact that human beings at birth differ enormously in mental capacities and that these differences are largely due to similar differences in their ancestry. All attempts to change human nature must accept as their most important condition the limits set by original nature to each individual. . . . It has been shown that the relative differences in certain mental traits which

---

[4] R. Freeman Butts: *op. cit.*, p. 561.

[5] See E. L. Thorndike: *An Introduction to the Theory of Mental and Social Measurements*, New York, Science Press, 1904, and *The Measurement of Intelligence*, New York, Teachers College Bureau of Publications, 1925. This latter work was written with E. O. Bregman, M. V. Cobb, Ella Woodyard and the staff of the Division of Psychology of the Institute of Educational Research of Teachers College.

[6] Thorndike: *Introduction to the Theory of Mental and Social Measurements*, p. v.

[7] Thorndike: *Educational Psychology*, p. 45. New York: Lemcke and Buechner, 1903.

[8] *Ibid.*, pp. 66-68.

were found in these one hundred children are due almost entirely to differences in ancestry, not in training." Training or education simply enables the individual to make better use of native ability, but does not increase it.[9] "Each nature in some measure selects its own environment, and each nature may get from an environment a different influence, so that the relative achievements of, say, the boys who this year begin school in America, will probably be more closely paralled to their relative original talents and interests than to their relative advantages in home and school environment." Accordingly, "specialization of schools," to take care of pupils of diverse abilities, is a necessity. It is more humane to be scientific in evaluating people than to be guided "by some customary superstition," such as, we can infer, radical democratic thinking.[10] It is therefore necessary to face realistically the fact "that racial differences in original nature are not mere myths."[11] This statement, one of Thorndike's central offenses to many, was, like his whole position, a product of his scientific methodology and measurements. Thorndike's conclusion was not one of racial prejudice; he recognized variations within groups and espoused the proper scientific utility of all human materials:

A city should try to improve the personal qualities of all its residents, native or foreign-born, white or black. In the conditions of city life, it is wasteful and dangerous, as well as cruel, to maintain Ghettos, black belts, Chinatowns, and the like, in space or in thought, as regions of inferiority, hopelessness, and neglect. Social stratification is probably unavoidable, and may be desirable, but it should be related to abilities and interests rather than to the pigment in one's skin or the church to which his parents belonged. It should be such as to encourage a good life within each stratum, and the utilization of the "higher" strata for the welfare of the lower, as well as conversely. Movement up of the capable and down of the in-

[9] Thorndike: *Measurements of Twins*, p. 11. Archives of Philosophy, Psychology and Scientific Methods, No. 1, September, 1905. New York: Science Press.

[10] Thorndike: *Individuality*, pp. 48, 51. Boston: Houghton Mifflin, 1911.

[11] *Ibid.*, p. 36. See also Thorndike: *Your City*, pp. 77-82. New York: Harcourt, Brace, 1939.

capable should be expected and facilitated. A stratum, white, yel-low or black, so low that it can do little beyond what an animal or a machine can do is an undesirable element in a modern city.[12]

Thorndike's position, therefore, was not the reflection of preju-dice but a scientist's version of Jefferson's aristocracy of talent and ability. Like Jefferson, Thorndike believed in equality of opportunity and of dignity as men, and also in natural inequali-ties which created a natural caste and inequalities. Society must remain free and fluid to permit the rise or fall of each to his natural level.

It is also an American habit to clamor about equality of oppor-tunity as the prime virtue of a school system. Equality at the start there should be, but the higher opportunities like the higher dis-tinctions should be, as they always have been, earned. The schools always have and always will work to create a caste, to emphasize inequalities. Our care should be that they emphasize inequalities, not of adventitious circumstances, but of intellect, energy, idealism and achievement.[13]

It becomes apparent why progressive educators have felt it neces-sary to go further than Thorndike did in departing from the more academic curriculum, which indeed served "to emphasize inequalities," as any truly educative process always must. To avoid inequalities, education in the historic sense must be avoided.

For Thorndike, then, education served to develop and make explicit the basic abilities of the individual, to be, in brief, *environment at its best.*[14] Thorndike was cynical, however, in his expectations of that environment. His study, for example, of *Ventilation in Relation to Mental Work* was upsetting to many who hoped it would be an argument in favor of better and more modern school buildings. The effect of conditions of air, temper-ature and ventilation upon the rate of improvement of mental

[12] Thorndike: *Your City*, p. 81f.
[13] Thorndike: *Educational Psychology*, p. 96.
[14] *Ibid.*, pp. 77-79.

functions indicated that poor conditions led to consistently better performance![15] Indeed, Thorndike went so far as to observe,

It is a common habit of pseudo-scientific writers about education to decry one thing or another in school practice on the ground that it causes arrested development. Such speculations lack any adequate basis of fact. We do not know whether any school methods can, much less whether they do, cause special or general arrest of mental growth.[16]

What then is education? As Thorndike saw it, it was as yet a primitive enterprise. "The work of education is to make changes in human minds and bodies. To control these changes we need knowledge of the causes which bring them to pass." This makes tests and measurements necessary and basic to education.[17] Education involves hygiene, to make growth possible and remove impediments, and involves providing opportunity, incentives, and deterrents, which meant also scientifically sound punishments.[18] Of education he said, "in all its usages it refers to *changes.*" It means "to change what is into what ought to be," which involves knowing what the laws of change are:

Education as a whole should make human beings wish each other well, should increase the sum of human energy and happiness and decrease the sum of discomfort of the human beings that are or will be, and should foster the higher, impersonal pleasures. These aims of education in general—good-will to men, useful and happy lives, and noble enjoyment—are the ultimate aims of school education in particular. Its proximate aims are to give boys and girls health in body and mind, information about the world of nature and men, worthy interests in knowledge and action, a multitude of habits of

[15] This study, undertaken with W. A. McCall and J. C. Chapman, is Teachers College Contributions to Education no. 78; 1916.

[16] Thorndike: *Educational Psychology,* p. 141.

[17] *Ibid.,* p. 3.

[18] *Ibid.,* p. 79. See also Thorndike: *An Experimental Study of Rewards,* Teachers College Contributions to Education No. 580, 1933; and *The Psychology of Wants, Interests and Attitudes,* New York: Appleton-Century, 1935; this latter was written with the assistance of the Staff of the Division of Psychology of the Institute of Educational Research, Teachers College.

thought, feeling and behavior and ideals of efficiency, honor, duty, love and service.[19]

All values, however, are for Thorndike, subjective, and, "in the last analysis, decisions as to the value and significance of things with which education is concerned are based on desires, wants, cravings, or urges."[20] All human activity, in child or adult, "is initiated and sustained by some urge, craving, desire, or want. . . . Value or worth or goodness means power to satisfy wants. . . . Life is activity instituted and sustained to satisfy wants. Since this is the case, we may say provisionally that the ultimate aim of education for man is to secure the fullest satisfaction of human wants." This means, since it calls for "the *fullest* satisfaction," "the advancement of mankind as a whole." "Education, then, aims at satisfying the wants of all people in order to give each person the fullest realization of his own desires. . . . The chief aim of education, then, is to realize the fullest satisfaction of human wants." This means *changing* human nature and human wants "which are futile or antagonistic to the satisfaction of other wants and to cultivate those wants which do not reduce or which actually increase the satisfaction of others." With Dewey, it must therefore be held that education "is not preparation for life, it is life."[21] Nature must be controlled "to increase the welfare of society at large," and this control and use must be a central goal of education also.[22] There must accordingly be a recognition of the value of "socialization in the school," and approval of the fact that "progressive schools are placing increasing emphasis on the process of socialization." Racially mixed classes are welcomed by progressive teachers "as a means of developing a consciousness of the interdependence of all peoples and an appreciation of the value of promoting the

[19] Thorndike: *The Principles of Teaching,* Based on Psychology, pp. 1, 3f, 7. New York: Seiler, 1906.

[20] E. L. Thorndike and Arthur I. Gates: *Elementary Principles of Education,* p. 16. New York: Macmillan, 1929.

[21] *Ibid.,* pp. 16-21, p. 33.

[22] *Ibid.,* p. 30.

interests of the Great Society."[23] Diversity of native endowment must lead to "specialization rather than general perfection." Not the well-rounded and classically educated man of the old school but the specialist is needed in the true society.[24] Indeed, even within the confines of educational research, strict specialization is and must be the general rule.[25] Each person, in his own particular way, must strive for that development and adjustment which will "contribute the most to the welfare of the Great Society."[26]

It is clearly apparent that for Thorndike values are relative to social wants, which change and develop, so that values, depending on wants, change also. Human wants must therefore be progressively improved in terms of the broader context of mankind. "The aim of education should then be: to make men want the right things, and to make them better able so to control all forces of nature and themselves that they can satisfy these wants."[27] This point is an especially significant one, in that it introduces the insistent note of *compulsion* in education. Men's *native abilities* cannot be changed; education only provides an environment for them. But men's *values* can be changed, and they *must* be changed to conform to the welfare of mankind, a natural and accordingly scientifically valid value. Education must therefore (1) "cultivate good will to men," which is "one of the best of wants, for it is a want which every satisfier of all will satisfy"; (2) "the second great means of making human wants better is to cultivate impersonal pleasures." How pleasures can be pleasure and still impersonal seems incongruous, but to Thorndike it meant "impersonal in the sense that for one to have the pleasure does not prevent anybody else from having it.

[23] *Ibid.*, p. 42f.

[24] *Ibid.*, p. 25.

[25] Thorndike, "Quantitative Investigations in Education: with Special Reference to Co-operation within this Association," pp. 33-52, in E. P. Cubberley, W. F. Dearborn, Paul Monroe, E. L. Thorndike: *Research Within the Field of Education, Its Organization and Encouragement. The School Review Monographs, No. I.* Chicago: University of Chicago Press, 1911.

[26] Thorndike and Gates: *Elementary Principles*, p. 59.

[27] Thorndike: *Education*, A First Book, p. 11. New York: Macmillan, 1912.

They are unlike the pleasures of eating or owning or wearing things, where the pleasure of one man usually uses up a possible means of satisfying other men." Men must be educated then to social or "unselfish pleasures." (3) The "third great means of making human wants better" is to eliminate or diminish "useless and harmful wants," which include "the wants represented by superstition." "Only those wants which the universe as it is may somehow satisfy are worth keeping."[28] "Morality in the broad sense is simply such thought and action as promote the improvement and satisfaction of human want." As a result, Thorndike could honestly hold that "the aims of education as a whole are identical with those of morality,"[29] because for him science and the schools had taken over the function of religion as the source of morality.

Thorndike saw the role of religion itself as "human betterment,"[30] rather than any theocentric motive, and naturally felt that science was the better instrument towards that end.

In his view of man, Thorndike was consistently post-Darwinian, ready to see man in terms of evolutionary thought. This meant a monistic rather than dualistic view of the mind-body relationship. Thorndike took this seriously, and held that there was "a close connection between motor and intellectual abilities."[31] The manually dexterous and the gifted intellectual are thus one and the same man.

But, more important, his stimulus-response (S-R) psychology presupposed a doctrine of man common to Enlightenment thought and to virtually all educators. Locke's conception of the mind as a blank tablet made the mind *essentially passive* and hence subject to *conditioning* and radical direction by the educator. Instead of a mind with a past, tradition, family and religion, coming to school to be *educated*, led out further into its own heritage, education in the tradition of Locke and the Enlighten-

[28] *Ibid.*, p. 12f.
[29] *Ibid.*, p. 29.
[30] Thorndike: *Your City*, p. 99.
[31] Thorndike and Gates: *Elementary Principles*, p. 139.

ment is essentially a *passive* activity and is *conditioning* rather than *education*. An important aspect of Thorndike's objection to transfer of training was his conception of the mind as essentially passive and hence incapable of such activity. It is significant that so much of the objection to Thorndike's attack on transfer of training came from religious and traditional sources opposed to the concept of the mind's passivity. Not only was Thorndike's S-R psychology passive as a result of its philosophical inheritance, but also because of its radically neurological conception of mind, so that the laws of learning meant repetition, conditioning, exercise, and the establishment of strong neurological patterns rather than sudden insight. Obedience to the laws of Readiness, Exercise and Effect meant neurological conditions were satisfied, and scientific requirements for the establishment of patterns of learning fully met.[32] Thorndike's laws of learning are based on thoroughly scientific logic, on the premise that man learns by the establishment of certain patterns in his nervous system, and that the older dualistic conception of the mind, by ascribing non-material powers to the mind, was guilty of unscientific thinking. Man cannot indeed be reduced to the level of other animals, but must be seen "as a king from the same race," and "his intellect we have seen to be a simple though extended variation from the general animal sort."[33] Thus, animal psychology is important, in that children are trained in exactly the same way, i.e., in terms of the same basic laws, as are animals—poets, preachers and artists to the contrary.

As a result, the child must be acted on; the mind is basically *passive*, malleable and open to direction. Lacking aggressive orientation except by way of reaction or frustration, the mind basically needs *conditioning* and *re-direction*. "The substitutive or directive methods" change men by "providing some positive

---

[32] See Thorndike: *Education*, 95ff.; *Principles of Teaching*, pp. 156ff.; *Animal Intelligence, Experimental Studies*, pp. 241ff., New York: Macmillan, 1911; *Educational Psychology*, vol. II, The Psychology of Learning, New York Teachers College, 1921; *Elementary Principles*, pp. 84ff.; *The Elements of Psychology*, New York: Seiler, 1905.

[33] Thorndike: *Animal Intelligence*, p. 294; cf. 127.

good tendency in place of the bad one, instead of simply avoiding or suppressing it."[34] In foreign policy, this has come to mean giving liberally to the aggressor nation to re-direct her energies. Thorndike believed this method to be effective, urged its use in education, courts, and internationally:

Similarly, a useful preventative of war between nations will be to habituate nations to positive cooperation in enterprises for the common good, such as charting the seas, exterminating contagious diseases, establishing international courts and international police, arranging for the migration of students and teachers, and the like.[35]

Lacking the biblical conception of evil as an aggressive, positive and ambitious power in creation, Thorndike was completely utopian in his conception of the treatment and cure of crime and war. And basic to this utopianism was his concept, in common with virtually all educators, of the essential passivity of the mind.

Similarly, in dealing with man's original nature,[36] Thorndike's faithfulness to evolutionary thought had its logical and dangerous implications. The *original* nature of man was distinguished from the " 'natural' proclivities of man." The original is basic, while the natural shifts from age to age.[37] For Thorndike, the original nature is "the ultimate source of all values."[38] Thorndike's lengthy evaluation of man's original nature is significant in that it is a catalogue of *primitive* and *infantile* traits, and this is an inevitable product of evolutionary thinking. Thorndike's list might differ from Freud's conceptions, but both were agreed as to the *primitive* and *infantile* character of man's basic, truest and determinative nature. *If man began from primitive origins, then primitive characteristics are most deeply inbedded in man. But, if in the biblical view, man was created as*

---

[34] Thorndike: *Education*, p. 200.
[35] *Ibid.*, p. 201.
[36] Thorndike: *Educational Psychology*, Vol. I, The Original Nature of Man, p. 198f. New York: Teachers College, 1921.
[37] *Ibid.*, p. 293.
[38] *Ibid.*, pp. 310-312.

*Adam, full-grown man, then the maturity of his manhood is the basic and determining aspect of his being, namely, that he was created in the image of God.* In the evolutionary view, infantilism has a priority, and educative and healing processes require a re-orientation and re-direction in terms of those primitive forces. *But, if man was created as man, infantilism has no priority, and the primacy of the child is arrant heresy, for man is either a covenant-keeper or a wilful covenant-breaker.* The modern world, of course, is in headlong flight from maturity in its rebellion against biblical faith.

Thorndike believed that education should be a science, but he recognized that one of the two questions a theory of education "must decide" is "what ought people to be?" He recognized that this question would be answered in terms of one's "conception of ultimate values."[39] His values being scientific, the man Thorndike was unable to do other than to reduce man's nature to infantilism. He saw "dangers" in too much education in childhood; education should accordingly be prolonged and tempered.[40] "A much larger fraction of schooling" should be left to "adult years" in terms of "the Dewey doctrine of 'First the need, then the knowledge or technique to satisfy the need.' "[41]

Thorndike hoped to replace controversy by science.[42] Instead, by means of science he deepened both the controversy and the rift at the heart of modern society.

[39] Thorndike: *Educational Psychology,* p. 163.
[40] Thorndike: *Elementary Principles,* pp. 202ff.
[41] E. L. Thorndike, E. O. Bregman, J. W. Tilton, E. Woodyard: *Adult Learning,* p. 190. New York: Macmillan, 1928. See also Thorndike: *Adult Interests.* New York: Macmillan, 1935; written with the staff of the Division of Psychology, Institute of Educational Research, Teachers College.
[42] Thorndike: *The Teaching of Controversial Subjects,* p. 39. Cambridge: Harvard University Press, 1937.

# 19. Boyd H. Bode:
## "Is Progressivism a New Absolutism?"

Boyd Henry Bode (born 1873), for many years professor of education at Ohio State University, was, with Kilpatrick, often identified as one of the two great followers of John Dewey in education. But a markedly different spirit sets off Bode from Dewey and Kilpatrick, however marked his common devotion to democracy. His casual observation, "a world-wide regeneration cannot take place over night,"[1] is an index to his temper. Again, he stressed the intellectual aspect of education more than other progressivists.

His purpose at all times, however, remained constant: "to interpret present-day educational problems from the standpoint of pragmatic philosophy."[2] His comments on education and democracy indicate his attitudes concerning them:

What counts, in short, is not only the materials that are taught, but the spirit in which they are taught, the spirit that is made to pervade our educational system. A system is not democratic simply because it is made available to everybody or because it is administered without distinction of persons. In a Spartan scheme of

[1] Bode: *Modern Educational Theories*, p. 224. New York: Macmillan, 1927.
[2] Bode: *Fundamentals of Education*, p. v. New York: Macmillan, 1922.

education all are included and all are treated equally, but it is not democratic because the individual is subordinated, is made a means to an end; and that end, the State. To be truly democratic, education must treat the individual himself as the end and set itself the task of preparing him for that intellectual and emotional sharing in the life and affairs of men which embodies the spirit of the Golden Rule. In proportion as common interests are permitted to outweigh special interests, the individual is becoming humanized and the successive adjustments of life will be made in the direction of democracy and in accordance with the needs of an expanding life.[3]

This statement makes apparent that democracy and man's fulfilment therein is an article of faith, not a pragmatic philosophy. His concept of social man is moreover a moral concept, because to be social is to be moral.

Most frequently, perhaps, the term "social" is applied to cooperative activities that are directed to a common end. In this sense the Allies in the recent war were social in their relations to one another, but not in their relations to Germany. When used in this sense the contrasting term is not nonsocial, but antisocial. But we are also inclined to describe the attitude of the sincere statesman or reformer as social because inspired by the desire to promote the well-being of others, even when those who are to be benefited resent what is being done in their behalf and unite against their would-be benefactor. That is, a man may be social, even though he stands all alone. He is called social not merely because his conduct has reference to the attitudes or activities of others, but because his conduct is the expression of a concern for the interests of others. Taken in this sense, social conduct is identical with moral conduct. Unless the word "social" is used with discrimination, it is bound to prove less serviceable as a means to insight than as a cover for our academic sins.

The common element in these different meanings, it will be observed, consists in the fact that we learn the meaning of our environment by discovering what things mean to others.[4]

In 1904, H. H. Horne, quoting Everett, had declared, "the indi-

[3] *Ibid.*, p. 61f.
[4] *Ibid.*, p. 43f.

vidual is *not* the universal but it will be."[5] Now in progressivism "the individual himself as the end," in Bode's words, had come into his own as the new universal by which all things are to be judged and in whom they have their being. This new universal, man, is moreover *social* man, against whom the purely *individual* or *personal* man dare not stand. Bode made the social reference always clear-cut. "Education is a process of growth; it means a liberation of capacity."[6] This growth is growth into social awareness and identity. "Speaking generally, we may say that education is a matter of gaining an understanding of the meaning which the things in our environment have to the members of our community."[7] Education must therefore be in terms of "a social outlook."

To repeat, the reconstruction of experience with reference to an ultimate standard of value is the outstanding concern of education. This concern or task is basic because democracy, as defined by pragmatic theory, is a challenge to every other system of belief and of education.[8]

However much progressivists protest that they are pragmatists, their essentially *religious* nature is apparent: in terms of "an ultimate standard of value" they assert a religious unity of belief as "a challenge to every other system of belief and of education." Moreover, by denying "the division of reality into a natural and a supernatural realm," and insisting "that the world is all of one piece,"[9] they prepare the way not only for the radical unity of man but for a radical totalitarianism. No law remains, or any universal, other than *social man,* before whom every *private man* must bow down and make obeisance.

This great democracy cannot be identified with a particular form of government.

When democracy is identified with established forms, it has ceased

---

[5] H. H. Horne: *The Philosophy of Education,* p. 286.
[6] Bode, *op. cit.,* p. 8.
[7] *Ibid.,* p. 30.
[8] Bode: *How We Learn,* p. 277. Boston: Heath, 1940.
[9] *Ibid.,* p. 264.

to be democracy. The letter killeth; it is the spirit that maketh alive.

The essential thing, then, about democracy is its attitude. To identify democracy, as Bryce does, with "the rule of the whole people expressing their sovereign will by their votes," is to invite the danger of accepting the form for the substance. Forms are important only in so far as they become a means for cultivating a democratic attitude.[10]

Since attitude is the essential thing, the private man is at the mercy of the new voices of the great god democracy whenever they choose to call his legal and formally democratic activity anti-social. Indeed, if he believes in *anything*, in heaven above or earth below, *other* than democracy, he is not truly democratic, for democracy requires that man think relatively, pragmatically and skeptically concerning all things save democracy. "Democracy requires the same open-mindedness toward values or interests as science requires toward evidence. In this aspect the spirit of science is the same as the spirit of democracy."[11] "There can be no final truth,"[12] and "practical" tests must be applied "to questions of truth and conduct."[13]

Progressive education, by seeking to avoid "compartmentalization" in education and experience,[14] was concerned with the restoration of a fundamental unity of learning and therefore of very great cultural importance. Bode, however, was not un-critical of progressive education. He even raised the question, "Is Progressivism A New Absolutism?" He insisted that the "individualism and absolutism of Rousseau" was the source of such absolutism as existed in current progressivism. His cure was more democracy of Dewey's sort.

A democratic program of education must necessarily rest on the perception that democracy is a challenge to all forms of absolutism,

[10] Bode: *Modern Educational Theories*, p. 13.
[11] *Ibid.*, p. 257.
[12] Bode: *Conflicting Psychologies of Learning*, p. 294. Boston: Heath, 1929.
[13] *Ibid.*, p. 251.
[14] Bode, "The Confusion in Present-Day Education," in W. K. Kilpatrick, ed: *The Educational Frontier*, p. 19. New York: D. Appleton-Century, 1933.

that it has its own standards, ideals, and values, and that these must pervade the entire program from end to end.[15]

How this new absolutism could itself end absolutism, we are not told. We are told that "when some one set of values is arbitrarily selected as final and absolute, we have the principle of dictatorship."[16] But this is only because such values are *external* to man. If things are seen as "operational" in value,[17] then the true value, *democratic or social man,* can become the universal instead of some abstract value. "Progressive education has a unique opportunity to become an avowed exponent of a democratic philosophy of life, which is the last remaining hope that the common man will eventually come into his own."[18] In other words, freedom and democracy mean liberation from all laws and standards external to man. Absolutism means subservience to any God or law external to man. In this scheme, *private* man because of his individualism, reflects the absolutism of Rousseau.

For Bode, democracy is more than a procedure. "It is important to note . . . that democracy, besides being a method, is also a faith or a creed or a theory of value or a social philosophy."[19] Democracy means freedom from authoritarian values other than social man and his democracy.

Authoritarianism places these values in the acceptance of certain habits for the guidance of belief and conduct. Democracy stresses the importance of keeping intelligence free for the continuous remaking of beliefs. The justification for this emphasis is the conviction that intelligence should function as a means of the "abundant life" and not as a means to the discovery of eternal and immutable truth.[20]

---

[15] Bode: *Progressive Education at the Crossroads,* p. 39f. New York: Newson, 1938.
[16] *Ibid.,* p. 119.
[17] *Ibid.,* p. 120.
[18] *Ibid.,* p. 122.
[19] Bode, "What is the Meaning of Freedom in Education?" in Harold B. Alberty and Bode, eds.: *Educational Freedom and Democracy,* p. 11. Second Yearbook of the John Dewey Society. New York: D. Appleton-Century, 1938.
[20] *Ibid.,* p. 15.

The choice, ultimately, is the basic one between democracy and traditional Christian theology. While Christianity has made some "invaluable contributions to the spirit of democracy," these contributions belong to the historical past. Any attempt to establish morality or education on supernatural Christianity, or to put religion in the schools, "would start us back on the road towards an evil past." It is an attempt to give the schools "a fundamental philosophy or way of life" but in actuality "promoting a way of life which competes with democracy. In effect it is an invitation to democracy to commit suicide."[21] Thus, the *totalitarian democracy* of progressive educators cannot tolerate Christianity because it is a rival religion. As totalitarian in nature, this democracy supplants all things in every area, art, economics, politics, athletics, and all else, with its own *democratic* interpretation, which is both total and totalitarian, and which usurps the total life of man and claims to be priest, prophet and king in and over every sphere of human activity. As Bode himself stated it,

We must face the fact that democracy in this modern world is no longer the simple concept that it was in earlier times, but that it involves the reconstruction of the whole mass of the traditional beliefs and attitudes and practices, so as to become the basis for a distinctive way of life. Such reconstruction obviously becomes a primary obligation for education.[22]

Does the individual have no place in this scheme of things? Indeed he does, for Bode insisted that democracy "stands or falls by its faith in the common man," and this faith alone is the "basis on which it can undertake to remold the sorry scheme of things so as to make it conform more nearly to the heart's desire."[23] Societies based on both common and uncommon man have alike collapsed; wherein is this new common man different?

[21] Bode: "Reorientation in Education," in Bode, etc.: *Modern Education and Human Values*, pp. 16-18. Pitcairn-Crabbe Foundation Lecture Series, Vol. I. Pittsburgh: University of Pittsburgh Press, 1947.

[22] Bode: *Democracy as a Way of Life*, p. viii. The Kappa Delta Pi Lectures Series. New York: Macmillan, 1943.

[23] *Ibid.*, p. 114.

Alfred L. Hall-Quest, in his editorial forward to Bode's *Democracy as a Way of Life,* declared,

> In essence democracy means the good life and the good life is basically social, and not individualistic. Freedom and equality involve an impartial distribution of the benefits for the assuring of which society exists.[24]

Others were soon to make very explicit that this democratic man in whom we can alone believe can only be this *social or mass man,* who has been conditioned to socialism by education and thinks the proper social thoughts with respect to all things, for, as Bode warned us, democracy cannot be limited to man's politics but has "implications with respect to his economic, ethical or religious beliefs."[25] Democracy "must signify a way of life" and hence cannot be "limited to majority rule." It is "a guiding principle for the formulation of national policy."[26]

How did Bode believe that such a scheme could avoid absolutism, dictatorship or totalitarianism? His answer was an amazingly naive one:

> The issue can now be sharply drawn. If judgments of good and bad, of right and wrong, must be made in terms of an antecedent "frame of reference," in the sense of a fixed scheme or creed, then the principle of dictatorship is vindicated, and democracy is plausible only because its basic absolutism is kept from view. The only liberty that is then permitted is liberty within the law, as laid down by absolutism. On the other hand, if there is no absolute standard of judgment, then our judgments must be made in terms of participation in common interests, regardless of other considerations. Conduct on the part of communities or individuals must be evaluated with reference to its effect on promoting common interests among men. Liberty grows as the area of common interests is widened. Democracy then becomes identified with this principle of relativity, as contrasted with the absolutism of dictatorships. There is no middle ground.

[24] *Ibid.,* p. xi f.
[25] *Ibid.,* p. 4.
[26] *Ibid.,* p. 15.

. . . No such end has any value except in so far as it increases our capacity for sharing in common concerns and thus contributes to human freedom. All creeds and social organizations are means to an end, and this end lies inside the process of living together and working together. . .[27]

Here is the same naive equation as in Dewey. Supernaturalism means dictatorship, and presuppositions and laws cease to be antecedent if natural! Because the divine process of Hegel has been fully naturalized by Dewey and Bode does not make it any the less absolutist. Because all laws and standards are absorbed into the being of social or mass man does not thereby rule out the obvious fact that not only does an absolute remain, but it has grown all the more powerful by being equated with the caprice of social man and is thus an unlimited tyranny. Heretofore, in the American tradition, liberty has been defined in relation to a fundamental and higher law; now it is no longer under law but beyond law.

Furthermore, the general will of this new mass man comes to focus, not in himself per se, but in the school, which then mediates it back to him. The school gives "clarification" to society. "In other words, the school is peculiarly the institution in which democracy becomes conscious of itself."[28] The platonic guardians of this new society are thus the educators, who, with becoming modesty, assume this determinative role in the name of that common or mass man who is refashioned according to the educator's proposed image!

[27] *Ibid.*, pp. 47-49.
[28] *Ibid.*, p. 95.

# 20. William Heard Kilpatrick:
## The Repeal of the Past

William Heard Kilpatrick (b. 1871) of Columbia Teachers College has long been the symbol of radicalism in education. Albert Lynd, for example, devoted a chapter to "The World of Professor Kilpatrick,"[1] while Augustin G. Rudd listed Kilpatrick as a leftist who, along with Harold Rugg and George S. Counts, is a contender for the honor of having "influenced more teachers and children than any person of this generation," according to many educators.[2] Kilpatrick had a part, moreover, in the Pasadena school controversy of 1948.

It would be a disservice to Kilpatrick to deny his markedly socialist tendencies, or to under-rate his influence. Because his students paid over a million dollars in fees to the university, he came to be known as "The Million Dollar Professor."[3] Kilpatrick was a devoted follower of Dewey, a dedicated and mis-

[1] Albert Lynd: *Quakery in the Public Schools*, pp. 212-254. New York: Grosset and Dunlap, 1950.

[2] Augustin A. Rudd: *Bending the Twig*, the Revolution in Education and its Effect on our Children, p. 194. New York: Sons of the American Revolution, 1957.

[3] The title comes from a copyreader's caption for an article by David Davidson in the New York *Post*, March 6, 1937. A chapter with the same title appears in Samuel Tenenbaum: *William Heard Kilpatrick*, Trail Blazer in Education, pp. 85-203. Intro. by John Dewey. New York: Harper, 1951.

sionary-minded socialist, and a crusading educator. But was Kilpatrick so radically dissimilar to other and ostensibly conservative educators? Was his power with teachers merely in his radicalism, or was it perhaps in a more honest and rigorous application of the basic premises of state-controlled schools and all contemporary educational thinking? Kilpatrick came to an open break with Thorndike's psychology, and was definitely at odds with William C. Bagley, whose appointed role at Teachers College was to counter-balance Kilpatrick. Dean James Earl Russell similarly differed with Kilpatrick, and, at the University of Chicago, Charles H. Judd tried to foster a more conservative educational theory. How basic were their differences with Kilpatrick?

When Kilpatrick came to Columbia Teachers College, he "found an institution pervaded with messianic zeal,"[4] and in this atmosphere Kilpatrick, son of a fundamentalist Baptist minister and a Southerner, found himself at home. Kilpatrick had been earlier destined for the ministry but had shown a disinclination to follow his father's wishes. He was, however, a strongly moralistic man throughout his life, proud of his chastity, not tempted by gambling or drinking, and, as a young man, always, so clear and clean of mind, Tenenbaum assures us, that "Freud would have had a difficult time explaining him. His libido and his subconscious did not bother him."[5] Kilpatrick taught mathematics at his own school, Mercer University, leaving subsequently because of attacks provoked by his radical departure from the faith. He never overcame, significantly, his irritation at this "unjust treatment,"[6] a revealing index to his outlook. Kilpatrick obviously did not share the fundamentalist faith of the school, and was thus on the faculty under false colors, but, for him, *loyalty to the past was always foolishness as contrasted to loyalty to that future envisioned by himself.* In an "open universe," the past had no right to bind man. In terms of such a faith, Kilpatrick and others could regard the "reactionaries," men with loyalties to past creeds and codes, as the truly disloyal and dishonest men. Kilpatrick was a crusading champion of loyalty to the future, and he inspired in his students a religious devotion. "In Kilpatrick's presence these everyday men and women became transformed."[7] The "open" universe was an area of new experiences because of its continuously new developments.

Kilpatrick rejected completely and unequivocally this static, fixed, predetermined universe, and withal he rejected the "closed system" approach to education—to learning as conceived in finding out eternal and unchanging laws, with its emphasis on hortatory, verbalized, authoritative doctrines, ethics, and morality; on so-called thinking, walled off from tested application; on all indoctrinations, whether they emanated from the Bible, religion, tradition, man-made institutions, folkways, or, for that matter, authoritarian textbooks.[8]

This position Kilpatrick derived from Dewey. As he noted in his Diary, May 14, 1909, "Prof. Dewey's fundamental point of view seems as unassailable as science," and the essence of this position was the faith in an "open" universe.[9] So "open" was Kilpatrick's universe, that he was indifferent to scientific training in education, and hostile to the attempts at scientific studies in education, as evidenced by Thorndike, for example.[10] His break with Thorndike's S-R psychology in favor of a more organismic psychology was grounded in rebellion against Thorndike's emphasis on the individual as against society, and on single responses as against a multiple reaction.[11] Accordingly, Kilpatrick opposed a science of education as theory predisposed to fixity, in favor of a philosophy of education, as theory open to change and hostile to law. This preference is all the more significant in that Kil-

[7] *Ibid.*, p. 186.
[8] *Ibid.*, p. 82.
[9] *Ibid.*, p. 77.
[10] *Ibid.*, pp. 105ff., 227f., 275ff.
[11] For instances of his hostility to Thorndike, see Tenenbaum, pp. 227f., 275ff; Kilpatrick: *Remaking the Curriculum*, p. 17, 116. New York: Newson, 1936.

patrick began his college teaching in the sciences, in mathematics specifically.

For Kilpatrick, "The inclusive aim of modern teaching is to help the child grow gradually into fullness of individual and social living." This involved certain democratic "principles of associated living," important to which was the limitation of the right to freedom by the more inclusive "equality of rights." The first goal "is that *all pupils shall learn to live well together*."[12] Alien standards cannot be imported into the educational process: "We begin where the young people are and build on their acceptance of responsibility."[13] Fixed standards, authoritative texts and tests, grading and other extraneous factors are thus undesireable.

And yet, in spite of this child-centered language, Kilpatrick could not give centrality to the child, because his concept of both mind and man was, in terms of the Enlightenment and virtually all modern thought, basically passive. While breaking with Thorndike's S-R psychology because of its individualism, Kilpatrick agreed with it in its passivity. Learning was in essence response to stimuli; the "challenge" came from without, not from man, whose role was "response."[14] Not only is learning passive, the environment and world doing the challenging, but that world is also determinative of the self: "the social element in the self is inherent and inextricable."[15] Kilpatrick tried to portray the self as active, but the activity was in essence response. This was so true, and the self so much social, that he could speak casually with the assumption that selfhood was a development of interaction. "The child . . . in his necessary interaction with the surrounding world is stirred, at first organ-

---

[12] W. H. Kilpatrick: *Modern Education and Better Human Relations*, p. 17f. New York: Anti-Defamation League of B'nai B'rith, 1949.

[13] W. H. Kilpatrick: *The Art and Practice of Teaching*, p. 14. New York: William R. Scott, 1937. A Commencement Address delivered at Bennington College, June, 1937.

[14] W. H. Kilpatrick: *A Reconstructed Theory of the Educative Process*, p. 4ff. New York: Teachers College Bureau of Publications, 1935.

[15] *Ibid.*, p. 10. See also Kilpatrick: *Philosophy of Education*, pp. 33-43. New York: Macmillan, 1951.

ically, but later—after selfhood is established—by the conscious choice of what promises to answer to his want."[16]

Kilpatrick could not give too great a scope of freedom and initiative to the individual, because for him the priority of society was the starting point of faith. Although he held that "the world, its institutions and its resources, are man's and exist for man, to develop and express him," he meant by this not man the individualist but social man. "As man comes to be man only in society, so each is to be developed and expressed in such a way as means simultaneously the development and expression of all, all together, no capable one at the mere expense of others."[17] Here is the essence of Kilpatrick's faith and educational theory: "Man comes to be man only in society." "Man's nature is social," and the greatest privation in life is "exclusion by others, the sense of not being accepted by the group." Hence integration of diverse racial and intellectual groups is a necessity. No social act is acceptable if it hurts another. "The pupils shall increasingly understand that freedom in a democracy is always limited by the requirement of equal regard for others. One is free to act only as his acts help, and do not hurt, all affected by them."[18] This means, of course, that competitive activity, educationally, socially or economically, is hurtful and hence wrong. Since "men become what they do,"[19] the competitive individualist obviously becomes a very bad character. The moral and truly purposeful act is the social act. And, since the child is "naturally social," if "the skillful teacher" guides "his purposing, we can especially expect that kind of learning we call character building."[20] The

[16] W. H. Kilpatrick in John L. Childs and W. H. Kilpatrick: *John Dewey as Educator*, p. 457. New York: Progressive Education Association, 1939
[17] W. H. Kilpatrick: *Education for a Changing Civilization*, p. 27f. New York: Macmillan, 1931.
[18] W. H. Kilpatrick in Kilpatrick and William Van Til: *Intercultural Attitudes in the Making*, pp. 3,4,6. Ninth Yearbook of the John Dewey Society. New York: Harper, 1947.
[19] *Ibid.*, p. 9.
[20] W. H. Kilpatrick: *The Project Method*, The Use of the Purposeful Act in the Educative Process, pp. 6, 18. New York: Teachers College, 1918. Teachers College Bulletin, Tenth Series, No. 3.

child must thus be group-centered rather than God-centered, other-directed rather than inner-directed, and more amenable to guidance than to resistance. After all, as Kilpatrick declared his "thesis" to be, "human personality, in any desirable sense, is inherently a social product."[21] Note the qualification: "in any desirable sense." Kilpatrick was clearly at war with that man who was not the creature of society, and for him society was in essence the sovereign and democratic state. This meant that the democratic group is the ultimate authority and source of final standards. Appeal cannot be made to tradition, the supernatural and God, or to intellectual absolutes. Conscience itself must bow before the group, the "competent others."

Either I must appeal to such further competent study as my final authority, or I renounce human effort, or I am insane. . . But my opinion is finally to be judged by competent others.

These facts mean, then, in spite of the emphasis of democracy upon the individual and its upholding of "freedom of conscience" . . , that I cannot appeal simply to myself to validate finally what I think. I may, to be sure, take my stand against the existing world, yes; but even so my appeal, if justifiable, is as always to the competent others.[22]

Who made these others competent, Kilpatrick did not say; it was an article of faith. Conscience, however, he saw as a product of culture, and very often no more than "customary morality demanding conformity with the *status quo*."[23] It cannot at its best set itself up against the group. The absolute is democracy, the group, and man only achieves selfhood by interaction with it.

As the title, *Selfhood and Civilization*, suggests, the book has two main aims. The first is to show how man in the human sense is a self-other compound such that within the resulting self there is a sense of others so inherently embedded that the person can act as others will see and judge him. This means that selfhood is essen-

[21] W. H. Kilpatrick: *Selfhood and Civilization*, A Study of the Self-Other Process, p. 1. New York: Macmillan, 1941.

[22] *Ibid.*, p. 82f.

[23] *Ibid.*, pp. 29, 41, 44. See also *Philosophy of Education*, pp. 93-112.

tially both self-conscious and other-conscious and therein can make use critically of experience after it has passed, both one's own and that of others. Out of this self-other origin of the human aspect of man comes the second aim of the book: to show how this self-other process thus basic to the creation of language and other cultural forms requires a favorable environment in order to realize its potentialities . . .

This view that normal man is a self-other compound, dependent on the civilization for his well-being, cuts deep in any study of man. So conceived, man is not born a self but achieves selfhood. He is at birth merely a higher animal, though crucially superior in his ability to learn.[24]

Kilpatrick recognized that education is in terms of a perspective or point of view, and is hence the teaching of a social philosophy:

Two things seem clear from all the foregoing discussion: (i) any distinctive social-political outlook, as democracy or Hitlerism or Communism or reactionary conservatism, will wish its own kind of education to perpetuate its kind of life; and (ii) each distinctive kind of teaching-learning procedure will, even if the teacher does not know it, make for its own definite kind of social life.[25]

Thus, a perspective or philosophy of education is inescapable, and the question of an educational philosophy cannot be evaded. Private and parochial schools isolate their students from democratic society and accordingly create national inconsistency and disunity. Kilpatrick, accordingly,

. . . calls in question . the practice found in certain of our cities of having three school systems, a public school system, a private school system, and a parochial school system. Any group shut off generation after generation from the rest is in danger of building attitudes which militate against conferring across the divisional lines corresponding to these . chool separations. The labor-management problem, for example, has almost surely been made more difficult by segregated schools for the better-to-do. In the degree

[24] *Selfhood and Civilization,* p. 228f.
[25] Kilpatrick: *Philosophy of Education* p. 11.

that any nation is cut up into groups which live separately from the rest, will that nation have difficulty in making up its mind on certain of its essential social problems. Such a nation is likely to act inconsistently with itself, and almost certainly not in consistency with democratic equality for all concerned.[26]

Kilpatrick does not consider the possibility that the separate or small group in a democracy can be in the right. Democracy is itself his supreme good, and truth in hostility to it is a contradiction which is inconceivable.

With Aristotle, Kilpatrick held that man is a social animal, and "Society is prior to any individual." True society is democracy, and, in terms of it, we must "identify individual welfare with group welfare."[27] Morality cannot be based on any absolute standard but must be social, and, therefore, changing and developing, since "we live in a world that develops in novel fashion."[28] In all of this, man remains basically passive: "Learning is the name we give to the twofold fact that the organism facing novelty may devise and create a new way of responding, and that this new response if accepted for action becomes thereby incorporated into the action system, or very being, of the organism itself, there to make available for the future the results of this experience."[29] Notice that the world presents man with "novelty"; man does not create it, but merely responds. It is natural therefore for Kilpatrick to speak of learning as "a continual rebuilding of the self."[30] When man is acted on, he is *rebuilt;* when man acts, he *develops.* For Kilpatrick, learning was not the development of the self, a purposeful and aggressive activity, but a passive rebuilding. "Under Professor Dewey's influence it has become a commonplace that no thinking worth the name goes on apart from a felt problem, a thwarted impulse."[31] It was in-

---

[26] *Ibid.*, p. 213.
[27] Kilpatrick: *Remaking the Curriculum,* pp. 42, 76.
[28] *Ibid.*, p. 83.
[29] *Ibid.*, p. 116.
[30] *Ibid.*, p. 28.
[31] Kilpatrick: *The Montessori System Examined,* p. 18. Boston: Houghton Mifflin, 1914.

evitable, therefore, for him to hold that the "social outlook must permeate and dominate the school system."[32] For Kilpatrick, the state is the absolute, and "the democratic outlook is . . . assumed."[33] Thus, Kilpatrick's "last word for moral education" is "zestful social living under the guidance of those who, on the one hand, appreciate social moral values and, on the other, love children and know how to lead them. Zestful social living under wise guidance. This must be our main reliance."[34]

In describing the details of this "zestful social living," Kilpatrick completely by-passed economics as a science and any concept of law in the realm of economics. Because he refused to believe in any predestination or absolute, he logically refused to recognize past laws as binding on the future. Man makes his own laws and binds himself thereto, and future laws can create a new economics entirely. There were three very closely related and interrelated aspects to this faith. *First,* the doctrine of *evolution* substituted chance and natural selection for the absolute and predestinating decree of God, so that *development and evolution mean the priority of future law rather than original and absolute law. Second,* the logical concomitant of evolution is an *"open" universe* which constantly creates its own future and its own laws. *Third, education* is the means whereby this evolution can be hastened and man delivered from the dead hand of the past, from the kingdom of necessity into the kingdom of freedom, to use Marxist terminology. The result is what Ludwig von Mises has called "the denial of economics."[35] *The presupposition of modern education is the repeal of the past in an evolving and "open" universe by means of education, and the creation of a future which is beyond good and evil and beyond*

[32] Kilpatrick in Kilpatrick, Bode, Dewey, etc.: *The Educational Frontier,* p. 286. New York: Century, 1933.

[33] Kilpatrick in H. B. Alberty and B. H. Bode: *Educational Freedom and Democracy,* p. 160. Second Yearbook of the John Dewey Society. New York: Appleton-Century, 1938.

[34] Kilpatrick: *Foundations of Method,* Informal Talks on Teaching, p. 343. New York: Macmillan, 1926.

[35] Ludwig von Mises: *Human Action,* A Treatise on Economics, pp. 235-237. New Haven, Yale University Press, 1949.

*law. Man makes his future, his world and his laws.* There can be no effective critique of contemporary education until this presupposition is recognized and challenged. And it cannot be challenged by those who hold to the presuppositions of the Enlightenment and modern man. *In this respect, Kilpatrick's thought had an inner integrity and consistency lacking in his opponents, who sought, for example, to hold to an evolving universe and an absolute law at one and the same time, despite their irreconcilable natures.* It is no wonder, therefore, that the new school in education has commanded the day. Having accepted the presuppositions of evolution, the conservative educators have then turned and bid the sun stand still, lest the darkness cover their old world and its laws.[36]

History and the past, therefore, have value only insofar as they serve the present. Only that element in history has meaning, accordingly, which can be seen as a "forerunner" of modern institutions and creeds. Thus, Kilpatrick, in his study of *The Dutch Schools of New Netherland and Colonial New York* (1912), while careful and thorough in his attention to detail, was not interested in the culture served and fostered by those schools but in their relation to modern state-controlled education. His study thus, beyond establishing the correct date of the first school in New Netherland and supplying masses of detail, has no meaning because it deals with a past that has no meaning except as a stepping-stone to Kilpatrick's present.

In this faith in the priority of the future, there is, however, an absolute and a sovereign law, *democracy and the group,* which must be served as surely as any god man ever worshiped. *Because reality is one and continuous in an "open" universe, there is of necessity a leveling of all values and meaning. The one common value is democracy, the unity and integration of all things, so that any other law, good or evil, God or Satan, become divisive elements and untenable in a continuous and democratic uni-*

[36] See R. J. Rushdoony, "The Concept of Evolution as Cultural Myth," pp. 6-13, *International Reformed Bulletin,* No. 5, April, 1960.

*verse.* A belief in the sovereign God means that history works to a division, as men are separated in terms of Him. Law is divisive always, and God's sovereign law especially divisive, so that history is a process whereby epistemological self-consciousness brings a progressive division and discrimination to focus.[37]

Accordingly, for Kilpatrick the primary purpose of education is not to be seen in terms of God, nor in terms of the development of individual man, but in social terms. This is the true purpose of education in a democracy, to fulfill the social functions required of democratic man:

> While parents and local communities have often, perhaps generally, been concerned rather with immediate educational returns, the more discerning and responsible educators and statesmen have throughout our national history upheld education and defended public schools mainly for their broad social effects, for the moral and social contribution they would make, immediately to a better citizenship but in general to the wider cultural welfare of the people taken as a whole.[38]

Notice the use of the word "responsible." For Kilpatrick, since democracy is the absolute, responsible men are not those who are loyal to an institution and its creed, to a past constitution or old faith, but men who act in terms of allegiance to this great democratic world of tomorrow. With Horace Mann, Kilpatrick saw education as the answer "not only to the problem of the distribution of wealth," but, in Mann's words, as "the great equalizer of the conditions of men—the balance-wheel of the social machinery."[39] To achieve this democracy, social planning is necessary by the state. There should be milk enough and material enough for all. The first control must thus be to balance "production against need." The second should be the balance of "income to buying needs" so that each can "buy their

---

[37] See Rushdoony: *Intellectual Schizophrenia.*
[38] Kilpatrick in Kilpatrick, Dewey, etc.: *The Teacher and Society*, p. 3. First Yearbook of the John Dewey Society. New York: Appleton-Century, 1937.
[39] *Ibid.*, p. 17, quoting Mann, *Annual Report on Education*, 1848, p. 669f.

full share" of goods. "These balances are essential to any way of life that shall be democratically satisfying" and "must be accepted as the aims of any democratic regime." Russia and Sweden alone, whatever their failings, have tackled the problem.[40]

Instead of seeing industrialism as the liberation of man from primitive conditions, Kilpatrick, in the Romantic tradition, saw it as bondage. Man must be saved from slavery to the machine by "a planning economy." The danger of being slaves to the state in such a system can be eliminated by democratic education. Political corruption is for him a natural correlative only of a capitalistic economy. The state must be free to plan continuously, having " a planning economy rather than a once-for-all planned economy." Such an economy will educate men into unselfishness, while "our business system" has "bad educational effects."[41]

The first step toward this ideal order involves, among other things, education, which "must give us practice in group thinking," which means also that "a new adult education is an essential step in the process."[42] Education "can hardly be true to itself or its obligation in any full sense unless it becomes in fact a profession organized and ready to assume its social responsibilities."[43] Every religion requires that man be responsible to his gods, and the god of Kilpatrick was democracy.

Along four general lines we shall expect to teach our pupils: (1) to expect social changes, that "becoming" is in fact the law of the life process, that wherever we look we see always something coming into being; (2) to wish the common good to seek it in season and out; (3) to learn to criticize in the light of the common good any existing and proposed institutions; (4) to seek to envisage a defensible social program, each thinking for himself and in behalf

[40] *Ibid.*, p. 57f.
[41] Kilpatrick: *Education and the Social Crisis*, A Proposed Program, pp. 9ff., 25f., 31f., 71, 82f. New York: Liveright, 1932.
[42] *Ibid.*, p. 41.
[43] *Ibid.*, p. 44.

of the whole. Along these lines we shall seek to have the pupils enrich their lives on the best attainable basis.[44]

But is not such education really *propaganda* and *"indoctrination"*? Can it be called education? Kilpatrick recognized this problem and called it a "complex" one. His answer was a varied one. The school has always taught some particular creed, and "the public school has never ceased to 'indoctrinate,' even in the matters of sectarian and partisan differences." Some kind of indoctrination is inevitable: why not intelligent democratic indoctrination?[45] Five years later, however, he declared that education is not indoctrination, and the democratic society cannot be brought in by teachers or schools alone. "Only the people themselves can change their culture."[46] Still a year later, in 1938, he asked, "What is the difference between education and propaganda? Is not good education always a kind of propaganda?" "Partisan propaganda" is partial, however, and does not have the wholeness of perspective and facts that true education has.[47]

Kilpatrick's philosophy of education was a consistent one, faithful to its premises and outspoken concerning the logical conclusions. What did the 'conservative' educators who were in clear dissent from him have to offer?

William C. Bagley (1874-1946) of Columbia Teachers College was clearly antagonistic to progressive education and spoke sharply of its attempt to avoid all compulsion, to escape tests and standards and called it "playing at the work of education."[48] Yet Bagley shared fully in Kilpatrick's belief in an "open" and evolving universe which was not bound by absolute law and was marked by a continuity of being.

[44] *Ibid.*, p. 60.
[45] *Ibid.*, pp. 65ff., 73ff.
[46] Kilpatrick: *The Teacher and Society*, p. 66.
[47] Kilpatrick: *Educational Freedom and Democracy*, p. 172f. Kilpatrick restated this position in more detail in 1951 in *The Philosophy of Education*, pp. 121, 307-310.
[48] W. C. Bagley: *Education, Crime, and Social Progress*, pp. ixf., 33, 77, 87-111. New York: Macmillan, 1931.

We need a theory of life and of morals that is adequate to explain these unquestioned facts of experience and the theory that higher-order functions may be and frequently are unique emergents transcending the laws governing lower-order functions offers such an explanation. Under this theory we find a firm place for the finest things in human experience without involving ourselves in treacherous dualisms, without bringing in a metaphysical element of any sort, without committing ourselves to supernaturalism. We can still hold to a thoroughgoing evolutionary hypothesis which links mankind structurally with the entire range of life from the simplest beginnings and yet recognizes in mankind a potential nobility. We can, in short, be both naturalists and idealists.[49]

Bagley thus was in basic agreement with Kilpatrick's concept of being; he differed only in trying to retain elements of an older perspective in a new setting, trying in effect to put an old patch on new cloth. Economically and politically, he was also close to Kilpatrick. Bagley noted that "the fact of social change is obvious. And yet it is seriously questioned whether changes in society always justify changes in education."[50] Bagley clearly lacked Kilpatrick's consistency of thought, and it is not surprising that Kilpatrick did not by and large, bother to answer his attacks.

Like Kilpatrick, Bagley turned to evolution as a means of escaping "the fetters of a mechanistic materialism and determinism" as well as supernaturalistic determination. For him "emergent evolution" was the answer; it enabled him to hold that, while capitalism was a "machine-slave civilization," and the profit motive must be modified and replaced in part by ideals of good workmanship, still emergent evolution uses man's failures as stepping stones to progress.[51] Bagley's faith was in democracy, and he held "that the interests and welfare of the social group are of primary significance."[52] He was critical of local control of schools and was a champion of both Federal sup-

---

[49] *Ibid.*, p. 122.
[50] *Ibid.*, p. 68.
[51] Bagley: *Education and Emergent Man*, pp. 165ff., 210ff. New York: Nelson, 1934.
[52] *Ibid.*, p. 126.

port and control of schools.[53] Moreover, he had a messianic faith in the role of the state school.[54] Bagley, thus, was conservative only when he was inconsistent.[55]

Dean James Earl Russell (1864-1945) of Columbia Teachers College was, like Bagley, hardly a champion of conservatism. While differing with Kilpatrick, he shared with Kilpatrick the emphasis on democracy. Russell, however, recognized the liberating power of the machine.[56] Education should have as its goal, according to Russell, the task of "proposing ways and means of making democracy safe for the world." The goal of history and of world striving is democracy, and "it is characteristic of the democratic mind to believe the best of all mankind, to have faith that somehow the good will triumph over the bad."[57] A new social order is in the making.

Call it what you will—socialism, Bolshevism, or something worse —we have passed the era of free competition, where each stood on his rights and was disposed to define his rights to suit himself, into another era, wherein the ideal is justice for all, and for each the right to get what he deserves. The majority may continue to rule, but it must be a majority that exercises the duty of protecting the rights of the minority. While philosophers are striving to define the meaning of democracy and statesmen are giving a civic form to social justice, schoolmasters will be wrestling with a new set of pedagogical problems. The doctrine that all shall get what they deserve presupposes that the largest possible number shall be taught to want what it is right that they should have. The fundamental problem of a democratic State, as I see it, is an educational one: the problem of teaching the proper appreciation of life-values and of training citizens to act in accord with the precepts of the Golden Rule.[58]

[53] *Ibid.*, pp. 124-132.
[54] Bagley: *A Century of the Universal School.* New York: Macmillan, 1937.
[55] For Bagley's more conservative educational theories, i.e., those having reference to pedagogy, see *The Educative Process*, New York, Macmillan, 1906; and *Educational Values*, New York, Macmillan, 1911.
[56] James Earl Russell: *The Trend in American Education*, p. 69. New York: American Book Company, 1922.
[57] *Ibid.*, p. 201f.
[58] *Ibid.*, p. 205f.

Since Russell was not sure that "the majority may continue to rule," it seems that even more force might be necessary to compel acceptance of this socialist version of the Golden Rule, "the right" to get what one "deserves." It is not surprising that now, in Russell's view, "teachers are servants of the State." Before this glorious day, "the teacher was a chattel sold in the open market," but the State has made for liberation. "The teacher as a civil servant whose foremost duty is the promotion of the welfare of the State is a new conception in American life," but a necessary one.[59] Education cannot be "the foremost duty" of the teacher, it appears. "The true aim of education" is social conformity and acceptability. "It is what we do that counts most in society. And every grade of society demands that its members conform to an accepted standard."[60] Since society has taken the place of God, it is natural that society should be accorded the same allegiance once given to God. This demands social utility: "The present trend in education has regard for the time when the man who is inefficient will be a disturber of the peace."[61] Social conformity, however, cannot be demanded of teachers without destroying democracy, nor can social utility be asked of the schools by the State without "autocracy." "Will democracy find it expedient to substitute for the established church of the old regime a state-supported and state-controlled school system? If that should come to pass, wherein would democracy essentially differ from autocracy?"[62] Thus, the school is given a freedom denied to other elements in the state. Russell, clearly, had no basic difference with Kilpatrick, however much the two men believed such a difference existed.

Charles Hubbard Judd (b. 1873) of the University of Chicago was another educator of stature who was regarded as a champion of conservatism as against Kilpatrick.[63] Judd held that

---

[59] *Ibid.*, p. 215.
[60] *Ibid.*, p. 175.
[61] *Ibid.*, p. 147.
[62] *Ibid.*, pp. 207-209.
[63] For his pedagogical views, see Judd: *Genetic Psychology for Teachers*, New York, Appleton, 1911, and *Introduction to the Scientific Study of Education*, Boston, Ginn and Co., 1918.

"the school is the chief agency which guarantees the perpetuation of civilization."[64] He believed in the local control of schools "guided by science."[65] On the other hand, he hoped for the state printing of textbooks and group rather than personal authorship as a step towards democratization.[66] He believed moreover in "a cooperative civilization" which would "find some way of equitably distributing the goods that it now produces in superabundance." This ideal democracy needs primarily "the cultivation of a new understanding of human relations" to be achieved. It is the "radicals" who ask the schools to "assume the role of leaders and direct the reorganization of the economic and political systems." This is rather the role of people and government, whereas "education trains minds to operate with clarity and independence. Education is a phase of civilization, not the whole."[67]

Moreover, Judd found impressive "The Children's Charter" of the White House Conference on Child Health and Protection, issued under President Hoover. The Charter is a children's "bill of rights" which in effect makes the child both the concern and ward of the State. Pre-natal care, love, understanding, "health protection from birth to adolescence," and "for every child the right to grow up in a family with an adequate standard of living and the security of a stable income as the surest safe guard against social handicaps," these and more were pledged by that Conference.[68] Nothing was said, of course, about guaranteeing the child the integrity of his life and home from interference by the State.

The opponents of Kilpatrick deservedly lacked his stature and

[64] Judd: *Teaching the Evolution of Civilization*, p. 43. New York: Macmillan, 1946.
[65] Judd: *The Unique Character of American Secondary Education*, pp. 56, 62. Cambridge: Harvard University Press, 1928.
[66] Judd: *The Evolution of a Democratic School System*, p. 109f. Boston: Houghton Mifflin, 1918.
[67] Judd: *Education and Social Progress*, pp. 265-268. New York: Harcourt, Brace, 1934.
[68] Judd: *Problems of Education in the United States*, pp. 30-32. New York: McGraw-Hill, 1933.

influence. They were inconsistent, and limited in vision. Kilpatrick, in breaking with biblical Christianity, was zealous and
consistent in his adherence to his new faith and accordingly
more influential.

The conservatives in education have been men of limited
views and perspectives. Lynd, in his thoughtful and earnest
book, *Quackery in the Public Schools,* does the "radicals" a serious injustice while strictly honest in his reporting. The same is
true of John Keats' *Schools Without Scholars.* The issue can be
joined in two citations from Keats. The first is his comment on
the N.E.A. document, *Education for All American Youth:*

> The document concludes it is the *job of the school* to meet "the
> common and specific needs of all youths," but this, naturally, is so
> much nonsense, because the common and specific needs of all youth
> include food, clothing, shelter and sexual gratification among many
> other things, and certainly it is not the job of the school to provide
> *them.*[69]
> The educational pragmatist says there are no objective standards
> in learning, but he nevertheless has a goal. His consuming desire
> is to turn each child into a well-behaved social function. The dean
> of one of our teachers colleges put it this way: "An educated man
> is one who is well adjusted and helpful in his community."
> Asked whether a man who was well adjusted and helpful could
> be considered educated without also being able to count his fingers
> or write his name, the dean said "Yes."[70]

Lynd and Keats are concerned with *literacy;* the educators under attack are concerned with a *consistent philosophy of education,* one in accord with scientific knowledge and contemporary
life. *Literacy* came into education as a necessity for mastery of
the Bible and the fulfilment of Christian vocation. What is its
scientific and philosophical rationale today? It is this question,
which the critics will not face squarely, which the educators are
answering. Some scholars today have developed better tech-

⁶⁹ John Keats: *Schools Without Scholars,* p. 19. Boston: Houghton Mifflin, 1958.
⁷⁰ *Ibid.,* p. 89.

niques for teaching reading, but they have not developed a philosophy for reading.[71]

The basic question, as of old, is this: what is man? *The New England Primer* had an answer to this question, and so does modern "radical" education. Too few others have concerned themselves with it, regrettably. For Kilpatrick and others, the doctrine of evolution has reinforced and developed Aristotle's basic premise, "that the state is a creation of nature, and that man is by nature a political animal."[72] The state, which "is the highest of all (communities), and which embraces all the rest, aims at good in a greater degree than any other, and at the highest good."[73] The doctrine of evolution has underscored man's status as "a social animal" and made it an unchallenged maxim of most sociology today. The net result of this has been to weaken man's freedom and to heighten the power of the state. Society is prior to man, as Kilpatrick concluded, and man is under the state.

In the biblical view, man was created as Adam, alone, and allowed to remain alone for some time, to know his calling as God's vicegerent and image-bearer before he knew himself in marriage and society. Thus, Adam had to know himself as man alone, before he was permitted to know himself as man in marriage and in human community. In a sense, "privation" and isolation, such as was not the case with the animal creation, was the first condition of man in Paradise and the ground of his status as man. As a consequence, marriage, the family, the church, the state, and every other God-ordained institution, while God-given and necessary in their respective spheres, were under man and never prior to him as the creature and image-bearer of God. Man is thus *not* a social animal who must run in the pack, and whose life is comprehended in the state, nor is he the creature of society or the state, but always and only the crea-

[71] See Sibyl Terman and Charles Child Walcutt: *Reading: Chaos and Cure.* New York: McGraw-Hill, 1958.
[72] *The Politics of Aristotle,* I, 1253a, Jowett trans.
[73] *Politics* I, 1252a.

ture of God, and, as redeemed man, having been "bought with a price," the blood of Christ, cannot become the servant of man (I Cor. 7:23), or of any institution. The centrality of this doctrine in Reformation teaching had vast libertarian and anti-statist effects and repercussions.

This doctrine, however, has virtually disappeared from the churches. The literal view of Genesis 1-11 is now not required of the members and clergy of the Church of Rome, and is indeed increasingly held in disrespect.[74] Very few Protestants hold to it, and even many fundamentalists who profess it content themselves with opposing evolution rather than teaching the doctrine of creation. And, in Reformed circles, Jan Lever has attacked the doctrine of creation in the name of orthodoxy![75] The doctrine has had some notable defenders,[76] but its implications are scarcely understood today.

The world of Aristotle is a world of statism, where every aspect of man's life is under the total jurisdiction of the state, whether tolerantly or otherwise, because man is a creature of the state. The N.E.A. document cited by Keats is simply in conformity to this premise, *and this premise is the only tenable one in terms of contemporary science and philosophy. Grant the premise that man is a social animal, and both statism and statist education are the necessary conclusions.* Thus, Keats and Lynd can win their little battles and still lose the war because they have not challenged the basic presupposition of modern education, namely, that man, a creature of the state, is truly man therefore in terms of the state rather than God. This man is the

---

[74] See Bernard J. Beolen, etc.: *Symposium on Evolution*, Duquesne University, Pittsburgh, Penn., 1959, and Knights of Columbus, pamphlet 48: *God's Story of Creation*, St. Louis, Mo., 1955; with imprimatur.

[75] Jan Lever: *Creation and Evolution*. Grand Rapids: International Publications, 1958.

[76] J. C. Whitcomb and H. M. Morris: *The Genesis Flood*, Philadelphia, Presbyterian and Reformed, 1961. R. E. D. Clark: *Darwin, Before and After*, Grand Rapids, International Publications, 1958. J. W. Klotz: *Genes, Genesis and Evolution*, St. Louis, Concordia, 1955. These are but a few from the scientific perspective. Cornelius Van Til, from the perspective of philosophy, is the great champion of the doctrine of creation: see *The Defense of the Faith*, Philadelphia, Presbyterian and Reformed, 1955, and his other works.

product of an evolving and "open" universe which has no absolute save that of the continuity of being; hence there is a basic
oneness of all peoples, values and things. If this be true, can we
have any other reason than nostalgia for binding ourselves to
past faiths and holding to past economic laws?

# 21. Harold O. Rugg:
## Democracy as a Messianic Religion

In Harold Ordway Rugg (b. 1886), the concept of democracy and democratic education was pushed to new developments with crusading fervor and ability. Rugg's religious faith in democracy as the answer to humanity's long struggle made him an effective educator, in that, in an atmosphere long surfeited with attempts at scientific exactness on the one hand, and pragmatic relativism on the other, he brought religiously oriented convictions which made him a compelling and influential educator. He labored as a man with a cause.

This cause was the fulfilment of democracy in the United States, and American leadership in the world-wide spread of democracy. This meant political action to implement democracy and to spread it, and political action must always, for Rugg, begin with economic necessities. Political freedom, he felt emphatically, was meaningless to hungry men. Hence, if the United States fed the world, "the world could be won over to democracy." Russia, he said, has had an appeal to the masses of the world by virtue of its economic planning during the years when the Western Nations were suffering from the depression of the 1930's.

Under these circumstances, democracy must be defended by a sincere counterforce. While Soviet propaganda makes Uncle Sam into Uncle Shylock, he must be busy converting himself into Uncle Savior. He can only do this by giving the answer that is always irrefutable: "The proof of the pudding is in the eating." If the world eats because of us rather than Russia, there will be a strong argument for democracy that no amount of propaganda can refute. Witness the sweeping trend of the voters away from communism in France and Italy after the adoption of the Marshall Plan.

A workable economic plan under democratic leadership that is sincerely in the interests of the world and not of any one nation is an unbeatable instrument to defend democracy.[1]

Rugg was serious in believing that the United States must become "Uncle Savior," and education for him was geared to this concept. While salvation was not bread, it was definitely by bread. Rugg was thus ready to see Satan's temptation of Christ as a sound world policy.

The two great problems of the second half of the twentieth century, as Rugg stated them, are "the Battle for Distribution" and "the Battle for Consent."[2] The first is the economic problem, the second the communications problem. *"He who controls the key agencies of communication is in a strategic position to control the understanding of the people."*[3] This battle belongs to the educators primarily, but the government itself must use the agencies of communication for an extensive program of education for consent. To this end, Rugg wrote to President Franklin D. Roosevelt during World War II, asking him to create an "Office of Education for Peace" to help further "the new world of abundance." Rugg wrote also to John Studebaker, U. S. Commissioner of Education, in the hopes that, with the president's legislative support, he could "launch an all-out campaign over every trunk line of communication in this country. It means a

[1] Harold Rugg and William Withers: *Social Foundations of Education*, p. 234. New York: Prentice-Hall, 1955.

[2] *Ibid.*, p. 282. See also Rugg: *Now is the Moment*, pp. 226ff. New York: Duell, Sloan and Pearce, 1943.

[3] Rugg: *Social Foundations of Education*, p. 291, italics are Rugg's.

nation-wide barrage of ideas and attitudes that will reach every city, town, and hamlet—a barrage day after day, month after month, not letting up for years to come." This meant "access" to movie theaters, radio, newspaper space, school and college classrooms and curricula.[4] Ten points were to be rammed home by this Battle for Consent:

—The idea that every nation on earth must be disarmed .. that all armaments be pooled and administered by a central world "police force."
—The idea that in worth and dignity, in sovereignty and personality all individuals and peoples of the earth are equal and there shall be no more imperial exploitation of the weak by the strong.
—The idea of the fragile interdependence of our people with the other industrialized peoples of the earth .. so that most of the human race now stand or fall together.
—The idea that now we have on this continent the makings of a great civilization—the abundant life . . . that things are plentiful, not scarce, as our fathers said.
—The idea that a people as rich as ours, need not fear a debt, even as large and growing as is ours.
—The idea that the farms and factories can safely be run at full employment in peace-time as well as in war.
—The idea that the government can take vigorous steps to prevent a depression at the close of Today's War Abroad.
—The idea that a people can afford whatever it can produce.[5]

Rugg earnestly issued these ten points or imperatives as a new Moses beckoning mankind to the promised land. Again, he cited "Ten Imperatives for a World Organization for Durable Peace" (in 1943), a statement for thorough-going international government.[6] He also cited Ten Imperatives for the Great Transition to Tomorrow. These included a call for extensive foreign aid, and the conduct of a "war at home . . . over property and security and social control," for "if our people turn their backs on a sick world, if we refuse to run our economic system

---

[4] Rugg: *Now is the Time*, pp. 225-238.
[5] *Ibid.*, p. 244. Rugg cites these as ten points while listing them as eight.
[6] *Ibid.*, p. 145.

full tilt, the engine of our domestic system will stall worse than ever before . . . and eventually break down. The alternative will be a fascist managed society."[7] Rugg was afraid of fascism, and the "chief" of the "seeds of incipient fascism . . is . . . 'laissez-faire' . . freedom to exploit your neighbor by preempting his means of pecuniary support." This evil had deep roots in America:

Thus, the word *fascism* as used currently is really only a new name for the characteristic method of government by the "best people" . . the leading citizens. It is one that the oligarchic minority in America—the rich, the wise, and the good—have employed since John Winthrop and his company locked the charter of the colony in their trunk and ruled the freemen of Massachusetts Bay as they saw fit.[8]

Rugg was confident, however, of the possibility "of a Great Society of abundance, democracy, and integrity of expression that can be achieved in the lifetime of the children now in our schools."[9] The creation of this Great Society is the American Problem for educators, statesmen and engineers to devote their energies to.[10] "The most urgent" imperative in a depressed society is *the problem of the control of the economic system.*"[11] In spite of this, Rugg did not regard himself as a Socialist, and disavowed any connection with that Party.[12] Moreover, he declared, "I believe in private enterprise. But I believe in social enterprise too."[13] His attitude towards Marx was partly uncomprehending and partly critical; he was also critical of Keynes.[14] On the other hand, in discussing TVA, he could declare:

Let us teach our young people two documented facts:
—that to plan and build and operate we must control the entire scope of the thing planned.

[7] *Ibid.*, pp. 1-21.
[8] Rugg, in Harold Rugg, ed.: *Democracy and the Curriculum*, p. 524f. Third Yearbook of the John Dewey Society. New York: Appleton-Century, 1939.
[9] *Ibid.*, p. 513.
[10] *Ibid.*, pp. v, 15ff., 19, 27.
[11] *Ibid.*, p. 117. Italics are Rugg's.
[12] Rugg: *That Men May Understand*, An American in the Long Armistice, p. 89. New York: Doubleday, Doran, 1941.
[13] *Ibid.*, p. xiv.
[14] Rugg and Withers: *Social Foundations Of Education*, pp. 70-85.

—that it is central control that the Americans have resisted throughout their history; this mood has carried over subtly and creates
opposition to government's participation in planning.[15]

Rugg could also write of "property barriers between the people
and the event" as a means of distortion of truth.[16] The lack of
property apparently gave no bias.

It would be easy to cite statement after statement from Rugg
which gives strong indication of socialist faith, but it would
nevertheless be a serious misunderstanding of the man. The
radicalism of Rugg lacked the primarily economic orientation of
the European socialist. Indeed, Rugg was not interested in economics as *economics,* and failed to recognize any laws in that
realm of either libertarian or socialist economic theory. Convinced of the boundless abundance of nature, and man's ability
to make his own laws, Rugg simply by-passed economics and
concerned himself with *the fulfilment of man in democracy.*
Rugg's radicalism was thus a romantic and sentimental humani-
tarianism, as much a part of the American tradition as was
Rugg's own ancestry.[17] His great-great-grandfather, fought at
Lexington and Concord in 1775, and others of his family fought
in every other American war. His cousin was the chief justice of
the Massachusetts Supreme Court. Rugg himself worked as a
youth as weaver in a New England textile mill.[18] Rugg's dedication to *Foundations for American Education* is an excellent
index to his American radicalism:

[15] Rugg: *Foundations for American Education,* p. 344. Yonkers-on-Hudson,
New York: World Book Co., 1947.

[16] *Ibid.,* p. 373.

[17] This did not, of course, make it any the less erroneous. Rugg's clearest statement of his position is in *The Great Technology,* Social Chaos and the Public
Mind; New York: John Day, 1933. Chapt. IX is especially revelatory of Rugg's
thinking in its title, "Plans for a Controlled Private Capitalism." Rugg was
ready to respect the achievements of the past, and hoped to retain them under
a radically different social and human order. Freedom has been more often buried
by its confused friends than by its enemies. It should be added that Rugg favored
"a planning economy" rather than "a planned economy," since he did not believe
in the fixity of economic law which a planned economy involved. A *planned*
economy is law-bound and past-bound, whereas a *planning* economy is *creative,*
(an important concept to Rugg), and makes its own conditions and laws.

[18] Rugg: *That Men May Understand,* p. 9.

Dedicated to Six Men Who Led Their Peers in Building an American Philosophy of Experience.

The Human Frontier—A New Biopsychology: Charles Sanders Peirce, William James, John Dewey.

The Social Frontier—A New Sociology: Thorstein Veblen.

The Esthetic Frontier—A New Esthetics: Walt Whitman.

The Frontier of Freedom and Control—A New Ethics: Oliver Wendell Holmes, Jr.

Other names might be added to this list, such as Emerson. The long American heritage of resistance to federalism and constitutionalism had its ardent representative in Rugg. Not law or constitution, nor God and Christianity, but *Man* was Rugg's orientation, and nothing could be permitted to gain priority or ascendency over man and his needs. It is important, then, to listen to Rugg's own "statement of position:"

I BELIEVE. I subscribe with profound admiration and deep loyalty to the historic American version of the democratic way of life, our greatest resource and possession. In essence it is sovereign personalities binding themselves together in that confederation known as society. Because in America it is a union which our people have created themselves, it gives greatest promise of guaranteeing personal sovereignty.

The American democratic outlook, I hold, is man-centered—it respects the dignity and worth of each personality, prizes human life above all things, values integrity, respect, tolerance and fair play, and it seeks to guarantee equal justice to all men. In these respects it differs sharply from the totalitarian—Communist, Nazi or Fascist—concept that the human being is a mere instrument of the state.

I believe that within the limits of Nature's bounty man is also master of his destiny. He is not poured into a rigid social matrix. Given the sculptural materials of social history, man as master craftsman carves out his own fortune. The day-by-day events which compound themselves into slow-moving glaciers of social trend and then precipitately become speeding avalanches are *human* events, and I believe, therefore, that men can give them intelligent direction.

It follows that I am a devotee of "progress." I believe that by taking thought man can build a better world in which to live. . . . Moreover, I believe that the social-economic changes and reforms necessary in this country can be accomplished under the American Constitution and the present framework of our government. But solutions will come, I believe also, only through thorough and long-time study and design by competent experts in economic, political and social affairs; our truly grave problems will not be solved by makeshift panaceas. . . .

I am convinced that the supreme problem that torments men's souls today is the redefinition of the concept of freedom to fit the changing conditions of our times . . . Confronted as we are by a social impasse in which the baffled supporters of private and social enterprise stand at loggerheads, the reconciliation of the conflict between the "I" and the "We" traits in human beings must be found . . .

. . . . Now is the time to build not a subject-centered school but a truly society-centered as well as a child-centered one . . .[19]

Rugg's position is very consistently "man-centered." The sovereignty of man means that law is under man and for man's service, not the manifestation of a higher and controlling order. Thus, "experts" can create the necessary economics to satisfy men; in every realm, man is to a great measure his own lawmaker. The problem is always one, therefore, for "experts" in democratic theory, even if not one for the "panaceas" of nondemocratic, laissez-faire or religious thinking. "The supreme problem" for man is "the reconciliation" of the "I" and the "We," of man and society. How is this to be done?

It is basically an educational problem. For Rugg, man is not a person created in the image of God, but the product of a social process. Rugg quoted Cooley with approval: "The Self idea is a social conception . . . 'I' is social in that the very essence of it is the assertion of self-will in a social medium of which the speaker is conscious."[20] "The Great Goal of Education" is "Developing

[19] Rugg: *That Men May Understand*, pp. xi-xv.
[20] Rugg: *Foundations for American Education*, p. 190, quoting C. H. Cooley: *The Rise of Self-Feeling*.

the Person."[21] "Since education is primarily devoted to the development of *persons,* the design of the curriculum must take cognizance of individual personality as well as social institutions. Its content and mode are as dependent upon personality as upon modes of living, social movements, and issues."[22] But, since man's personality itself is a social product, concern with the development of persons is a social concern, since the true and healthy personality is the democratic and social personality. Thus, "the primary educational problem" for educators is to *"transform their formal schools of literacy into dynamic schools for understanding and creative imagination."*[23] Indeed, schools have been in error in over-stressing literacy. *"Literacy must not be confused with education. There is grave doubt, indeed, whether it should have been taken as the first objective of education."* Primary stress on literacy has led to unhappy results. "Every country which has done so has produced a top-heavy, white-collar class, a false hierarchy of social classes. Also, the literate masses of the people have been made easy subjects for propaganda."[24] True understanding is not through literacy but the realization of human personality in a democratic society. Families would be the ideal means to this end, but, unhappily, families reveal "cultural immaturity" in appraising the culture and interpreting it properly, and hence "We are forced, therefore, to turn to professional teachers to find the greatest competence to *pass* on the culture while passing it *on* to our youth."[25] Notice the dual role of the teacher: first, he passes judgment on the culture, and then he passes on those aspects deemed worthy. Rugg, however, hoped that the family would "assume a role of educational leadership today." A "few" of "the great imperatives" Rugg listed:

[21] *Ibid.,* p. 203.
[22] Rugg and Withers: *Social Foundations of Education,* p. 40.
[23] *Ibid.,* p. 41, italics are Rugg's.
[24] Rugg: *The Great Technology,* p. 102.
[25] Rugg and Withers: *Social Foundations of Education,* p. 37f.

1. The family should help its members to understand the great world problem of organization for peace.

2. It should also help its members to understand, as well as possible, the problem of full employment and full production and the political and economic issues involved in it.

3. It should help children and youth to become aware of the great forces that have been, and are now, changing American life. The family should not resist cultural change. It must assist youth to understand change, to adjust to change, and to begin to assess what is good and bad in the new and old.

4. The family also should make youth realize the great influence of science and free thought in promoting American social progress, the importance of facts and reason, and the great and cherished American heritage of intellectual and personal freedom.

5. The family must finally play its part in creating an awareness of the need for greater social control in a society that is becoming interdependent, of the need for cooperation as well as individual freedom, and of group objectives and behavior as well as purely individualistic goals and behavior.[26]

It becomes immediately apparent that Rugg's conception of the family is markedly different from the Christian conception so influential in American life. The orientation of the family, as well as of human personality, is not in terms of God but in terms of the democratic state and the social order. And, just as the personality is a social product, so the family is a social product and must serve therefore as a social agency. If God is the Creator, then man the family and society must serve Him and move in terms of His law, *but if society is the maker of man and his family, then man and the family must move in terms of true society and become agencies thereof. Man is bound by the laws of his nature and of his creation, and if man is a social product, then the law of his being is the law of the pack, and the greater the pack the truer its law.* Everything done by the group, by democratic society, is hence a shaping of man, its creature. *"In a truly democratic society government is the entire social process in so far as it bears on collective life, and the very essence of that process is education. Thus in our kind of society education is not a casual institution, it is crucial.*"[27] Education becomes therefore a form of conditioning. Man is no longer man, the creature made in God's image and as powerful in godly potentiality as in apostate revolt. Man is no longer a *thing*: he is a *function*. "The Great Dichotomy," as Rugg more than once declared, is between "The Thing People" who "Define the world in terms of Substance—the thing," and "The Force People," who "Define the world in terms of function—the relations between things."[28] This concept, derived from Dewey and the new psychologies, meant also the de-emphasis on mind and the functional emphasis on the body, since "mind" tends to connote a thing or substance, i.e., man as an individual in and of himself, whereas the body is an instrument and functional. Accordingly, after 1900, as Rugg noted, "The Body as the Primary Instrument in the New Education" came to be recognized and stressed.[29] As Rugg declared, "I would base the whole reconstructed education on the use of two primary instruments (1) the social group, that is, the life of the school as a whole; (2) the human body. These are basic to all other phases of the education of a man, since they induct him into his culture and practice him in the control of the self. In saying *basic* to all others, I mean indisputably the instruments; that the others cannot advance except through the use of these two. Hence I subscribe completely to the view that the body and the social group are the basic instruments of human education."[30]

All this adds up to a radically different doctrine of man than has previously characterized American history, and at this point Rugg went far beyond the older tradition of American radicalism. For him, the culture makes the individual, and man is

[27] Rugg: *Foundations for American Education*, p. 6., italics are Rugg's.

[28] *Ibid.*, p. 69. See also Rugg: *The Teacher of Teachers,* Frontiers of Theory and Practice in Teacher Education, pp. 142, 159.

[29] Rugg: *American Life and the School Curriculum,* Next Steps toward Schools of Living, p. 386. Boston: Ginn and Company, 1936.

[30] *Ibid.*, p. 388.

molded by group experiences. For earlier American theory, man was the shaper of society, and group experience was not his molding but rather his testing and refining. Not so for Rugg: man is the child of society,[31] and the proper goal of education is to give man "the Democratic Vista," to make him a consenting partner of the social whole.[32] It is to Rugg's credit and characteristic of the man that he himself raised the very pertinent question, "Can Man, Then, Really Be 'Free'?"

We can see now that in the modern complex world no individual is really "free." Hour after hour, year after year, he is poured into the mold of existing family, neighborhood, and national culture. He becomes essentially what his psychological environment makes him. . . . This is not to deny the large role of inherited capacities for original invention. Because of them a few individuals of unusual initiative do break through the molding influences of the family, the neighborhood, and the other groups in which they live, reacting against certain aspects of the culture and perhaps succeeding in making some of them over. But the ingrained idea of the "free" individual, certainly as freedom was conceived of in the simple frontier world of earlier days, must be given up. The social structure today impinges heavily and inescapably on each individual life. Individual and society form a single integral organic structure from which no separate individual can escape to lead a "free," uninfluenced life.[33]

Much of this is a truism as old as society. Men have always been aware of social influences, but they have also been confident in man's ability to transcend those influences in terms of a basic faith which can move the simplest man as powerfully as the greatest. Rugg, however, could see only a few as capable of transcending social influences. Rugg's earnest concern for a democratic society rested on this belief. Without democracy and social control, society would quickly move into control by the few. Education cannot be in terms of the few but must be in terms of the many.

[31] *Ibid.*, pp. 280ff.
[32] *Ibid.*, p. 265ff.
[33] *Ibid.*, p. 296.

In Rugg's view, man and society are organismic, not mechanistic. These for him were the two alternatives. The older humanistic and Christian views were not live choices. The "integrated organism" was his ideal.[34] Rugg was profoundly influenced by Walter Lippmann's *Public Opinion* (1922) and his concept of the stereotype: "we tend to perceive that which we have picked out in the form stereotyped for us by the culture."[35] Thus, while Rugg defined man in part as a "goal-seeking organism," "the psychology of consent" involved building *"better stereotypes"* for man. The self is formed by interaction between the individual and his environment; "the individual learns to adjust to his world by patterns of behavior which have been selected and stereotyped for him by the culture."[36]

This organismic view was one of the three concepts which were the "essential basis for the new educational experiments:"

1. The concept of life and education as growth.
2. The concept of meaning through active response; growth as the continuous reconstruction of experience.
3. The concept of the human being as an organism and of his responses as integrated.[37]

These three concepts are in effect statements that (1) growth, lacking any transcendent criterion, is animal growth, and hence the primacy of the body; (2) response emphasizes the passive character of man and his learning and makes him essentially a product and not a producer; (3) the emphasis on unity and integration radically side-steps the moral issue: should man at times not be in conflict within himself and with society? *Man has lost more than freedom in Rugg's conception; he has lost his manhood and become no more than a biological entity whose main role is to be acted upon.*

Thus, however much Rugg sought man's solutions in his

[34] See Rugg: *Foundations for American Education*, pp. 59-69; 392; *American Life and the School Curriculum*, 1-236; *Democracy and the Curriculum*, pp. 233ff.; *That Men May Understand*, pp. 287ff.; *Social Foundations of Education*, p. 36.
[35] Rugg: *The Teacher of Teachers*, p. 87.
[36] Rugg: *That Men May Understand*, pp. 224-239, p. 290.
[37] Rugg: *American Life and the School Curriculum*, p. 236.

democratic state, he sought them at the cost of man's manhood, and at the sacrifice of all standards to the one, democracy. For Rugg, morals meant the "rules of conduct developed through the social practices of the people," and "ethics, the principles which determine the rules."[38] The "Self and its interests" lead to the moral problems of our age.[39] Rugg was in agreement with Dewey and Tufts in their view of ethics, in the main, with his own romantic additions. Two men are "in everyman," "the aggrandizing I . . . and the balancing We. But to make these two men one—That is the eternal problem."[40] The answer, of course, is education.

The Exploitive Tradition has emphasized the I; The Great Tradition, of which Jesus is for Rugg a part, leads to democracy. Freedom as defined by the Exploitive Tradition is "absence of restraint," and this tradition, paradoxically, "crystallized in its most extreme form in the Nazi creed, which takes its cue from the philosophers of the superman."[41] This statement is especially revelatory of Rugg's thinking. The traditional American concept of freedom and of liberty spelled only exploitation for him, because in his view, if man is not protected by a welfare society, he is inevitably exploited by the strong few. Thus, his view of man is not that man is a sinner, but that man is more sheep than man, and is best suited for fleecing when not protected by the state. Thus, he was fully in accord with the National Resources Planning Board's New Bill of Rights, or "Nine Freedoms," a statement of man's "right" to cradle to grave security from the state.[42] He was in accord with Henry Wallace's concept of "The People's Revolution."[43] School was for him therefore "an enterprise in guided living"[44] whereby both man and society would be harmoniously integrated and made crea-

---

[38] Rugg: *Foundations for American Education*, p. 475.
[39] *Ibid.*, p. 496.
[40] *Ibid.*, p. 505; Rugg: *Now is the Moment*, p. 49.
[41] Rugg: *Now is the Moment*, p. 83.
[42] *Ibid.*, p. 88f.
[43] *Ibid.*, pp. 4, 115f.
[44] Rugg: *Foundations for American Education*, p. 650.

tive, and the teacher is the "chosen change agent, the clear guide for the culture-molding process."[45]

What will man become in this strange world of Rugg's? With man's every need taken care of, would man remain man without the experiences of trial and testing, dissatisfaction and purposive striving, and without those aspects of an insecure world which challenges man? In 1952, Rugg showed a mild awareness of this problem, and gave it a brief consideration:

> There are three alternatives before us: first, a society of robots, operating clever machines on the order of George Orwell's *1984;* second, a society of idle degenerates, stomachs full, but minds and souls empty; third, a society of happy craftsmen engaged in labor adapted to their creative abilities, but *not competing with the standardized products of the automatic factory!* There are no other choices. In the next generation we have to decide which we want. . . . The task is clear: *we must invent jobs that cannot be mechanized.*[46]

For Rugg, every problem is as simple as that. Let the social engineers take care of the details; we have only to establish the proper democratic goals.

"Creative labor" is the need, but how can mass man become creative man? This problem Rugg did not face. For him, all virtues were synonymous with democracy and would accompany it. The schools should teach, in his opinion, "sex and home life," "religion" and other subjects.[47] The state should provide man with thorough security; the American Bill of Rights needs to be balanced with a Bill of Duties, promising "to provide work, a place on the land, and credit or monetary means . . . health and enjoyment of life, social security, education, rest, recreation, and adventure," and other things in other areas.[48] *"Meaning is something which we create for ourselves,* first and

[45] Rugg: *The Teacher of Teachers,* pp. 3, 169.
[46] Rugg: *The Teacher of Teachers,* p. 8f.
[47] Rugg: *Foundations of American Education,* p. 674.
[48] Rugg and Withers: *Social Foundations of Education,* p. 631.

foremost by doing or feeling something with our bodies."[49] What is to prevent this statist, democratic man, cared for in all things, from seeing meaning as no more than a full stomach and an empty mind? Neither freedom nor character are the properties of animal nature or of biological organisms but of man, whose mind enables him to surpass the limitations of his body. In Rugg's thinking, *in the name of democratic equality, man is degraded to less than man as the means of his liberation! The freedom envisioned is freedom from the necessity of failure, from the necessity of suffering and privation, from the necessity of testing in school and in life, in short, freedom from the necessity of character.* The net result will be, as Ludwig von Mises has pointed out, the very world of *1984* which the planners decry:

The common man will be freed from the tedious job of directing the course of his own life. He will be told by the authorities what to do and what not to do, he will be fed, housed, clothed, educated and entertained by them. But, first of all, they will release him from the necessity of using his own brains. Everybody will receive "according to his needs." But what the needs of an individual are, will be determined by the authority. As was the case in earlier periods, the superior men will no longer serve the masses, but dominate and rule them.[50]

None of this Rugg saw. With very earnest fervor, he wrote:

As the twenty years have passed I have become convinced that the life and program of the school, like life in the American democracy itself, must be focused and given motive power by a great purpose. Professor (Boyd H.) Bode said to me recently: "To make democracy work we must make a religion of it!" I feel the same way about making education work. We must give it a driving

---

[49] H. Rugg and B. Marian Brooks: *The Teacher in School and Society,* An Introduction to Education, p. 133. Yonkers-on-Hudson, New York: World Book, 1950.

[50] Ludwig von Mises, "On Equality and Inequality," in *Modern Age,* vol. 5, no. 2, Spring, 1961, p. 147. See also von Mises: *Human Action,* pp. 279-285. New Haven: Yale University Press, 1949.

purpose, so clear and magnetic that thousands of teachers and millions of parents and youth will be energized by it.[51]

In this respect, Rugg was a thorough success. He brought religious fervor to both democracy and education and the immense success and popularity of his textbooks is due to this fact. Unlike other textbooks, Rugg's were always *alive* with a passionate desire to teach, and, moreover, to make democracy the religious faith of the people. Rugg's capabilities as a teacher through textbooks far outran his theories. Much as he defended the child-centered school,[52] Rugg himself was zealously subject-centered in his texts, and the subject was always democracy. He was often partial, "slanted" in his approach, but always concerning with *understanding,* giving time, effort, and factual detail to make every subject comprehensible. Thus, his treatment of Jackson's abolition of the National Bank is far superior to that in many college histories, not because its point of view is necessarily to be approved, but because, here as elsewhere, where others felt the subject too difficult for the average student, Rugg was *intensely concerned with making it understandable to all.*[53] In theory, Rugg devalued the mind as against the body; in practice, he was primarily concerned with the mind of man, and with ideas. He was fond of Comte's dictum, "Ideas rule the world or throw it into chaos."[54] Today, millions of Americans who were educated on Rugg's readable and crusading textbooks are ruled by his ideas—and by his chaos.

[51] Rugg: *That Men May Understand,* p. 277.

[52] See H. Rugg and Ann Shumaker: *The Child-Centered School,* An Appraisal of the New Education. Yonkers-on-Hudson, New York: World Book, 1928.

[53] Rugg: *A History of American Government and Culture,* America's March to Democracy, pp. 238-243. Boston: Ginn and Co., 1931. See also Rugg: *Teacher's Guide for A History of American Government and Culture,* Boston: Ginn and Co., 1931. Equally able were Rugg's *Changing Governments and Changing Cultures,* The World's March toward Democracy, 1932; *Changing Civilizations in the Modern World,* a Textbook in World Geography with Historical Backgrounds, 1930, and others of the social studies textbooks, published by Ginn, which Rugg wrote.

[54] Rugg: *That Men May Understand,* pp. 210, 213.

# 22. George S. Counts:
## Who Shall Control Education?

A vice-principal once declared that the "law" of writing in educational studies is in essence simply this: Never state in a sentence what can be said in a paragraph, nor in a paragraph what can be said in a chapter, nor in a chapter what can be said in a book! There is an unhappy element of truth in this, and not only among professors of education, be it added. A clear-cut exception to this is to be found in George S. Counts (born 1889), one of the most dedicated of recent educators. The influence of Counts has been great, but that it has not been greater is no tribute to most educators, who in principle share certain common assumptions with Counts but do not equal him in his intelligent and unflinching application of them. It is easy to differ with Counts, but no careful reading of him can lead to other than a recognition of his integrity and his intelligence, as well as his awareness of at least a few of the problems inherent in his position.

Counts is well known for his insistence that a new social order, a planned economy, must be built, and that the schools must help build it. What is the nature of that order as Counts has seen it?

Like other educators after Dewey, Counts has not seen history as bound by law, and hence with them refused to recognize the validity of economics. History accordingly has been made, by such thinkers, merely man's struggle against the tyranny of law and of anti-democratic powers. The goal of history is, for both Marxist and pragmatist, the abolition of history. Molnar and Kirk have called attention to Dewey's hostility to the inner life. For Dewey, in *Democracy and Education*, the "inner" man is a socially divisive concept and denotes that "which is not capable of free and full communication," and "spiritual culture has usually been futile, with something rotten about it, just because it has been conceived as a thing which a man might have internally—and therefore exclusively." As Kirk has commented, the drift of such thinking is the creation of "an impersonal society," and "Dewey's 'education for democracy' may become education for tyranny."[1] Such an outcome is inevitable. *If the universe is ultimately and essentially impersonal, then man and his society are at their highest development when most impersonal. But if the universe has its creation at the hands of a highly and totally self-conscious God, then man and society are at their best when most personal.* Modern education is in large measure a schooling for impersonality and the submergence of the person into the impersonal group. With intelligence tests, "the more depersonalized the tests, the more they are supposed to 'identify' talent and dictate vocational and professional orientation."[2] The break with the past that characterizes education since Dewey is not only a break with law and history, but a break with personality. It is a faith that the future of man rests, not in his inner character, but on his outward circumstances, the form of his society in particular. In Molnar's words, "thus a social gospel and technological method were combined in one simple statement: From our material well-being, a new man and a better society will arise."[3] This, of course, was precisely

[1] Russell Kirk in foreword to Thomas Molnar: *The Future of Education*, p. 11f. New York: Fleet, 1961. See Molnar, p. 121f.

[2] Molnar, p. 65; cf. pp. 119, 125, 133, 150.

[3] *Ibid.*, 130.

the program proposed to Jesus in the Temptation. But, as a subcommittee of the House of Representatives has pointed out, "The average delinquent is considerably more socialized than his non-delinquent contemporaries. It is partly through his group interests and activities that he gets into trouble in the first place."[4]

All this is relevant to Counts, who, like Washburne, has spent little or no time in criticism of earlier educators and has been sensitive to at least some of the dangers of his concept of democracy. A brief summary of the development of Counts' concept of the role of education and its problems is necessary in order to see his awareness of the developing problems. Loyal to Dewey, he went far beyond Dewey. A champion of the impersonal society, he also feared it.

Counts, as a follower of Dewey and a champion of democracy, was early concerned with *The Selective Character of American Secondary Education* (1922).[5] The high school, he believed, because of its academic and scholastic emphasis, had given "education for the selected few, whether by birth or by talent," instead of the education into adolescence and into political democracy which some educators desired.[6] Immediately a characteristic note of the new education becomes apparent: intellectualism is aristocratic, and a scholastic emphasis, anti-democratic, even though it be available to all who are capable. No such prejudice against art, for example, was manifested, although artistic ability is, like high intellectual aptitudes, not the common possession of all students. Somehow, as many educators saw it, the mind is peculiarly divisive. This common fallacy Counts avoided. His approach was from the standpoint of taxes and their use in a democracy. Secondary education, made possible by the taxation of all, was serving the selective few and thus doubly undemocratic, both in its use of funds and its

[4] *Ibid.,* p. 96.
[5] Supplementary Educational Monograph No. 19, May, 1922, Chicago, The University of Chicago.
[6] *Ibid.,* p. 3.

limited student body. Counts, thus, was far from being anti-intellectualistic as were some of his colleagues. It was his concern, in 1922 and always, to "put the high school at the service of every class without distinction, and at the same time render the largest service to the entire community."[7] Counts' position, then, from his earlier years, had a different emphasis than was prevalent in certain quarters. His premise was the tax structure of the schools, which taxed all. The tax funds could therefore not be used to educate the few, as the academic high school did, but must educate all classes, providing for the needs of every calibre of student as well as the needs of society. For the intelligent, an academic program is excellent; for others, a more 'practical' kind of training is necessary and desirable.

For Counts, "education, as a social process, is nothing more than an economical method of assisting an initially ill-adapted individual, during the short period of a single life, to cope with the ever-increasing complexities of the world."[8] Thus, education is a differing process from person to person in terms of their abilities and goals. The school is "a purified environment" designed to lead to the purification of "our present social, industrial, and political order."[9] This "advantageous environment" of the school cannot be unduly prolonged or overdone, lest "prolonged guardianship foster social parasitism." Such parasitism comes, in rich or poor, when they are "reared in a system which satisfies their wants, without requiring service in return." The postponement of marriage through prolonged immaturity is a second evil of "prolonged guardianship."[10] And yet, in spite of this remarkable emphasis, Counts could at the same time (1924) declare that "our educational program . . . must recognize the distribution of income as equal in importance to production itself."[11] The guardianship Counts feared

[7] *Ibid.*, p. 156.
[8] J. Crosby Chapman and George S. Counts: *Principles of Education*, p. 11. Boston: Houghton Mifflin, 1924.
[9] *Ibid.*, p. 165.
[10] *Ibid.*, p. 168f.
[11] *Ibid.*, p. 248.

in the schools he was ready, in allegiance to Dewey's "Great Society,"[12] to impose on the people at large in the name of democracy. On the other hand, his concept of education was, very early, more religiously oriented than most, in that he recognized the fundamentally religious nature of education, a recognition his later studies of Russian education underscored. Thus, "the elementary school would seek to further health, promote the family life, order and humanize the economic life, advance the civic life, enrich the recreational life, and foster the religious life."[13] Nothing is said about teaching the child to read, an omission somewhat surprising in Counts. The high school must become, for Counts, "the people's university" and "the central agency through which the ideal America may be brought into the world of reality."[14] The college should train the leaders of the Great Society.[15] The teacher thus has "a unique position in controlling the evolution of society" and in exercising a "regenerating influence."[16] Counts returned, as he often did, to the subject of the support and control of the schools. Tax support is justifiable in a democracy, where all give and all receive equally, and, where education is selective, it is to prepare the few for the good of all. However, local control of schools sometimes leads to control by powerful minorities. On the other hand, the interests of the state are not always or necessarily good and can endanger education.

To the writers there seem to be three ways in which the educational interest must be safeguarded against the undue interference of the state. First, practically complete freedom should be given to private initiative in the promotion of different forms of educational enterprise; second, the centralization of educational control in the hands of federal authorities should be extremely carefully watched and, in our opinion, vigorously opposed; and third, wide liberty of

12 *Ibid.*, p. xiif., 30ff., 40ff., 503f.
13 *Ibid.*, p. 435.
14 *Ibid.*, p. 476f.
15 *Ibid.*, p. 505.
16 *Ibid.*, p. 598f.

action, especially on the upper levels of the educational system, should be guaranteed the teacher in the discharge of his task.[17]

Thus, Counts was very early both an advocate of "practically complete freedom" for private education, and fearful of state and especially federal control.

In *The Senior High School Curriculum,* Counts called attention to the changes towards the new education in current secondary education.[18] In *The Social Composition of Boards of Education, A Study in the Social Control of Public Education* (1927), Counts called attention to the non-democratic nature of most school boards, failing as they did to represent the worker and minority groups.[19] Counts cited an American Federation of Labor recommendation concerning this proposed amendment to state educational law:

That a State Board of Education if hereby created, to consist of five members to be appointed from the state at large; two members to be representatives of education, one to be a representative of the manufacturing and commercial interests, one a representative of the agricultural interests, and one a representative of labor. The governor shall appoint the members of the board for a term of five years.[20]

Counts felt that other interests also should be recognized, but that "some such provision should be made." The implications here are far-reaching: In the name of democracy, class differences are written into society and made permanent. No man is seen as capable of representing anything other than his environment. The farmer is thus always and only a farmer, and the Negro permanently a Negro. The more democracy tries to equalize classes, the more it emphasizes and creates classes and castes, and democratic society becomes caste society and status-

[17] *Ibid.,* p. 621.
[18] Supplementary Educational Monograph No. 29, February, 1926, Chicago: The University of Chicago.
[19] Supplementary Educational Monograph, No. 33, July 1927, published in conjunction with The School Review and The Elementary School Journal.
[20] *Ibid.,* p. 96f. Cited from *Education for All,* p. 17; Washington: AFL, 1922.

conscious society. The state, as the social arbiter, becomes man's all in all. Thus, "education is one of the highest forms of statesmanship. The educator working in the public schools is a servant of the state."[21] A managed economy is necessary,[22] and perhaps socialized medicine as well.[23]

The great purpose of the public school therefore should be to prepare the coming generation to participate actively and courageously in building a democratic industrial society that will co-operate with other nations in the exchange of goods, in the cultivation of the arts, in the advancement of knowledge and thought, and in maintaining the peace of the world. A less catholic purpose would be certain, sooner or later, to lead the country to disaster.[24]

In view of this, when all else is managed and socialized, how can the schools escape the same fate? Counts believed that schools and educational movements should have "a solid social foundation."[25] How can they have such a grass roots foundation when controlled from the top? As Counts himself saw, the Soviet Russian schools "have faced very squarely such questions as the purpose of education, the relation of education to society, the role of science in the study of education, the place of the school among the educational agencies, and the function of education in the evolution of culture."[26] Such an answer can come very neatly, but not necessarily ably or accurately, from a centralized authority, one which Counts feared, but can a managed society do other than produce a managed school? For Pinkevitch, "by social education we mean that education which aims to develop man first as a member of society and then as an individual." Thus, the individual is to be subordinated to the mass, and

[21] Counts: *The Social Foundations of Education*, p. 4. Report of the Commission on the Social Studies, Part IX, American Historical Association. New York: Scribner, 1934.

[22] *Ibid.*, pp. 185ff., 450ff., 501ff.

[23] *Ibid.*, p. 247-9.

[24] *Ibid.*, p. 544.

[25] Counts: *Secondary Education and Industrialism*, p. 68. The Inglis Lecture, 1929. Cambridge: Harvard University Press, 1929.

[26] Counts in Albert Petrovich Pinkevitch: *The New Education in the Soviet Republic*, p. xii. New York: John Day, 1929.

more than that, to be manure for the future, according to Pinkevitch:

> The idea of social education and social pedagogy in its most general form was formulated by Kant who in his lectures on pedagogy expressed among other things the following thought: Children must be trained not for the present but for the future improvement of the human race and in accordance with some conception of the destiny of mankind.[27]

If morality is completely non-supernatural and man-centered then it must serve, not the insignificant individual, but the whole, the state or world order, and Lenin is on the right track in declaring, "We say that our morality is entirely subservient to the interests of the class struggle of the proletariat."[28] The Soviet Russians thus are more consistent than Counts: a managed society means a managed school in terms of a social morality which must subordinate the individual to the group. How could Counts' educator, "a servant of the state" in his own words, hope for a liberty which the state denies to all other orders? How can democracy, in eliminating differences, escape destroying the liberty which creates differences?

Counts, always strongly hostile to Soviet Russian dictatorship, espoused democracy in the hope that it means freedom for the common man. But the common man, "the people as a whole," do not possess "the revolutionary spirit of their ancestors,"[29] and as a result they will not make the schools the force for social change which it should be. The schools simply reflect the culture of the day, which can be analyzed into "ten principles:"

> They may be styled the principle of faith in education, the principle of governmental responsibility, the principle of local initiative, the principle of individual success, the principle of democracy, the principle of national solidarity, the principle of social conformity,

[27] *Ibid.*, p. 32.
[28] *Ibid.*, p. 27.
[29] Counts: *The American Road to Culture*, A Social Interpretation of Education in the United States, p. 27f. New York: John Day, 1930.

the principle of mechanical efficiency, the principle of practical utility, and the principle of philosophic uncertainty.[30]

Together with this there is a messianic expectation of the school: "education is identified with the work of the school. As a consequence the faith in education becomes a faith in the school, and the school is looked upon as a worker of miracles. *In fact, the school is the American road to culture.*"[31]

The people will not act; it is dangerous for the state to assume the prerogative of action. Who then should act? The schools, the teachers. Hence the challenge in 1932: *Dare the Schools Build a New Social Order?*[32] The schools must redeem society, and "society is never redeemed without effort, struggle, and sacrifice."[33] Progressive Education "has elaborated no theory of social welfare, unless it be that of anarchy or extreme individualism."[34] Education cannot escape dealing with the issues of life; hence, social welfare, religion, morality, every important issue, is inextricably tied up with education, and some kind of indoctrination is inevitable. It must be recognized as always present and necessary, must be conducted in truth and honesty, with distortion and suppression of facts avoided.

I am prepared to defend the thesis that all education contains a large element of imposition, that in the very nature of the case this is inevitable, that the existence and evolution of society depend upon it, that it is consequently eminently desirable, and that the frank acceptance of this fact by the educator is a major professional obligation.[35]

This pamphlet by Counts has been frequently cited as a manifesto for a planned economy. This element was clearly present. Society, Counts held, is moving from a political to an economic democracy, and the schools must help create that new order.

[30] *Ibid.,* p. 10.
[31] *Ibid.,* p. 16f. Italics are Counts'.
[32] No. 11, The John Day Pamphlets.
[33] *Ibid.,* p. 4.
[34] *Ibid.,* p. 7.
[35] *Ibid.,* p. 12.

The machine and industry must be socially owned, and capitalism must be recognized as dead.[36] Democracy means "the moral equality of men," and the repression of "every form of privilege and economic parasitism"; it must "manifest a tender regard for the weak, the ignorant, and the unfortunate; place the heavier and more onerous social burdens on the back of the strong" and seek the triumph of man in equality of opportunity. It must "direct the powers of government to the elevation and the refinement of the life of the common man" and destroy all special privileges and must resort to revolution if necessary.[37] This is, of course, in large measure *the subsidy, special privilege, and social parasitism of the weak on the strong* which has come into being since 1932.

The radical element in *Dare the Schools Build a New Social Order?* was neither political nor economic, containing as it did nothing not previously held by Counts in these spheres or shared by others, but was *religious and philosophical.* Counts broke radically with the modern conception of autonomous man who, in his autonomy is capable of objectivity and impartiality. The whole myth of scientific and modern man was sharply shattered in Counts' unflinching rejection of the pure and objective reason as educator. Education was *inevitably* "imposition" to a large measure, and the impossibility of impartiality made "the frank acceptance" of partiality a necessary means to truth and "a major professional obligation." At this point, Counts met the vulnerability of western, humanist education before the Marxist, Fascist and Nazi educational onslaughts that were already beginning to mount. These new tyrannies had seen the absurdity and impossibility of the old ideal of objectivity. *Their answer was to make the state the only organ of objectivity as alone capable of transcending personality and hence subjectivity.* As a result, they turned from one fallacy only to plunge into another. Counts rejected the first. His problem was how to avoid the second and make personal humility and self-recog-

[36] *Ibid.,* pp. 32, 37, 44f., 46f.
[37] *Ibid.,* p. 41f.

nition of partiality as itself the ground of reaching truth. Counts as a result broke at the one and same time from the anarchism of Progressive Education, the old humanistic myth of objectivity, capitalism, and the state as the new order of truth. This left him in the precarious position of espousing a statist and managed economy while fearing the state's claim to be the vehicle of truth. For the biblically consistent Christian, God is both the source of the order of life and the order of truth. For Counts, the state had become the order of life, but, contradictorily, he feared it and sometimes fought it as the order of truth. The two orders, however, remain as the two faces of a common coin.

Somehow, Counts hoped, the teachers would strike a balance and become the saving factor. "Teachers are at the same time the loyal servants and the spiritual leaders of the masses of the people."[38] The teacher must become the cultural agent.

Above all, the teacher is a bearer of culture and a creator of social values. The need therefore is for a training of great breadth and depth. A teachers college, to be worthy of the name, should be a center of truly liberal education. The emphasis on methodology should be secondary; the emphasis on ideas and understanding primary. Education itself should be recognized, not as an independent and universal technique, but as an inseparable aspect of a particular culture in evolution.[39]

Here again, but more mildly stated, is a denial of the independence of education from subjectivity and partiality; it is a representative of and an aspect of a culture and a faith in process of evolution. If no more than this, why not accept the totalitarian and medieval subservience of education to a "superior" institution or order as the true voice and vehicle of that culture? Counts' hope for order was social democracy and the

---

[38] Counts: *A Call to the Teachers of the Nation*, p. 19. John Day Pamphlet No. 30, 1933, by The Committee of the Progressive Education Association on Social and Economic Problems, George S. Counts, Chairman.
   [39] *Ibid.*, p. 25.

democratic state and world. Why should the school be anything more than an instrument of that order?

Counts knew the potential dangers in democracy. He favored a managed economy because he believed that technology has made "old conceptions and practices obsolete."[40] On the other hand, he recognized that "it is not impossible that the American people might be led into the camp of dictatorship flying the flag of democracy."[41] Hence, it was necessary to *organize* the masses as completely as possible, as though organization would preserve liberty! "If free institutions are to be preserved and employed in social reform, the people must capture the state." Hence, "the organization of the people, as producers, consumers, and citizens, should be promoted on the broadest possible basis."[42] But might this not array "class against class" and hence destroy "the unity of the nation?" "But this should arouse anxiety in no real friend of democracy."[43] But, with modern technology, is mass man the power, or is it the man or state that controls the machines? Who is the true power? "Can it be that democracy will retreat, as it advanced, with the infantry?" Counts' hope is that vigilance will prevent this eventuality by assuring government "a complete monopoly of the police and military power."[44] This only compounds the problem, however, rather than solves it. Counts, contradictorily, trusted the concentration of economic power and control in the hands of the state, but doubted at times the state's trustworthiness to control education to the same degree.

Who shall control education? Counts recognized that in the past the American "aristocracy" did not govern education merely in terms of class interest but in terms of "faith in popular government, in the potentiality of common people, in the wisdom of the free play of reason, and in the indefinite perfectibility of

[40] Counts: *The Prospects of American Democracy*, p. 172. New York: John Day, 1938.
[41] *Ibid.*, p. 171.
[42] *Ibid.*, p. 183.
[43] *Ibid.*, p. 184.
[44] *Ibid.*, p. 197.

man and human institutions.[45] In short, the "aristocracy" governed in terms of a faith shared with "the common man." "Every educational program embraces the apparently logically contradictory process of molding and enlightenment."[46] There must be a balance between the two, which statism destroys. Education, "without presuming to shape the entire social process, . . should accept its share of responsibility for the reconstruction of society." To be guided in terms of its full responsibility and to avoid becoming a mere tool, "two closely related conditions must be achieved: education must attain a relative measure of independence of the state and escape the domination of the contemporary aristocracy." The teacher's "deepest" loyalty cannot be statist.[47] The teacher must be the representative of a broad democratic faith,[48] that is, his role is inevitably religious. Thus, the state must triumph in every area except one, the school, which is man's new church, and the teacher his new clergy, who must be kept free of state control—while on state support!

Counts failed to pursue his thinking past this point. Beginning with World War II, fear of world despotism made him overlook certain issues in terms of a call to arms.[49] On the other hand, his conception of the religious nature of education remained unchanged: "A truly great education must express a truly great conception of life."[50] He recognized that "the contemporary dictatorships . . have demonstrated the political dangers inherent in a highly centralized system of educational control." Some solution to the problem must be sought.[51] Counts' solution, strangely, included what he once decried, namely, federal aid to education! It involved, moreover, a

[45] *Ibid.*, p. 301; cf. p. 319.
[46] *Ibid.*, p. 302.
[47] *Ibid.*, p. 304f.
[48] *Ibid.*, p. 346f.
[49] Counts, "Education for a New World," in Ernest O. Melby, editor: *Mobilizing Educational Resources, For Winning the War and the Peace,* p. 3. Sixth Yearbook of the John Dewey Society. New York: Harper, 1943.
[50] *Ibid.*, p. 12.
[51] *Ibid.*, p. 15.

"national emergency educational board" of tentatively eleven members, five to be educators. Another five "would be drawn from each of the following five groups of the American community: business men, industrial workers, farmers, Negroes, and youth." The eleventh "should be a great national figure familiar with the many facets of our complicated life." As a further goal, an international board of education was proposed.[52] The five educators would seemingly protect the independence of education. But how independent would any state "selected" and appointed men be? And would not the board ensure a permanent caste and class system, with Negroes, for example, always subject to representation as Negroes and not as men and citizens at large?

And how could the school transcend the state if the state and civilization are made identical by the concentration of control into the hands of the state? As Counts insisted, "education is always a function of some particular civilization at some particular time in history."[53] If civilization and the state are made identical, education and religion also become identical with the state. Counts' passionate hope for educational freedom was in contradiction to his statism.

From his studies in Soviet Russian pedagogy, Counts saw Russian education to be "education in communist morality" or "education in the qualities of Bolshevik character."[54] When the state knows no law beyond itself, whether that law be communism or democracy, the state, in controlling the schools, will make its goals and morals the goals and morals of the children. It knows no other law. Counts criticized progressive educators for holding to anarchistic individualism and the Great Society at one and the same time. Counts was guilty of the same sin: his teachers and schools were to have an independence denied to all others in the name of the Great Society.

[52] Counts, "Needed New Patterns of Control" in Melby, *op. cit.,* p. 233.

[53] Counts: *Education and the Promise of America,* p. 23. Kappa Delta Pi Lecture Series, v. 17. New York: Macmillan, 1945.

[54] Counts, introduction to B. P. Yesipov (or Esipov) and N. K. Goncharov: *"I Want to be Like Stalin,"* p. 5; cf. 13ff. New York: John Day, 1947.

Counts continued to call attention to the dangers inherent in the Soviet Russian system.[55] He could warn of tyranny, stating, *"Nineteen Eighty-Four* may be closer than you think!"[56] But he continued to believe that somehow education could escape management and control in an increasingly managed and controlled society. In respect to Counts, however, it must be recognized that he saw issues and problems which many educators failed to see or deal with. There was in Counts not only a dedication to statism but a dedication to liberty which made this awareness possible.

[55] See Counts: *Khrushchev and the Central Committee Speak on Education;* Pittsburgh, University of Pittsburgh Press, 1959. *American Education Through the Soviet Looking Glass,* an Analysis of an article by N. K. Goncharov entitled "The School and Pedagogy in the USA in the Service of Reaction; New York: Teachers College, Columbia, 1951. *The Challenge of Soviet Education;* New York: McGraw-Hill, 1957.
[56] *American Education through the Soviet Looking Glass,* p. 48.

# 23. Theodore Brameld:
## Democracy and Consensus

In the writings of Theodore Burghard Hurt Brameld (born 1904), a forthright attempt has been made to cope with some of the developing problems confronting "progressivism" in education.[1] In some respects, Brameld has made the most notable attempt in education within the United States to broaden its foundations and increase its general relevance. In spite of these earnest efforts, Brameld's philosophy remains rather the culmination and end product of a perspective that began in U. S. education with Mann, rather than a new beginning. The future may well be determined by Brameld's kind of concept, but it will remain an end of the line product and a culmination philosophy, the doctrine of radical democracy come to full flower.

Brameld is, like Dewey, an advocate of relativism up to a point. "Even Deweyism," he is ready to grant, "despite the loud protests we may expect to hear from certain advocates, is perhaps ironically the rather too dispassionate myth of the scientific-technological culture through which we have been

[1] Brameld's teaching appointments have included Long Island University, University of Wisconsin, University of Minnesota, New York University, University of Puerto Rico, New School for Social Research, and visiting lecturer at Columbia and Dartmouth.

speeding."[2] Myths are "true" or "false" "depending upon the extent to which they serve to unveil, or to disguise, the common character, the 'folk-life,' of the periods when they are influential."[3] In education, progressivism or reconstructionism must create a "true" myth.

The myth to be created is a cultural therapeutic: first, to lessen the tensions and bewilderments from which too many of us suffer; second, to substitute for these a constructive aim in which we can join and for which we can fight, knowing that we are once more on the side of righteousness.[4]

How "righteousness" can be man's concern in a totally relative and mythological world, we are not told. The myth becomes "more and more real as we share in its fulfilment" and as it expresses man's deepest communal instincts, experiences and needs.[5] Thus, it becomes an instrument for the apprehension of reality, since, for reconstructionists, "all beliefs about reality ultimately have a cultural context."[6] This reality is best apprehended if "the cultural determinants of human experience" are properly governed and resolved.[7] To see "History as Reality" means to view it "in terms of a philosophy of history as social struggle, as expansion and contraction of freedom, as organism, and as future."[8] And all this spells democracy.

Brameld's devotion to democracy is beyond question. It constitutes for him the wholeness and soundness of life, so that all else is fragmentary, partial and unsound. The champions of democracy are defenders of truth, whereas all others are "pressure groups" representing "cultural lags."[9] Education must be

[2] Brameld: *Patterns of Educational Philosophy, A Democratic Interpretation*, p. 501f. Yonker-on-Hudson: World Book Co., 1950.

[3] *Ibid.*, p. 502.

[4] *Ibid.*, p. 503.

[5] *Ibid.*, p. 504f.

[6] *Ibid.*, p. 413.

[7] *Ibid.*, pp. 412-425.

[8] *Ibid.*, pp. 425-436.

[9] George S. Counts and Theodore Brameld, "Relations with Public Education: Some Specific Issues and Proposals," in Brameld, ed.: *Workers' Education in the United States*, p. 254. Fifth Yearbook of the John Dewey Society. New York: Harper, 1941. See also Brameld: *Patterns of Educational Philosophy*, A Democratic Interpretation, p. 278ff.

in terms of a basic philosophy and is an expression of the faith and perspective of that philosophy. "And it is democracy, after all, which rightly stands at the apex of our beliefs."[10] In the realm of beliefs, "it would seem certain that the deepest, most universal of all is an unqualified respect for the decency, worth, and promise of the ordinary human being." This human being has not only "indispensable *needs*" but "dynamic *wants*" as well, and "human living means far more than just keeping alive: it means *the greatest possible development of the whole person*—his abilities, his desires, his interest, his understanding."[11] This means democracy and democratic education. Workers' education should also be in terms of these needs and wants as democratic goals. Workers moreover should be educated in terms of their democratic requirements, and "the publicly supported university or college" should include "a school or department of labor." Public education seen in its true perspective and development "can and should become one highly effective instrument in the struggle of organized labor against the inhuman forces which would destroy it."[12]

Brameld, however, believes he is "most vehement" in his rejection of statism; for him the state is not an end in itself but a means.[13] Marxism regards the state as an evil destined to wither away, but it has nonetheless been unable to escape statism. But Brameld, while opposing statism, does not share Marx's ostensible horror of the state. With respect to "the bugaboo of federal control" of education, Brameld insists that "the word 'control' is entirely amoral. It connotes neither good nor bad as such. It becomes good or bad only in the context of specific methods and purposes—in other words, according to how control is exercised and for whose purposes."[14] Again, *"Federal authority as such is neither good nor bad; it becomes good or*

[10] Brameld, "Toward a Philosophy of Workers' Education" in Brameld: *Workers' Education*, p. 286.

[11] *Ibid.*, p. 283. Italics are Brameld's here and in all succeeding quotations.

[12] Counts and Brameld, "Relations with Public Education," p. 276f.

[13] Brameld, "Towards a Philosophy of Workers' Education," p. 281.

[14] Brameld: *Education for the Emerging Age*, Newer Ends and Stronger Means p. 145. New York: Harper, 1961.

*bad as it does, or does not, support the consensus of the majority in satisfying their universal wants.*"[15] Thus, the powers of the truly democratic state are good powers and to be trusted.

"The history of democracy" is that of a "people's revolution."[16] When the schools "come under the indisputable control of that immense majority which alone is sure to care that free education should become the revolutionary weapon of a people's peace," then they will be "directed toward the *future* of democracy."[17] It is Brameld's "conviction" that *"democracy, more than any form of society devised thus far by man, is capable of providing greatest happiness for the largest number of people on the earth."*[18] With Brameld, there is an "equation of democracy and happiness" on the basis of "self-evidence." This self-evidence arises from the fact that,

since these values flow from springs of nature of which each person is himself a part, each person must testify to their vitality and then, with others who so testify, arrive at mutual agreement that here are indeed the values which they share. Precisely in this sense majority rule is also the expression of agreement by the largest number as to what, from mutual experience, these values mean to *them*.[19]

Majority rule, or consensus, thus appears as a major aspect of Brameld's philosophy.

But what of majority rule when the majority opinion differs with Brameld's definition of democracy, or rejects it altogether? In dealing with such a school and community situation, Brameld does not speak of majority rule. Instead, he speaks of developing a "future-looking" perspective in students.[20] At the beginning of the special project in Floodwood, Minnesota, the students' attitudes were described as "cynical, pessimistic and

[15] Brameld: *Patterns of Educational Philosophy*, p. 658.
[16] Brameld, "The Organized Working People," in E. O. Melby, *op. cit.*, p. 101.
[17] Brameld, "Toward a Democratic Faith," in Melby, p. 187.
[18] *Ibid.*, p. 177.
[19] *Ibid.*, pp. 182-4.
[20] Brameld: *Design for America*, An Educational Exploration of the Future of Democracy for Senior High Schools and Junior Colleges, p. 16. Written with the collaboration of Kenneth Hovey, Dorothy O'Shaugnessy and Donna Traphagan. New York: Hinds, Hayden and Eldredge, 1945.

apathetic" about man and society, according to one teacher, and special tests revealed the students believed the following things:

> Human nature cannot be altered; the profit system is the only possible incentive; sports must have competition, for what else is there to strive for than a victory over others?; big business is good for the country—its profits and motives are acceptable. The wealthy have a right to excessive profits, for haven't they acquired them because of their diligence and abilities?; munitions and manufacturers cause war; everyone has a right to free speech, press, religion; crime is inevitable (why the prisons and punishment, then?).
>
> They glibly repeat the Bill of Rights and the Four Freedoms but they have no realistic conception of their true meaning and implications. They cannot envisage their status under a fascist state, which they do not believe is coming. They have no conception of the difficulties and obstacles they will meet upon leaving Floodwood.[21]

Happily, the students did not long remain in this benighted state; they were soon equally glib with other opinions. The group was taught to *"build a definition out of its own experiences and expectations as to what it would suppose a good society should provide."*[22] "The problem arising from this inductive discussion of wants was, 'What Kind of Society will best guarantee the maximum fulfillment of our wants?' "[23] Here humanism and democracy come to full flower. Not God but man is the measure. The past is cancelled, and man makes his own law, science, society and future in terms of his wants. In place of the Bible as the infallible word to order all things by, we have man's infallible wants, as properly and democratically understood under guidance.

Before too long, the students were expressing themselves thus:

> Before reading something about art in a democracy, I didn't think the government should assist or help artists, but now I have changed my mind. Art is important to the government as a whole . . .

[21] *Ibid.*, p. 18.
[22] *Ibid.*, p. 20.
[23] *Ibid.*, p. 21.

The movies and radio are also used for getting people to believe and think along certain lines. However, there should be more education in the radio programs than there is. As for having the government take over the radio entirely, that wouldn't be right, but it should regulate the programs more . . .

SCIENCE could do better than it does if it were not so clamped down. A company such as DuPont can hire the best chemists and thus monopolize many products produced by their chemists. They can do this because they have money and power. This should be broken because it hinders progress.[24]

In the "economic-political area," no student now inclined to the "right," a minority were to the "left," but the majority "inclined strongly toward a 'center' solution, especially of the type recommended by 'Charter for America.' "[25] True education is thus equated with a politico-economic orientation rather than with scholarship in any historical sense. *The task of the schools has become religious conversion to a politico-economic statist order rather than education.* Indeed, insistence on education proper is a sign of "reaction." If the critic of the schools, like Robert M. Hutchins, is himself a champion of the same "liberal" politico-economic order, then he is separated from the "voices of the old reaction" and called "The New Reaction."[26] Anything short of total subscription to the new education is a heresy which bespeaks the presence of the cloven hoof and the demonic forces of reaction Democracy is Brameld's goal, method and answer in every situation, and hence his intense concern for integration as an *educational* goal as well as a social one.[27] He sees "Democracy as Value,"[28] and hence all else is to be judged in terms of this non-supernatural absolute.

The *religious* task of the schools is seen as a *philosophical* one by Brameld, a merely verbal difference, in that democracy

[24] *Ibid.*, p. 65f.

[25] *Ibid.*, p. 105.

[26] Brameld: *Education for the Emerging Age*, p. 40.

[27] Brameld: *Minority Problems in the Public Schools*, A Study of Administrative Policies and Practices in Seven School Systems. New York: Harper, 1946. See also *The Remaking of a Culture*, Life and Education in Puerto Rico; New York: Harper, 1959.

[28] Brameld: *Patterns of Educational Philosophy*, p. 125.

is by his own statement the basic premise and "faith." For him, philosophy is the "pattern of basic beliefs—political, economic, religious, moral, esthetic, scientific—which provides those who accept that culture with a sense of consistency and significance." Accordingly,

Education, in its most universal meaning, may be regarded as the effort to translate this philosophy into practice by showing those members of a society who are considered most important to its welfare how to serve it most fruitfully. If philosophy articulates the beliefs of a culture, education helps to carry them out, and in doing so generates additional experience useful to that articulation.[29]

First of all, the honesty of this position is clearly apparent and of course commendable. Second, its radical break with the science and humanism of which it is the ostensble fulfilment, is even more apparent. The old secular order, wherein man lived in detachment of faith and in terms of science, has been buried irretrievably. A new democratic one-world and one faith is the new medievalism and holy faith; but it is also the old secularism baptized and tonsured. Education must work to preserve and further this new faith against the assaults of the infidel. Brameld's "central theme is that education can and should dedicate itself centrally to the task of reconstructing a culture which, left unreconstructed, will almost certainly collapse of its own frustrations and conflicts."[30] Like Dewey, Brameld believes himself to be a pragmatist, and is ready to apply a corrosive relativism against all positions other than his own. Thus, in speaking of "the third major concealment" of the essentialist position in education, Brameld asserts, "the whole doctrine of a pre-existent and indubitable reality becomes a powerful cultural device to reinforce attitudes of compliance with objective institutional arrangements or subjective wishes and habits or both."[31] This statement, of course, is premised on a faith without evidence.

---

[29] Brameld: *Ends and Means in Education: A Midcentury Appraisal,* p. 222f. New York: Harper, 1950.

[30] *Ibid.,* p. ix.

[31] Brameld: *Philosophies of Education in Cultural Perspective,* p. 281. New York: The Dryden Press, 1955. See also *Patterns of Educational Philosophy,* pp. 277-285.

For Brameld, progressivism does not necessarily believe even in a *universe*, but it does believe in *democracy* and *one-world*.[32] Creation is not necessarily a unit or one world, but man is and must be! Only occasionally does Brameld seem conscious of the arbitrariness of his position. Why should human freedom or democracy (for him the two are inseparable and virtually synonymous) be a value in a relative world?

> Why human *freedom*? Why not some other encompassing goal —love, for example? I am forced to admit an element of arbitrariness in this selection, but my defense is that given the kind of planet we live upon today no other value is of equal urgency.[33]

The "urgency" is the rise of threats to democracy from dictatorships abroad and menaces within. These menaces serve to reveal that Brameld's position is, in his own words, "an unqualified belief in democracy."[34]

Brameld does seek *support* (or proof-texts) for his faith in democracy in the sciences, i.e., in psychology and anthropology in particular, both of them new disciplines and still largely philosophical in their essence. Brameld's position is one of *faith*, and hence his philosophy of education is a demand for democratic indoctrination. Thus, he can title chapters "The Philosophy of Education as Philosophy of Politics."[35] Moreover, democracy is its own proof; man's needs, wants and wishes have an infallibility *when democratically expressed*. Hence, *consensus* is basic to his approach. Of course, a cultural consensus is not necessarily a personal consensus, although Brameld is unwilling to speak strongly against majority rule. His belief in the consensus is a part of his concept of society: "consensus . . . always pervades cultural patterns." Very few cultures, however, are dedicated to freedom. How then can Brameld assert:

[32] Brameld: *The Remaking of a Culture*, p. 419, for example, speaks of the "affinity" of all men possible with democracy.

[33] Brameld: *Cultural Foundations of Education*, An Interdisciplinary Exploration, p. 225. New York: Harper, 1957.

[34] Brameld: *Ends and Means*, p. 4.

[35] *Ibid.*, pp. 57-70; *Education for the Emerging Age*, pp. 79-90.

Meanwhile, this much we can affirm at least for educational theory. *The ultimate justification for our commitment to the goal of freedom lies in the social consensus—a consensus that most of us do or share—that real people living in real cultures reach in behalf of that commitment.*[36]

This is as much an absolute, and as "authoritarian," as anything "organized religion" presents. And for Brameld, organized religion is to be barred from education because it is authoritarian.[37] But Brameld's democracy outdoes organized religion with its authoritarianism as well as its demands on credulity. Note Brameld's "scientific" conclusion regarding values: *"the final criterion of intercultural values is the social consensus that can be attained about them."*[38] What does the consensus give us? According to Brameld,

And when it is done, is the social consensus always identical, always unanimous? Of course it is not. To a remarkable extent, however, that consensus, epitomized by self-realization, may be stated like this:

Most men do not want to be hungry: they cherish the value of *sufficient nourishment.*

Most men do not want to be cold or ragged: they cherish the value of *adequate dress.*

Most men do not want uncontrolled exposure either to the elements or to people: they cherish the value of *shelter and privacy.*

Most men do not want celibacy: they cherish the value of *sexual expression.*

Most men do not want illness: they cherish the value of *physiological and mental health.*

Most men do not want chronic insecurity: they cherish the value of *steady work, steady income.*

Most men do not want loneliness: they cherish the value of *companionship, mutual devotion, belongingness.*

Most men do not want indifference: they cherish the value of *recognition, appreciation, status.*

[36] Brameld: *Cultural Foundations of Education,* p. 246.
[37] Brameld: *Ends and Means,* pp. 81-85.
[38] *Ibid.,* p. 44f. See also *Toward a Reconstructed Philosophy of Education,* p. 166; New York: The Dryden Press, 1956.

Most men do not want constant drudgery, monotony, or routine: they cherish the value of *novelty, curiosity, variation, recreation, adventure, growth, creativity.*

Most men do not want ignorance: they cherish the value of *l'teracy, skill, information.*

Most men do not want continual domination: they cherish the value of *participation, sharing.*

Most men do not want bewilderment: they cherish the value of *fairly immediate meaning, significance, order, direction.*[39]

Assuming for the moment the accuracy of this consensus, a question arises. If this indeed is the human consensus, then is not man amazingly stupid not to have attained his ends, and, rather, to have worked so contrarily to his own desires? Moreover, if man is so stupid and perverse in attaining his values, how can he be trusted to express values? Brameld operates on the old humanist premise of faith in the goodness of man rather than the biblical doctrine of man the sinner. Both positions are equally religious. How can Brameld hold that reactionaries prevent the true order from being realized when he begins with the premise the "consensus . . . always pervades cultural patterns?" This means that *every* culture exists in terms of a cultural consensus, so that, instead of a universal consensus for freedom, many contradictory consensuses exist. Brameld recognizes the reality of *cultural pluralism,* but he wants nonetheless an *ethical universalism* in a cosmos that may not even be a *uni*verse but a *multi*verse. Moreover, some of his values are in essence hopeful and idealistic expressions of faith, or involve a *prior* presupposition. For example, what is mental health? Mental and physical sickness are more natural and common (more a consensus) than health. Mental health, moreover, is a value variously defined by Aquinas, Calvin, Freud, and Dewey. Which definition is Brameld's value? And is this value of any significance as a value to Communists, Christians, Hindus, Moslems, animists and others? How can a consensus of conflicting

[39] Brameld: *Ends and Means,* p. 46.

values give a single value? To assume that there is a common core of religion behind all religions, or a common core of values behind all ethics, is to assume a radically self-contradictory faith and one totally without warrant.[40] Brameld is therefore far more guilty of authoritarian dogmatism than the "organized religion" he discounts. His entire system of values runs in direct contradiction to the anthropological and psychologcal "evidences" he adduces so earnestly and conscientiously. His "majority-defined values"[41] are simply Brameld-defined values and no more. He more accurately expresses his position in titling a chapter, "Toward a Democratic Faith."[42] It is a future consensus. He often shows awareness of the fact that men today, and America in its origin, are at odds with him. But his trinity of values (democracy, freedom and happiness), are in essence one god, inseparable though triune, and hence man cannot truly seek one without seeking all. Therefore the true consensus can only be the democratic consensus:

Here moreover is *the reconstructed democratic import of intelligence; it is human nature become collectively aware of and agreed upon what human nature wants, and of the steps necessary at a given time to satisfy its wants.*[43]

The social consensus as law is "a practical necessity" in order to avoid total relativism or an untenable resort "to a supernatural or metaphysical authority."[44] Majorities are thus "supreme judges of values," for

if we accept democracy we must accept also the belief that no more reliable or ultimate criterion of practical, social judgment can be found in political experience than that reached by the method of

[40] See Gordon H. Clark: *Religion, Reason and Revelation,* pp. 1-27. Philadelphia: Presbyterian and Reformed, 1961.
[41] *Ibid.,* p. 85.
[42] Brameld: *Education for the Emerging Age,* pp. 222-230; *Ends and Means,* pp. 230-240.
[43] Brameld: *Ends and Means,* p. 235; *Education for the Emerging Age,* p. 226.
[44] Brameld: *Patterns of Educational Philosophy,* p. 465.

communication and agreement about evidence by the widest possible majority.

In view of this, "the giant political task of our time is, then, to build a new and far more genuine consensus."[45]

Since this is a "reconstructed" and "collectively aware" intelligence and consensus, which, only when so is "genuine," it becomes very clear now that *Brameld's consensus is that old mainspring of all modern tyranny, Rousseau's general will,* the old priest now writ large. Much as Brameld may hate the comparison, his democracy and Hitler's National Socialism have a common origin and are sisters under the skin. Both alike create and require a new and more powerful order of Platonic guardians to become the focus, expression and idea of man in the name of the (folk) people. They become the voice of the consensus, or general will. This authoritarian consensus is somehow good, whereas the authoritarianism of God is the defect of organized religion. Man is safe with powers God dare not be trusted with![46]

What about the old fashioned champions of liberty, who cling to Calvinist, constitutional or other grounds in their resistance to this new leviathan? One of Brameld's comments on democracy is sufficient answer:

For *democracy is that form of society in which all physical and spiritual resources of life are in fact available to and under the control of the majority of people; and in which the minority is always free to criticize while obedient to policies authorized by the majority.*[47]

Thus, if churches, private schools, private property, or any other thing be outlawed by the majority, the minority has no right to do other than obey the great god consensus, beyond whom and apart from whom no value exists. Polite criticism will be chari-

[45] *Ibid.,* p. 485f.
[46] See *ibid.,* p. 665.
[47] Brameld: *Ends and Means,* p. 96.

tably granted to the warped minority, but no more. For no law exists beyond the consensus. Not only is economics eroded of law, but science as well. "To paraphrase a famous dictum about history by one of our great nineteenth-century thinkers, Marx, the operational philosophy of science means, above all, that man makes science; science does not make man."[48]

This is "progressivism" or "reconstructionism" in education. Against it, "essentialism" and "perennialism" are weak and impotent, and are philosophies more often found in critics of education rather than among educators themselves. Moreover, these two dissident positions are in a measure early and retarded forms of progressivism and are equally statist in orientation.[49] In progressivism, and in Dewey, the philosophy of life formulated in Descartes on the premise of autonomous man has come to full fruition. Even as philosophy from Augustine to Duns Scotus and Occam explored and exhausted a particular foundation in philosophy and led to the reign of the dunces, so the mined out vein from Descartes to Kant and Dewey is already leading to a similar reign of dunces. The dunces then as now are often brilliant and dedicated men, but they move beyond absurdity in attempting to dig new ore from exhausted veins.

Herman Dooyeweerd, who together with Vollenhoven and Cornelius Van Til, has, after Abraham Kuyper, broken radically with the philosophy of autonomous man, has described the fundamental motive of the modern era as *nature* and *freedom*.[50] These, although radically in contradiction one to another, have been the presuppositions of modern philosophy and the sources of the modern mythology of man. Nature has lost its normative status, and humanistic freedom has been replaced by security as a human ideal. Educators reflect the tension and insecurity of cultural crisis and collapse. Some, like Brameld, seek to help

---

[48] Brameld: *Education for the Emerging Age*, p. 180.
[49] See Rushdoony: *Intellectual Schizophrenia*.
[50] Dooyeweerd: *A New Critique of Theoretical Thought*, 4. v. Philadelphia: Presbyterian and Reformed, 1953-58.

create a new order because, in advance of others, they recognize the crisis. But, although he fails to recognize it, Brameld's "future" is a return to the worst evils of the old order and is in essence a recapitulation of them.

# 24. The Kindergarten:
## Model for a New Eden

When Emma Marwedel (1818-1893), pioneer of the kindergarten in California, lay dying in the German Hospital in San Francisco, she "implored" former pupils who came to visit her to hold fast to Froebel's teaching and the ideal of the kindergarten. Her last words to one group were urgent: "Have faith in the kindergarten, strive to represent Froebel in his essence. I believe in the power of the kindergarten to reform the world."[1] For Miss Marwedel, the kindergarten was the means for "the regeneration of the human race."[2] According to Earl Barnes, who knew her, "She was the typical educational reformer, and about equally interested in the details of kindergarten education and in schemes of world regeneration through education."[3] Miss Marwedel spoke with passion of the role of the child. "The child's first mission opens with its helplessness, which is its great silent claim to be saved from the evils under which it is born, and from which it suffers while passing

[1] Fletcher Harper Swift: *Emma Marwedel, 1818-1893, Pioneer of the Kindergarten in California*, p. 144. University of California Publications in Education, Vol. 6, no. 3. Berkeley, California, 1931.
[2] *Ibid.*, p. 151.
[3] *Ibid.*, p. 176.

through life. The child is man's civilizer, purifier, and re-deemer." On this educator Swift commented, "Few educational reformers have stated more convincingly the social and racial importance of the child."⁴

The kindergarten thus was born into an exalted role. It was to be the child's garden through which the world-wide Garden of Eden, paradise remade, was to be established.

Its champions took their role very seriously. Horace Mann's sister-in-law, Elizabeth P. Peabody, one of the two 'great' figures in American kindergarten history, in her lectures on Froebel and the kindergarten, underlined the fact that, "I feel, as it were, *Divinely authorized* to present him to you as an authority which you can reverently trust; and so be delivered from the uncertainties of your own narrow and crude notions, inexperienced and ignorant as you undoubtedly are, however talented."⁵ For her, the child is a "seer blest," whose teaching must be in terms of its "trailing clouds of glory from God,"⁶ (God being here pantheistically defined as "one in substance with the deepest consciousness of self"⁷), and hence to be gently "cultivated" and by no means "drilled."⁸ "Kindergartning" is "true education;" more than that, "it is a religion; not an avocation, but a vocation from on High."⁹ It is the means to the true millennium.

Childhood understood, leading in the promised millennium of peace on earth and good will among men, will make mankind forget the Babel confusion of its first experimenting, and enter into the mutual understanding of the Pentecostal miracle.¹⁰

---

⁴ *Ibid.,* p. 183.
⁵ Elizabeth P. Peabody: *Lectures in the Training Schools for Kindergartners,* p. 28f. Boston: Heath, 1886.
⁶ *Ibid.,* p. 70.
⁷ *Ibid.,* p. 108.
⁸ *Ibid.,* p. 5.
⁹ *Ibid.,* p. 88.
¹⁰ *Ibid.,* p. 131. Of Elizabeth Peabody's dedication and faith, a biographer has written: "Elizabeth believed with all her fervent heart that education was the best means to bring about the answer to her daily prayer—that God's will should be done on earth as it is in heaven. If people only knew the right, they would never do wrong. Horace Mann had believed that a people taught to rule them-

Basic to this goal is its means, love. As she stated it, with all her typographical eloquence, "LOVE, *when it is understood, is irresistible.*"[11] The child must be made to surrender its alien selfishness and blossom into its truly good nature under love. Under such a kindergarten regime, great wonders will be wrought, even to the curing of color-blindness.[12] The hopes of men for the kindergarten movement were thus clearly optimistic. It was intended to be, in the words of the title of one manual, *The Paradise of Childhood.*[13]

The fountain-head of all this, Friedrich Froebel (1782-1852), well before Darwin, not only held to cosmic evolution but saw education as a major element in that continuing process. For Froebel, the entire universe was a living, evolving organism, the unity of which is called God. Its evolution is possible because of the law of activity, the law of action, reaction, and equilibrium, a broader application of the intellectual principle of process, i.e., thesis, antithesis, and synthesis. This process has come to self-consciousness in man; thus man, who is evolving to a higher order of being, can guide that process through education. Evil is faulty education which interferes with the fundamental nature and direction of the cosmic process. The individual repeats his racial development (the culture-epoch theory in education, the recapitulation theory in biology), but, as a self-generating force by virtue of his participation in the Absolute, man's growth is not merely imitative but creative. Hence,

---

selves could eradicate poverty, prevent war and see to it that dictators should rise no more. And William Ellery Channing had held that the child comes into this world free of sin. Evil, then, must be given to the child by means of evil environment. It must be corrected by education. Adding her own unquenchable faith to the teachings of the two men she had loved, Elizabeth conceived the idea that the kindergarten could correct evil environment—if placed in slum districts where the evil lay. Free public kindergartens were the answer, but until the public could be convinced of the value and allocate the funds, Elizabeth proceeded, with private donations, to lead the way." Louise Hall Tharp: *The Peabody Sisters of Salem,* p. 320f. Boston: Little, Brown, 1951.

[11] *Ibid.,* p. 177.

[12] *Ibid.,* p. 51.

[13] Edward Wiebe: *The Paradise of Childhood:* A Manual for Self-Instruction in Friedrich Froebel's Educational Principles and a Practical Guide to Kinder-Gartners. Springfield, Mass.: Milton Bradley, 1869.

self-expression is necessary to growth and to self-realization. Thus, Froebel markedly advanced as well as clearly formulated the fundamental thesis of modern education: learning by living, and learning by *play*. For Froebel, play was basic to education and essential to the development of the group spirit and group unity he so greatly desired.

Every town should have its own common playground for the boys. Glorious results would come from this for the entire community. For at this period games, whenever it is feasible, are common, and thus develop the feeling and desire for community, and the laws and requirements for community.[14]

For Froebel, the child, through play "is working out his own education."[15] This play needs the guidance of knowing educators to reach its true goal. As a result, education becomes guided living and play. The true teacher stands back and allows, through proper guidance, the potentialities of the child to come forth.

For the purpose of teaching and instruction is to bring ever more *out* of man rather than to put more and more *into* him; for that which can get *into* man we already know and possess as the property of mankind, and every one, simply because he is a human being, will unfold and develop it out of himself in accordance with the laws of mankind. On the other hand, what yet is to come *out* of mankind, what human nature is yet to develop, that we do not yet know, that is not yet the property of mankind; and, still, human nature, like the spirit of God, is ever unfolding its inner essence.[16]

Here is one of the typical myths of modern man nakedly stated. Culture and civilization are biological products which are now permanent data of man's nature. As Ortega y Gasset said of the modern specialist and barbarian, "He also believes that civilization is *there* in just the way as the earth's crust and the forest primeval."[17] Culture and civilization for Froebel were *there*

[14] Friedrich Froebel: *The Education of Man*, p. 114. New York: Appleton, 1891.
[15] Froebel: *Autobiography* and Materials to Aid Comprehension of the Work of the Founder of the Kindergarten, p. 104. New York: Kellogg, 1887.
[16] Frobel: *The Education of Man*, p. 279. Italics in original.
[17] Jose Ortega y Gassett: The Revolt of the Masses, p. 126. New York: Norton, 1932.

even as man's hands and feet are his natural "properties." Thus, the educator can "desert" culture and civilization in the confidence that it cannot "desert" him! He presses on, instead of dealing with permanently conquered and developed areas, to bring new properties of man into being, to discover through applied evolution the true involution of man, in short, to evolve what is involved rather than to remain at his present stage. But, since what is to be brought out is what the state educators first believe is there, this doctrine involved, not a respect for the child's nature or for cultural inheritance, but rather an insistence on a new doctrine of man and the re-creation of child, state and school in terms of it. Since each individual is an aspect of that fundamental unity, the Absolute, his true development is into unity with other men; hence education is in large measure social activity. Since for Froebel play constituted the truest expression of the inner and true nature of man, play is basic to and the means of educating children. As a result, Froebel was insistent on the centrality of activity and play, not only to the kindergarten, but to elementary education in general. Since the Absolute best expresses itself in man impulsively and instinctively, it follows that *symbolism* rather than *learning* dominates true education. Accordingly, Froebel developed his doctrine of correspondences, whereby various natural forms are manifestations of eternal truths, because mind and nature "are parallel manifestations of God."[18] As a result, every form in nature has as its very essence a symbolic meaning.[19]

The main principles, it will be remembered, whose applications form Froebel's system, are: *self-activity*, to produce development; all-sided *connectedness* and unbroken *continuity*, to help the right acquisition of knowledge; *creativeness*, or expressive activity, to produce assimilation of knowledge, growth of power, and acquisition of skill; well-ordered physical *activity*, to develop the physical body and its powers; and *happy and harmonious surroundings*, to foster and help all these. If a school, therefore, includes amongst its aims

[18] W. H. Kilpatrick: *Froebel's Kindergarten Principles Critically Examined*, p. 31. New York: Macmillan, 1916.

[19] H. Courthope Bowen: *Froebel and Education Through Self-Activity*, p. 46. New York: Scribner, 1897.

the true acquisition of knowledge—as distinct from the more or less temporary possession of information—and with this the development of power and the production of skill—and most schools at least profess to do so—it follows at once that the school must look to these same principles for continued guidance and help, unless it denies their efficacy altogether, or holds that the life of a human being is a series of discontinuous separate existences, the natural laws of which differ for each successive existence.[20]

These words of a dedicated disciple of Froebel, H. C. Bowen, first a headmaster, and then University Lecturer at Cambridge on the theory of education, give us the fundamentals of what later came to be known as progressive education. The separation of true knowledge from mere learning and information was an emphatic note. True knowledge is a mystical social experience for this school of educators.

The mystical aspect was very prominent in Froebel. As Butts has observed,

The handling of a ball or sphere was somehow supposed to give the child a sense of the perfect unity of all things, and sitting in a circle was supposed to make him feel his identification as an individual with his social group and eventually with the unity of all mankind in the Absolute.[21]

For Froebel, every life-form was a mystical pointer to "God," the unity of being. "The things of nature form a more beautiful ladder between heaven and earth than that seen by Jacob; not a one-sided ladder leading in one direction, but an all-sided one leading in all directions."[22] Man is in essential unity with all things because everything is a manifestation of divine being, and this apprehension is basic to his education and religion.[23] Every form of nature is thus a witness to that unity. "So man, even when a child  by games with the ball is placed in the centre

[20] *Ibid.*, p. 180f.
[21] R. Freeman Butts: *A Cultural History of Western Education*, p. 403.
[22] Froebel: *The Education of Man*, p. 203.
[23] S. S. F. Fletcher and J. Welton, translators: *Froebel's Chief Writings on Education*, p. 17. London: Edward Arnold, 1912.

of his own life and of all life."[24] The development of this experience led to total identification with all being and mystical love of all, so that the dying Froebel could say, "I love flowers, men, children, God! I love everything!"[25]

Because of this mysticism, Emma Marwedel held that the ideal schoolhouse would be a circular building.[26] Froebel's rationale for this symbolism was both his view of the *continuity* of being, and his radical *empiricism, things* having a primacy to *words,* and hence *experiences* having a primacy to *information and book-learning* in education. As Froebel stated it,

> The A, B, C of things must precede the A, B, C of words, and give to the words (abstractions) their true foundations. It is because these foundations fail so often in the present time that there are so few men who think independently and express skillfully their inborn divine ideas . . .
>
> Perception is the beginning and the preliminary condition for thinking. One's own perceptions awaken one's own conceptions, and these awaken one's own thinking in later stages of development. Let us have no precocity, but natural, that is consecutive, development . . .
>
> The correct perception is a preparation for correct thinking and knowing.[27]

Later followers of Froebel such as Dewey dropped the symbolism, but, *by retaining the concept of continuity retained the emphasis on socializing the child, and by retaining the empiricism, retained the primacy of experience in education.* Thus, social experience constitutes the core of true education for Froebel and for all his successors to the present.

Froebel's kindergarten "gifts" were these basic symbolic forms whose experience opened up reality for the child. The ball or sphere is a symbol of the one, and of unity, whereas the cube

[24] *Ibid.,* p. 180.
[25] Froebel: *Autobiography,* p. 118.
[26] Swift, *op. cit.,* p. 187.
[27] Kate Douglas Wiggin and Nora Archibald Smith: *Froebel's Gifts,* p. 1f. Boston: Houghton, Mifflin, 1895.

symbolizes variety or manifoldness in unity, so that, by these two symbols, the great principles of the one and many, and their inseparable unity, are set forth.[28] The other "gifts" or forms had like mystical meanings.

Another fundamental principle of Froebel's educational philosophy was aimed against the Christian doctrine of original sin. As Froebel expressed it himself in his Mother Songs, the "soft and pure" child was to teach its mother the truth and purity of life.

> Dear little children, we will learn from you;
>   Gardens we'll make, and you the flowers shall be;
> Our care shall seem no tedious drudgery—
>   Only a happy trust that's ever new.
> We'll guard you from the great world's strife and din;
>   But, ah, our chiefest, gladdest care shall be
> To *give you your own selves!* to help you see
>   The meaning of each opening power within.
> Oh, blessed thought, that God to us has given
>   The finishing of that which He has planned;
>   And as we help your young souls to expand,
> Our own, in the sweet task, shall grow toward heaven.[29]

Behind this ecstasy stands certain self-assured claims. First, the child is naturally good and pure, as against the doctrine of original sin. Second, the Absolute, the pantheistic God or unity of all being, has turned over the government and shaping of these children to these enlightened new educators and to their agencies, later increasingly identified with the democratic state. Third, these educators will give to children their true selves, whereas others would ostensibly rob them of it.

The child's kindergarten play must be used to reveal the true symbols of nature. Thus, the familiar nursery game, pat-a-cake, truly means that there is a "great chain of life and service"

---

[28] *Ibid.*, p. 6, 31, 50. See also K. D. Wiggin and N. A. Smith: *Froebel's Occupations.* Boston: Houghton Mifflin, 1896.

[29] Henrietta R. Eliot and Susan E. Blow: *The Mottoes and Commentaries of Friedrich Froebel's Mother Play*, p. 230f. New York: Appleton, 1895.

and human interdependence.[30] Hide-and-seek reveals that "The goal of life is unity. The yearning for estrangement merely points to the path by which unity may be attained."[31] Thus, long before Jung, Froebel saw symbols and activities as expressions of a racial unconscious which in turn reflected the essential forms of the Absolute. The children were to learn the basic unity of all things and restore that unity by love, so that, children reared on the "Flower Song" would learn to exclaim, "O mother, the plants and flowers love us, just as you do!"[32] The effect of play, therefore, play in terms of true kindergarten principles, is "blessedness."[33]

The goal of this kind of education is the "perfect man."[34] For Froebel and his followers, "the destiny of nations lay in the hands of women" as they apply these principles, and follow Froebel's "Mother-Play," "The Kindergarten Bible" which "must be studied."[35] The result of such application would be world history begun anew.[36] The purpose of the kindergarten is in terms of this, "to develop the spiritual nature of the child and prepare him for ideal citizenship."[37] As they dedicate themselves to this task, women will find that, "like St. Christopher, we have borne the Christ upon our shoulders."[38] The kindergarten movement thus, by its own avowed declaration, "proclaimed a new gospel."[39] It is "education by development" of the potentialities of the holy child and is thus "something more

[30] *Ibid.*, pp. 124-127.
[31] *Ibid.*, p. 258.
[32] *Ibid.*, p. 98. See also Susan E. Blow: *The Songs and Music of Friedrich Froebel's Mother Play*, p. 15. New York: Appleton, 1895.
[33] K. D. Wiggin and N. A. Smith: *Kindergarten Principles and Practices*, p. 169f. Boston: Houghton Mifflin, 1896.
[34] Nora A. Smith: *The Kindergarten in a Nutshell*, p. 3. Ladies' Home Journal Practical Library. New York: Doubleday, Page, 1907.
[35] *Ibid.*, pp. 6, 13.
[36] *Ibid.*, p. 21.
[37] *Ibid.*, p. 36.
[38] *Ibid.*, p. 134.
[39] Nina C. Vandewalker: *The Kindergarten in American Education*, p. 1f. New York: Macmillan, 1908.

fundamental than instruction in the Three R's."[40] This principle holds good for all education:

That education is a process of development rather than a process
of instruction; that play is the natural means of development during
the early years; that the child's creative activity must be the main
factor in his education; and that his present interests and needs
rather than the demands of the future should determine the material and method to be employed,—all these principles underlying
kindergarten procedure the psychologist approved, not for kindergarten alone, but for all education.[41]

These principles of the kindergarten have steadily prevailed and
reached up through the elementary and secondary school into
the college and university. Long before progressive education
was formally born, it existed in kindergarten theory. Since man
is "in essence good, and education is a natural process of unfolding his spiritual capacities, in accordance with the universal
laws of evolution,"[42] it follows that education is not only permissive in nature but that it is the unfolding of the new democratic god in all his glory.

The pervasive influence of the kindergarten is seldom appreciated. It early infected every church in Western Europe and
America and was carried by them into missionary practice the
world over, into church schools and parental training. The
Women's Christian Temperance Union championed it widely.[43]
Later, Russia made it basic to its statist education, starting full-
schoolday kindergartens for children at the age of three, and
nursery schools for younger children. G. Stanley Hall, John
Dewey and others in large measure expanded and developed the
fundamental principles of the kindergarten movement in terms
of a world-view. In a new and radically alien sense, it was held
that a little child should lead humanity to a new paradise. Unhappily, instead of being the beginnings of a new Garden of

[40] *Ibid.*, p. 3.
[41] *Ibid.*, p. 245.
[42] *Ibid.*, p. 25.
[43] *Ibid.*, p. 103, cf. 95.

Eden, the kindergarten, by its induction of the young into a radically false concept of life, has come closer to being *a child's garden of neurosis.*

Moreover, while the symbolism of Froebel receded, his emphasis on evolution and his anti-intellectualism increased in subsequent theory. According to the doctrine of evolution, man's emotional and instinctual responses have a priority to his intellectual activities, preceding them in development, and hence are more basic to man. Truly basic education is thus in terms of this basic nature of man. Hence the emphasis on play, activity, physical education, art, music and the like. As Frederic Burk stated it, "So far as neurological data gives evidence, the order of development is ever from those structures which are oldest in the race towards those which are the most recent."[44] Thus, this is both basic and scientific education. There was, of course, resistance to it from many first grade teachers:

First grade teachers confide to their superintendents that they would prefer children who have not attended the kindergarten to those who have. They fail to find any product in the kindergarten training of which the school can make use, and, on the other hand, they whisper that the kindergarten children are unruly, lack a spirit of obedience, are dependent, and continually expect to be amused. It may be, of course, that the primary school teacher does not know a good thing when she sees it, but the upshot of the matter is that the kindergarten is having a hard time of it in establishing its place in the educational system. The least we can say is that the school and the kindergarten are out of joint.[45]

These whispered complaints, however, were futile. By and large, the kindergarten was immensely popular both with educators and parents. Indeed, prominent personages, and politicians in Washington, D. C., early took the lead in giving both their children and their approval to the new gospel of childhood. In later years, educators, pitting the hold-out children against the kin-

[44] Frederic Burk: *A Study of the Kindergarten Problem in the Public Kindergartens of Santa Barbara, California, for the year 1898-9,* p. 29. San Francisco: Whitaker and Ray, 1899.

[45] *Ibid.,* p. 6.

dergartners, were able to find "scientific evidence" to prove the slight superiority of the kindergarten trained children to these others.[46] This superiority applied to the early grades, indicating that the kindergarten children had better learned to deliver what was expected of them.

The kindergarten ably caught the spirit of the age and uttered its truisms with telling effectiveness. Thus, when Katherine Beebe declared "the necessity" of "self-expression," ("we must admit that it is absolutely essential to the growth of body, mind, and soul"),[47] it had the ring of infallible and necessary truth. All else must be eliminated, to give this over-riding concept free play. Not what the child *learned* from wiser heads, but what the child, this new fount of wisdom, *expressed* was the hope of the future. Play, from Froebel on, was the means to this wisdom. In play, the child sought, not mere amusement, but to give expression to basic and important impulses arising out of the vast racial and personal unconscious mind. And, as Froebel had stated it, "Unconsciousness is raised to consciousness chiefly by action."[48] This cause was carried forward by many dedicated champions, including William Torrey Harris, Col. Francis W. Parker, Frederic Burk, John Dewey, Maria Montessori, and many others. Montessori strongly emphasized "the social aspect of the school," and Dewey added to the growing philosophy the faith that "the present as well as the future is of importance to the child. Education is not all preparation for what is to come, but it is also the enriching and interpreting of the experiences of the present."[49]

The purpose of the kindergarten has thus remained basically

[46] Edward William Goetch: *The Kindergarten as a Factor in Elementary School Achievement and Progress,* University of Iowa Studies in Education, 1925-27, Vol. III, no. 4; Iowa City, Iowa.

[47] Katherine Beebe: *The First School Year,* For Primary Workers, p. 79. Chicago: Werner, 1895.

[48] Edna Dean Baker, ed., *The Kindergarten Centennial, 1837-1937,* A Brief Historical Outline of Early Childhood Education, p. 6. The Association for Childhood Education, Washington, D. C., 1937.

[49] Josephine C. Foster and Neith E. Headley: *Education in the Kindergarten,* p. 17. Second ed. New York: American Book Company, 1948.

the same through the years. The addition of reading to the program does not alter its basic nature, which is education by means of activity and experience. This philosophy is characteristic of the school as a whole and not of the kindergarten only. This philosophy was well summarized some years ago by Ada Van Stone Harris, Supervisor of Kindergarten and Primary Education, Rochester, New York: "The kindergarten offers the child experience instead of instruction; life instead of learning; a miniature world, where he lives, grows, expands, and learns."[50] Nina C. Vandewalker measured the success of the kindergarten by the application of its principles to all grades.[51] These guiding principles are self-activity, experience as a means of self-discovery and self-revelation, "all education" made "relative to the society in which it is given," generalizations based on evolutionary theory, and belief in the importance and "organic unity of experience."[52] The essence of education is thus activity in terms of the child's self-expression and social adjustment. The kindergarten is thus education by activity.[53]

This activity is itself learning. "We learn through experience. Learning by doing" is the essence of the program.[54] Learning by studying and by means of books is somehow either reprehensible or at best secondary. An activity program is a "problem-solving approach,"[55] and is thus apparently more scientific. The

[50] Harris, "Introduction," in Manfred J. Holmes, ed., *The Kindergarten and its Relation to Elementary Education,* p. 18. The Sixth Yearbook of the National Society for the Scientific Study of Education, Part II. Chicago: University of Chicago Press, 1907.

[51] N. C. Vandewalker, "The History of Kindergarten Influence in Elementary Education," in Holmes, p. 116.

[52] Harriette Melissa Mills, "The Evolution of the Kindergarten Program," in Holmes, pp. 89-99.

[53] For the activities, and their basically constant nature, see Katherine Beebe: *Kindergarten Activities.* Akron, Ohio: Saalfield, 1904. Helen Bartlet Hurd: *Teaching in the Kindergarten,* With Emphasis on the What and the How to Teach. Minneapolis: Burgess, 1956. For a religious adaptation of these activities, see Mamie W. Heinz: *Growing and Learning in the Kindergarten.* Richmond, Virginia: John Knox Press, 1959. Note the primacy given to growing in this title.

[54] Clarice Dechent Wills and William H. Stegeman: *Living in the Kindergarten,* A Handbook for Kindergarten Teachers, p. 77. Chicago: Follett, 1950.

[55] *Ibid.,* p. 73.

kindergarten is usually a child's first introduction "to a large social group,"[56] and is therefore of tremendous importance in "meeting social-emotional needs." The teacher must thus remember that "she is a guide and leader of children rather than a teacher of specific facts."[57] The truisms which kindergartners remind us of, as though they alone are aware of them, are sometimes startling: we are assured that "kindergarten children are human beings, as they have been since birth, and will continue to be until death." After this profound bit of wisdom, we are warned, "They have a right to the privileges and responsibilities which come with membership in a democratic society."[58] But are children only human when the world is turned into a child's paradise and an adult's hell? Is the child truly *human* to kindergartners who *divinize* him? Are not the tantrums of this new god more reminiscent of the old devil?

But, since the aim of education is now *"self-realization,"*[59] external standards have no place. The self-expressing individual and a society designed for the social unity of such individuals is the essence of education. "The kindergarten is pre-eminently an ethical institution," because it is a *social* setting,[60] and ethics today is thoroughly social in reference. Therefore, "education is an interactionary process" of assimilation and adjustment.[61]

J. B. Watson's Behaviorism furthered the anti-intellectualism of education and aided kindergarten theory.[62] Man being a social being,[63] his truest learning is in terms of the group. Hence, "socializing the class"[64] is a kindergarten procedure and goal.

[56] *Ibid.,* p. 29.
[57] *Ibid.,* pp. 55-57.
[58] *Ibid.,* p. 36.
[59] Nora Atwood: *Theory and Practice of the Kindergarten,* p. 75. Boston: Houghton Mifflin, 1916.
[60] *Ibid.,* p. 54.
[61] *Ibid.,* p. 50.
[62] L. A. Pechstein and Frances Jenkins: *Psychology of the Kindergarten-Primary Child,* pp. 63-67. Boston: Houghton Mifflin, 1927.
[63] Lucy Weller Clouser and Chloe Ethel Millikan: *Kindergarten-Primary Activities Based on Community Life,* p. 2. New York: Macmillan, 1929. "The activity or experience must meet the need of society," p. 3.
[64] Pechstein and Jenkins, *op. cit.,* p. 202-206.

For old-fashioned people complaining about the results, educators had answers most satisfying to themselves:

Asked if a room was too noisy, another supervisor replied: "Are you judging by the noise inherent in the situation, or by your inherited prejudices?" How many of us have prejudices to overcome![65]

And, in this day and age, to accuse anyone of prejudice is assumed to be sufficiently crushing.

The nursery school began together with the kindergarten and was championed as necessary for "mental hygiene."[66] Children apparently need such mental hygiene to recuperate from their families. The nursery school from the beginning has been especially popular, not only with working mothers, but with intellectuals and pediatricians.[67] According to the high priestesses of the kindergarten cult, to further mental hygiene, a new literature is needed for children, realistic "here and now" stories.[68]

The kindergarten, although play, is serious business and has a curriculum which is "social science." After all, "a large part of kindergarten experience has to do with learning to live happily, comfortably, and constructively with other people. This is perhaps the most important thing that the child learns in kindergarten."[69]

The cult of the child has exalted the kindergarten into a position whereby it has undercut and devalued the great Christian rites of baptism and confirmation. Their great function, entrance into the covenant and culture of God's church and people, has given way to a new rite, the first day at kindergarten, which is a divorce from family and past. The comparison to rites is not a hostile or critical one: indeed, in a handbook

[65] *Ibid.,* p. 241.
[66] Ilse Forest: *The School for the Child from Two to Eight,* p. 42. Boston: Ginn, 1935.
[67] *Ibid.,* p. 46.
[68] *Ibid.,* p. 176.
[69] Charlotte Gano Garrison, Emma Kickson Sheehy and Alice Dalgliesh: *The Horace Mann Kindergarten for Five-Year-Old Children,* p. 29. Teachers College, Columbia University: Bureau of Publications, 1937.

for parents of prospective kindergarten children, Part I is titled "Initiation Rites."[70] While study may be out for most little children, it is the order of the day for some parents. "Many kindergartens have a study group for parents." At these meetings, the parents not only study the meaning of the child but repair toys, paint furniture and become involved "in greater community activities."[71] The family can no longer see itself as the central institution. Family life and activity must give way to greater things.

The dying Emma Marwedel said, "I believe in the power of the kindergarten to reform the world." To a large measure, the Western world in particular has been re-formed in the original sense of that word, *re-shaped*, but, Miss Marwedel to the contrary, it has *not* been *regenerated*. The kindergarten model for a new Garden of Eden has better reflected the fall of man than paradise. "In the modern school, *play* and *learn* are different aspects of the same situation, each one a natural supplement to the other."[72] Some Romans once charged that Nero played while Rome burned. In terms of the coming conflagration that world events increasingly promise, educators have thoughtfully taken pains that we do not lack our Neros.

The main responsibility, however, cannot be ascribed to educators but must be firmly laid at the door of parents, mothers in particular. In spite of all the honors and high praise accorded them, more than a few of the earnest pioneers of the kindergarten movement had more than a slight air of absurdity in the eyes of their contemporaries. Indeed, one of the most dedicated of these women was sometimes seen as amusing by uncouth kindergarten pupils. Certainly neither mothers nor prominent personages were deceived in this matter. Why then did the kindergarten succeed? The answer was and is clear-cut: the desire of women to get rid of their children. Educators have had

[70] Minnie Perrin Berson: *Kindergarten, Your Child's Big Step*, pp. 19-53. New York: Dutton, 1959.

[71] *Ibid.* p. 106f.

[72] Ruby Minor: *Early Childhood Education*, Its Principles and Practices, p. 159. New York: Appleton-Century, 1937.

to set an age requirement for kindergarten children, else they would be deluged with mothers trying to push very young children into their hands. Thus, kindergarten has proven to be in part *a polite and oblique form of infanticide,* one which hypocritical women can indulge in while getting credit for solicitous motherhood. The kindergarten movement was born out of romantic and idealistic philosophy and its idealization of the child. It prospered because women, drinking the heady wine of feminism, had come to regard womanhood and motherhood as burdensome, and lacked the honesty to say so. The nursery school and the kindergarten were thus admirable as respectable escapes from responsibility.

What health there is in the kindergarten has come, not from the educational philosophers, but from loving and healthy-minded teachers. These women, oblivious of theory and curriculum, have taken shy children, awed by the world of learning, gently in hand and led them toward the world of books. The introduction in some areas lately of reading into the kindergarten has been in a measure the formal adoption of informal practice.

# 25. Is the University Beyond the Law?

In the name of academic freedom, the modern university today claims to be beyond the law, and a law unto itself. In this stand, the universities have been under serious attack of late, and there is no question but that some or many of these attacks have been ill-advised, too sweeping, or too vague. But the defense of the universities has often been equally precarious, and the "academic freedom" too often asserted has been a modern variation of an ancient dogma which divides responsibility in human society and creates a segment which is its own law. The roots of the concept of academic freedom are medieval, and akin to canon law. The universities are heirs of a concept of law which makes them free of all courts save their own. Is this new canon law to be recognized as such? Are the professors the new clerks of society and thereby exempt from its law? For the roots of this current claim are medieval and represent a dogma of long-standing history. To assess its merits, the background must be understood.

One of the persistent problems of medieval life, one which in many respects lingers to this day, was the relationship of church and state. We have seen that it was the claim of the Roman see that the Church was beyond the reach of secular law and subject only to its own authority. Thus, if a member of the clergy was charged with any crime, whether an offense against the moral law, murder, theft or the like, he could escape the arms of the secular courts. The poet Ben Jonson, for example, in 1598 escaped the gallows for the murder of Gabriel Spencer by pleading benefit of clergy, for which he had only a technical qualification. Only after long controversy was the present precarious compromise attained in most modern states, whereby the state surrenders claims to jurisdiction in the spiritual realm in return for the recognition of one law in the temporal realm. In the American compromise, the state recognized a common law Christianity in the form of a recognition of a general conformity to its norms (as with the ban of polygamy, the support of a chaplaincy, etc.) in a settlement which can be better termed disestablishment than separation.

But the crisis of modern civilization is in part the break-down of the concept of authority. As long as the idea of law retained its validity and was undergirded by a belief in the absolute and transcendant God behind and beyond it, Western society had vitality. But justice is a metaphysical concept, as is law, and the break-down of metaphysical validity for law has been the break-down of society. When natural law and reason were regarded as the immanent principle of the deity, man was the substance and end of society, and society itself was accident and relation. As a result, man's natural rights were championed against the claims of the state. Subsequently, as Romanticism developed this doctrine, the divine immanence was transferred from reason to the folk and the State. The divine reason was immanent in the human will, the common will, and the State was the expression of the general will, thus giving priority to the State and limiting man to a merely formal freedom. Rights passed over to the State. The decline was furthered by the positivist destruction of the metaphysical concept of justice, making true law and justice merely the product and will of the strongest force.[1]

[1] See Peter F. Drucker: *The End of Economic Man*, N.Y., John Day, 1939, and *The Future of Industrial Man*, N.Y., John Day, 1942, and especially John H. Hallowell: *The Decline of Liberalism as an Ideology*, with particular reference to German Political-Legal Thought. Berkeley, University of California Press, 1943.

Modern society believes it has solved the matter of the relationship of church and state by granting freedom of worship, which is a declaration of the irrelevancy of worship to society. And yet this freedom of worship is not a reality. What, for example, the United States has is a toleration of all religions *insofar* as their practices are not offensive to common law Christianity and morality. Thus, religious polygamy, as with Mormonism, was forbidden, and cannibalism, human sacrifice, and other cultic practices offensive to Christian and modern secular sense, were also banned. But in so ruling the Supreme Court repudiated the right and power of religion to dictate our acts:

"Can a man excuse his practices . . . because of his religious belief? To permit this would be to make the doctrines of religion superior to the law of the land; and in effect to permit every citizen to become a law unto himself. Government could exist only in name."[2]

As far back as 1927, a secular writer like Leon Whipple recognized the dilemma of modern man in this situation. This concept of religious liberty leaves nothing to religion except mere belief and opinion and establishes as final authority the will of the majority as expressed in the state.[3] The older conception of an established church, to the exclusion of all others, made an ecclesiastical institution the expression of the divine will; the modern conception of religious liberty makes the state the vehicle of truth. But because the state now lacks the backing of metaphysical truth, every citizen has become a law unto himself and his own tyrant, and the State an unlimited and uncontrollable god. And, because of the usually mutually exclusive claims of church and state, each can accord the other only a basically subordinate role. Furthermore, because of the relationship of authority and liberty, to deny authority to or limit the authority of either church or state is to limit its liberty. Similarly, when the university claims to be beyond the law in manners pertaining to academic freedom, it denies both the authority and liberty

2 United States v. Reynolds, 98 United States Reports 145.
3 Leon Whipple: *The Story of Civil Liberty in the United States,* p. 272.

of church and state. Thus, church-controlled colleges not infrequently deny that the church or state has any authority to limit their teaching or writing, that, although a church may be supporting the school in order to promote a particular theology, it cannot control that school without offense.

The Church thus was not alone in claiming to be a separate realm. The school advanced a like claim, patterned after that of the Church, and we have seen that German universities did succeed in gaining their own jails, and English universities at least gained their own representatives in parliament. Originally, they held to a concept of responsibility under God. Most American colleges and universities share with their continental cousins an ecclesiastical origin or purpose, now in most instances lost. To replace the old responsibility and function, the new concept of academic freedom has been developed. The university is responsible *to itself,* a poor substitute for God, and its liberties cannot be infringed by society without destroying the concept and practice of freedom.

Is this doctrine either true or realistic? The first challenge to it comes from the modern state. The state has replaced the church as the significant sponsor of education. Not even Protestant and Roman Catholic colleges and universities are free from this sponsorship in the form of various subsidies, whether veterans' educational provisions, military training programs, special research grants, and the like. The price of support is always control, and the university cannot complain of government interference when it accepts so readily the government's support. In a day when the universities most loudly proclaim their autonomy, they are most rapidly, and too often willingly, succumbing to the encroachments of statism. A kept woman has no honest protest against adultery or claim to virginity. The position of the university today is analogous: the charge against her is that she is guilty, in many areas, of promoting statism. Her answer is that she has no entangling alliances with anyone, and that she is beyond the challenge of church, state or society, because the new canon law of academic freedom makes her a law unto herself, subject only to self-discipline, and with offenders in her circle liable only to the academic courts.

As long as the university does either or both of two things, this claim and hope is totally unrealistic. First of all, the university cannot accept the support of any local, state or federal agency, without rendering itself into the hands of that body as a ward. Even as a farmer cannot accept price supports without being legally liable to government restrictions and controls, so no institution, the university included, can commit itself to any measure of wardship without a surrender of liberty. If the restrictions and pressure are lightly exercised, it is only because the sponsoring agencies have been lax in exercising their rights. But it is significant that the main area of pressure on universities, and the institution of loyalty oaths, has been in state universities. The state rightly asserts its title to loyalty from its wards, and the university cannot protest legitimately without also renouncing the funds which give jurisdiction. The free university, like the free society, is ultimately incompatible with state support and control. The university has failed to see the irony of its position in defending or protecting its Communist or ostensibly Communist faculty members: it insists on protecting the promulgation of the most insistent and tyrannous statism while at the same time wailing against a minor assertion of statism in the form of the loyalty oath and government investigation!

This points clearly to the second step. Not only must the university, if it be consistent, reject statism internally and externally, but it must recognize that the free university can exist only in a free society, and that it has an obligation to promote that society. The university cannot shirk its cultural and sociological obligation without ruin to itself. A major and insistent threat to academic freedom today is the decline of private giving to education. The mainsprings of freely given financial support are drying up as a result of the rise of statism. A confiscatory system of taxation and a policy of government encroachment on a free economy increasingly render it difficult for the university to command a financial support from a financially free population. Lacking these sources, the university finds very tempting the constant flow of government funds. Today atomic research, and, with it, allied avenues of study, has largely passed into the hands of the government and its subsidized allies. The temptation grows to emphasize the value of research in terms of governmental needs. Today even anthropology has come to represent in some instances the viewpoint of the Department of the Interior in financed researches which are congenial to the outlook of the Indian Service. But such support is unavoidable when private sources are drying up. To assert the irrelevance of this social problem to the university is as weak a viewpoint as art for art's sake. The university is an instrument of society (rather than of church or state) and can only sever itself from it at the price of its relevant existence.

Assuming that the free society is firmly established, can the university then make good its claim to be beyond the law? Can it defend its right to protect from external criticism men guilty of sexual perversion, many of whom find a convenient and safe asylum in university circles? Can it challenge the right of society to charge its faculty members with treasonable associations and acts? Can it properly claim to be the possessor of a new canon law which places its members beyond the pale of all other law?

The university must certainly be free from the state and subject essentially to the government of its boards and academic senate. But in an interdependent society, the university is never free of obligations and never beyond the law. It cannot be free from the requirements of either God or society except at the peril of ruin. Society is not the state; it is the root and ground which nourishes the state, church and university, and to separate itself from society means a withering away of university life in the anemic isolation of decadence. The university cannot renounce society, its laws or its norms. It is *free under law;* to be free beyond the law means the tyranny of irresponsibility, and it is this tyranny which today manifests itself in too many university circles and cloaks itself in the claim to academic freedom.

In a sense, as Buckley has pointed out, the *laissez-faire* concept has heavily influenced educational thinkers.[4] Having denied the validity of *laissez-faire* in economics, the university in particular has been emphatic in asserting its radical validity in educational controls. But there is a difference: *laissez-faire* economic theory insisted on the sovereignty of law, each sphere of human activity being in itself a law-sphere and strictly circumscribed by the laws thereof. But modern educational relativism is hostile to this concept of law. Wherever else some relativistic concept of law might or must be utilized, in the university not even this measure of law can be tolerated, it is held. Here, in the quest for knowledge, man must be beyond the law. Here the autonomy of his being is to be manifested. Here, in "the one place," "by concession of state and society a given epoch may cultivate the clearest possible self-awareness . . . For it is a human right that man must be allowed somewhere to pursue truth unconditionally and for its own sake."[5]

What is basic to this concept of academic freedom? What presupposition undergirds its claim to be beyond the law? As Russell Kirk has asked, "Can there be an end or aim to anything without a religious interpretation of life? . . . I repeat that we all have our absolutes, our dogmas, if we are reflective men, whether we acknowledge them or treat them as bastards."[6]

When institutions, through loss of rationale, begin to move in terms of *power* instead of *meaning*, their end is in view. The university has clearly revealed this grasping for power in faculty and administration, and the same trend is apparent also in the state. The objective *idea* or *world reason* of modern man is no longer the university, and, though having long served the state, is less and less identifiable with it. It is now increasingly incarnated in autonomous man, who is held to be beyond the law. This autonomous man demands of the universe not law (with

[4] William F. Buckley, Jr.: *God and Man at Yale*, The Superstitions of "Academic Freedom," pp. 157, 160. Chicago, Regnery, 1951.

[5] Karl Jaspers: *The Idea of the University*, p. 1. Boston: Beacon Press, 1959.

[6] Russell Kirk: *Academic Freedom*, An Essay in Definition, p. 49. Chicago: Regnery, 1955.

its implication of judgment and punishment by a superior power) but unlimited and unconditional love and freedom. For the existentialist and the radical relativist, God is no longer a problem; other people are. His own unconditional autonomy must require the lawless love which is beyond good and evil, and this constitutes a societal problem. Whatever concessions are made on this societal level, however, none can be made where the pursuit of truth is concerned. Here man functions as the autonomous seeker and interpreter, and as the source of law and meaning. He is beyond the law even as in orthodox Christian theology God is beyond the law—by virtue of his total sovereignty.

# 26. The Freedom of Higher Education

The university has also been bitterly criticized in recent years by its own members and friends. Thus, some faculty members have been very ready to see administrative power as the prime evil. This was perhaps best stated by J. McKeen Cattell some years ago: "In the academic jungle the president is my black beast . . . I once incited one of my children to call her doll Mr. President, on the esoteric ground that he would lie in any position in which he was placed."[1]

Thorstein Veblen saw the evil in vocationalism, or professional schools in the university, which he deemed incompatible with true learning.[2] Hutchins likewise saw a conflict between "the pursuit of truth for its own sake" and "the preparation of men and women for their life work."[3] This made the university in his eyes "anti-intellectual." The Christian presupposition that *truth* and *calling* are inseparable was nowhere in consideration in the thinking of either Veblen or Hutchins.

[1] J. McKeen Cattell: *University Control*, p. 31. New York: The Science Press, 1913.

[2] Thorstein Veblen: *The Higher Learning in America*, New York: Sagamore Press, 1957.

[3] Robert Maynard Hutchins; *The Higher Learning in America*, pp. 33ff. New Haven: Yale University Press, 1936.

Jaspers has called attention to the anti-intellectualism of the university as an institution. In appointments, "The excellent are instinctively excluded from fear of competition, just as the inferior are rejected out of concern for the prestige and influence of the university."[4]

A more persistent charge is with reference to the radical inferiority of science departments. Some research scientists in private laboratories hold that, not only could they give better advanced academic training, but that they often find it necessary to retrain university graduates whom they employ.

Other charges can be mentioned briefly in passing. Administrators state that professors, while ostensibly dedicated to higher learning and often contemptuous of the profit motive, are, whatever their pay, still as avaracious and status-conscious a group of men as ever existed. This charge can be dismissed, in that it is equally true of great segments of the clergy and other "non-profit" callings. Nothing makes a man more prey to the most vicious avarice than to believe that his service to God, humanity, science, art, or scholarship makes him immune to particular sins.[5]

Similarly, it is charged that, inadequate as elementary and secondary schools may be, the failures of higher education are greater: more curriculum padding, more watering down of im-

---

[4] Jaspers, *op. cit.*, p. 71.

[5] A revealing incident of the importance of the profit motive is the Buell G. Gallagher case. Dr. Gallagher, minister, professor and college president, a dedicated socialist and champion of the service motive, is one of the ablest of teachers and an experienced administrator. Gallagher left New York's City College in 1961, where he was paid $30,000, and was under a pension plan which would have paid him $16,000 annually. In California to head the state college system as the first chancellor, a system with 108,000 students on fifteen campuses, his pay was $32,000, second only to the governor in the state salary hierarchy. To his dismay, he found the pension under the new position to be equal only to half that in New York, and with no housing provided with the position. He quickly and secretly re-applied for his New York post before his pension credits expired there, returning in February 1962. Again, typical of the mentality of the left, Governor Brown promptly declared that the resignation had been forced by the John Birch Society, whom he was "going to fight from hell to hell." Gallagher, with his usual forthrightness, denied this as in any sense a cause for his action. See *Newsweek*, February 26, 1962, p. 82, and Caspar W. Weinberger, "California Commentary," *Santa Cruz Sentinel*, p. 15, Tuesday, February 20, 1962.

portant subjects in the quest for popularity, more social passing, and more irrelevances exist in colleges and universities than in lower schools, where more public control exists. There is a measure of truth in this, but it is a charge equally applicable to church, state and other spheres, in all of which such irrelevancies, typical of the end of an age, prevail.

Again, it is charged quite frequently that professors, once having attained that eminence, lose interest in further learning and represent a low calibre of intellectual curiosity. Indeed, one faculty member has stated that the majority of his full professor colleagues limit their total annual reading to one or two periodicals. Such men then communicate the lust for position rather than of learning to their students. This is true, however, of most professional men, and some telling evidence of this professional lack of learning is cited by Dr. Sigerist.[6]

Our concern, however, is with principial rather than procedural issues. This concern is tellingly illustrated by a facetious quip: "Why do Harvard men confuse themselves with God? Because they have a high opinion of God!" With the Enlightenment, man became increasingly the new universal, supplanting God. The result was a Messianic Utopianism which held that "the approaching Millennium" would be a product of (1) man's rejection of the past and of history, in terms of his sovereign ability to create a new, revolutionary culture. (2) Similarly, institutions and customs were to be rejected, since man's reason and science was to be the one true source of all these things. (3) It was further held that man is basically good, and that evil is not in man but in his environment. (4) "By changing human institutions human nature itself will be born again." (5) The new managers of man will be "the scientific moralists and lawgivers, the educators, the statesmen."[7] Education in the modern age is a Messianic and Utopian movement born of the Enlight-

[6] Henry M. Sigerist, M.D.: *The University at the Crossroads,* Addresses and Essays, pp. 92-105. New York: Henry Schuman, 1946.

[7] Louis L. Bredvold: *The Brave New World of the Enlightenment,* pp. 111ff. Ann Arbor: The University of Michigan Press, 1961.

enment hope of regenerating man in and through his autonomous reason. This faith was greatly furthered by Kant's concept of the role of reason, whereby the ontological trinity was replaced by autonomous man and his reason. In man, being is exhausted in relation, and that relation is exclusively internal. Knowledge ceased to be the correlation of mind and matter, of the knower and reality, but rather became the synthesis, the unifying of human experience, the synthetic power of the mind. Knowledge is thus creative, constitutive and interpretive. The world is man's representation, and the basic reality is the Self, which is hence not an object of knowledge. Thus, Kant heightened the Enlightenment faith. At times, he spoke of the goodness of man as earlier thinkers of the Enlightenment had. Thus, "Evil is only the result of nature not being brought under control. In man there are only germs of good."[8] But he also asserted, "But is man by nature morally good or bad? He is neither, for he is not by nature a moral being." His reason by its sway produces virtue, and his "natural inclination," vice. "Vices, for the most part, arise in this way, that civilisation does violence to Nature."[9] "Moral culture must be based upon 'maxims,' not upon discipline; the one prevents evil habits, the other trains the mind to think. . . . 'Maxims' ought to originate in the human being as such. . . . If we wish to establish morality, we must abolish punishment."[10] The development in Kant becomes apparent. As the new universal, man is in a sense beyond good and evil, as Nietzsche was more logically to assert, because he is himself the source of law and hence superior to it. His virtue is his freedom to be pure reason, and his dedication to this purpose and achievement in terms of it. "Our ultimate aim is the formation of *character*. Character consists in the firm purpose to accomplish something, and then in the actual accomplishing of it."[11]

[8] Emmanuel Kant: *Education,* p. 15. Ann Arbor: The University of Michigan Press, 1960.
[9] *Ibid.,* p. 108.
[10] *Ibid.,* p. 83f.
[11] *Ibid.,* p. 98f.

The developed creed of the Enlightenment is thus the authoritarian faith of the modern university, held as tenaciously as any medieval university held to its dogmas. This new 'catholic' faith is moreover held naively, in that it is assumed that the modern scholar, impartially, without prejudice or presupposition, seeks truth, when in actuality rigid presuppositions and axioms govern his every thought. The hard core of doctrine of this new 'catholic' faith includes the following ideas:

1. The autonomy of man and of his reason are assumed, and the penetrability of all things to man's reason and its scientific or philosophical methodology. Thus, what cannot be comprehended by this methodology, or measured by it, is not real. While man will not limit reality to what the baboon can grasp, he does limit it to his own apprehensibility, since man, and not God or the baboon, is the measure and the true universal.

2. The evolutionary hypothesis is similarly assumed as an article of faith.

3. The natural order is assumed to be self-sufficient and a law in and of itself.

4. Education is held to be the instrument of social salvation.

5. The state is viewed as the primary order of man's life.

6. The primary responsibility and accountability of man to man (as against man to God) is maintained.

7. True learning is of necessity assumed to be religiously secular, i.e., divorced from God, and academic freedom requires a radical absolution from all theistic ties.

8. The priority of science and learning to ethics, and the determination of true ethics by means of autonomous man's own resources is maintained. Furthermore, even as morality is subordinate to and a product of human activity and intelligence, so true religion is subordinate to and a product of ethics.

9. Intelligence is the desired and necessary agency of social planning and control.

10. Evil is a social product because man is essentially a passive

creature, so that the "moral education of the individual is purely and simply the management of his environment."[12] The mind is passive in that its every activity or idea is empirically aroused. Nothing can exist in the mind that is not first in the senses. While, in the Kantian sense, knowledge is not the correlation of mind and object, it is still passive in that it is the synthesis which stimulus produces. Thus, delinquency is not seen as more than a response, i.e., to a lack of love in the environment, and social evils as responses to environmental factors. Activity is hence seen as conditional and responsive, and thus the assumption of the basic passivity and ostensible malleability of the mind.

11. Nature is infinite and uncreated; hence the problem in economics and life is not one of limitations of creation and of scarcity, but a problem of distribution and use.

Many of these tenets characterized the 19th century college, but the facade of Christian faith nonetheless prevailed, albeit a Christian position syncretistically maintained at best. However, there was enough opposition to one or more of these tenets to make the 19th century a relatively dark period to the modern champions of academic freedom.[13] Some universities were founded by men with a generally religious outlook, whose presidents however rapidly made the new institutions leaders of the new faith.[14]

Basic to the modern university and its concept of its role as well as of its academic freedom, is, as Metzger has clearly seen, its rejection of doctrinal moralism. This "assault on doctrinal moralism was mounted on two major premises—the ethical neu-

[12] Bredvold, *op. cit.*, p. 108.

[13] See Richard Hofstadter: *Academic Freedom in the Age of the College*, New York: Columbia Paperback, 1961, and Ernest Earnest: *Academic Procession*, An Informal History of the American College, 1636 to 1953, Indianapolis: Bobbs-Merrill, 1953.

[14] See Carl L. Becker: *Cornell University*, Founders and the Founding; Ithaca Cornell University Press, 1944; and Frederick Rand Rogers: *Treason in American Education*: A Case History; New York: Pleiades, 1949. For some of the tensions between old and new, see John Chamberlain, "The End of the Old Education," *Modern Age*, I, 4, 343-354, Fall, 1960.

trality of science and the experimental status of ethics."[15] This "ethical neutrality" has been maintained inconsistently at times but is nonetheless basic to the modern university, as is "the experimental status of ethics." The university and its scholar are thus *beyond good and evil.* The clearest, and indeed only expression of consistent doctrinal moralism, which subordinates both man and moralism to a theological faith, is orthodox Christianity. As the Westminster divines stated it, "truth is in order to goodness." That is, character, morality, and true goodness cannot exist in any true sense apart from the foundation of truth, truth which is to be identified only with the personal God of Scripture and His word and its order of knowledge. This faith is an affirmation of universal causality of a personal nature. Cause and effect move thus in terms of the absolute and personal will of a personal God. For the modern university, if causality exists, it is only an impersonal causality, and hence *ultimately indifferent* to the matter of personal morality. As a result, in terms of this ultimate impersonalism, *man's salvation is technological and scientific* and so to be sought, rather than in terms of faith and obedience to a very personal and jealous God. For orthodox Christianity, it is not a question of *manipulation and control,* but rather of *faith and obedience,* not external works. To the extent that a theology allows the existence of an unconscious potentiality in God, to that extent it allows for the efficacy of *works* rather than of *faith.* Man's faith today is in an impersonal universe and an impersonal or slightly personal God, and hence his hope is in technology and science, in manipulation and control. But to presuppose an *ultimate impersonalism* is to assume as a necessary consequence *the priority and determinative power of an immediate impersonalism.* Hence, for Freud man is basically governed by sub-personal and subconscious forces. Hence, for Dewey man is basically social and not personal. Hence too external means are basic to his life and welfare. Chemistry will cure his mental illness, and techniques his social, sexual and

---

[15] Walter P. Metzger: *Academic Freedom in the Age of the University,* p. 82. New York: Columbia Paperback, 1961.

personal problems. *A cosmic impersonalism leads inevitably to the depersonalization of man.*

The effects of the rejection of doctrinal moralism have been most clearly seen in those areas of culture which are new to the 20th century, as witness motion pictures and television. As an anthropologist has pointed out, Hollywood's predominant approach to life is one of radical mechanization and impersonalization, so that love, life and all things are reduced to techniques of manipulation and control.[16] According to Dr. Powdermaker, "Hollywood represents totalitarianism. . . . In Hollywood, the concept of man as a passive creature to be manipulated extends to those who work for the studios, to personal and social relationships, to the audiences in the theaters and to the characters in the movies."[17] "Hollywood has the elaborated totalitarian elements we have described: the concept of people as property and as objects to be manipulated, highly concentrated and personalized power for power's sake, an amorality, and an atmosphere of breaks, continuous anxiety and crises."[18] Here, ironically, from the lips of a university scholar, is a pointed description of the consequences of the very faith held by the modern university, albeit held with more sophistication. It is not surprising that a comparison between Dr. Powdermaker's Hollywood and the university reveal very real similarities. Self-pity and a martyr-complex seem moreover to characterize the modern professor, as he finds society reluctant to accept his gospel of total manipulation.[19]

The rejection of doctrinal moralism is the rejection of per-

[16] Hortense Powdermaker: *Hollywood, The Dream Factory*, p. 317f. Little, Brown, 1950.

[17] *Ibid.*, p. 327.

[18] *Ibid.*, p. 332.

[19] For academic self-pity, see Theodore Caplow and Reece J. McGee: *The Academic Marketplace*, p. 7f. New York: Basic Books, 1958. For the "martyr complexes," see Paul F. Lazarfeld and Wagner Thielens, Jr.: *The Academic Mind*, pp. 11, 14. Glencoe, Illinois: Free Press, 1958. For the liberal intellectuals' habit of regarding themselves as victimized, see David Riesman: *Selected Essays from Individualism Reconsidered*, p. 110ff. Garden City: Doubleday Anchor Books, 1955.

sonal responsibility. The resultant concept of academic freedom is a demand for *total license* and a *freedom from all consequence*. It is the lust for a world without personal consequence, and an unwillingness to risk anything for one's faith. This concept of academic freedom, wedded as it is increasingly to pragmatism and relativism, holds in effect that nothing matters, whether the man is atheistic, Marxist, or a sexual pervert, if he is competent in his field. But, in this sea of relativism, what can be called competence? And if intelligence be made a criterion, on what ground is it held to have value? And as for Dewey's standard of the Great Community, what gives that community any value in a valueless world? The doctrine of academic freedom, as held today, has no foundation other than autonomous man's claim to be the universal as he manifests himself as reasoner and researcher. It is thus a modern and *totally immanent* version of an ancient dogma: *divine right*. In the theory of academic freedom, *this divine right is now incarnate in the university and its scholar, and is hence beyond all law*. The school has thus been instrumental in overthrowing the divine right of church, state, and artist, but only to assert its own claim.

This trend was not challenged but rather furthered by John Henry Cardinal Newman by his insistence on the supremacy of human reason.[20] Newman's position was that this autonomous reason, if true to itself, would ultimately be true to God; but the fallacy of this position was its failure to recognize that basic to this faith in the autonomous mind is the claim of that reason to function as God rather than reason.

Another brilliant religious attempt to wed faith and the university is seen in George Huntston Williams' hope that man "may be citizen . . . of three cities: Of Jerusalem, which is the church of all ages and climes. . . . Of Athens, which is the university where reason—that in us whereby we of all His creatures reflect uniquely the image of the Creator—is free to pursue its

---

[20] See Wilfred Ward's introduction to Newman: *The Scope and Nature of University Education*, p. xv. New York: Dutton, 1958. Ward gives evidence of this without intending to do other than commend Newman.

inquiries to the very brink of human perception; and Of the City of Man, the free society grounded in law . . ." This is to be "under the continuous and searching judgment of Christ."[21] But, as in every merger, priority goes to a particular partner. Although he believes very earnestly in the "christological sanction of the spiritual autonomy of the Christian professor,"[22] Williams regrettably finds in the Synoptic Gospels "faint echoes within echoes of oral tradition."[23] Since the only Christ who can be known is the Christ re-constructed by the professors, "the continuous and searching judgment" of that Christ is more likely to be, and usually has been, a letter of marque for the academic privateers of liberal Protestantism.

"Christian" education in the 19th century was non-theological,[24] and there is no evidence of any real change in its character since then. Harbison, for example, rejects the idea of a "Christian curriculum" with a "Christian sociology" or the like. There is for him no full revelation of God in history, only a "balance between concealment and revelation," which "the Christian has to find."[25]

When ostensibly Christian thinkers have been so lacking in any substantial answer to the prevailing relativism, it is not surprising that the direction of educational theory proceeds more rapidly than ever towards the vast ocean of inchoate relativism. Within the ranks of the scholars themselves, there has been discontent. Riesman, in criticizing anthropological relativism, has

[21] George H. Williams: *The Theological Idea of the University*, p. 95. New York: National Council of Churches, 1958. See also George H. Williams, ed.: *The Harvard Divinity School*, Its Place in Harvard University and in American Culture, p. 247f.

[22] Williams, in *The Christian Scholar*, Special Issue, Autumn, 1958, p. 199, cited by Cornelius Van Til, "The Christian Scholar," *Westminster Theological Journal*, XXX, 157, May, 1959.

[23] Williams, p. 207, in Van Til, p. 162.

[24] H. Richard Niebuhr, "Some Recent Trends in Theological Education," in H. R. Niebuhr, D. D. Williams and J. M. Gustafson: *The Advancement of Theological Education*, p. 4. New York: Harper, 1957.

[25] E. Harris Harbison, "Liberal Education and Christian Education," in Edmund Fuller: *The Christian Idea of Education*, pp. 67f., 82f. New Haven: Yale University Press, 1960.

commented: "As many observers have pointed out, it was all very well to seek neutrality towards the exotic behavior of the vanishing Dobrans or Nanda—but not towards the racist behavior of the Nazis or the suppression of cultural pluralism and the extirpation of whole peoples in the Soviet Union."[26] The problem, however, is not easily solved. How can neutrality be set aside in one realm when posited for all reality? How can any absolute be introduced into a sea of relativity? If democracy be introduced, as some would do, as a moral standard against the vast realm of neutrality, Mark Van Doren's observation holds true that "there is no such thing as democratic morals and ideas. Morals are either bad or good."[27] Majorities do not ensure morality. If attempts be made to "develop and enforce a group conscience,"[28] the problem remains how a conscience can be developed with reference to an ultimate relativism. Biddle has declared that "growth of responsible personalities is the basic aim of all education."[29] Responsible to whom? When man is himself the universal, there can be no question of responsibility: man is a law unto himself. If the group is the universal, then there is no value apart from the democratic majority, or any appeal against it. As Fustel de Coulanges has shown in *The, Ancient City*, the absence of transcendence was the root and ground of tyranny and of the impossibility of freedom. Man had no frame of reference beyond himself or his group. In the closed universe of modern thought, i.e., a universe without transcendence and wholly comprehensible in terms of itself, man is also wholly comprehended by his society, appetites and his subconscious. His reason itself is passive, an evolutionary, racial and social product. As a result, he has no law to appeal to against his group, or against himself for deliverance from himself. Total

[26] David Riesman: *Constraint and Variety in American Education*, p. 93; cf. p. 75f., 94. Garden City: Doubleday Anchor Books, 1958.

[27] Mark Van Doren: *Liberal Education*, p. 38. New York: Henry Holt, 1943.

[28] Wallace Brett Donham: *Education for Responsible Living*, The Opportunity for Liberal-Arts College, p. 143. Cambridge: Harvard University Press, 1944.

[29] William W. Biddle, with the collaboration of Loureide J. Biddle: *Growth Toward Freedom*, A Challenge for Campus and Community, p. 11. New York: Harper, 1957.

tyranny is the inevitable product of every closed universe in human thought. Only the open universe of biblical faith allows for true transcendence and for human liberty. And the hand of the modern intellectual is raised against the true transcendence of the ontological trinity. Holmes well expressed this temper in a letter to Laski: "I detest a man who knows that he knows."[30] University scholars have of late begun to join the ranks of anti-intellectual intellectualism, although not without resistance from some, as witness Jacques Barzun's *The House of Intellect*. But the lack of any true concept of freedom is all too clear. During World War II, the universities saw the virtual suspension of liberal education[31] with scarcely a murmur. It was no longer seen as essential to true liberty and was an expendable luxury. A committee of the American Council of Learned Societies, writing during that war, observed that "our greatest weakness today is our lack of genuine culture."[32] Such culture as existed was seen as in a sense retrogressive because technology and mechanization had gained priority over traditional cultural values: "Nothing is more amazing than the forms of idolatry which have shown themselves through the ages. It seems hardly credible that men would make a golden calf and then worship the product of their own workmanship; yet something of the same fear and awe appeared in the twentieth century attitude toward the machine."[33]

As a result of the basic impersonalism of contemporary philosophies, the university and college have moved steadily to the left, to politics and economics of manipulation and control. Lazarfeld and Thielens might call the new attitude "permissive" in their study of *The Academic Mind,* but it is more clearly to be defined as statist, and it is in clear-cut revolt against

---

[30] Edmund Wilson: *Eight Essays,* p. 235. Garden City: Doubleday Anchor Books, 1954.

[31] Van Doren, *op. cit.,* p. vii.

[32] Theodore M. Greene in T. M. Greene, C. C. Fries, H. M. Wriston, W. Dighton: *Liberal Education Re-examined,* Its Role in a Democracy, p. 115. New York: Harper, 1943.

[33] Wriston, in Greene, etc., p. 6.

individualism and against freedom.[34] The long-standing demand for federal assistance has accordingly been stepped up.[35]

Two challenges to the neutralism of the modern university have arisen in recent years, both denying the moral neutralism as well as denying the myth of scholarly objectivity. Both, however, were philosophies of a closed universe. These challenges came from the Nazi German and the Soviet Russian universities.[36] The German universities surprised the world by their readiness to turn to the Nazis. In so doing, they were (1) reacting against the liberal myth of inherent equality in favor of another myth, inherent racial superiority. (2) They were reacting against the myth of objectivity in favor of a new, existential subjectivism. (3) They were reacting against the myth of relativism in favor of an immanent concept of truth, truth as comprehended and manifested in the process of the German nation. This was, of course, simply a form of the Hegelian dialectic which also commands the allegiance of Soviet Russia. The Soviet Russian university was not so radical as the Nazi university in its break with the past, retaining in part the liberal mythology and also the liberal incarnation of process in the state rather than the race. The belief, however, of the Marxist scholar in this bastard version of "truth," and his insistence on the reality of truth, has given him, in Western universities, a power far beyond his numbers. The Marxist professor, as a "crusader for truth," and a believer in the reality of his Hegelian-Marxist truth, has had a compelling power as he teaches in the midst of academic relativism. As the world crisis has deepened, the popularity of the relativists has given way in turn to the Marxists, and now, with disillusionment over their tyrannies, to a new and implicitly religious as well as explicitly political and economic conservatism.[37]

---

[34] See V. Orval Watts: *Away from Freedom,* The Revolt of the College Economists. Los Angeles: The Foundation for Social Research, 1952.

[35] See The American Assembly, Columbia University; Douglas M. Knight, ed.: *The Federal Government and Higher Education.* Englewood Cliffs, N. J.: Prentice-Hall, 1960.

[36] See Arnold S. Nash: *The University and the Modern World,* An Essay in the Philosophy of University Education. New York: Macmillan, 1943.

[37] M. Stanton Evans: *Revolt on the Campus.* Chicago: Regnery, 1961.

By and large, however, the university is content to see its problem as basically twofold: a need for more money, and a need for more license so that it can indulge in that total irresponsibility which it calls academic freedom. But, as Stanley Baldwin once observed, "power without responsibility" is "the prerogative of the harlot throughout the ages."[88]

[88] Cited by Denis Baly: *Academic Illusion,* p. 9. Greenwich: The Seabury Press, 1961.

# 27. "Education as a Religion"

In the United States, it has been customary to regard Adolph
Hitler as a man who was at once both a stupid and an amusing
figure, albeit a vicious one. There has thus been little intelligent
understanding of the rise and triumph of National Socialism in
Germany (where it was destroyed only from without), and
hence no ability to cope elsewhere with these same dangers,
which are endemic to modern culture. Hitler not only controlled the most educated and advanced of modern states, but he
thoroughly commanded the loyalties of educators and scientists
because he understood and was able to use their myths and tools.
The genius of Hitler, in its grasp of modern realities, is sharply
seen in his soliloquy at an automobile show:

Strange that these machines and all the thousands of other machines
in our factories should be changing the human character. But they
are. The man who drives his car at top speed has developed a
totally new set of reflexes. He does not think any more before he
makes a move—there is no time to think. For his own safety he
must react with lightninglike speed. There he must act automati-
cally, almost like a machine. A good part of his energy goes into
automatic reflexes instead of into thought. That is why in our day

and age the number of people who think for themselves is dwindling.[1]

It is possible to assert, and with very good cause, that the machine can be an instrument of liberation, but the fact remains that, culturally, modern man has seen fit to liken himself to a machine, deny his transcendence to the material order (which has again often been seen mechanistically), and to pattern his life to the machine's. With Hitler, all these aspects of modern culture were deliberately accepted and utilized to create a post-Christian and scientific barbarianism. Before Hitler's rise to power, Jose Ortega y Gasset had called attention to the coming scientific barbarism in *The Revolt of the Masses,* citing its origins in 19th century civilization, in particular its liberal democracy and technicism.[2] One aspect of Hitler's goal was noted by Erika Mann in her study of *School for Barbarians,* but she failed to recognize the importance of the emphasis on science.[3]

What was the significance of the Nazi approach to education? The matter can be briefly summarized as follows:

1. For National Socialism, man was truly man in terms of the group or the state, and the true state was an expression of *the folk,* in their case the Germanic folk.
2. True education and true psychological and spiritual health required the acceptance of the group and of one's racial identity.
3. Scientific *objectivity* was seen as mythological. Every conclusion represents a point of view.

---

[1] Cited from Sigrid L. Shulz: *Germany Will Try It Again,* p. 181, Reynal and Hitchcock, N. Y., 1944, by Wallace Brett Donham: *Education for Responsible Living,* p. 79. Cambridge: Harvard University Press, 1944.

[2] See Gasset: *The Revolt of the Masses,* pp. 119-126.

[3] Erika Mann: *School for Barbarians.* New York: Modern Age Books, 1938. It is significant of its day that Thomas Mann, in his introduction to daughter Erika's book, commended it because "the author's sense of humor, her power of seeing 'the funny side,' the gentle mockery in which she clothes her scorn, go far to make our horror dissolve in mirth" (p. 5). Post-war studies have sometimes been designed more to make our sense dissolve by horror into an anti-German racialism which is equally incapable of understanding National Socialism.

4. Modern science was nonetheless basic to National Socialism and essential to its new order. *Science and scientific methodology* must be both furthered and dedicated to the service of the state.

Thus, a *scientific barbarianism*, an advanced, scientific and post-Christian order, was systematically created and furthered by every means possible, in particular military, educational, and scientific. What, in this scheme of things, constituted a liberal education, i.e., education for 'true' freedom as seen in terms of the cultural goals? The answer is readily apparent: it meant an education which was scientific, and which called for the radical identification of the individual with the group, an abandonment of freedom in its historic sense.

Soviet Russia, meanwhile, was developing its own concept of 'liberal' education. Its educational policy has been militantly materialistic in and through every change of policy, strictly Pavlovian, ready to call even Freudian theory "idealist."[4] Scientific socialism requires scientific materialism, and the enthronement of scientific *methodology* as the instrument of social liberation. Scientific *objectivity* was, as with the Nazis, more or less denied by the theory of the economic conditioning of man. Education is thus to be materialistic in the Marxist sense, scientific, and further, dedicated to the service of the dictatorship of the proletariat and to world revolution. To be usable in terms of this goal, a man must be educated. "In the Soviet Union people without education are not considered people. They are just like horsepower."[5] The "link between life and school" demanded by Khrushchev means "that education serve the aims of the Soviet state."[6] Accordingly, the only measure of freedom open to a

---

[4] See G. I. Kositsky, "The Subconscious, Dreams and Intuition: A Materialist View," in *The Soviet Review*, II, 4, April, 1961, p. 61.

[5] George Z. F. Bereday, "Class Tensions in Soviet Education," in Bereday and Joan Pennar: *The Politics of Soviet Education*, p. 85. New York: Praeger, 1960. See also Christopher Jencks, "Platonism, Soviet Style," in *The New Republic*, vol. 144, no. 17, April 24, 1961, p. 31f.

[6] Fred M. Hechinger: *The Big Red Schoolhouse*, p. 152. Garden City: Doubleday Dolphin Books, 1962. New revised edition.

man is in terms of utility to the state. The result has been a desperate dedication to study as the only readily accessible escape from a grim, grinding and sub-human status in Soviet society. Any means possible, including bribery, to gain the necessary grades for educational advancement towards status in Soviet society, have been readily used. Because Soviet Russia is a police state, there is no real security such as freedom makes possible. The logical end, of course, of every form of statism, however much an ostensibly welfare society dedicated to furthering security, is the destruction of every form of genuine security. In such a society, man's only hope is to become a member of the ruling class and to share in its precarious privileges, however briefly. The result, in education as in all society, is a grim competition for survival and the rule of jungle law. A fiercely competitive spirit such as leftists normally ascribe to "predatory capitalism" is the normal life of the police state. In all of this, education becomes radically divorced from learning and becomes an instrument of state and a means of social advancement. Academic freedom is an impossibility, because the laissez-faire presupposition inherent in it, i.e., the independence of education and learning from the state and its own integrity as a separate sphere of activity, is totally rejected.

In the United States, and throughout the Western world, there has been an equally strong emphasis on the group or the state, and on education in terms of utility to the state or group, as against the traditional faith in education in terms of utility to God. Man has ceased to regard himself as created in the image of God and insists on seeing himself materialistically as a social animal and a creature of the state. The forms of the faith differ, but the essence remains the same. The roots of this new concept of man are in part in Darwin and Freud, whose influence has led to anti-intellectualism in a variety of forms. With respect to the role of science, the influence of Auguste Comte (1798-1857) has been decisive. As Comte observed in *The Positive Philosophy*, "Ideas govern the world, or throw it into chaos; in other words, . . . all social mechanism rests upon Opinion." The opinions of our age derive substantially from Comte. In contrasting the "Theological, or fictitious" form of knowledge, and "the Metaphysical, or abstract," with "the Scientific, or positive," Comte insisted on the supremacy of the last, which is strictly a methodology, and believed that *true liberty is deliverance from meaning to method.* He failed to recognize that his methodology had implicit in it both a religion and a metaphysics, as does every methodology, but he did give to his successors, Dewey included, *an ostensibly scientific tool for dispensing with meaning and the disciplines of meaning.* We have already noted the allegiance given to scientific methodology by German National Socialism and by Soviet Russia. It should be noted how extensive is the allegiance to it in the West, and in the United States. Thus, for Sidney Hook, the meaning of liberalism in education is "the centrality of method."[7] Similarly, Arthur Bestor, a conservative and a classicist in education, insists on identifying liberal education, not in terms of meaning, but in terms of a training in method, "to weigh evidence, to reason logically," and so on.[8] It escapes Bestor that prior to weighing is a standard of weighing, and prior to logical thought a concept of logic. The Marxist insistence that an ideology predetermines a methodology has not been appreciated; it has been written off as characteristic surely of Marxists, but liberals have a god-like objectivity. If meaning enters in, they create rather than presuppose meaning!

The emphasis on scientific methodology, on method rather than meaning, has inevitable cultural repercussions. Methodology is *economical.* The shortest distance between two points is, so to speak, its constant goal. Moreover, methodology is *functional.* It calls for the elimination of what appears to be unessential and of duplications. Hence, a scientific sociology leads to centralization: family, township, county, state and even nation

[7] Sidney Hook: *Education for Modern Man,* pp. 112-138. New York: The Dial Press, 1946.

[8] Arthur Eugene Bestor: *The Restoration of Learning,* A Program for Redeeming the Unfulfilled Promise of American Education, p. 411. New York: Knopf, 1955.

are costly and uneconomical duplications. Hence, man's true home and family is the world state. Furthermore, individual and cultural differences among men are deemed to be unessential to the essential mathematical equality of men seen as similarly constructed biological entities. Hence equality, a purely mathematical term in essence, is applied to men, and, if it is challenged, it is again in the name of mathematics, i.e., in terms of inequality, as though man were a fragment of an equation.

American education, and virtually all education today, is committed to this methodological fallacy. It is committed to universal education on the "grounds both of democratic principles and of the need to make the most of our human resources as a people."[9] This national goal in education must be compromised in its scientific methodology by a very anti-scientific entity, the family. James Bryant Conant has, more honestly than others, stated the dilemma:

> Wherever the institution of the family is still a powerful force, as it is in this country, surely *inequality* of opportunity is automatically, and often unconsciously, a basic principle of the nation; the more favored parents endeavor to obtain even greater favors for their children. Therefore, when we Americans proclaim an adherence to the doctrine of equality of opportunity, we face the necessity for a perpetual compromise. Now it seems to me important to recognize both the inevitable conflict and the continuing nature of the compromise.[10]

It should be noted that Conant believes both in the inevitability of the conflict between that anti-democratic institution, the family, and the democratic state, and in the necessity "for a perpetual compromise." Others, facing the same problem, have been less past-bound and have rejected compromise, as in Nazi Germany and Soviet Russia. The increasing hostility to local control of education in the United States, and the demand for

[9] The Fund for the Advancement of Education: *A Report for 1954-1956*, p. 17. New York, 1957.
[10] James Bryant Conant: *Education in a Divided World*, The Function of the Public Schools in our Unique Society, p. 8. Cambridge: Harvard University Press, 1948.

federal aid, has in part behind it a distrust of the local power of anti-democratic and methodologically uneconomic and non-functional groups, such as the family, the church, local clubs, lodges, business and other interests.

The triumph of methodology has thus been *the enthronement of anti-meaning*. Thus, in a two and half hours conversation by six prominent Stanford faculty members on "the problem of the relationship of the humanities and the sciences in the modern American university," the discussion was in essence financial and administrative, in short, methodological. When it was observed that "It's hard to justify classics and folklore in terms of national defense," it was with reference to securing further federal funds for such studies under the National Defense Education Act.[11]

The differences thus in Nazi German, Soviet Russian, and Western scientifically oriented educational philosophies are, while very real, nonetheless differences in degree rather than in kind, all alike regarding *methodology* as basic to the education of the truly free man as each defines it. The West, however, has presented a mixed picture, in that older views of liberal education have co-existed with or extensively leavened the new methodological orientation. An able champion of this older concept, Robert Maynard Hutchins, has stated, "The aim of liberal education is wisdom."[12] This wisdom is appreciation of and participation in the great moving ideas of Western culture. But, basic to this classical concept of liberal education, is the radically syncretistic and anti-historical belief that Western culture from the Greeks to the present has been one culture. The West has been a battlefield of very diverse and hostile cultures. What constituted the free man in Greek and Roman cultures sharply differed from Christianity's conception of the free man. The various forms of Christianity, and the Enlightenment, also differed in their concept of the free man and of liberal educa-

[11] Stanford University Bulletin, *Stanford Today*, Series 14, no. 7, Spring, 1962.
[12] R. M. Hutchins: *The Conflict in Education in a Democratic Society*, p. 90. New York: Harper, 1953.

tion. Much of the continuing weakness of Western cultures has been due to retrogressive educational practice, to the continued use of the Greek concept of a liberal education, which had meaning in terms of Greek society, in cultures radically alien to Hellenism. In such cultures, Greek liberal education has successively and successfully acted as a destroying power. Progressive education was justified in its hostility to traditional education as essentially alien to the modern era, but, for answer, it turned at first from the classical Greek tradition to the mystical Greek tradition, from an emphasis on the Greek arts and sciences to an emphasis on Greek enthusiasm, the mystical and religious use of the dance, drama, physical education, and other activities.

Traditional liberal education has thus been consistently antiliberal because in essence alien to the current cultural concept of the free man. A few instances can be cited. With the rise of Rome, civilization generally found a new basis, one previously existing mainly among the Jews, *law*. The Jewish and Roman concepts of law differed, but both cultures rested on law and made law basic to social and personal emancipation. Every Western culture since, save Nazi Germany, and Fascist Italy, which sought a return to the corporate state, has been established on one or another of these concepts of law. In spite of this, law has had scant attention in liberal education. In terms of Greek society, literature and music have outweighed, in traditional thought, the significance of law. But a liberal education cannot exist, in view of the present nature of the West, unless it asks and answers satisfactorily the question, What is law?

The essentially religious nature of every culture must again be dealt with. What are the religious presuppositions of a culture? Are they valid, and are we aware of our pre-theoretical religious commitments?

Economics again is basic to life in a radically interdependent world, wherein man's relationships to his fellow men are heightened and at the same time his ability to specialize and individualize his existence increased. A liberal education which bypasses economics is destined to become a slave's education.

Again, science has given man not only the ability to create great technological tools but also, sometimes very unhappily, to become reshaped by his own creations. Thus, television is made by man, but it then proceeds to reshape man. Men bring highways into their isolated communities, and then are permanently influenced by those highways. Man cannot thus create blindly, as though he were a god capable of meeting every contingency, but must create under God, with wisdom, humility and an awareness of the double edge of his activities. Ecology is thus a necessary discipline to freedom and important to a liberal education.

From even this hasty survey, it is apparent that *traditional concepts of liberal education, because they are often pre-Roman, are certainly inadequate for our era and in essence hostile to every aspect of modern culture.* Their rout certainly constitutes one of the clearest gains from the modern philosophies of education, however inadequate their substitution of pragmatism or other forms of the methodological faith of positivism. Moreover, nothing can be more ill-advised than the attempt of some Christian thinkers to champion the classical concept; it is a nullification of the victories of Augustine, Anselm and Calvin. The attempt of secular thinkers, such as Walter Lippmann, to champion the old cause is again futile; it is a centuries-old corpse rapidly turning to dust.[13]

But man cannot live by bread alone, nor by methodology alone. As a result, the exaltation of the group, whether humanity, democracy, the proletariat or the folk, has steadily become religious, and the state school a religious institution. As pointed out in *Intellectual Schizophrenia,* the public school is the established church of today and a substitute institution for the medieval church and dedicated to the same monolithic conception of society. Some years ago, Dewey very candidly dis-

[13] See Walter Lippmann, "Education Destroying Western Culture," in *The Key Reporter,* the Phi Beta Kappa News Magazine, vol. VI, no. 2, Spring, 1941, pp. 1-4; see also *The American Scholar,* Spring, 1941. For a like opinion, see also Sir Richard Livingstone: *On Education;* New York: Macmillan, 1945.

cussed "Education as a Religion."[14] Commenting on this, John S. Brubacher has observed:

What now of making education the object of religion? In religion's long history many things have been declared to be god. At a time when race, nationality, and the state have each been raised up as objects of worship, one could certainly do worse than to make education a religion. The fundamental principle of faith of such a religion would be belief in the possibility of human achievement. Education would then become at once the symbol of humanity's as yet unrealized potentialities and the means of its salvation. Such a religion, however, would have the drawback of the political religion already mentioned. It would only be fragmentary; it would be worshipping the part for the whole. This might be a misdirection of religious endeavor if religion be taken, as it generally is, to denote inclusiveness of viewpoint. On the other hand, at least one outstanding advantage could be claimed for such a religion. It would not be in conflict with science! On the contrary, it would be based on science. Indeed without the invigorating vitality of science, such a religion would be in danger of lapsing into the dogmas of pedagogy and the rituals of educational administration. At all events in view of man's innumerable previous mistakes and discouraging backslidings, it takes courage, if nothing else, to hold to a faith in education as a religion.[15]

The issue lies deeper, however. If education is in any sense a preparation for life, then its concern is religious. If education is at all concerned with truth, it is again religious. If education is vocational, then it deals with calling, a basically religious concept. It would be absurd to reduce preparation for life, truth and calling to an exclusively religious meaning in any parochial sense, but it is obvious that these and other aspects of education are inescapably religious. As Whitehead observed, "The essence of education is that it be religious."[16]

[14] John Dewey, "Education as a Religion," *The New Republic,* August, 1922, p. 64f.
[15] John S. Brubacher: *Modern Philosophies of Education,* p. 321f. New York: McGraw-Hill, 1939.
[16] Alfred North Whitehead: *The Aims of Education,* p. 26. New York: Mentor Books, 1952.

The public or state schools have thus been inescapably religious. Their "common faith" has been described as "made up of elements provided by Rousseau, Jefferson, August Comte, and John Dewey. 'Civil religion' is an apt designation for this faith."[17] As one educator has observed, "America's faith in education has been called by a European visitor the 'national religion of America.' "[18]

Not only is education a new religion, but it rests on a specifically anti-Christian doctrine of man. "What is perhaps most important, the entire educational enterprise today is based not on the assumption of the wickedness of child nature, but on the child's natural human goodness and almost infinite improvability."[19] It has a full-fledged soteriology, "faith in the power of education."[20] As a result, delinquency in the child (or adult) is not an evidence of sin or any desire to do evil, but is rather an aspect of learning experience, since "all behavior is developmental."[21] As a result, maladjustment or delinquency is to be traced to such "causes" as poor health, intense worry, frustrated needs, over-loaded life schedules, rigid class structures, environment, instructor's disregard for the learning process, inadequate preparation for the learning experience, unreasonable pressures in the form of unreachable standards, unfair competition, scholarship tests (since "overemphasis on test results frequently leads to nervousness and maladjustment"), and so on.[22] From all this it follows that teachers and parents are to blame rather than the children, for according to Margaret Mead's studies, educators can infer "that the status of children is a function of the

[17] George Huntston Williams: "The Church, the Democratic State, and the Crisis in Religious Education," p. 41; Address at the Opening Session of the Harvard Divinity School, 1948-1949, delivered September 28, 1948; *Harvard Divinity School Bulletin*, 1948-1949.

[18] Ward G. Reeder: *A First Course in Education*, p. 8. New York: Macmillan, 1950. Third edition.

[19] Kenneth H. Hansen: *Public Education in American Society*, p. 9. Englewood Cliffs, N. J.: Prentice-Hall, 1956.

[20] *Ibid.*, p. 71.

[21] *Ibid.*, p. 105.

[22] C. B. Mendenhall and K. J. Arisman: *Secondary Education, Guidance and Curriculum-Method*, pp. 204-206. New York: William Sloane, 1951.

environment and that youth respond accurately to the cultural conditions about them and become products of those conditions."[23]

*It is apparent that any religion which frees man from the burden of original sin also frees him from the "burden" of responsibility. Responsible man gives way to man the pawn of environment and heredity.* Here the old conflict between pagan philosophers and Christian thinkers, culminating in Augustine's writings, is reproduced. When man is freed from God and His eternal decree, man does not thereby eliminate the problem of evil. *By denying his culpability, man denies his responsibility and therewith his manhood.* As a consequence, the pagan philosophers ended by destroying the dignity of man which they sought to establish, whereas Augustine, with his insistence on predestination and original sin, restored responsibility, order and manhood. To assert the basic neutrality of man does not serve to avert this dilemma.[24] Neutral man is bland and blank man, whose direction of development is again a social product.

But whenever and wherever the doctrine of total depravity (with its analogue, total responsibility) is eroded, or absent, then responsibility, which is essential to social order, devolves upon the state. Hellenic culture was thus thoroughly statist, and the religious entity was the *polis,* the city-state. Aristotle believed in "the adaptation of education to the form of government,"[25] because "the citizen should be moulded to suit the form of government under which he lives." Education should be public or statist, not private, because education must be "the business of the state." We must not "suppose that any one of the citizens belong to himself, for they all belong to the state, and are each of them a part of the state, and the care of each part is inseparable from the care of the whole."[26]

Since responsibility is in this faith a state affair, man is not

[23] *Ibid.,* p. 134.
[24] For such an assertion, see the Report of the Harvard Committee: *General Education in a Free Society,* p. 169. Cambridge: Harvard University Press, 1945.
[25] Aristotle: *Politics Bk. V,* Chapt. 9.
[26] *Ibid.,* Bk. VIII, Chapt. 1.

man apart from the state or the group. For Aristotle, as we have seen, the care of the citizen was inseparable from the care of the state. This is again an article of faith in the new civil religion. Thus, Melby and Benne assert, "We tend to associate freedom with lack of social responsibility. In reality, true freedom has a social origin. A person who is alone is not free. Man's freedom has been developed through his interaction with other personalities."[27] According to Kelley and Rasey, "Man, then, is a social creature, or he is nothing."[28] Man is free thus only through the group. The biblical doctrine of Adam, who first had to know himself and develop his sense of vocation in radical isolation is of course denied. The theocentric constitution of man, created in God's image, and his need for privacy in order to grow in terms of God rather than man, is denied by the civil religion, with its emphasis on "the social constitution of the human personality."[29] It speaks instead of the 'fact' that "everyone needs to belong."[30] Everyone needs to belong, and the state is man's true society, and the world commonwealth his "sacred city."[31] Much earlier, Nietzsche, in his attack on statist education, declared that the interest of the state in education is to ensure that the "masses" follow "the guiding star of the State!"[32] In such thinking, freedom means freedom for the state, and true education is in terms of citizenship and service to the sovereign state.[33]

[27] Ernest O. Melby and Kenneth Benne, "The Needed New Conception of Educational Control," in E. O. Melby, ed., *Mobilizing Educational Resources,* p. 22f.

[28] Earl C. Kelley and Marie I. Rasey: *Education and the Nature of Man,* p. 30. New York: Harper, 1952. Cited by Franz E. Winkler: *Man: The Bridge Between Two Worlds,* p. 196. New York: Harper, 1960.

[29] V. T. Thayer: *American Education Under Fire,* p. 9. New York: Harper, 1944.

[30] Henry J. Otto: *Principles of Elementary Education,* p. 318. New York: Rinehart, 1952.

[31] Maxwell Garnett: *The World We Mean To Make,* And the Part of Education in Making It, p. 57. London: Faber and Faber, 1943.

[32] F. W. Nietzsche: *On the Future of our Educational Institutions,* p. 89. Edinburgh: Foulis, 1909.

[33] See James Bryant Conant: *The Child, the Parent, and the State,* Cambridge: Harvard University Press, 1959; and Hyman George Richover: *Education and Freedom,* New York: Dutton, 1959.

Since in civil religion the state is god, and there is no right beyond the state (or the state's concept of its goal and the goal for humanity), it follows that right is what the state requires, and the normal or healthy man that which the society requires man to be. Bryson, from 1935 to 1953 professor of education at Columbia University, has thus stated it:

One of the great contributions to our thinking about this was Ruth Benedict's famous book, *Patterns of Culture* (a book, happily, that was read by millions in paperback editions). Mrs. Benedict made it clear that most of us are normal and that the normal person finds it easy to live by the rules and expectations of his tribe, whatever they may be. The striking differences, which the anthropologist finds among the various peoples of the earth, modern or ancient, primitive or developed, are not caused by differences in race or by any other physical difference. They are all "normal" patterns and had he chanced to be born in a society in which they were accepted, any normal person would have learned happily to adjust to them.

By molding and forming the varied and adaptable natures of most of the young people in any society, education aims to make "normal" persons of them.[34]

According to Benjamin, "the end products in education should be human beings who have been substantially changed by their years of schooling."[35] This substantial change is being wrought, with the result that mass man, dedicated to radical conformity, is the normal product of statist education. Thus, Dirk Jellema, in reporting on the composite attitudes of college students, reported these questions and answers:

Q. *What is the purpose of education?*
A. To enable the student to adjust to the group and thus gain emotional security.
Q. *But to what group should the student be trained to adjust?*
A. To the dominant group in this country.

[34] Lyman Bryson: *An Outline of Man's Knowledge,* p. 374. Garden City: Doubleday, 1960.
[35] Harold Benjamin, "The Problems of Education" in Bryson, ed., *op. cit.,* p. 383.

Q. *And what does it want?*
A. A high standard of living.
Q. *Is this good?*
A. Obviously, since the group wants it.
Q. *Is Communism good?*
A. Not in this country, since we don't think it is. It is good for the Russians, since they believe in it.
Q. *Is science true?*
A. Yes, since it raises the standard of living, which the group believes in.[36]

It is apparent that Mortimer Smith's observation on education in California, "that the primary task of the school is not education but social conditioning,"[37] has application far beyond the borders of that state.

Education is thus seen as "a function of the state."[38] Since it is a state function, it must steadily be removed from local control. This is being steadily done, so that today "some 40 Federal agencies" are "spending about $2,000,000,000 a year on programs covering nearly the entire spectrum of our schools and colleges."[39] To be opposed to federal aid to education, is, in this line of reasoning, to be opposed to education, which can only be education if its character as a function of the state is furthered. Thus, Secretary of Welfare Abraham Ribicoff could reprimand a thousand college presidents and deans meeting in Washington for their failure to *crusade* for (rather than merely support) federal aid: "I don't think you really care about education, or are going to do anything about it."[40] More than bad taste was

[36] Dirk Jellema, "Christianity and the 'New Faiths'," in *Christianity Today*, June 20, 1960, Vol. IV, no. 19, p. 13.

[37] Mortimer Smith, "How to Teach the California Child," in *The Atlantic*, September, 1958. Vol. 202, no. 3, p. 33. See also Mortimer Smith: *The Diminished Mind*, A Study of Planned Mediocrity in our Public Schools; Chicago: Regnery, 1954.

[38] W. W. Eshelman, N.E.A. president, "The Road Ahead," in N.E.A.: *Addresses and Proceedings*, 98th annual meeting, June 26-July 1, 1960, p. 13. Washington: N.E.A., 1960.

[39] "Washington, D. C., A Department of Education?," in *Christian Heritage*, Vol. 23, no. 4, April, 1962, p. 14.

[40] San Jose, California, *Mercury*, Friday, October 6, 1961, p. 6.

involved in this outburst, which revealed clearly that to Ribicoff education to be education requires the entrance of federal power. But, since the holy city of man is humanity, it is not enough to bring education under the authority of the national state: it must be subordinated to the United Nations. Accordingly, a United Nations' resolution, called a Draft Convention Against Discrimination in Education, has been framed to control *all* education, 'public,' private and parochial. Only schools fulfilling the qualifications laid down by UNESCO are to be permitted. If approved, every school in every subscribing country will be under the far-reaching control of an international body and will exist only on its permission.[41]

There are those who increasingly call for the prohibition of all non-statist education,[42] but, even more significant is the curious reasoning of some who insist on the constitutionality of "the right to establish and to attend private, church-run schools." Thus, the New Republic, in an editorial, went on to declare,

But we misunderstand the scheme if we think of the state as neutral. It is neutral in that it must prefer none of our many religions and cultural strains. But it is itself committed to exerting a secular, unifying, equalitarian force. While required impartially to accept the presence in society of sectarian influences, the state is nevertheless a party in the contest. To accept the principle of general support of public and private schools equally out of public funds is to abandon the mission of the state, since it removes the single most effective inducement available to the state to draw people to its system of schools and away from centrifugal systems. To this extent,

[41] See I. E. Howard, "Will the UN Control the Little Red Schoolhouse?" in *Christian Economics*, vol. XIV, no. 2, January 23, 1962, p. 4. See also, with reference to the Pennsylvania and Ohio actions against Amish fathers, Howard's "Our Children Belong to God!" in *Christian Economics*, vol. XII, no. 12, June 14, 1960, p. 4. See also the editorial, "Is UNESCO's Design Subversive?" in *Christian Home and School*, February, 1962.

[42] See Rushdoony: *Intellectual Schizophrenia*, pp. 76, 90; see also Russell Kirk, "Enemies of the Public Schools," in *National Review*, vol. XI, no. 2, July 15, 1961, p. 18; and Kirk, "Intolerance Among the Educationists," *National Review*, vol. XIV, no. 20, November 19, 1960, p. 306. See Staff Study for the Association for Christian Schools: *Schools Weighed in the Balances*, pp. 8-26. Houston: St. Thomas Press, 1962.

it is the mission of the state to discourage parochial schools, just as it is the mission of the Catholic Church, for example, to discourage Catholic attendance in public schools.[43]

The editorial spoke of "the mission of the state" and its lack of neutrality, but it failed to see that this mission is a religious mission, and it is a lack of religious neutrality that characterizes this civil religion.[44]

Early in the history of the United States, the courts had no doubt that education was a function of the parents and no more a function of the state than is the begetting of children. Education was seen as an aspect of child-rearing.[45] With the birth and development of state schools, however, the courts steadily invaded the area of parental authority, and the school came to be seen, not as an aspect of family government, but of civil government. Numerous decisions established that "Public education is not merely a function of government; it is of government. Power to maintain a system of public schools is an attribute of government in much the same sense as is the police power or the power to administer justice or to maintain military forces or to tax."[46] The state thus assumed an important aspect of parental authority. It is supposed by many that the ground of this assumption is the welfare of the child; the courts, on the contrary,

[43] *The New Republic*, "Parochial and Public," vol. 144, no. 12, March 20, 1961, p. 4.

[44] Strangely, Thomas J. O'Toole, responding to this editorial in "School Aid— A Catholic View," *The New Republic*, vol. 144, no. 15, April 10, 1961, pp. 13-15, failed to call attention to this civil religion espoused by *The New Republic*, although calling attention to the absurdity of speaking of "an impartial party to a contest," and adding, "I fear to know the writer's definition of the term 'the state'."

[45] See Neil G. McCluskey, S.J.: *Catholic Viewpoint on Education*, p. 126f., for citations from several early decisions. Garden City: Hanover House, 1959.

[46] Newton Edwards: *The Courts and the Public Schools*, The Legal Basis of School Organization and Administration, p. 23. Revised edition. Chicago: University of Chicago Press, 1961. For additional data on the legal aspects, see Alvin W. Johnson: *The Legal Status of Church-State Relationships in the United States*, with Special Reference to the Public Schools. Minneapolis: University of Minnesota Press, 1934. For a brief survey of recent legal decisions, see NCWC Legal-Department Study, "The Constitution and Parochial Schools," *The Catholic Digest*, vol. 26, no. 7, May, 1962, pp. 16-20. See for an interpretation of the historical and legal meaning of the first amendment, Henry P. Van Dusen: *God in Education*, pp. 99ff; New York: Scribner's, 1951.

have made clear that it is in terms of *the welfare of the state.* "The primary function of the public school, in legal theory at least, is not to confer benefits upon the individual as such, the school exists as a state institution because the very existence of civil society demands it."[47] Of course, civil society existed securely in the United States and elsewhere before state schools were established; its "very existence . . . demands it" only when the state becomes the civil religion, the father of its people, and the ground of their true existence. In recent years, the courts have done much to erode and deny the validity of absolutes. The late Chief Justice Vinson declared, "Nothing is more certain in modern society than the principle that there are no absolutes." One certainty which has not been eroded, but rather much strengthened and developed, is the police power of the state.

Statist education increasingly assumes that (1) the child is the child of the state or the property of the state, which can therefore interfere extensively with parental authority. (2) The state "priesthood" of educators are best able to rear the child and prepare him for life, viewed as statist life. (3) Statist education is alone "objective" and hence true, the state having the impartiality and transcendence of a god. Statist education is thus entrance into the true catholicity of the civil religion of the modern state. It is the religious ideal of the French Revolution realized.

In terms of this, it is not surprising that the private life of the child, and his family relationships, even when congenial, become increasingly a province of statist educators, and diaries, parental interviews, and very personal questionnaires become tools of the educator.[48] It is to be expected then, in view of this social orientation, that an educator should declare, "An edu-

[47] Edwards, p. 24.

[48] See, for example, Hilda Taoba: *Studies in Intergroup Relations, With Perspective on Human Relations,* A Study of Peer Group Dynamics in an Eighth Grade; Washington: American Council on Education, 1955; and Hilda Taoba, Elizabeth Hall Brady, John T. Robinson and William E. Vickery: *Studies in Intergroup Relations, Diagnosing Human Relations Needs*; Washington: American Council on Education, 1951.

cated man is one who is well adjusted and helpful in his community."[49] In terms of this, "basic education" is criticized as not being *basic,* i.e., aware that the fundamental fact of our time is *democracy* and not the creation of an intellectual elite.[50]

In some respects, the advance has been very real. The older higher education was the education of an elite who sought college education as a mark of social status. High seriousness was not common among such students. Democracy in education, while in itself in the hands of its philosophers is hostile to middle class ideals, in the hands of teachers it has actually furthered the rise of middle class education and brought a new earnestness to colleges and universities and made possible their rapid development in the 20th century. In the hands of many dedicated teachers and administrators, the new movement in education has often been an extension of the middle class revolution.[51] It has, however, also been an anti-cultural movement hostile to excellence as anti-democratic. Witness thus the minority of college professors of English who "suggested that the reading of Shakespeare's plays had a harmful effect on the democratic education of youth" because "the Bard lived under a monarchy and was therefore the representative of a totalitarian mentality."[52]

Moreover, ostensibly democratic statist education has had, by virtue of its statism, *a radically anti-democratic bias. To assume the right and need of the state to provide for its citizens is to assume the basic incompetence of man.* Thus, Robinson, in questioning that basic education is truly basic, states, in the course of an able analysis, that, because "mass education is here to stay," to insist on "basic education" is to "cheapen scholarship by trying to make scholars of everyone." "Or has he (Arthur Bestor) discovered a new process for the manufacture of silk purses?"[53] What Robinson is not honest enough to add is

[49] Cited by John Keats: *Schools Without Scholars,* p. 89.

[50] Donald W. Robinson, "How Basic is Basic Education?" in *California Teachers Association Journal,* vol. 53, no. 7, October, 1957, pp. 30, 40, 41.

[51] Without intending to, Martin Mayer gives an excellent report of this fact in his survey, *The Schools;* New York: Harper, 1961.

[52] Thomas Molnar: *The Future of Education,* p. 38.

[53] Robinson, *op. cit.,* p. 41.

that the non-scholars are for him sow's ears. Similarly, George H. Henry holds that "the lower one-third" of pupils are a "non-verbal" type and hence cannot be taught to read.[54] The result is a "retreat from learning" in the name of this new education.[55] As a consequence, in many cities, schools have become custodial rather than educational institutions, subject to violence and mob control, and held behind locked doors. The purpose in retaining these children and young people, in some cases psychotics, delinquents and even prostitutes, is the idea that the social situation provided by the school, apart from all learning, is therapeutic. Thus, pupils can graduate from high school unable to read their diploma.[56] Yet it is assumed that somehow, in spite of all failures, the healing situation can be created so that salvation can be socially dispensed to the state's children.

This messianic faith in education is held in circles far beyond the state and its schools. Accordingly, every group in society seeks to load the curriculum with courses and data designed to create the law-abiding citizen and perfect man. As a result, in addition to basic education and the various forms of new education, the curriculum is under the impact of demands for education in temperance, driver's training, soil conservation, hygienic practices, narcotics education, pre-marital or sexual education, social adjustment, personal hygiene and etiquette, "personal problems," and so on. All or most of these may be good, but are they the province of the schools? Is education to become totally institutional? And do not many of these require primarily a good character more than good information in order to be achieved?

Messianic institutions are not new in history, and the West has seen a variety of them. The church early claimed prerogatives belonging to the Christ, only to be surpassed in these claims by the state. The university and school have also asserted claims, and art has been often militantly and obsessively messianic. The

---

[54] G. H. Henry, *op. cit.*

[55] See Joan Dunn: *Retreat from Learning*, Why Teachers Can't Teach—A Case History. New York: David McKay, 1955.

[56] For a well documented statement of this kind of situation in New York City, see George N. Allen: *Undercover Teacher*. Garden City: Doubleday, 1960.

school has served ably in limiting the effectiveness of the churches' claims, but only at the price of advancing often more extravagant ones.

And, like all monolithic and messianic institutions, it seeks increasingly to limit the freedom of man in the name of its own freedom. A state school system, like a state church system, is unable to please all men or meet all needs. The more catholic or democratic it strives to be, the more it must compromise the integrity of its own mission. Moreover, being unable to satisfy all, it must defend itself against enemies who are by compulsion within its ranks. Total systems lead to an *Index* and an *Inquisition* in order to maintain their strength as a total system. Their very totality hinders the freedom of inconspicuous trial and error, freedom to experiment with willing subjects, and the humility of competition. State establishment gives to particular schools or churches delusions of grandeur and a sense of historical necessity which makes them intolerant of rivals as well as of critics.

Thus, when Jerome Ellison wrote a popular article on college cheating, he was thereupon given notice by the university that his services were no longer wanted.[57] In Holland, Michigan, the Holland Christian High School was "disaccredited" by the North Central Association of Colleges and Secondary Schools for refusing to include cooking and shop training in its curriculum. This became the subject of editorials in various popular periodicals, such as *The Saturday Evening Post* and *Life*.[58] As a result, the NEA sought immediately to retaliate against publications daring to call attention to the Holland case. The National Association of Secondary School Principals recommended the ban of offending periodicals from high schools. In Chicago, how-

[57] Jerome Ellison, "American Disgrace: College Cheating," in *The Saturday Evening Post*, vol. 232, no. 28, January 9, 1960, pp. 13, 58f. For a report of the consequences, see Russell Kirk, "May Professors Profess Principles?" in the *Southwest Review*, vol. XLV, no. 4, Autumn, 1960.

[58] "Don't Put Hobbles on Schools that Really Teach," *The Saturday Evening Post*, vol. 230, no. 39, March 29, 1958, p. 10. "The Deeper Problem in Education," *Life*, vol. 44, no. 13, March 31, 1958, p. 32.

ever, the AFL-CIO American Federation of Teachers' executive council opposed the ban.[59] As Kandel has observed, "The more professionalized the administration of education has become, the greater has been the tendency among its practitioners to become complacent and to resent criticism from any source."[60] The rift also between administrator and teacher has grown, so that the NEA, because of its administrative orientation, is now called "a company union" used by administrators to bring teachers further under their control.[61] But, more important, educators have increasingly lost any goal other than more money and more federal aid; statism is a singularly static and uninspiring god. The result has been a growing stagnation in educational thinking; education has no real goal left. Hence, the inability now of such an important center as Columbia Teachers College to stimulate its students.[62] A mined-out vein yields no more ore.

It would be a very great injustice, however, to see the school's failure only; the school shares in the general cultural crisis. Moreover, the schools are by no means primarily at fault; their role, while very important, has not been primary. In their emphasis on man as a social product, to cite a single instance, they have merely shared in a common cultural opinion. Religious leaders, for example, who should provide leadership in another direction, have themselves echoed the dehumanization chorus. Thus, Arthur G. Coons, a United Presbyterian lay leader and president of Occidental College, has declared, "The self itself is

[59] See Russell Kirk, "The Educationist Book-Burners," in *National Review*, vol. V, no. 13, May 10, 1958, p. 453; and *The San Francisco Chronicle*, May 11, 1958, p. 14. For an instance of slander of a variety of critics, see the California Teachers Association "Memorandum" of May 4, 1961, to all members; this was subsequently repudiated when it received widespread publicity.

[60] Isaac Leon Kandel: *American Education in the Twentieth Century*, p. 7. Cambridge: Harvard University Press, 1957.

[61] See the editorial, "The Professional Teacher," *The New Republic*, vol. 145, no. 24, December 11, 1961, p. 3f.

[62] For a study of that school, see Miriam Borgenicht, "Teachers College: An Extinct Volcano?" in *Harper's*, vol. 223, no. 1334, July 1961, pp. 82-87. The author is anxious to see the current need for educational "powerhouses" met by more than "bland liberality that was good enough twenty and fifty years ago."

largely or considerably a social product." He cites approvingly "one writer" to the effect that "The fully developed individual is the consummation of a fully developed society."[63] Thus, for him society creates man, and not man society.

Again, Randolph Crump Muller of Yale Divinity School and the Episcopal ministry, has declared, "Education is what happens to a person in community."[64] "Men become persons within community."[65] Furthermore, "An individual isolated on a desert island would not become a person."[66] This is a radical denial of the biblical doctrine of Adam. Adam, created in the image of God rather than of society or the state, was at first in isolation from men and in relationship to God in order that he might know himself and his calling. If society or the state makes man, then man must know himself in terms of society and the state. He then cannot be a person apart from the group. But if God created man in His own image, then it is God alone who enables man truly to know himself. The society which is equally ultimate with man is his society with God, and the Kingdom of God. For Coons and Miller, man is a social creature primarily, and it is his relationship to the group that makes or breaks him.

But Coons and Miller are modernists. Is there a better report from other circles? The influence of Aristotle's social theory of man on the Church of Rome is well-known. What about Protestant fundamentalism? Billy Graham, in a book[67] designed to effect our "peace with God," begins his chapter on "The Christian and the Church" with the assertion, "Man is a social animal!"[68] Graham in this instance has made better contact with Aristotle than with God! The impotence of his Christ is apparent when he repeats the ancient heresy, "The only feet that

---

[63] A. G. Coons, "Why Are We Here?", Convocation Address, September 25, 1947, in *Occidental College Bulletin*, vol. XXV, no. 1, November, 1947, p. 14.

[64] R. C. Miller: *Christian Nurture and the Church*, p. 1. New York: Scribner's, 1961.

[65] *Ibid.*, p. 119.

[66] *Ibid.*, p. 120.

[67] Billy Graham: *Peace With God*, p. viii. New York: Permabooks, 1955.

[68] *Ibid.*, p. 188.

Christ has are your feet. The only hands that He has are your hands. The only tongue that He has is your tongue."[69] Christ is thus scarcely to be seen as Lord, and "man is a social animal." The logical conclusion, which Graham does not make and which educational thinkers have made, is that the social group is a kind of god, creative and redemptive.

And yet, in the face of the extensive religious, political and educational enthronement of the group (church, society, state, folk, proletariat), the independent school movement has grown steadily. It is, in fact, the one area in which statism in the United States is definitely losing ground. At present, sixteen percent of school children are not in state schools. The critical issue is being increasingly recognized: statist education is the socialization of the child. If the state can own and socialize our children, then it can most certainly own and socialize our property. We cannot legitimately surrender our children to the state and its schools and then claim the right to withhold our property. The major concession makes objection to the lesser absurd, and an instance of misplaced values.[70]

An able system of common schools provided universal education before state control existed. A treatise written in 1800 at the request of Thomas Jefferson gives a telling account, not of the mere literacy, but literate capability, of America:

Most young Americans . . can read, write and cipher. Not more than four in a thousand are unable to write legibly—even neatly; while in Spain, Portugal, Italy, only a sixth of the population can read; in Germany, even in France, not more than a third; in Poland, about two men in a hundred; and in Russia not one in two hundred.

England, Holland, the Protestant Cantons of Switzerland, more nearly approach the standard of the United States, because in those

[69] *Ibid.*, p. 200.

[70] See on this subject two recent pamphlets, T. Robert Ingram: *Schools: Government, or Public?*; Houston: St. Thomas Press; and Oscar B. Johannsen: *Private Schools for All*; Roselle Park, N. J.: Committee of One. See also Irving E. Howard, "Who is Responsible for Education?" in *Christian Economics*, vol. XIV, no. 10, May 15, 1962, p. 4.

countries the Bible is read; it is considered a duty to read it to the children; and in that form of religion the sermons and liturgies in the language of the people tend to increase and formulate ideas of responsibility. Controversy, also, has developed argumentation and has thus given room for the exercise of logic.

In America, a great number of people read the Bible, and all the people read a newspaper. The fathers read aloud to their children while breakfast is being prepared—a task which occupies the mothers for three-quarters of an hour every morning. And as the newspapers of the United States are filled with all sort of narratives—comments on matters political, physical, philosophic; information on agriculture, the arts, travel, navigation; and also extracts from all the best books in America and Europe—they disseminate an enormous amount of information, some of which is helpful to the young people, especially when they arrive at an age when the father resigns his place as reader in favor of the child who can best succeed him.

It is because of this kind of education that the Americans of the United States, without having more great men than other countries, have the great advantage of having a larger proportion of moderately well-informed men; although their education may seem less perfect, it is nevertheless better and more equally distributed. But that does not mean that the general education cannot be improved.[71]

The education provided then, in terms of the times, was both able and truly democratic in the best sense of that word, in that it assumed the capacity of every American child to understand and participate intelligently in the basically Christian republican culture of the day. Modern 'democratic' education is often radically contemptuous of most students, and it lowers standards, fights testing, and debases education in the name of its ostensible democracy but actual oligarchy. Local control of education is fought by this faith in oligarchical principles, and the possibility of free schools discounted in horror: people are not capable of maintaining and supporting their schools. The high calibre of political thought in that era reflected an audience capable of

[71] DuPont de Nemours: *National Education in the United States of America*, pp. 3-5. Newark, Delaware: University of Delaware Press, 1923.

understanding sustained argument. The *Federalist* papers were popular arguments for the Constitution a few years earlier; today, university students have been known to complain when compelled to read such "heavy" material.

Moreover, education then provided for its day not only literacy but a Christian republican framework of reference and a general concept of law which had marked social effects. From the early 19th century to mid-20th century, the average age of the criminal has dropped from 45 to 19. This reflects more, far more, than education. The general cultural restraint, the more disciplined family life, the more theological and authoritative ministry of the church, as well as the content of education, provided the individual with a structure and discipline which often took some time to erode, even if the person's character were alien to it. Today, the scientific barbarian has no structure or discipline to erode; hence, he is very early in trouble. And the fault cannot be limited to education, nor even primarily be laid there, however important the role of the schools. It is, basically, a failure of character. It was once assumed, as Garet Garrett pointed out, that "Government is the responsibility of a self-governing people." Today, the "democratic" assumption is "that people are the responsibility of government."[72] This assumption was operative as early as Horace Mann, many of whose contemporaries were radical statists.

But, with all of this, the successes of statist education must be clearly recognized. The scientific barbarian is still a genuinely scientific man. No better tribute to the schools exists than the vast technical competence of the average man. This is certainly due in part to the technological temper of the age, the popularity of such mechanical inventions as the automobile, radio and television, and to other factors, but the role of the school is nonetheless very real. It is absurd to believe that Russian or European schools surpass the United States in these respects, and such claims involve the use of doctored statistics. The contempo-

[72] G. Garrett: *Rise of Empire,* p. 7. Caldwell, Idaho: Caxton, p. 1961.

rary scientific ascendency of the United States is by no means un-
related to the calibre of the schools, and it would be wrong to
think otherwise. The "educational boondoggle" is a very real
and sickening fact, as are the existence of such college courses,
and in great numbers, as "Square Dance and Square Dancing,"
"Analysis of Problems of Dance Education," "Fly and Bait
Casting;" similar courses exist in some high schools. But, more
important, the serious courses are also taught and are studied by
vast numbers of youth, earnest and studious youth. The excellence of technical and vocational education is clear-cut and commendable. The failure has been elsewhere: a liberal education
has not been developed. And liberal education is inevitably
pluralistic. The difference between an orthodox Christian and
a humanist conception of the free man is very great, and is productive of a different philosophy of education. Moreover, progressivism, while justified in its challenge of the traditional and
long obsolete conception of liberal education, has further
clouded the issue by transferring freedom from man to society.
Society, not man, is seen as the free agency, a theory which in
effect denies the possibility of true freedom. In terms of this
faith, man has been increasingly depersonalized and society
deified. Dewey's "great society" produces very small men. The
process, however, has not been all loss. The issues have been
accordingly sharpened as never before, and therefore clarified.

And, for the present, most people, including most critics of
the state schools, are getting better schools than they deserve.
The state as yet does not hinder men from establishing and
maintaining schools to further their own faith and principles.
The future has never been shaped by majorities but rather by
dedicated minorities. And free men do not wait for the future;
they create it. The difficulties and problems in that venture are
to them not a hindrance but a challenge that must be met.
Those critics of the schools who wait for the state or society to
act work on the same premise of the primacy of the group. The
futility of their cause is thus foreordained. Free men do not look
to the state for the opportunities and results of freedom.

# 28. The Lowest Common Denominator

The Messianic Utopianism of early educators often took extravagant form, as claims were made that prisons, crime, sin, war, tyranny, and every form of evil and disharmony would disappear with the triumph of universal statist education. This same expectation, in more sophisticated form, is the premise of the more modern drive to attain the "Great Community." But, it should be noted, that in the early years the educators were far surpassed in their extravagance by the Unitarian clergy. Although other churches made their contributions to the movement, and the New England 'theocracy' absorbed the cause, as we have seen with reference to Sheldon, it was Unitarianism in particular which gave itself whole-heartedly to the cause of messianic education and statism. The influence of that church on 19th century America is too seldom appreciated. Unitarianism was in a sense the American establishment of its day, and its influence was so pervasive as to render institutional Unitarianism as at best peripheral. Other churches felt its influence, and the schools reflected its faith. The McGuffey Readers, in spite of their author's own background, reflected the non-theological and Unitarian common faith of their day and served ably to further it. Institutional Unitarianism under-rated itself because it had a marginal doctrine of the church; it sought "establishment," in a very real sense, in and through the schools, and the schools became the embodiment and establishment of Unitarian faith. The church thereafter became progressively irrelevant to the American scene as the schools became steadily the working embodiment of the Unitarian faith in salvation by statist education. The relationship of Unitarianism, statism, and statist education in the United States is an important if neglected area of 19th century history.

There was resistance from various sectors, however, and notably from the orthodox Calvinists of the day, who viewed with suspicion not only the Unitarians but the developments of New England's ostensible orthodoxy. For them, New England Puritanism and Congregationalism, however much professing adherence to Calvinism, had departed from it at least since Jonathan Edwards' day. Edwards' neo-Platonism had extensively colored subsequent New England "orthodoxy." The departures of such men as Hopkins and Bellamy from the faith have often been noted, although their greatness has been too little appreciated. Unitarianism, however, was the consistent development of their anthropocentric premises and carried the day.

Against all these theological tendencies, and against statist education, Archibald Alexander Hodge, Princeton theologian and orthodox Calvinist, made a forthright stand. He saw the statist claim, that "self-preservation" of the State required statist education, as a denial of the competence of other agencies as well as of their right to self-preservation. Moreover, "The tendency of the entire system . . . is to centralization." It enthroned also the radically fallacious idea that secular and atheist opinions and approaches to education were "neutral" while religious approaches were partial and prejudiced. Hodge insisted that the statist approach was as fully committed and sectarian as any other, that it was indeed an establishment of an immediate minimum theism but in actual fact an ultimate atheism.

I am as sure as I am of Christ's reign that a comprehensive and centralized system of national education, separated from religion, as is now commonly proposed, will prove the most appalling enginery for the propagation of anti-Christian and atheistic unbelief, and of anti-social nihilistic ethics, individual, social and political, which this sin-rent world has ever seen.[1]

But, more than that, Hodge saw as basic to the whole concept of statist education and its hostility to religion a dangerous principle in operation, that of *the supremacy of the lowest common denominator:*

The tendency is to hold that this system must be altogether secular. The atheistic doctrine is gaining currency, even among professed Christians and even among some bewildered Christian ministers, that an education provided by the common government should be entirely emptied of all religious character. The Protestants object to the government schools being used for the purpose of inculcating the doctrines of the Catholic Church, and Romanists object to the use of the Protestant version of the Bible and to the inculcation of the peculiar doctrines of the Protestant churches. The Jews protest against the schools being used to inculcate Christianity in any form, and the atheists and agnostics protest against any teaching that implies the existence and moral government of God. It is capable of exact demonstration that if every party in the State has the right of excluding from the public schools whatever he does not believe to be true, then he that believes most must give way to him that believes least, and then he that believes least must give way to him that believes absolutely nothing, no matter in how small a minority the atheists or the agnostics may be. It is self-evident that on this scheme, if it is consistently and persistently carried out in all parts of the country, the United States system of national popular education will be the most efficient and wide instrument for the propagation of Atheism which the world has ever seen.[2]

[1] A. A. Hodge: *Popular Lectures on Theological Themes*, p. 283f. Philadelphia: Presbyterian Board of Publications, 1887. These lectures were prepared and delivered to women's groups, first in Princeton then in Philadelphia, several years prior to their publication.

[2] *Ibid.*, p. 280f.

This statement, widely reprinted in recent years, was of course prophetic. The principle of the lowest common denominator steadily excluded not only religious teaching, and, of late, even Christmas carols in some schools, but also subjects regarded as anti-democratic or too scholastic. It has led to a steady lowering of reading requirements and the debasing of the curriculum in the name of democracy.[3]

But the effect of this principle of the lowest common denominator has been more than educational. As a political philosophy, it has been "nothing less than a new religion" whose "character is essentially totalist."[4]

In terms of this faith, which is the lode-star and guiding principle of contemporary foreign and domestic policies, *integration downward* becomes a religious necessity. Christian missions reach out to the lowest, in the faith that the highest, God, can by His sovereign grace exalt them. Contemporary foreign aid is based on a leveling principle whereby the most advanced nation has a guilty obligation to the most backward and must impoverish itself for absolution from this sin. The property owner must be taxed heavily to provide for the indigent, who has a privileged status with the state as the lowest common denominator. Indeed, the welfare recipient is today the central object of care and subsidy, which, instead of removing the evils it seeks to cure, furthers them.

Basic to the principle of the lowest common denominator is a hatred of excellence and of any law other than that which emanates from the lowest. The state, in terms of this radical democracy, ceases to be the instrument of justice and social order and becomes a class weapon, and the law of the state becomes the law of the pack.

The Constitution embodied a different conception of the state. First of all, it set forth, not the principles of majority or

[3] See, with reference to second grade readers, Francis Russell, "New Friends and Second Readers," in *National Review*, vol. VI, no. 18, January 31, 1959, p. 500f.

[4] Lord Percy of Newcastle: *The Heresy of Democracy*, A Study in the History of Government, p. 16. Chicago: Regnery, 1955.

minority rule, but the supremacy of law, law understood in terms of a higher law or absolute law background.[5] Second, the Constitution and the Bill of Rights saw liberty as "the by-product of limitations on governmental power, not the objective of its existence. . . . Our rights, as the framers conceived them, were essentially certain specified immunities. They were not claims on, but assurances against, the government."[6] Third, it followed from this that "government is the responsibility of a self-governing people," not as now "that people are the responsibilities of government."[7] The principle of the lowest common denominator is reducing a self-governing and free people to a governed and slave people.

The enthronement of this principle has coincided with imperialism, whether in Rome, Russia or the United States. We have seen Col. Parker's enthusiastic faith: "I await the regeneration of the world from the teaching of the common schools of America." The dying Emma Marwedel declared, "I believe in the power of the kindergarten to reform the world." The principles of the kindergarten are today enthroned in Congress and in the White House. The "children" of the state, its citizens, and the "children" of the world, are to be saved by this messianic state. The enthronement of the lowest goes hand in hand with the assumption that the messianic state can assume the responsibilities of all men and nations, keep world peace, save world civilization, and usher in paradise regained.

But, inevitably, the lowest common denominator is chaos. In ancient fertility cults, which, as genetic faiths, enthroned the lowest as the primary, a ritual return to chaos was held to be the means to social regeneration. The fixed, lawful and rational were late and higher developments and hence less basic and also seen as essentially sterile. Closeness to the primitive was

[5] Edward S. Corwin: *The "Higher Law" Background of American Constitutional Law.* Ithaca: Great Seal Books, 1955.

[6] Mark de Wolfe Howe, "The Constitutional Question," in W. L. Miller, etc.: *Religion and the Free Society*, p. 58f. New York: The Fund for the Republic, 1958.

[7] Garet Garrett: *Rise of Empire*, p. 7. Caldwell, Idaho: Caxton, 1961.

closeness to creativity and vitality, and chaos itself was the principle of regeneration. Saturnalia, the primitive festival, orgies, rituals involving confusion in the forms of incest, bestiality or perversion, were necessary rites and means of social regeneration. "In fact, the festival is presented as a re-enactment of the first days of the universe, the *Urzeit*, the eminently creative era."[8] The rebirth of nature and the rebirth of society both require the return to chaos as the principle of life. "The festival is thus celebrated in the context of the myth and assumes the function of regenerating the real world."[9]

Beginning with the Romantic movement, art, poetry, music and novel have vigorously pursued the principle of primitivism, the genetic faith in the lowest common denominator. This genetic faith has had its scientific versions in Darwin and post-Darwinian thinking, and in Freud. Politically, the faith in rootless revolutions, revolutions dedicated to radical destruction and a break with the past, is another instance of the myth of the creative power of chaos. Lenin defined both the class struggle and true morality as in essence the destruction of existing order.[10] In Western democracies, this same faith in revolution has been held with variations; revolution is believed in, as far as other countries, backward ones in particular, are concerned. Somehow, the destruction of existing if faulty order will thereupon enable the society to transcend itself by virtue of the mystical baptism in chaos. The genetic fallacy, as an aspect of the scientific mythology of the age, has permeated an education already dedicated to the principle of the lowest common denominator. Evolution sees primitive world forces as determinative and creative. Psychoanalysis sees the libido, or whatever else it holds to be the primal power, as the basic life force. The varied world of art seeks creativity in primitive chaos, or in primal forms and impulses. Foreign policies are

---

[8] Roger Caillois: *Man and the Sacred*, p. 103. Glencoe, Illinois: The Free Press, 1959.

[9] *Ibid.*, p. 108.

[10] See David Shub: *Lenin*. New York: Mentor, 1948.

geared to the lowest common denominators, or to hopes in revolutionary chaos. The total result is, to use Cornelius Van Til's apt expression, a vast "integration into the void."

A realistic appraisal of our time requires recognition of this grim fact: chaos is the goal of contemporary human endeavor. Chaos is thus not a threat but an objective.[11]

For those who believe that liberty is the concomitant of law and of order, the answer rests clearly upon man to accept, instead of the genetic fallacy, the sovereignty of the ontological trinity, God the sovereign creator and redeemer. God, the self-determined one, has created man in His image, and man's self-government and responsibility under God in Christ is a restoration of liberty and order to a fallen world. Men who truly know themselves to be bought with a price and adopted into the glorious liberty of the sons of God will not become the slaves of men and of the state. James Oppenheim, in his poem, "The Slave," expressed it thus:

> They can only set free men free . . .
> And there is no need of that:
> Free men set themselves free.

[11] See Samuel J. Warner: *The Urge to Mass Destruction*. New York: Greene and Stratton, 1957.

# APPENDIX

# A Selective Commentary on Principal Individuals Mentioned or Cited in the Narrative Text

(With Biographical Data, and Major Relevant Works)

by DAVID L. HOGGAN

ARROWOOD, CHARLES FLINN

Presbyterian scholar; his main fields are American education, 1750-1850, and medieval and modern British ecclesiastical history (he has translated and edited many important British Latin texts, i.e., *De Jure Regni apud Scotus,* etc.); he collaborated on two important books on American education with Frederick Eby, cited below under Eby; he is also editor and commentator on a book dealing with Jefferson's educational theories and policies.

He was born on November 9, 1887, in Cabarrus County, North Carolina; he received his AB from Davidson College, 1909, BD from Union Theological Seminary (Virginia), 1915, AM, Rice Institute, 1921, and PhD, University of Chicago, 1924; he was on the faculty of Rice Institute, later Rice University, from 1926 to 1955; he was visiting professor at Teachers College, Columbia University; University of Illinois; University of Colorado; and Duke University.

*Thomas Jefferson and Education in a Republic,* N.Y.: McGraw-Hill, 1930, 184pp.

## BAGLEY, WILLIAM CHANDLER

He was born on March 15, 1874, in Detroit, Michigan; he received his BS from Michigan State College, 1895, MS, University of Wisconsin, 1898, PhD, Cornell University, 1900; his initial teaching experience was in public secondary and normal schools, 1895-7, 1901-8; he was professor of education at the University of Illinois, 1908-17, and at Teachers College, Columbia University, 1917-40; he was president of the National Society for the Study of Education, 1911-12, and he wrote some history texts, including one with Charles Austin Beard in 1918; he received a Commonwealth Fund grant in 1924 to lead a study of California public education; he died in 1946.

*The Educative Process,* N.Y.: Macmillan, 1905, 358pp. (2nd ed., 1906, 3rd ed., 1908, 4th ed., 1912).
*Educational Values,* N.Y.: Macmillan, 1911, 267pp.
*School Discipline,* N.Y.: Macmillan, 1914, 259pp.
*An Introduction to Teaching* (with John Keith), N.Y.: Macmillan, 1924, 400pp.
*The California Curriculum Study* (with George Kyte), Berkeley, Calif.: University of California Press, 1926, 430pp.
*Education, Crime, and Social Progress,* N.Y.: Macmillan, 1931, 150pp.
*Standard Practices in Teaching: a Summary of the Standards Generally Recognized as Governing Good Practice in Typical Teaching Procedures* (with Marion Macdonald), N.Y.: Macmillan, 1932, 189pp.
*Education and Emergent Man,* N.Y.: Nelson, 1934, 238pp.
*The Teacher of the Social Studies* (with Thomas Alexander), N.Y.: Scribner's, 1937, 328pp.
*A Century of the Universal School,* N.Y.: Macmillan, 1937, 85pp.

## BARNARD, HENRY

Episcopalian 19th century American champion of public education, and, together with Carter and Mann, one of the three most important founders of the present American system of public education; his private means enabled him to travel extensively in Europe on behalf of comparative educational studies; he was a disciple of the Enlightenment of the 18th Century in general, with its dominant secular impulses, and of the educational theories of Pestalozzi in particular; he saw the future of all American education in uniform and standard public instruction.

He was born on January 24, 1811, in Hartford, Connecticut; he attended the Monson Academy in Massachusetts prior to entering Yale in 1826, where he was active in the Linonia Literary Society; he received his BA from Yale in 1830 and taught school in Wellsboro, Pennsylvania, prior to entering the Yale Law School, 1833-4; after admission to the bar and several years of travel in Europe, he was elected to the Connecticut Legislature in 1837; he became the first secretary to the Board of Commissioners of Common Schools in Conn., 1838-1842, and from 1843-9 he was state superintendent of schools in Rhode Island; he was principal of the New Britain, Conn., Normal School, 1849-1854, and from 1855-81 he published his general encyclopedia of education, *The American Journal of Education,* in 31 volumes; from 1858-1860 he was chancellor of the University of Wisconsin and agent for the Wisconsin Normal School Regents; he was president of St. John's College, Maryland, 1866-7, and the first United States Commissioner of Education, 1867-1870; he died in Hartford in 1900.

*First* (Second, Third, Fourth) *Annual Report of the Board of Commissioners of Common Schools in Connecticut, Together with the First* (Second, Third, Fourth) *Annual Report of the Secretary of the Board,* Hartford: Case, Tiffany & Burham, 1839-1843.

*Report on the Condition and Improvement of the Public Schools of Rhode Island, for 1845* (1846, 1847), Providence: B. Cranston & Co., 1846-1848.

*Reports and Documents Relating to the Public Schools of Rhode Island, for 1848* (1849), Providence: B. Cranston & Co., 1849-1850.

*Normal Schools and other Institutions, Agencies and Means Designed for the Professional Education of Teachers,* 2 vol., Hartford: Case, Tiffany, 1851.

*Practical Illustrations of the Principles of School Architecture,* Hartford: Case, Tiffany, 1851, 175pp.

*National Education in Europe: being an Account of the Organiza-*

*tion, Administration, Instruction, and Statistics of Public Schools of Different Grades in the Principal States,* N.Y.: C. B. Norton, 1854, 890pp.

*Reformatory Education: Papers on Preventive, Correctional and Reformatory Institutions and Agencies in Different Countries,* Hartford: F. C. Brownell, 1857, 363pp.

*American Educational Biography,* Syracuse, N.Y.: C. W. Bardeen, 1859.

*Pestalozzi and Pestalozzianism,* 2 vol., N.Y.: F. C. Brownell, 1859.

*Science and Art,* N.Y.: E. Steiger, 1872, 807pp.

*American Educational Biography: Memoirs of Teachers, Educators, and Promoters and Benefactors of Education, Science and Literature,* Syracuse, N.Y.: C. W. Bardeen, 1874, 526pp.

*American Pedagogy: Education, the School, and the Teacher,* Hartford: Brown & Bross, 1876, 570pp.

*Analytical Index to Barnard's American Journal of Education* (31 vol., 1855-1881; *vide* also *Library of Education,* 52 vol.), Washington, D.C.: Government Printing Office, 1892, 128pp.

BESTOR, ARTHUR EUGENE, JR.

He was born on September 20, 1908, in Chautauqua, New York; his father was president of the Chautauqua Institution (for his father's views on education, *vide* Arthur E. Bestor, Sr., *Organized Popular Education,* Washington, D.C.: Government Printing Office, 1917) ; A. E. Bestor, Jr., received his PhB, Yale University, 1930, and PhD in history, Yale University, 1938; at Yale he instructed in literature (1930-1) and history (1934-6) ; he instructed in history at Teachers College, Columbia University, 1936-1942; he was assistant professor of humanities at Stanford from 1942-6, and lecturer in history at the University of Wisconsin, 1946-7, prior to receiving a permanent appointment in history at the University of Illinois in 1947, where he has been a full professor since 1951; he was a Newberry Fellow at Chicago in 1946, and a Guggenheim Fellow, 1953-4, 1961-2; he received the Albert J. Beveridge memorial award of the American Historical Association in 1946, and he instructed at Oxford on a Fulbright grant, 1956-7; his major field, in addition to American education, is socialist theory.

*Chautauqua Publications: an Historical and Bibliographical Guide,* Chautauqua, N.Y.: Chautauqua Press, 1934, 67pp.

*Backwoods Utopias: the Sectarian and Owenite Phases of Communitarian Socialism in America, 1663-1829,* Philadelphia: University of Pennsylvania Press, 1950, 288pp.

*Educational Wastelands: the Retreat from Learning in our Public Schools,* Urbana, Illinois: University of Illinois Press, 1953, 226pp.

*The Restoration of Learning: a Program for Redeeming the Unfulfilled Promise of American Education,* N.Y.: Knopf, 1955, 459pp.

*American Phalanxes: a Study of Fourierist Socialism in the United States,* 2 vol. ms., Madison, Wisconsin: University of Wisconsin microfilm, 1956.

BIDDLE, WILLIAM WISHART

He was born on June 19, 1900, in Chicago, Illinois; he received his BA from Pomona College, 1923, prior to study at the Union Theological Seminary in New York City, 1924-6; he received his PhD in social psychology from Columbia University, 1932; he was a research assistant at Columbia, 1927-1930, and an instructor of applied social science, Western Reserve University, 1930-3; after teaching education at Colgate, 1933-5, he was professor of education and head of the department at Wisconsin State Teachers College, Milwaukee, 1935-1944; he was senior health specialist, United States Department of Agriculture, 1944-7, and professor of social psychology, Earlham College, 1947-60; he has been employed as an administrator by the Board of National Missions, United Presbyterian Church, since 1960.

*Propaganda and Education,* N.Y.: Teachers College, Columbia University, 1932, 84pp.

*The Cultivation of Community Leaders: up from the Grass Roots,* N.Y.: Harper, 1953.

*Growth toward Freedom: a Challenge for Campus and Community,* N.Y.: Harper, 1957, 171pp.

BODE, BOYD HENRY

He was born on October 4, 1873, in Ridott, Illinois; he studied at Yankton College in South Dakota prior to attending Penn College, where he received his AB in 1896; he received his AM, University of Michigan, 1897, and PhD, Cornell University, 1900; he was instructor and assistant professor of philosophy at the University of Wisconsin, 1900-1909, and associate professor and professor of education, University of Illinois, 1909-1921; from 1921-1944 he was professor of education at Ohio State University; he did education work for the federal government after retirement, and he was visiting professor at the Institute of Education, Cairo, Egypt, 1944-5; he died at Gainesville, Florida, March 29, 1953.

*An Outline of Logic,* N.Y.: Henry Holt, 1910, 324pp. (2nd ed., 1914).

*Fundamentals of Education,* N.Y.: Macmillan, 1921, 245pp. (2nd ed., 1922).

*Modern Educational Theories,* N.Y.: Macmillan, 1927, 351pp.

*Conflicting Psychologies of Learning,* Boston: Heath, 1929, 305pp.

*Democracy as a Way of Life* (the Kappa Delta Pi Lecture Series), N.Y.: Macmillan, 1937, 114pp. (2nd ed., 1943).

*Progressive Education at the Crossroads,* N.Y.: Newson, 1938, 128pp.

*Educational Freedom and Democracy* (2nd Yearbook of the John Dewey Society), N.Y.: D. Appleton-Century, 1938 (with H. B. Alberty).

*How We Learn,* Boston: Heath, 1940, 308pp.

*Modern Education and Human Values* (Bode, ed.), Pittsburgh, Pa.: University of Pittsburgh Press, 1947.

BRAMELD, THEODORE BURGHARD HURT

He was born on January 20, 1904, in Neillsville, Wisconsin; he received his BA from Ripon College, 1926, and PhD, University of Chicago, 1931; his thesis was on *The Role of Acquiescence in Leninism,* and Soviet education and society has remained one of his major fields along with American educational theory; he was Field Secretary for Ripon College, 1926-28, and University of Chicago Fellow, 1928-31; he instructed philosophy at Long Island University, 1931-35, and Adelphi College, 1935-9; he taught philosophy at the University of Minnesota, 1939-47, where he first attained the rank of full professor in 1945; from 1947-1958 he was professor of education and philosophy at New York University, and since 1958 at Boston University; he has been a visiting professor at Columbia, Dartmouth, University of Wisconsin and University of Puerto Rico; he was chief American delegate to the International Education Conference in Australia in 1946.

*A Philosophical Approach to Communism,* Chicago: University of Chicago Press, 1933, 242pp.

*Worker's Education in the United States* (5th Yearbook, John Dewey Society), N.Y.: Harper, 1941.

*Design for America: an Educational Exploration of the Future of Democracy for Senior High Schools and Junior Colleges, et al,* New York: Hinds, Hayden & Eldridge, 1945.

*Minority Problems in the Public Schools: a Study of Administrative Policies and Practices in Seven School Systems,* N.Y.: Harper, 1946.

*Ends and Means in Education: a Midcentury Appraisal,* N.Y.: Harper, 1950.

*Patterns of Educational Philosophy: a Democratic Interpretation,* Yonkers-on-Hudson: World Book Co., 1950.

*The Battle for Free Schools,* Boston: Beacon Press, 1951, 79pp.

*Philosophies of Education in Cultural Perspective,* N.Y.: Dryden Press, 1955, 446pp.

*Toward a Reconstructed Philosophy of Education,* N.Y.: Dryden Press, 1956, 417pp.

*Cultural Foundations of Education: an Interdisciplinary Exploration,* N.Y.: Harper, 1957.

*The Remaking of a Culture: Life and Education in Puerto Rico,* N.Y.: Harper, 1959.

*Education for the Emerging Age: Newer Ends and Stronger Means,* N.Y.: Harper, 1961, 244pp.


BREDVOLD, LOUIS IGNATIUS

Specialist in 17th and 18th centuries of English literature and culture; an expert on the poetry of Dryden and the politics of John Wilkes; author of numerous monographs and articles dealing with special aspects of the English enlightenment; his importance in this context is his illuminating analysis of certain superficial 18th century ideas which have been of guiding importance to many American educators.

He was born on July 20, 1888, in Springfield, Minnesota; he received his AB from the University of Minnesota, 1909, and his AM there the following year; he was a University of Chicago Fellow, 1913-14, and a University of Illinois Fellow, 1920-1, where he received his PhD in 1921; he instructed English at Iowa State, 1914-16, and at the University of Illinois, 1916-17, 1919-20 (he served in the United States Army), 1917-1919; he taught English literature at the University of Michigan from 1921-1955; he was appointed full professor in 1930, and he was chairman of the department from 1936-1947.

*The Philosophy of Edmund Burke* (ed., with R. G. Ross), Ann Arbor: University of Michigan Press, 1960, 276pp.

*The Brave New World of the Enlightenment,* Ann Arbor: University of Michigan Press, 1961.

### BRUBACHER, JOHN SEILER

He was born October 18, 1898, in Easthampton, Massachusetts; he received his AB from Yale University in 1920, his LL.B. from Harvard, 1923, and his PhD from Columbia, 1928; he was in the United States Army, 1918-19, and he was an instructor in history at Dartmouth, 1924-5; after serving as an assistant professor of education at Columbia, 1927-8, he went to Yale in 1928 to teach history and the philosophy of education; he has been a full professor since 1946.

*The Judicial Power of the New York State Commissioner of Education,* N.Y.: Teachers College, Columbia, 1927, 173pp.

*Henry Barnard on Education,* N.Y.: McGraw-Hill, 1931, 298pp.

*Modern Philosophies of Education,* N.Y.: McGraw-Hill, 1939, 370pp. (2nd ed., 1950, 349pp.; 3rd ed., 1962, 373pp.).

*The Public Schools and Spiritual Values* (7th John Dewey Society Yearbook), N.Y.: Harper, 1944, 222pp.

*A History of the Problems of Education,* N.Y.: McGraw-Hill, 1947, 688pp.

### BRYSON, LYMAN LLOYD

He was born on July 12, 1888, in Valentine, Nebraska; he received his AB from the University of Michigan in 1910 and his AM there in 1915; he was employed on the editorial staffs of the Omaha *Daily Bee,* 1907-1911, Omaha *Daily News,* 1911-12, and Detroit *Evening News,* 1912-13; he was instructor and assistant professor of rhetoric and journalism, University of Michigan, 1913-17; from 1917-20, he was employed by the Red Cross in Washington, D.C. and Paris, France; from 1920-1934, he was employed as a public relations expert by the League of Red Cross Societies; during this period he was also an extension lecturer for the University of California, 1925-32; he was invited to Columbia as visiting professor of education, 1934-5, and he remained there on a permanent appointment, 1935-1955, except for his three years in the crucial post of chief, bureau of special operations, Office of War Information, 1942-5; he died in 1959.

*A State Plan for Adult Education* (California), N.Y.: American Association for Adult Education, 1934, 69pp.

*Which Way America? Communism—Fascism—Democracy,* N.Y.: Macmillan, 1939, 113pp.

*Adult Education,* N.Y.: American Book Co., 1936, 208pp.

*The New Prometheus,* N.Y.: Macmillan, 1941, 107pp.

*Science and Freedom,* N.Y.: Columbia U. Press, 1947, 191pp.

*The Next America: Prophecy and Faith,* N.Y.: Harpers, 1952, 248pp.

*An Outline of Man's Knowledge,* Garden City, N.Y.: Doubleday, 1960, 692pp.


BUCKLEY, WILLIAM F., JR.

He was born on November 24, 1925, in New York City; he studied at the University of Mexico in 1943 prior to serving in the United States Army, 1944-6; he entered Yale University and received his BA in 1950; he served as senior editor for *American Mercury* in 1952; he has been editor-in-chief of *National Review* and one of its principal contributors since 1955.

*God and Man at Yale: the Superstitions of Academic Freedom,* Chicago: Regnery, 1951, 240pp.

*McCarthy and his Enemies: the Record and its Meaning* (with L. Brent Bozell), Chicago: Regnery, 1954, 413pp.

*Up from Liberalism,* N.Y.: McDowell, Obolensky, 1959, 205pp.

*The Committee and its Critics: a Calm Review of the House Committee on Un-American Activities,* et al, N.Y.: Putnam, 1962, 352pp.

### BUTLER, NICHOLAS MURRAY

He was born on April 2, 1862, in Elizabeth, New Jersey; he received his AB from Columbia University in 1882, his AM there in 1883, and his PhD there in 1884; from 1884 to 1886 he engaged in post-graduate studies in education at Paris and Berlin; returning to the United States, he launched and directed the New York College for the Training of Teachers in 1886 and directed it until 1891, when he became dean of the faculty at Columbia, of which the teachers college was a part; from 1901 to 1945 he was president of Columbia; he was also president of the Carnegie Endowment for International Peace, 1925-45; he died in New York City on December 7, 1947.

*Education in the United States:* (Butler editor and contributor) *a Series of Monographs Prepared for the United States Exhibit at the Paris Exposition, 1900,* 2 vol., Albany, N.Y.: Lyon, 1900.

*True and False Democracy,* N.Y.: Macmillan, 1907, 111pp. (2nd ed., 1940).

*The International Mind: an Argument for the Judicial Settlement of International Disputes,* N.Y.: Scribner's, 1912, 121pp.

*A World in Ferment: Interpretations of the War for a New World,* N.Y.: Scribner's, 1917, 254pp.

*Is America Worth Saving?,* N.Y.: Scribner's, 1928, 398pp.

*The Faith of a Liberal: Essays and Addresses on Political Principles and Public Policies,* N.Y.: Scribner's, 1924, 369pp.

*Between Two Worlds: Interpretations of the Age in Which We Live,* N.Y.: Scribner's, 1934, 450pp.

*The Family of Nations, its Need and its Problems,* N.Y.: Scribner's, 1938, 400pp.

*Liberty, Equality, Fraternity: Essays and Addresses on the Problems of Today and Tomorrow,* N.Y.: Scribner's, 1942, 240pp.

### BUTTS, R. FREEMAN

He was born on May 14, 1910, in Springfield, Illinois; he received the following degrees from the University of Wisconsin: AB, 1931, AM, 1932, PhD, 1935; after a period of post-graduate instruction in Wisconsin, he joined the faculty of Teachers College, Columbia, in 1938, where he has remained (as a full professor since 1947); he was executive officer, division of foundations of education, Teachers College, 1946-1956, and director of the division, 1956-60; since 1961, he has been director of International Studies, Teachers College.

*The Development of the Principle of Election of Studies in American Colleges and Universities,* unpubl. PhD thesis, U. Wisconsin, 1935 (abstract, *Phi News,* vol.13, no.1, Feb.,1936).

*The College Charts its Course: Historical Conceptions and Current Proposals,* N.Y.: McGraw-Hill, 1939, 464pp.

*A Cultural History of Education,* N.Y.: McGraw-Hill, 1947, 726pp.; (2nd ed., *A Cultural History of Western Education,* Ibid., 1955, 645pp.).

*The American Tradition in Religion and Education,* Boston, Beacon Press, 1950, 230pp.

*A History of Education in American Culture* (with L.A. Cremin), N.Y.: Holt, 1953, 628pp.

## CARR, WILLIAM GEORGE

He was born June 1, 1901, in Northampton, England, and he came to the United States with his parents at the age of 14, in the autumn of 1915; he studied at the University of California at Berkeley, 1920-3, prior to attending Stanford, where he received the following degrees: AB, 1924, AM, 1926, PhD, 1929; he taught in the Roosevelt Junior High School at Glendale, Calif., 1924-5; he was instructor in education, Pacific University, 1926-7; in 1928-9, he was director of research for the California Teachers' Association; the National Educational Association appointed him assistant director of research in 1929, and promoted him to director, 1931-40; he was associate secretary of the National Educational Association from 1940 to 1952, and he has been executive secretary since 1952; he has been visiting professor of education, summer sessions, at Stanford, 1929, 1931, 1942; at the University of Michigan, 1930, 1933, 1934, 1936, 1937, 1938; at University of California at Los Angeles, 1935; at University of California at Berkeley, 1939; at University of Oregon, 1940; at University of Pennsylvania, 1941; in addition to his regular work for UNESCO, he was consultant, United States delegation, UNESCO Mexico City conference, 1947; he was also in charge of the American delegation at the Mid-East Teacher Exchange conference, Cairo, Egypt, 1951.

*Education for World-Citizenship,* Stanford, Calif.: Stanford U. Press, 1928, 225pp.
*The County Unit of School Administration,* N.Y.: H.W. Wilson, 1931, 144pp.
*The Lesson Assignment* (with John Waage), Stanford, Calif.: Stanford University Press, 1931, 98pp.
*John Swett, the Biography of an Educational Pioneer,* Santa Ana, Calif.: Fine Arts Press, 1933, 173pp.
*The Purposes of Education in American Democracy,* Washington, D.C.: National Educational Association, 1938.
*Educational Leadership in this Emergency* (Cubberley lecture, July 20, 1941), Stanford, Calif.: Stanford University Press, 1942, 32pp.
*International Frontiers in Education,* Philadelphia: American Academy of Political and Social Science, 1944, 180pp.

CARTER, JAMES GORDON

Educator and dedicated disciple of Pestalozzi; he was the decisive leader of the movement for free state education; he began the campaign in 1820 which attracted the attention of Horace Mann only much later; he was virtually a broken man after being superseded by Mann in 1837 and did little for his cause after that time; his main academic field was geography, and he published several textbooks on the geography of Massachusetts and New Hampshire.

He was born on September 7, 1795, in Leominster, Massachusetts; his father, Captain James Carter, was a prosperous man; he attended Groton Academy prior to entering Harvard College, where he received his BA in 1820; he was director and teacher at the Cohasset School, 1820-3, and at the Lancaster School, 1823-30; he published articles advocating state education in the 1820's in the Boston *Transcript* and the Boston *Patriot*; his effort on behalf of a state normal school failed by only one vote in the Massachusetts Senate in 1827; he entered the Massachusetts House of Representatives in 1835, where he was chairman of the committee on education; after 1837, when Mann was placed in charge of the public education program, he served a term in the Massachusetts Senate; he died in Chicago, July 21, 1849.

*Letters to the Honorable William Prescott on the Free Schools of New England, with Remarks upon the Principles of Instruction,* Cummings, Hilliard & Co., Boston, 1824, 123pp.

*Essays upon Popular Education, Containing a Particular Examination of the Schools of Massachusetts, and an Outline of the Institution for the Education of Teachers,* Bowles & Dearborn, Boston, 1826, 60pp.

## CATTELL, JAMES MCKEEN

He was born on May 25, 1860, in Easton, Pennsylvania; his father, Reverend William C. Cattell, was president of Lafayette College; he received two degrees from his father's college: AB, 1880, AM, 1883; he then studied at Goettingen, Leipzig, Paris, and Geneva, 1880-1882; he was a Johns Hopkins fellow, 1882-3, prior to returning to Europe, where he was a student and scientific assistant at the University of Leipzig, 1883-6; he received his Leipzig PhD in 1886; he lectured at University of Pennsylvania and Bryn Mawr, 1886-8; in 1888, he was also invited to offer a course of guest lectures in educational psychology at the University of Cambridge, England; he was professor and chairman of the department of psychology, University of Pennsylvania, 1888-91; he was professor of psychology and education at Columbia from 1891 to 1917; from 1894 to 1904, he was editor of the *Psychological Review,* and in 1915 he founded *School and Society,* taking the name from the title of the famous book by John Dewey; he remained editor of this publication until 1939; he was named trustee of Science Service in 1920, and he was president of this foundation from 1928 to 1937; he died on January 20, 1944.

*American Men of Science: a Biographical Directory* (founder, and editor of the first six editions), N.Y.: Science Press, 1906, 1910, 1921, 1927, 1933, 1938.

*University Control,* N.Y.: Science Press, 1913, 484pp. (2nd ed., N.Y.: Sagamore Press, 1957).

*Carnegie Pensions,* N.Y.: Science Press, 1919, 253pp.

*Leaders in Education* (founder, and editor of the first two editions), N.Y.: Science Press, 1932, 1941.

CLARK, GORDON HADDEN

He was born on August 31, 1902, in Philadelphia, Pennsylvania; he received the following degrees from the University of Pennsylvania: AB, 1924, PhD, 1929; he was instructor and assistant professor of philosophy at the University of Pennsylvania from 1924 to 1937, and associate professor of philosophy at Wheaton College, 1937-43; since 1945 he has instructed at Butler University, where he has been a full professor since 1948; he was visiting professor, Theological Seminary of the Reformed Episcopal Church, 1931-6.

*A Christian View of Man and Things,* Grand Rapids: Eerdmans, 1952, 325pp.
*Dewey,* Philadelphia: Presbyterian and Reformed Publishing Company, 1960, 69pp.
*Religion, Reason and Revelation,* Philadelphia: Presbyterian and Reformed Publishing Company, 1961, 241pp.
*Karl Barth's Theological Method,* Philadelphia: Presbyterian and Reformed Publishing Company, 1963, 275pp.
*James,* Philadelphia: Presbyterian and Reformer Publishing Company, 1963, 58pp.


CONANT, JAMES BRYANT

Scientist and educator; example of the scientist in education; he made the following declaration at the massive Harvard tercentenary celebration in 1936, when 67 honorary degrees were awarded: "The origin of the constitution . . . must be dissected as fearlessly as the geologist examines the origin of rocks."

He was born on March 26, 1893, in Dorchester, Massachusetts; from Harvard he received his AB, 1913, and his PhD, 1916; he joined the chemistry department at Harvard the same year, and he was promoted to full professor in 1927; he succeeded Lowell as president of Harvard in 1933; his influence as president was slight, and in 1953 he resigned to become United States High Commissioner in West Germany; after his return from Germany in 1957, he was given a permanent assignment by the Carnegie Foundation to investigate American education; he was chairman of the National Defense Research Commission from 1941 to 1946.

*Speaking as a Private Citizen: Addresses on the Present Threat to our Nation's Future,* Cambridge, Mass.: Harvard University Press, 1941, 38pp.

*Education in a Divided World: the Function of the Public Schools in our Unique Society,* Cambridge, Mass.: Harvard University Press, 1948, 249pp.

*Education and Liberty: the Role of the Schools in a Modern Democracy,* Cambridge, Mass.: Harvard University Press, 1953, 168pp.

*Recommendations for Education in the Junior High School Years,* Princeton, N.J.: Princeton University Press, 1960, 46pp.

*Slums and Suburbs: a Commentary on Schools in Metropolitan Areas,* N.Y.: McGraw-Hill, 1961, 147pp.


COUNTS, GEORGE SYLVESTER

Educator; member of the Liberal Party since 1955, and formerly member of the American Labor Party; as a teacher, writer, and chairman of the Committee of the Progressive Education Association on Social and Economic Problems, he has exerted an extensive influence on American education.

He was born on December 9, 1889, in Baldwin City, Kansas; he received his AB from Parker University in Kansas, 1911, and his PhD, University of Chicago, 1916; he was head of the department of education at Delaware College, 1916-18, professor of education and sociology at Harris Teachers' College, St. Louis, 1918-19, and professor of secondary education at the University of Washington in St. Louis, 1919-20; he was professor of education at Yale, 1920-6, and at the University of Chicago, 1926-7; from 1927 to 1956, he was professor of education at Teachers College, Columbia University, 1927-56, until retirement from teaching; in 1946, he headed the United States education mission to Japan.

*The Selective Character of American Secondary Education,* Chicago: University of Chicago Press, 1922, 162pp.

*Principles of Education* (with J. Crosby Chapman), Boston: Houghton Mifflin, 1924.

*The Senior High School Curriculum,* Chicago: University of Chicago Press, 1926, 160pp.

*The Social Composition of Boards of Education: a Study in the*

*Social Control of Public Education,* Chicago: University of Chicago Press, 1927, 100pp.

*School and Society in Chicago,* N.Y.: Harcourt, Brace & Co., 1928, 367pp.

*Secondary Education and Industrialism,* Cambridge, Mass.: Harvard University Press, 1929, 70pp.

*The American Road to Culture: a Social Interpretation of Education in the United States,* N.Y.: John Day, 1930, 194pp.

*A Ford Crosses Soviet Russia,* Boston: Stratford, 1930, 223pp.

*The Soviet Challenge to America,* N.Y.: John Day, 1931, 372pp.

*Dare the Schools Build a New Social Order?,* John Day Pamphlets, N.Y.: John Day, 1932, 56pp.

*A Call to the Teachers of the Nation,* John Day Pamphlets, N.Y.: John Day, 1933, 44pp.

*The Social Foundations of Education,* et al, N.Y.: Scribner, 1934, 579pp.

*The Prospects of American Democracy,* N.Y.: John Day, 1938, 370pp.

*The Relations of Public Education and Private Enterprise,* N.Y.: Teachers College, Columbia U. Press, 1938, 33pp.

*Education and the Promise of America* (Kappa Delta Pi lecture series, vol.17), N.Y.: Macmillan, 1945.

*The Challenge of Soviet Education,* et al, N.Y.: McGraw-Hill, 1957, 330pp.

CUBBERLEY, ELLWOOD PATTERSON

He was born on June 6, 1868, in Andrews, Indiana; he received his AB from Indiana University, 1891, AM, Columbia, 1902, PhD, Columbia, 1905; he was professor and president at Vincennes University, 1891-6, and city superintendent of schools, San Diego, Calif., 1896-8, prior to joining the Stanford University faculty as associate professor of education in 1898; he was promoted to full professor in 1906, and from 1917 until his retirement in 1933, he was dean of the Stanford school of education; during his Stanford career, he also directed municipal school surveys in Portland, Oregon, and Salt Lake City, Utah; he died on September 15, 1941.

*Syllabus of Lectures on the History of Education, with Selected Bibliographies,* 2 vol., London: Macmillan, 1902.

*School Funds and their Apportionment: a Consideration of the Subject with Reference to a more general Equalization of both the Burdens and the Advantages of Education*, N.Y.: Teachers College, Columbia University Press, 1905, 255pp.

*Changing Conceptions of Education*, Boston: Houghton Mifflin, 1909, 69pp.

*State and County Educational Reorganization: the Revised Constitution and School Code of the State of Osceola*, N.Y.: Macmillan, 1914, 257pp.

*School Organization and Administration: a Concrete Study Based on the Salt Lake City School Survey*, et al, Yonkers-on-Hudson, N.Y.: World Book Company, 1916, 346pp.

*Public Education in the United States*, Boston: Houghton Mifflin, 1919, 517pp. (2nd ed., 1934, 782pp.).

*The History of Education: Educational Practice and Progress Considered as a Phase of the Development and Spread of Western Civilization*, Boston: Houghton Mifflin, 1920, 849pp.

*The Principal and his School*, Boston: Houghton Mifflin, 1923, 571pp.

*An Introduction to the Study of Education*, Boston: Houghton Mifflin, 1925, 476pp. (2nd ed., 1933, 532pp.).

*State School Administration: a Textbook of Principles*, Boston: Houghton Mifflin, 1927, 773pp.


## CURTI, MERLE EUGENE

He was born on September 15, 1897, in Papillon, Nebraska; from Harvard he received the following degrees: AB, 1920, AM, 1921, PhD, 1927; he instructed history at Beloit College, 1921-2, and studied at the Sorbonne, 1924-5; he taught at Smith College from 1925 to 1937, and he was promoted to full professor in 1929; he was professor in the history of education at Teachers College, Columbia, from 1937 to 1942; since 1942 he has been professor of history at the University of Wisconsin; he was visiting professor in India, 1946-7, and Japan, 1959-60.

*The Social Ideas of American Educators*, N.Y.: Scribner's, 1935, 613pp. (2nd ed., with new preface, Paterson, N.J.: Littlefield, Adams, 1959, 613pp.).

*Peace or War: the American Struggle, 1636-1936,* N.Y.: W. W. Nor-
ton, 1936, 374pp.
*American Scholarship in the 20th Century,* et al, Cambridge, Mass.:
Harvard University Press, 252pp.
*Probing our Past,* N.Y.: Harper, 1955, 294pp.


DEARBORN, NED HARLAND

He was born on June 2, 1893, in Conneautville, Pennsylvania; he
graduated from the State Normal School at Edinboro, Pennsylvania
in 1912, and began his career as a secondary school teacher in Erie
and Crawford counties, Pa., where he was also a principal and school
superintendent, 1912-21; from 1921 to 1923, he was training director
at the State Normal School, Oswego, N.Y.; he was assistant to the
director of the Commonwealth Fund in New York City from 1923
to 1925, and during this period he completed his graduate studies;
from Columbia he received the MA, 1924, and PhD, 1925; from
1925 to 1929 he was director of the teacher training division of the
N.Y. State Department of Education; from 1929 to 1959, he was professor of education at New York University; he was appointed dean
of the division of general education, NYU, 1934, executive vice
president, 1942, and from 1944 to 1959 he was president of the
division; during the latter years he was also director of the National
Safety Council.

*The Oswego Movement in American Education,* N.Y.: Columbia
University Press, 1925, 189pp.
*An Introduction to Teaching,* N.Y.: D. Appleton, 1925, 337pp.
*Once in a Lifetime: a Guide to the CCC Camp,* N.Y.: Merrill, 1935,
302pp. (2nd ed., 1936, 308pp.) .


DE GARMO, CHARLES

Quaker educator and leading American proponent of the Herbartian doctrine; many of the American educators, such as Kilpatrick, have testified to the decisive influence he exerted upon their
thinking; he was an indefatigable lecturer, and he traveled throughout the country expounding his ideas after becoming president of
Swarthmore.

He was born on January 7, 1849, in Mukwanago, Wisconsin; he graduated from the Illinois State Normal School in 1873; from 1873-6 he was a secondary school principal; he returned to Illinois State Normal School to instruct in education, 1876-83, and during this period he edited the *Illinois School Journal*; from 1883-6 he studied at Jena and Halle in Germany, receiving his PhD from Halle in 1886; he returned to the Illinois State Normal School to teach modern languages, 1886-90, and he was professor of philosophy at the University of Illinois, 1890-1; he was appointed the third president of Swarthmore College in 1891, where he remained until 1923; during this period he was also visiting professor of education at Cornell University; he died in 1934.

*The Essentials of Method: a Discussion of the Essential Form of Right Methods in Teaching*, Boston: Heath, 1889, 119pp.

*Herbart and the Herbartians*, N.Y.: Scribner, 1895, 268pp. (2nd ed., 1896).

*Apperception, a Monograph on Psychology and Pedagogy* (by Karl Lange, ed., trans. by C. De Garmo), Boston: Heath, 1896.

*Language Lessons*, N.Y.: Werner, 1897, 256pp.

*Outlines of Educational Doctrine* (J.F. Herbart, annotated and translated by C. De Garmo), N.Y.: Macmillan, 1901.

*Interest and Education: the Doctrine of Interest and its Concrete Application*, N.Y.: Macmillan, 1902, 230pp. (2nd ed., 1903).

*Principles of Secondary Education*, 3 vol., N.Y.: Macmillan, 1907-1910.

*Aesthetic Education*, Syracuse, N.Y.: Bardeen, 1913, 161pp.

*Essentials of Design* (with Leon Loyal Winslow), N.Y.: Macmillan, 1924, 225pp.

## DEWEY, JOHN

He was born October 20, 1859, in Burlington, Vermont; he received his BA from the University of Vermont in 1879, and he taught secondary school in Vermont and Pennsylvania before entering the Johns Hopkins graduate school, where he received his PhD, 1884; he instructed in philosophy at the University of Michigan from 1884 to 1894, except for one year as visiting professor of philosophy, University of Minnesota, 1888-9; he was head of the department of philosophy, psychology and education at the University of Chicago, 1894-1904; in 1896, he established his University of Chicago laboratory school for progressive education; this school soon included 23 instructors, 10 assistants, and 140 experimental students; he was professor of philosophy at Columbia University from 1904 to 1930; he visited the Soviet Union in 1928 and he returned impressed with the Marxist experiment in Russia; in 1937, he conducted a famous mission to Mexico with respect to Leon Trotsky; he died in New York City on June 1, 1952.

*Psychology*, N.Y.: Harper, 1886, 427pp. (2nd ed., 1887, 3rd ed., 1891).

*My Pedagogic Creed*, Washington, D.C.: Progressive Education Association, 1897 (2nd ed., 1929).

*The School and Society*, Chicago: University of Chicago Press, 1899, 125pp. (1st revised ed., 1900, 129pp.; 2nd revised ed., 1915, 164pp.).

*The Educational Situation*, Chicago: University of Chicago Press, 1902, 104pp.

*The Child and the Curriculum*, Chicago: University of Chicago Press, 1902, 40pp.

*Ethical Principles Underlying Education*, Chicago: University of Chicago Press, 1903, 34pp. (2nd ed., 1908).

*Moral Principles in Education*, N.Y.: Philosophical Library, 1959; original edition, Boston: Houghton Mifflin, 1909, 60pp.

*Educational Essays*, London: Blackie & Son, 1910, 168pp.

*The Influence of Darwin on Philosophy, and Other Essays in Contemporary Thought*, N.Y.: Henry Holt, 1910, 300pp.

*Interest and Effort in Education*, Boston: Houghton Mifflin, 1913, 101pp.

*The Schools of Tomorrow* (with Evelyn Dewey), N.Y.: Dutton, 1915, 316pp.

*German Philosophy and Politics*, N.Y.: Henry Holt, 1915, 134 pp.

*Democracy and Education: an Introduction to the Philosophy of Education*, N.Y.: Macmillan, 1916, 434pp. (2nd ed., 1923, 3rd ed., 1929).

*Human Nature and Conduct: an Introduction to Social Psychology*, N.Y.: Henry Holt, 1922, 336pp.

*The Public and its Problems*, N.Y.: Henry Holt, 1927, 224pp. (2nd ed., N.Y.: Minton, Balch, 1930).

*Characters and Events: Popular Essays in Social and Political Philosophy*, 2 vol., N.Y.: Henry Holt, 1929.

*Impressions of Soviet Russia and the Revolutionary World*, N.Y.: New Republic, 1929, 270pp. (2nd ed., 1932).

*The Sources of a Science of Education*, N.Y.: Liveright, 1929, 77pp.

*Individualism, Old and New*, N.Y.: Minton, Balch, 1930, 171pp.

*Philosophy and Civilization*, N.Y.: Minton, Balch, 1931, 334pp.

*American Education, Past and Future*, Chicago: University of Chicago Press, 1931, 14pp.

*The Way Out of Educational Confusion*, Cambridge, Mass.: Harvard University Press, 1931, 41pp.

*A Common Faith*, New Haven, Conn.: Yale University Press, 1934, 87pp.

*Education and the Social Order*, N.Y.: League for Industrial Democracy, 1934, 14pp.

*Art as Experience*, N.Y.: Minton, Balch, 1934, 355pp.

*Liberalism and Social Action*, N.Y.: Putnam, 1935, 93pp.

*Experience and Education*, N.Y.: Macmillan, 1938, 116pp. (2nd ed., 1948).

*Intelligence in the Modern World*, N.Y.: Modern Library, 1939, 1077pp.

*Freedom and Culture*, N.Y.: Putnam, 1939, 176pp.

*Problems of Men*, N.Y.: Philosophical Library, 1946.

DONHAM, WALLACE BRETT

Lawyer and university administrator; his book on education in 1944 was regarded at Harvard as an advance dissent from the famous Aristotelian Harvard report on education in a free society directed by Professor Demos and published the following year; Donham urged a return to the earlier traditions of American individualism.

He was born on October 26, 1877, in Rockland, Massachusetts; he received his AB from Harvard in 1898, and his LL.B. there in 1901; after admission to the bar that year, he served in the legal department of the Old Colony Trust Co. from 1901 to 1919, and he was vice-president, 1906-19; from 1919 to 1942, he was dean of the Graduate School of Business at Harvard, where he was also professor of public administration from 1942 to 1948; he was visiting professor of human relations, Colgate University, 1948-9, and from 1950 to 1954, he was managing director of the Harvard-Yenching Institute;

he died at Cambridge, Massachusetts on November 29, 1954; his son, Richard Donham, is dean of the School of Business at Northwestern University.

*Business Adrift*, N.Y.: McGraw-Hill, 1931, 165pp.
*Business Looks at the Unforseen*, N.Y.: McGraw-Hill, 1932, 209pp.
*National Ideals and Internationalist Idols* (address, Mar.23, 1933)
  N.Y.: Chemical Foundation, Inc., 1933, 19pp.
*Education for Responsible Living: the Opportunity for Liberal-Arts College*, Cambridge, Mass.: Harvard U. Press, 1944.

EBY, FREDERICK

He was born on October 26, 1874, in Berlin, Ontario, Canada; he received his BA at McMaster College, 1895; the following three years he studied at Chicago before going to Clark, where he received his PhD in 1900; he spent one year in post-doctoral research at the University of Berlin, 1905-6; his first teaching experience was at the Morgan Park Academy in Illinois, 1897-8; from 1900 to 1909, he was professor of philosophy and education at Baylor University, and from 1909 to 1941 he was professor of education at the University of Texas; he was Holland Foundation lecturer at the Southwest Baptist Theological Seminary in 1935 and 1955; in 1947 and 1948 he lectured at the Austin Presbyterian Theological Seminary.

*The Reconstruction of the Kindergarten*, Worcester, Mass.: J. H. Orpha, 1900, 58pp.
*Christianity and Education*, Dallas, Texas: Baptist General Convention of Texas, 1915, 298pp.
*Education in Texas: Source Materials*, Austin, Texas: University of Texas Press, 1921, 963pp.
*The Development of Education in Texas*, N.Y.: Macmillan, 1925, 354pp.
*A Study of the Financing of Public Junior Colleges in Texas* (with Benjamin Pittenger), Austin, Texas: University of Texas Press, 1931, 8opp.
*The Development of Modern Education in Theory, Organization and Practice* (with C.F. Arrowood), N.Y.: Prentice-Hall, 1934, 922pp. (2nd ed., 1947).
*Graduate Theses and Dissertations in Education: Baylor, Southern*

*Methodist, Texas Christian, Texas Tech, University of Texas, West Texas State Teachers College; a Bibliography* (with S.E. Frost, Jr.), Austin, Texas: University of Texas Press, 1934, 77pp.

*Early Protestant Educators: the Educational Writings of Martin Luther, John Calvin, and other Leaders of Protestant Thought,* N.Y.: McGraw-Hill, 1935, 312pp.

*The History and Philosophy of Education, Ancient and Medieval* (with C.F. Arrowood), N.Y.: Prentice-Hall, 1940, 966pp.

*Reorganizing American Education for World Leadership,* Austin, Texas: University of Texas Press, 1958, 74pp.

EVANS, MEDFORD STANTON

He was born on July 20, 1934, in Kingsville, Texas; he received his BA from Yale University in 1955, and he has carried on further studies at New York University; he has worked in the field of journalism since 1955 with a primary interest in American education; he was assistant editor of *The Freeman,* 1955, assistant editor of *National Review,* 1955-6, managing editor of *Human Events,* 1956-9, publications director for the Intercollegiate Society of Individualists, 1956-9 (since 1959 he has been one of their trustees); he was chief editorial writer for *Indianapolis News,* 1959-60, and he received Freedom Foundation awards for editorial writing, 1959, 1960; he has been editor of the *Indianapolis News* since 1960.

*Revolt on the Campus,* Chicago: Regnery, 1961, 248pp.

GALLAGHER, BUELL GORDON

He was born on February 4, 1904, in Rankin, Illinois; he received his AB at Carleton College in 1925, and his BD at Union Theological Seminary, N.Y.C., 1929; he was ordained a Congregationalist minister prior to departing for England, where he studied at the London School of Economics, 1929-30; he received his PhD from Columbia in 1939; from 1930 to 1931 he was national secretary of the interseminary movement; he was minister of a Congregational Church in Passaic, New Jersey, 1931-3, and from 1933 to 1943 he was president of the Talladega College for Negroes in Alabama; he was professor of Christian Ethics at the Pacific School of Religion,

Berkeley, Calif., 1943-9, and educational consultant, United States government, 1949-52; he was appointed president of City College in N.Y.C. in 1952; he consented to serve as first chancellor of the California State College System in 1961, but he resigned and returned to City College in 1962.

*American Caste and the Negro College* (with a foreword by W.H. Kilpatrick), N.Y.: Columbia U. Press, 1938, 463pp.
*Color and Conscience: the Irrepressible Conflict*, N.Y.: Harper, 1946, 244pp.


HALL, GRANVILLE STANLEY

He was born on February 1, 1844, in Ashfield, Massachusetts; he attended the Ashfield and Williston academies prior to entering Williams College, where he received his BA, 1867; he abandoned seminary study in favor of graduate education in Germany at Bonn University, 1868-71; he instructed in literature and philosophy at Antioch College, 1872-6, and he received his PhD at Harvard, 1878; he instructed in English, German literature, and education at Harvard, 1876-82, and psychology and education at Johns Hopkins, 1882-8; Jonas Gilman Clark agreed to appoint him president of a new graduate university at Worcester, Mass., in 1888; Hall spent one year in Germany, 1888-9, prior to opening the new university in October, 1889; Hall taught psychology full time at Clark from 1893 until he retired as president in 1921; he died on April 24, 1924.

*Aspects of German Culture*, Boston: J.R. Osgood, 1881, 320pp.
*Hints toward a Select and Descriptive Bibliography of Education*, (with J.M. Mansfield), Boston: Heath, 1886, 309pp.
*How to Teach Reading and What to Read in School*, Boston: Heath, 1886, 40pp.
*The Contents of Children's Minds on Entering School*, N.Y.: Kellogg, 1893, 56pp.
*Adolescence: its Psychology, and its Relations to Physiology, Anthropology, Sociology, Sex, Crime, Religion and Education*, 2 vol., N.Y.: D. Appleton, 1904.
*Youth: its Education, Regimen, and Hygiene*, N.Y.: D. Appleton, 1906, 379pp. (2nd ed., 1908).
*Aspects of Child Life and Education*, et al, Boston: Ginn, 1907, 326pp. (2nd ed., 1921).

*Educational Problems,* 2 vol., N.Y.: D. Appleton, 1911.

*A Genetic Philosophy of Education: an Epitome of the Published Educational Writings of President G. Stanley Hall of Clark University,* N.Y.: Sturgis & Walton, 1912.

*Jesus, the Christ, in the Light of Psychology,* 2 vol., Garden City, N.Y.: Doubleday, Page & Co., 1917.

*Morale, the Supreme Standard of Life and Conduct,* N.Y.: D. Appleton, 1920, 377pp.

*Recreations of a Psychologist,* N.Y.: D. Appleton, 1920, 336pp.

*Life and Confessions of a Psychologist,* N.Y.: D. Appleton, 1923, 622pp. (2nd ed., 1927).

HARRIS, WILLIAM TORREY

He was born on September 10, 1835, on a farm near North Killingly, Connecticut; after attending the Worcester and Andover academies, he was a student at Yale, 1854-6, but he did not like the curriculum; he taught secondary school in St. Louis, 1857-68; in 1858, Henry Brokmeyer introduced him to Hegel, and this event determined the balance of his intellectual career; he founded the *Journal of Speculative Philosophy,* with its Hegelian slogan: "God, Freedom, and Immortality," in 1867, and he edited it until 1893; he was superintendent of schools in St. Louis from 1868 to 1880, and he issued thirteen annual reports on St. Louis education; from 1880 to 1889 he instructed at the Concord, Massachusetts School of Philosophy; he was United States Commissioner of Education from 1889 to 1906; he died at Providence, Rhode Island, on November 5, 1909.

*Hegel's Doctrine of Reflection,* N.Y.: D. Appleton, 1881, 214pp.

*Hegel's Logic: a Critical Exposition,* Chicago: S.C. Grigg, 1890, 406pp.

*The Theory of Education,* Syracuse, N.Y.: Bardeen, 1893, 54pp.

*Horace Mann,* Syracuse, N.Y.: Bardeen, 1896, 34pp.

*The Spiritual Sense of Dante's Divina Comedia,* Boston: Houghton Mifflin, 1896, 193pp.

*Psychologic Foundations of Education,* N.Y.: D. Appleton, 1898, 400pp.

*Elementary Education* (Nicholas Murray Butler, ed.) , Albany, N.Y.: J.B. Lyon, 1900, 63pp.

HAROUTUNIAN, JOSEPH

He was born on September 18, 1904, in Marash, Ottoman Empire; he studied at the American University of Beirut, Lebanon, 1919-23, prior to entering the United States, where he is a naturalized citizen; he received his AB at Columbia in 1926, and his PhD there in 1932; in the meantime, he had received his BD from Union Theological Seminary, N.Y.C. in 1930 and entered the ministry; he was assistant professor of Biblical history at Wellesley College, 1932-1940, and he has been professor of systematic theology at the Mc-Cormick Theological Seminary, Chicago, since 1940; at the Centenary Convocation of Knox College, September 24, 1958, he delivered a sermon, *How to Hear the Gospel,* which attracted wide attention.

*Piety versus Moralism: the Passing of the New England Theology,*
N.Y.: Henry Holt, 1932, 329pp.
*Wisdom and Folly in Religion: a Study of Chastened Protestantism,*
N.Y.: Scribner's, 1940, 174pp.
*Calvin: Commentaries,* Philadelphia: Westminster, 1958, 414pp.

HOFSTADTER, RICHARD

Historian of politics, ideas and education; he first made his reputation with a brilliantly written monograph on social Darwinism; he then turned to political history and political theory, but in recent years he has been increasingly concerned with the history of American education.

He was born on August 6, 1916, in Buffalo, New York; he received his BA from the University of Buffalo in 1937; his graduate degrees are from Columbia: MA, 1938; PhD, 1942; he first instructed in American history at Brooklyn College, 1940-1; he was assistant professor of American history at the University of Maryland, 1942-6; he has been on the history staff at Columbia since 1946, and in 1958-9 he was visiting professor of American history at Cambridge University, England; he received the Pulitzer Prize in History for his book *The Age of Reform,* which appeared in 1956.

*Social Darwinism in American Thought, 1860-1915,* Philadelphia: University of Pennsylvania Press, 1944, 191pp. (revised edition, Boston: Beacon Press, 1955, 248pp.).

*The Development and Scope of Higher Education in the United States* (with C. Hardy), N.Y.: Columbia University Press, 1952, 254pp.

*The Development of Academic Freedom in the United States* (with Walter P. Metzger), N.Y.: Columbia University Press, 1955, 527pp.

*Academic Freedom in the Age of the College,* N.Y.: Columbia Paperback, 1961.

## HORNE, HERMAN HARRELL

Educator and philosopher; attempted to reconcile the idealistic philosophy of Hegel and the pragmatism of Peirce.

He was born on November 22, 1874, in Clayton, North Carolina; he received his AB from the University of North Carolina, 1895, and his graduate degrees from Harvard: AM, 1897, PhD, 1899; he did one year of post-doctoral study at the University of Berlin, 1906-7; his first teaching was in the field of modern languages, University of North Carolina, 1894-6; he instructed in philosophy and education at Dartmouth, 1899-1909, and from 1909 to 1942 at New York University; he undertook extensive guest lecturing at seminaries and colleges, including Southern Baptist Theological Seminary, Harvard Summer School of Theology, Martha's Vineyard Summer Institute, Columbia University, University of California at Berkeley, and Union Theological Seminary in N.Y.C.

*The Philosophy of Education, Being the Foundations of Education in the Related Natural and Mental Sciences,* N.Y.: Macmillan, 1904, 295pp. (revised edition, 1927, 329pp.).

*The Psychological Principles of Education, a Study in the Science of Education,* N.Y.: Macmillan, 1906, 435pp.

*Idealism in Education, or First Principles in the Making of Men and Women,* N.Y.: Macmillan, 1910, 183pp.

*Story-Telling, Questioning and Studying: Three School Arts,* N.Y.: Macmillan, 1916, 181pp.

*The Teacher as Artist: an Essay in Education as an Aesthetic Process,* Boston: Houghton Mifflin, 1917, 62pp.

*Modern Problems as Jesus Saw Them,* N.Y.: Association Press, 1918, 137pp.

*Jesus, the Master Teacher,* N.Y.: Association Press, 1920, 212pp.

*This New Education,* N.Y.: Abingdon, 1931, 280pp.

*The Essentials of Leadership and other Papers in Moral and Religious Education,* Nashville, Tenn.: Cokesbury Press, 1931, 136pp.

*The Democratic Philosophy of Education,* N.Y.: Macmillan, 1932, 547pp. (2nd ed., 1946).

*The Philosophy of Christian Education,* N.Y.: Revell, 1937, 171pp.

## HUTCHINS, ROBERT MAYNARD

He was born on January 17, 1899, in Brooklyn, New York; he studied at Oberlin College, 1915-17, prior to spending two years with the United States Army Ambulance Service, 1917-19; he entered Yale after returning from Europe; from Yale he received his AB, 1921, AM, 1922, and LL.B., 1925; he was master of literature and history at the Lake Placid School, 1921-3, and administrative secretary, Yale University, 1923-7; he was a lecturer in the Yale Law School, 1925-7, and professor of law, 1927-9; he was dean of the Yale Law School, 1927-9; in 1929, he was appointed president of the University of Chicago; he served first as president and then in the new office of chancellor from 1929 to 1951; he was an associate director of the Ford Foundation, 1951-4; since 1954, he has been president of the Fund for the Republic, and he resides at Santa Barbara, Calif.

*Inaugural Address of Robert Maynard Hutchins, Fifth President of the University of Chicago, November 19, 1929,* Chicago: Chicago University Press, 1929, 15pp.

*No Friendly Voice,* Chicago: University of Chicago Press, 1936, 196pp.

*The Higher Learning in America,* New Haven, Conn.: Yale University Press, 1936, 119pp.

*The Conflict in Education in a Democratic Society,* N.Y.: Harper, 1953, 112pp.

## JAMES, WILLIAM

He was born on January 11, 1842, in New York City; much of his youth was spent with his family in European travel (1855-8; 1859-60); at the age of eighteen he decided to become an artist, but he abandoned the idea the following year and began to study science at Harvard and the Lawrence Scientific School; he received his BA from Harvard in 1864 and entered the Harvard medical school; he accompanied the Louis Agassiz expedition to Brazil, 1865-6, and he spent the year 1867-8 visiting universities in Germany; he received his MD from Harvard in 1869; he returned to teach at Harvard after further travel in 1872; he instructed in physiology from 1872 to 1882, and in psychology and philosophy from 1882 to 1907; he became a pragmatist and disciple of Peirce in 1890; he played a prominent part in an anti-Hegel philosophical society in England, and he joined E. L. Godkin of the *Nation* in 1898 for a public campaign against American annexation of the Philippine Islands, and, following annexation, on behalf of de-annexation; he maintained an extensive correspondence with German, French, Italian, and British scholars; during his last years he spent some time in California; he died on August 26, 1910.

*Psychology,* N.Y.: Henry Holt, 1892, 478pp. (revised ed., 1910).
*The Principles of Psychology,* 2 vol., N.Y.: Henry Holt, 1890.
*Talks to Teachers on Psychology,* N.Y.: Henry Holt, 1899, 301pp.
  (the 1938 revised edition, *Ibid.,* 238pp., was edited and abridged by Dewey and Kilpatrick).
*Pragmatism: a New Name for some old Ways of Thinking,* N.Y.: Longmans, Green, 1907, 308pp.
*The Meaning of Truth: a Sequel to "Pragmatism,"* N.Y.: Longmans, Green, 1909, 297pp.
*Essays in Radical Empiricism,* N.Y.: Longmans, Green, 1912, 282pp.


JUDD, CHARLES HUBBARD

He was born on February 20, 1872, in Bareilly, Indiana; he received his AB from Wesleyan University in 1894, and his PhD from Leipzig University in Germany, 1896; he was instructor of philosophy, Wesleyan, 1896-8, and assistant professor of psychology, New York University, 1898-1901, and University of Cincinnati, 1901-2; from 1902 to 1909 he was associate professor of psychology at Yale, and from 1909 to 1938 he was professor of education and chairman of the department at the University of Chicago; he resigned ahead of his scheduled retirement in 1938 to accept a New Deal appointment as director of education for the National Youth Administration; he held this position for three years.

*Genetic Psychology for Teachers* (W.T. Harris, ed.), N.Y.: D. Appleton, 1903, 329pp. (2nd ed., 1911).

*Measuring the Work of the Public Schools,* Cleveland, Ohio: Cleveland Foundation, 1916, 290pp.

*Problems Involved in Standardizing State Normal Schools* (with S.C. Parker), Washington, D.C.: Government Printing Office, 1916, 141pp.

*The Evolution of a Democratic School System,* Boston: Houghton Mifflin, 1918, 118pp.

*Introduction to the Scientific Study of Education,* Boston: Ginn & Co., 1918, 333pp.

*The Psychology of Social Institutions,* N.Y.: Macmillan, 1926, 346pp. (2nd ed., 1931, 3rd ed., 1936).

*The Psychology of Secondary Education,* Boston: Ginn & Co., 1927, 545pp.

*The Unique Character of American Secondary Education* (Inglis lecture) Cambridge, Mass.: Harvard University Press, 1928, 53pp.

*Problems of Education in the United States* (in the *Recent Social Trends* series), N.Y.: McGraw-Hill, 1933, 214pp.

*Education and Social Progress,* N.Y.: Harcourt, Brace, 1934, 285pp.

*Education as Cultivation of the Higher Mental Processes,* et al, N.Y.: Macmillan, 1936, 206pp.

*The Preparation of School Personnel,* N.Y.: McGraw-Hill, 1938, 151pp.

*Educational Psychology,* Boston: Houghton Mifflin, 1939, 566pp.

*Teaching the Evolution of Civilization,* N.Y.: Macmillan, 1946.

KILPATRICK, WILLIAM HEARD

Progressive educator; Dewey regarded him as his model disciple and remarked that progressive education and the work of Kilpatrick were synonomous concepts; Kilpatrick was always an aggressive fighter for his conception of education and culture.

He was born in 1871 at White Plains, Georgia, the son of a Baptist minister; he reluctantly joined the Baptist Church in 1885, only to revolt from it a few years later; he received his AB in 1891 from

Mercer University, a Baptist college at Macon, Georgia; he studied at Johns Hopkins in 1891-2, and returned to Mercer to receive his MA in 1892; he was a high school principal at Blakely, Georgia, 1892-5; he studied again at Johns Hopkins, 1895-6, and he was a high school principal at Savannah, Georgia, 1896-7 prior to joining the Mercer faculty in 1897 as professor of mathematics; in 1898, he attended the University of Chicago summer school, and in 1900 the summer school at Cornell, where he studied under Charles De Garmo; he was acting president of Mercer University from 1902 to 1905; he was forced to leave Mercer in 1906 because of objections to his ideas; he was principal of a high school at Columbus, Georgia, 1906-7, prior to entering Teachers College of Columbia University as a graduate student in 1907; from 1907 to 1913 he was a part-time instructor at Teachers College and at the Pratt Institute; he received a full-time appointment at Teachers College in 1913, where it is estimated that he taught 35,000 students during his subsequent teaching career; he was usually in conflict with President Butler of Columbia; in 1926 he visited India, and in 1929 the Soviet Union, where he was warmly welcomed; he accepted the Soviet ideal of a supranational government to be achieved by the employment of the national state in a revolutionary program; during the 1930's he was involved in public controversies with Hutchins, Thorndike, and William Randolph Hearst, Sr.; he retired from teaching on July 1, 1938.

*The Dutch Schools of New Netherland and Colonial New York,* Washington, D.C.: Government Printing Office, 1912, 239pp.

*The Montessori System Examined,* Boston: Houghton Mifflin, 1914, 71pp.

*Froebel's Kindergarten Principles Critically Examined,* N.Y.: Macmillan, 1916, 217pp.

*The Project Method: the Use of the Purposeful Act in the Educative Process,* N.Y.: Teachers College, Columbia, 1918, 18pp.

*Foundations of Method: Informal Talks on Teaching,* N.Y.: Macmillan, 1925, 383pp. (2nd ed., 1926, 3rd ed., 1935).

*Education for a Changing Civilization,* N.Y.: Macmillan, 1926, 143pp. (2nd ed., 1927, 3rd ed., 1928, 4th ed., 1931).

*Education and the Social Crisis: a Proposed Program,* N.Y.: Liveright, 1932, 90pp.

*The Educational Frontier* (with Bode, Dewey, et al), N.Y.: Century, 1933, 325pp.
*A Reconstructed Theory of the Educative Process*, N.Y.: Teachers College, Columbia, 1935.
*Remaking the Curriculum*, N.Y.: Newson, 1936, 128pp.
*The Art and Practice of Teaching* (Bennington College commencement address), N.Y.: William R. Scott, 1937, 14pp.
*John Dewey as Educator* (with J.L. Childs), N.Y.: Progressive Education Association, 1939.
*Selfhood and Civilization: a Study of the Self-Other Process*, N.Y.: Macmillan, 1941, 243pp.
*Intercultural Attitudes in the Making* (with William Van Til; 9th Yearbook, John Dewey Society), N.Y.: Harper, 1947.
*Modern Education and Better Human Relations*, N.Y.: Anti-Defamation League of B'nai B'rith, 1949.
*A Philosophy of Education*, N.Y.: Macmillan, 1957.

KIRK, RUSSELL AMOS

Political philosopher and journalist; he has been an active ally of William Buckley in investigating the American educational scene during the past decade and in reporting his observations to the American public.

He was born on October 19, 1918, in Plymouth, Michigan; he received his BA from Michigan State University, 1940, MA from Duke University, 1941, and D.Litt., St. Andrews University, Scotland, 1952; he served in the United States Army, 1942-6; he was assistant professor of civilization, Michigan State, 1946-53; in 1954-5 he was a Guggenheim research fellow; since 1955, he has been a leading contributor to *National Review*, and since 1956, editor of *Conservative Review*; he has also been professor of political science at Post College, Long Island, since 1956.

*The Conservative Mind, from Burke to Santayana*, Chicago: Regnery, 1953, 458pp.
*A Program for Conservatives*, Chicago: Regnery, 1954, 325pp.
*Academic Freedom: an Essay in Definition*, Chicago: Regnery, 1955, 210pp.

## LEIDECKER, KURT FRIEDRICH

Linguist (modern European languages and Sanskrit); he has changed his field of teaching and research since World War II to include teaching and research in philosophy and cultural history, in addition to further language research; he has advocated a strong federal role in education throughout his academic career.

He was born on September 11, 1902, in Gera, Germany and is a naturalized American citizen; from Oberlin College he received his BA, 1924, and MA, 1925; from 1925 to 1927 he was a fellow at the University of Chicago, where he received his PhD in 1927; from 1927 to 1944 he instructed modern languages, especially scientific German, at the Rensselaer Polytechnic Institute; from 1944 to 1948 he instructed in scientific German for the United States Air Force; he taught philosophy during the summer session at Lehigh University in 1948; he has been professor of philosophy at Mary Washington College, Virginia, since 1948; he received a Fulbright research grant for India, 1950-2, and he was a United States Department of State lecturer on education in West Germany, 1954-5; he was employed by the United States Information Service in Thailand, 1955-7, and in 1956-7 he was visiting American lecturer in philosophy at the Buddhist University, Bangkok, Thailand.

*Josiah Royce and Indian Thought,* N.Y.: Kailas, 1931, 32pp.
*A Pragmatic Approach to Scientific German,* Troy, N.Y.: Swift, 1941, 209pp.
*Yankee Teacher: the Life of William Torrey Harris,* N.Y.: Philosophical Library, 1946, 648pp.

## MANN, HORACE

Lawyer, politician, education administrator; he had little to do with the pre-1837 Massachusetts movement for public education, but he espoused the cause of state schools with zeal for the remainder of his life and many of his ideas found wide acclaim; he is traditionally regarded as the father of American state education.

He was born on May 4, 1796, in Franklin, Massachusetts; he received his BA from Brown University in 1819; he was tutor of Latin and Greek at Brown from 1819 to 1821; he graduated from the

Litchfield, Connecticut Law School, the most famous in New England, in 1823, and he was admitted to the Massachusetts Bar the same year; from 1823 to 1833, he practiced law at Dedham, Mass.; he married Charlotte Messer, the daughter of President Asa Messer of Brown, in 1830; she died in 1832; he served in the Massachusetts House of Representatives, 1827-33, and in the Mass. Senate, 1833-7; he was president of the Senate, 1835-7; with the passage of the education law on April 20, 1837, he was appointed state secretary of education in place of James Carter, who had been the principal lobbyist for the bill; this was mainly due to the influence of Edmund Dwight, a leading Boston industrialist, and later president of the Western railway; Dwight actually placed considerable funds at the disposal of Mann on behalf of the state education program; Mann resigned to succeed John Quincy Adams in the United States House of Representatives in 1848; Dwight died the next year; Mann's political position in his native state was further injured by a conflict with Daniel Webster, and he was defeated as candidate for governor, 1852; at this point, Mann, a Unitarian, was called upon to be first president of the new college, Antioch, at Yellow Springs, Ohio; during his seven years as president he also taught philosophy, political economy, and theology; the college was sold for debt in 1859, partly due to Mann's mismanagement; Mann had a nervous breakdown and died the same year; the college was reorganized and restored; Mann was survived by his second wife, Mary Peabody Mann (the sister of Elizabeth Peabody), and their three children.

*The Life and Works of Horace Mann,* 5 vol., Boston: Lee & Shepard, 1891.

*Lecture on Education,* Boston: Marsh, Capon, Lyon & Webb, 1840, 62pp.

*Answer to the "Rejoinder" of 29 Boston Schoolmasters,* Boston: W.B. Fowle & N. Capon, 1845, 124pp.

*Lectures on Education,* Boston: L.N. Ide, 1850, 338pp.

*The Demands of the Age on Colleges,* N.Y.: Fowler & Wells, 1857, 86pp.

## MARBLE ALBERT PRESCOTT

Education administrator; he opposed the child-centered educational philosophy of Francis Parker on the ground that it would result in the corruption of the children; the progressive educators have unanimously recognized in Parker their most significant practical forerunner; therefore, Marble launched the first conscious counter-attack against what later came to be known as progressive education.

He was born on May 21, 1836, in Vassalboro, Maine; he received his BA from Waterville (later Colby) College in 1861; he went to Wisconsin where he instructed in mathematics at Wayland University, 1861-6, and served as a recruiter for the Union Army; he was principal of the Worcester Academy, 1866-8, and superintendent of public schools, Worcester, Mass., 1868-93; from 1893-6, he was superintendent of schools at Omaha, Nebraska, and from 1896 to 1902 he was the superintendent of high schools in New York City; Marble was president of the Massachusetts State Teachers Association for three terms, and he served for many years as secretary, and later, president, of the National Educational Association; he was also a member of the board of visitors of Wellesley College for twenty years; he died on March 25, 1906; several of his standard school textbooks on geography were still in use at the time of his death.

*The Powers and Duties of School Officers and Teachers,* Syracuse, N.Y.: Bardeen, 1887, 27pp.
*Sanitary Conditions for School Houses,* United States Bureau of Education, Washington, D.C., 1891, 123pp.

METZGER, WALTER PAUL

Historian; he has worked extensively with Richard Hofstadter during the past ten years on projects relating to the history of education (*vide* Hofstadter); he is also concerned with the role of religion in American education.

He was born on May 15, 1922, in New York City; his undergraduate study at City College was interrupted by service in th United States Army, 1942-5; he received his BS from City College, 1946, his MA from Columbia, 1947, and his PhD from the State University of Iowa, 1950; he was an instructor in history at Iowa from 1947-50, and at Columbia from 1950-3; he was promoted to assistant professor at Columbia in 1953, and to associate professor in 1956.

*Academic Freedom in the Age of the University,* N.Y.: Columbia Paperback, 1961.

## MOEHLMAN, CONRAD HENRY

Congregationalist educator and professor of theology; he has been a leading spokesman for many years on behalf of eliminating Christian observances in the public schools; he considers such observances contrary to the separation of church and state and an unnecessary affront to Jews and other non-Christian religious groups.

He was born on May 26, 1879, in Meriden, Connecticut; he received his AB from the University of Michigan in 1902; he taught secondary school prior to entering the University of Rochester for graduate study; he received his MA from Rochester in 1907, and from 1907 to 1944 he was faculty member of the Colgate-Rochester Divinity School; he received his PhD in the field of art criticism from the University of Michigan in 1918, and he was awarded an honorary DD by Rochester in 1929; from 1952 to 1955 he was visiting professor of education at the University of Southern California.

*The Catholic-Protestant Mind: some Aspects of Religious Liberty in the United States,* N.Y.: Harper, 1929, 211pp.
*The Christian-Jewish Tragedy: a Study in Religious Prejudice,* Rochester, N.Y.: Leo Hart, 1933, 285pp.
*The American Constitutions and Religion,* Berne, Indiana: n.p., 1938, 142pp.
*Protestantism's Challenge: an Historical Study of the Survival Value of Protestantism,* N.Y.: Harper, 1939, 286pp.
*In Defense of the American Way of Life,* Berne, Indiana: n.p., 1939, 31pp.
*School and Church: the American Way, an Historical Approach to the Problem of Religious Instruction in Public Schools,* N.Y.: Harper, 1944.

## PARKER, FRANCIS WAYLAND

Educational administrator, noted for his educational experiments; he was praised by John Dewey in the *New Republic,* July 9, 1930, as the father of progressive education; the most decisive phase of his

child-centered experiments was in Massachusetts during the 1880's.
He was born on October 9, 1837, in Bedford, New Hampshire; he
attended school at Mt. Vernon, New Hampshire, until 1853; then,
at the age of fifteen, he began teaching elementary school himself;
he taught school in New Hampshire from 1853 to 1859, and in
Illinois from 1859 to 1861; he hastened home on the outbreak of the
Civil War to join a New Hampshire regiment; he was commissioned
lieutenant at once, and he had been promoted to lieutenant-colonel
in August, 1864; shortly afterward he received a battle wound; after
convalescence, he retired from military service and returned to
teaching in New Hampshire; he was normal school director at
Dayton, Ohio, 1870-2; he visited German universities from 1872 to
1875 and acquired many new ideas on educational techniques; he
began his own experiments in 1875 after he was appointed superintendent of schools at Quincy, Mass.; from 1880-3 he was Boston
school supervisor, and in 1883, he was appointed principal of the
Cook County Normal School in Chicago; he also established a private institute of education in Chicago, which was transferred to the
University of Chicago in 1899; as a result, Parker served as first director of the school of education, University of Chicago, from 1899
until his death in 1902.

*Notes of Talks on Teaching* (July-August, 1882, lectures), N.Y.:
Kellogg, 1883, 182pp. (2nd ed., 1903).
*How to Study Geography,* Englewood, Illinois: Parker, 1888, 400pp.
(2nd ed., 1890, 3rd ed., 1892).
*Uncle Robert's Geography* (with Nellie Helm; ed. by W.T. Harris)
4 vol., N.Y.: D. Appleton, 1897-1904.
*Talks on Pedagogics: an Outline of the Theory of Concentration,*
(based on the July, 1891, Chautauqua lectures), N.Y.: John Day,
1937, 342pp.

PEABODY, ELIZABETH PALMER

Founder of the American kindergarten and precursor of progressive education; she was a champion of the experiments of Colonel
Parker at Quincy and Boston, and her campaigns for educational
reform are widely regarded as having prepared the way for the later
acceptance of Dewey's educational theories.

She was born on May 16, 1804, in Billerica, Massachusetts; her father was a medical doctor, and her mother, Elizabeth Palmer Peabody, conducted a private school; she studied at her mother's school prior to opening one of her own at the age of sixteen in Lancaster, 1820; two years later she started another school in Boston, and began to study Greek under Ralph Waldo Emerson, who converted her to transcendentalism; her modest efforts at starting schools proved abortive, and from 1823 to 1825 she was a governess in Maine; then, for nine years, she was secretary to the Unitarian philosopher, William Ellery Channing; from 1834 to 1836, she was the assistant of Bronson Alcott at his Temple School; from 1836 to 1839 she was at home with her parents; returning to Boston, she founded a successful book shop, where the transcendentalist *Dial* was published, 1842-3; she founded and conducted the first American kindergarten, 1860-7; from 1867 to 1868 she studied at Hamburg, Germany, and from 1873-5, she published the *Kindergarten Messenger*; in her later years, she traveled and supported numerous educational enterprises, including one by Sarah Winnemucca for the education of the Indians in Nevada, which turned out to be nothing more than a clever fraud, in which she and her friends, due to their financial assistance, were the victims; she died on January 3, 1894.

*Record of a School* (Bronson Alcott's school), N.Y.: Leavitt, Lord, 1835, 198pp. (revised edition, 1874, 297pp.).

*Reminiscences of Reverend William Ellery Channing, D.D.*, Boston: Roberts, 1880, 459pp.

*Lectures in the Training Schools for Kindergartens*, Boston: Heath, 1886, 226pp.

*A Last Evening with Allston and other Papers*, Boston: Lothrop, 1886, 350pp.

### POWDERMAKER, HORTENSE

She was born on December 24, 1901, in Philadelphia; she received her BA from Goucher College, 1920, and her PhD in anthropology from the University of London, 1928; she was a specialist for the Australian government, 1928-30, and a research assistant at Yale University, 1930-2, 1934-8; she worked on a Social Science Research Council grant in Mississippi, 1932-4; she has been professor of cultural anthropology at Queens College, Flushing, N.Y., since 1938; she was president of the American Ethnological Society in 1946, she was visiting professor at Yale, 1943-4, UCLA, 1946-7, and Columbia, 1958-9; she was research associate at the William Alanson White Institute of Psychiatry, 1947-54, and in 1954-5 she was a Guggenheim research fellow in Africa.

*Physical Education Play Activities for Girls in Junior and Senior High Schools,* N.Y.: A. S. Barnes, 1938, 369pp.
*After Freedom: a Cultural Study in the Deep South,* N.Y.: Viking, 1939, 408pp.
*Visual Aids for Teaching Sports,* N.Y.: A. S. Barnes, 1940, 28pp.
*Hollywood: the Dream Factory,* Little, Brown: Boston, 1950, 342pp. (London: Secker & Warburg, 1951).

PRESSEY, SIDNEY LEAVITT

He was born on December 28, 1888, in Brooklyn, New York; he received his AB from Williams College, 1912, and his graduate degrees from Harvard: AM, 1915, PhD in psychology, 1917; he was instructor of psychology at Indiana University, 1917-21; from 1921 to 1959 he instructed in the field of educational psychology at Ohio State University, where he was appointed full professor in 1929; he was visiting professor of educational psychology at UCLA, 1959-60.

*Introduction to the Use of Standard Tests* (with Luella Cole Pressey) Yonkers-on-Hudson, N.Y.: World Book Co., 1922, 263pp. (2nd ed., 1926, 3rd ed., 1931).
*Mental Abnormality and Deficiency* (with Luella Cole Pressey), N.Y.: Macmillan, 1926, 356pp.
*Research Adventures in University Teaching,* et al, Bloomington, Illinois: Public School Publishing Co., 1927, 152pp.
*Psychology and the New Education,* N.Y.: Harper, 1933, 594pp.
*A Casebook of Research in Educational Psychology* (with J. E. Janney), N.Y.: Harper, 1937, 432pp.
*Life: a Psychological Survey,* et al, N.Y.: Harper, 1939, 654pp.

PRUETTE, LORINE LIVINGSTON

She was born on November 3, 1896, in Millersburg, Tennessee; she received her BS from Chattanooga, 1918, her MA from Clark, 1920, and her PhD from Columbia, 1924; from 1924 to 1926, she was research psychologist for Macy Department stores, and from 1926 to 1927, she was research associate in psychology at the New York University graduate school; from 1927 to 1932, she was lecturer and director of research for the New York Committee on Social Attitudes; she was study director for the National Council on Women, 1932-3, and editor of personnel studies for the American Woman's Association, 1934-5; from 1936 to 1938, she was research consultant for the Progressive Education Association; from 1938 to 1943, she was an editor for the National Bureau of Economic Research, and from 1943 to 1945, she was a supervisor of radio propaganda broadcasts overseas for the Office of War Information; she has been a consulting psychologist in New York City since 1945; since 1954, she has also served on the staff of the Flower Fifth Avenue Hospital in New York City, and as research associate with the New York Medical College.

*Women and Leisure: a Study of Social Waste* (introduction by H. E. Barnes), N.Y.: Dutton, 1924, 225pp.
*G. Stanley Hall: a Biography of a Mind,* N.Y.: D. Appleton, 1926, 266pp.
*The Parent and the Happy Child,* N.Y.: Henry Holt, 1932, 290pp.
*School for Love,* Garden City, N.Y.: Doubleday, Doran, 1936, 277pp.
*Working with Words: a Survey of Vocational Opportunities for Young Writers,* N.Y.: Funk & Wagnalls, 1940, 210pp.

RIESMAN, DAVID

He was born on September 22, 1909, in Philadelphia; from Harvard he received his BA, 1931, and LL.B., 1934; he was admitted to the Massachusetts and Washington, D.C. Bars in 1935, after working a further year at Harvard as research fellow, 1934-5; from 1935 to 1937, he was law clerk to Justice Louis D. Brandeis of the United States Supreme Court; he was professor of law at the University of Buffalo, 1937-42; from 1942 to 1946, he was assistant to the treasurer of the Sperry Gyroscope Company, Lake Success, New

York; from 1946 to 1958, he was professor at the University of Chicago; since 1958, he has been Henry Ford II Professor at Harvard; he was visiting professor at Yale University, 1948-9.

*Constraint and Variety in American Education,* Garden City, N.Y.: Doubleday Anchor Books, 1958.

## ROSENSTOCK-HUESSY, EUGEN

He was born on July 6, 1888, in Berlin, Germany; he studied at the universities of Zuerich and Berlin, and from Heidelberg he received his JD, 1909, and PhD, 1923; he was an assistant instructor at Heidelberg for several years prior to joining the factulty of law at the University of Leipzig, 1912-19; he edited the newspaper of the Daimler-Benz automobile company at Stuttgart, 1919-21, and the following year he served as director of the Labor Academy at Frankfurt, a.M.; he taught psychology at the Karlsruhe Institute of Technology, 1922-23, and sociology and the history of law at the University of Breslau, 1923-33; from 1933 to 1936, he was visiting professor at Harvard; he became a naturalized American citizen and he was professor of social philosophy at Dartmouth from 1936 until his retirement in 1957; he was visiting professor of social philosophy at the University of Koeln, Germany, 1961-2.

*Out of Revolution: an Autobiography of Western Man,* N.Y.: Morrow, 1938, 795pp.

## RUGG, HAROLD ORDWAY

He was born on January 17, 1886, in Fitchburg, Massachusetts; he reluctantly agreed to leave high school in 1902, at the age of sixteen, in order to help his family by working in a mill for two years during a temporary emergency; this experience had a basic effect on his views; he completed his high school study in the summer of 1904, and then entered Dartmouth, where he received his BS in 1908, and his MS in engineering in 1909; he taught at Dartmouth prior to studying at Columbia, where he received his PhD in 1915; he was consultant for the Grand Rapids School Project, 1915-16, and an investigator for the Civil Service Commission, Washington,

D.C., 1916 to 1920; he was professor of education at Teachers College, Columbia, from 1920 to 1956; he died on May 17, 1960.

*Statistical Methods Applied to Education* (E. P. Cubberley, ed.) Boston: Houghton Mifflin, 1917, 410pp.

*The Child-Centered School: an Appraisal of the New Education* (with Ann Shumaker), Yonkers-on-Hudson, N.Y.: World Book Co., 1928, 359pp.

*Teacher's Guide for a History of American Government and Culture*, Boston: Ginn & Co., 1931.

*A History of American Government and Culture: America's March to Democracy*, Boston: Ginn & Co., 1931, 635pp. (2nd ed., 1937).

*Changing Governments and Changing Cultures: the World's March toward Democracy*, Boston: Ginn & Co., 1932, 701pp. (2nd ed., 1933; the revised 3rd ed., 1937, 752pp., carried a different subtitle: *Democracy vs. Dictatorship*).

*The Great Technology: Social Chaos and the Public Mind*, N.Y.: John Day, 1933, 308pp.

*Social Reconstruction: Study Guide for Group and Class Discussion* (with Marvin Krueger), N.Y.: John Day, 1933, 140pp.

*American Life and the School Curriculum: Next Steps toward Schools of Living*, Boston: Ginn & Co., 1936, 471pp.

*America's March toward Democracy: a History of American Life, Political and Social*, Boston: Ginn & Co., 1937, 515pp.

*Changing Civilizations in the Modern World: a Textbook in World Geography with Historical Backgrounds*, Boston: Ginn & Co., 1938, 586pp.

*Democracy and the Curriculum* (3rd Yearbook of the John Dewey Society), N.Y.: Appleton-Century, 1939.

*That Men May Understand: an American in the Long Armistice*, N.Y.: Doubleday, Doran, 1941, 355pp.

*Now is the Moment*, N.Y.: Duell, Sloan & Pearce, 1943.

*Foundations for American Education*, Yonkers-on-Hudson, N.Y.: World Book Co., 1947.

*The Teacher in School and Society: an Introduction to Education*, Yonkers-on-Hudson, N.Y.: World Book Co., 1950.

*The Teacher of Teachers: Frontiers of Theory and Practice in Teacher Education*, N.Y.: Harper, 1952.

RUSSELL, JAMES EARL

He was born on July 1, 1864, in Hamden, New York; he received his AB from Cornell in 1887; from 1887-90 he taught high school in Ithaca, N.Y., and from 1890-3 he was principal of the Cascadilla School in Ithaca; he studied at Jena University in Germany, 1893, and Leipzig, 1893-4, where he received his PhD in 1894; he continued with a year of post-doctorate study at the University of Berlin, 1894-5; during these years in Germany he was European agent for the United States Bureau of Education, and he subsequently held this position from 1904 to 1927; from 1895-7, he was professor of education at the University of Colorado; from 1897 to 1927, he was dean of Teachers College, Columbia University; after retiring as dean, he was Richard Hoe Foundation professor of education from 1927 to 1932, and from 1932 to 1940 he was a member of the New Jersey State Board of Health; he died on November 4, 1945.

*The Extension of University Teaching in England and America: a Study in Practical Pedagogics*, New York University Press, 1895, 247pp.

*German Higher Schools: the History, Organization, and Methods of Secondary Education in Germany*, N.Y.: Longmans, Green, 1899, 455pp. (2nd ed., 1907, 489pp.) .

*The Trend in American Education*, N.Y.: American Book Co., 1922, 240pp.

*Founding Teachers College*, N.Y.: Columbia University Press, 1937, 106pp.


SHELDON, EDWARD AUSTIN

He was born on October 4, 1823, on a farm near Perry Center, New York; he attended the Perry Center Academy and Hamilton College, 1844-7; a temporary illness discouraged him from continuing toward a degree; he was partner in a landscape nursery enterprise at Oswego, New York in 1847 until the business failed; he founded the Orphan and Free School Association of Oswego, New York, on November 28, 1848; he married Frances Stiles, the daughter of the famous Congregationalist minister, Ezra Stiles, on May 16, 1849; he resigned from the School Association and founded a private school; he was an active lobbyist for a public education law in New York; the law was passed in 1853, and he served as superintendent of public schools at Syracuse, N.Y., 1853-60; he became president of the New York State Teachers' Association and editor of the *New York Teacher* in 1860; from 1862 until his death in 1897 he was principal of the first municipal teacher training school in the United States, at Oswego, N.Y.

*A Manual of Elementary Instruction . . . Containing a Graduated Course of Object Lessons,* N.Y.: Scribner, Armstrong, 1862, 465pp. (revised ed., 1873, 471pp.).

*The Teacher's Manual of Instruction in Reading* (with E. H. Barlow) N.Y.: Scribner, Armstrong, 1875, 159pp.

*Autobiography of Edward Austin Sheldon,* N.Y.: Ives-Butler, 1911, 252pp.

## SIGERIST, HENRY ERNEST

He was born on April 7, 1891, in Paris, France; he studied at the Zuerich Gymnasium, 1904-10, University of London, 1911-12, University of Munich, 1914-15, and the University of Zuerich, 1912-13, 1915-17; he received his MD at Zuerich in 1917; following several years of private practice, he was lecturer in the history of medicine at the universities of Zuerich, 1921-5, and Leipzig, 1925-31; he emigrated to the United States in 1931; from 1932 to 1947, he was director of the Institute for the History of Medicine, Johns Hopkins University; from 1947 to 1956, he was research associate in medicine at Yale University; he edited the *Bulletin of the History of Medicine,* 1933-1947, and the *American Review of Soviet Medicine,* 1943-8; he died at Zuerich on March 17, 1957.

*The Great Doctors: a Biographical History of Medicine,* N.Y.: W. W. Norton, 1933, 436pp. (1st ed., Munich, 1932; trans by Eden and Cedar Paul).

*Socialized Medicine in the Soviet Union,* N.Y.: W. W. Norton, 1937, 378pp.

*The University at the Crossroads: Addresses and Essays,* N.Y.: Henry Schuman, 1946.

## SWETT, JOHN

He was born on July 31, 1830, on a farm near Pittsfield, New Hampshire; after a rudimentary education, he began his own career as a teacher at Buckstreet, New Hampshire, 1847-8, and West Randolph, Massachusetts, 1849-50; he sailed from Boston to San Francisco, via Cape Horn, 1852-3, following a protracted illness; he tried his hand at mining and ranching prior to his return to teaching; he taught at the Rincon School in San Francisco, 1853-62; in the latter year, he married Mary Tracy, the daughter of Frederick Tracy, a San Francisco judge; a few months later, he campaigned successfully for the elective post of California state school superintendent, 1862-8; in this capacity he left a lasting imprint on the California school system; from 1868-95, he was active in the San Francisco schools and he served a term as San Francisco city school superintendent; he retired to his farm at Martinez, Calif., in 1895; he was a close friend of Henry George; he died on August 22, 1913.

*The History of the Public School System of California,* San Francisco: Bancroft, 1876, 246pp.

*Methods of Teaching,* N.Y.: Harper, 1880, 326pp. (2nd ed., American Book Company, 1880).

*American Public Schools, History and Pedagogics,* N.Y.: American Book Company, 1900, 320pp.

*The Elementary Schools of California,* San Francisco: Department of Education, 1904, 16pp.

*Public Education in California . . . with Personal Reminiscences,* N.Y.: American Book Company, 1911, 320pp.

## TENENBAUM, SAMUEL

Clinical psychologist and educator; the success of his biography of Kilpatrick in 1951 has prompted him to devote his full time to teaching and writing in the field of American education; his biography was an uncompromising defense of Kilpatrick's progressive education ideas.

He was born on January 12, 1902, in New York City; he received his BS from the University of Missouri, 1924, his MA from Columbia, 1927, and his PhD from New York University in 1939; his work from 1927 to 1959 was mainly in clinical psychology at the Lafargue Clinic in New York City and the Adler Institute of Individual Psychology; he was visiting professor of education at Brooklyn College, 1947-8; he has been associate professor of education at Yeshiva University in New York City since 1959.

*William Heard Kilpatrick, Trail Blazer in Education,* N.Y.: Harper, 1951.

### THORNDIKE, EDWARD LEE

Pragmatist educator; he was considered conservative by some colleagues, but he never disagreed with Dewey on major issues; he subscribed to the idea originally held by Herbert of Cherbury that controversy could be eliminated by so-called objective science.

He was born on August 31, 1874, in Williamsburg, Massachusetts· he received his AB from Wesleyan University, 1895, his MA fron Harvard, 1897, and his PhD from Columbia, 1898; he was instructor of education at Western Reserve University, 1898-9; from 1899 tι 1941, he was professor of educational psychology at Teachers College, Columbia; he was William James lecturer at Harvard, 1942-3; he died on August 9, 1949.

*Educational Psychology,* N.Y.: Lencke & Buechner, 1903, 177pp. (2nd ed., revised, 1910, 248pp.; 3rd ed., revised, 3 vol., 1913-14: vol. 1: *The Original Nature of Man,* vol. 2: *The Psychology of Learning,* vol. 3: *Mental Work and Fatigue;* 4th ed., 1921).

*Aᵣ Introduction to the Theory of Mental and Social Measurements,* N.Y.: Science Press, 1904, 212pp.

*The Principles of Teaching, Based on Psychology,* N.Y.: Seiler, 1906, 293pp.

*Individuality,* Boston: Houghton Mifflin, 1911, 55pp.

*Animal Intelligence: Experimental Studies,* N.Y.: Macmillan, 1911, 297pp.

*Education: a First Book,* N.Y.: Macmillan, 1912, 292pp.

*Ventilation in Relation to Mental Work,* et al, N.Y.: Teachers College, 1916, 83pp.

*The Measurement of Intelligence,* N.Y.: Teachers College, 1925, 613pp.

*Adult Learning,* et al, N.Y.: Macmillan, 1928, 335pp.

*Elementary Principles of Education* (with A. I. Gates), N.Y.: Macmillan, 1929, 335pp.

*An Experimental Study of Rewards*, N.Y.: Teachers College, 1933, 72pp.

*The Psychology of Wants, Interests and Attitudes*, N.Y.: Appleton-Century, 1935, 301pp.

*Adult Interests*, et al, N.Y.: Macmillan, 1935, 265pp.

*The Teaching of Controversial Subjects* (Inglis lecture, 1937), Cambridge, Mass: Harvard University Press, 1937, 39pp.

*Your City*, N.Y.: Harcourt, Brace, 1939, 204pp.

*Human Nature and the Social Order*, N.Y.: Macmillan, 1940, 1019pp.


## Van Dusen, Henry Pitney

He was born on December 11, 1897, in Philadelphia; he received his AB from Princeton, 1919, his BD from Union Theological Seminary, 1924, and his PhD, Edinburgh University, 1932; he became an ordained Presbyterian minister in 1924, and he joined the faculty of Union Theological Seminary in 1926; he was dean of students, 1931-9, full professor since 1936, and president of Union Theological Seminary and Auburn Theological Seminary since 1945; he is editor of the *Ecumenical Review*, director, *Fund for the Republic*, trustee, Rockefeller Foundation, and a member of the Board of Foreign Missions, United Presbyterian Church.

*In Quest of Life's Meaning: Hints toward a Christian Philosophy of Life for Students*, N.Y.: Association Press, 1926, 140pp.

*God in these Times*, N.Y.: Scribner's, 1935, 194pp.

*God in Education*, N.Y.: Scribner's, 1951.


## Van Til, Cornelius

Philosopher, Christian apologist. Born on May 3, 1895 in the Netherlands, coming to U.S. in 1905. Graduate, Calvin College, Princeton Seminary, Princeton University (Ph.D., 1927). Taught at Princeton Seminary, resigned in dissent at Seminary reorganization. Joined faculty of Westminster Seminary. Author of numerous works: *The New Modernism, Common Grace, The Defense of the Faith,*

*Christianity and Barthianism,* etc. Author of various articles on education, including widely circulated pamphlet, reprinted from a symposium, on *The Dilemma of Education.*

### WASHBURNE, CARLETON WOLSEY

He was born on December 2, 1889, in Chicago, Illinois; he received his AB at Stanford, 1913, and he taught in the Frederic Burk school, San Francisco, 1914-19; he married Heluiz Chandler in 1912; she became a feature writer for the Chicago *Daily News* after he obtained control of the Winnetka public schools and began his experimental progressive school program in 1919; he visited Russia in 1925 and 1927, where he approved of what he called the comparable Soviet experiment in progressive education.

*New Schools in the Old World* (with Myron M. Stearns), N.Y.: John Day, 1926, 174pp.
*Results of Practical Experiments in Fitting Schools to Individuals: a Survey of the Winnetka Public Schools* (with Mabel Vogel and William S. Gray), Bloomington, Illinois: Public School Publishing Co., 1926, 135pp.
*What Children Like to Read: the Winnetka Graded Book List* (with Mabel Vogel), N.Y.: Rand McNally, 1926, 286pp.
*Better Schools: a Survey of Progressive Education in American Public Schools* (with Myron M. Stearns), N.Y.: John Day, 1928, 342pp.
*Adjusting the School to the Child: Practical First Steps,* Yonkers-on-Hudson, N.Y.: World Book Co., 1932, 189pp.
*Remakers of Mankind,* N.Y.: John Day, 1932, 339pp.
*A Living Philosophy of Education,* N.Y.: John Day, 1940, 585pp.
*The World's Good: Education for World-Mindedness,* N.Y.: John Day, 1954.

### WATSON, JOHN BROADUS

He was born on January 9, 1878, in Greenville, South Carolina; he received his AM from Furman University in 1900; he was a graduate student at the University of Chicago from 1900 to 1903, where he studied under Dewey; he received his PhD in psychology from the University of Chicago in 1903; he was a research associate and instructor in psychology at the University of Chicago, 1903-8; he was professor of psychology at Johns Hopkins University, 1908-1920; from 1908 to 1915, he was editor of *Psychology Review*, and from 1915 to 1927, he was editor of the *Journal of Experimental Psychology;* he was appointed vice president of J. Walter Thompson Co., 1924, and vice president of William Estly & Co., 1936; he died in 1958.

*Animal Education,* Chicago: University of Chicago Press, 1903, 122pp.

*Behavior: an Introduction to Comparative Psychology,* N.Y.: Henry Holt, 1914, 439pp.

*Suggestions of Modern Science Concerning Education,* et al, N.Y.: Macmillan, 1917.

*Psychology from the Standpoint of a Behaviorist,* Philadelphia: Lippincott, 1919, 429pp. (revised ed., 1924, 448pp.).

*Behaviorism,* N.Y.: The People's Institute, 1924, 251pp. (2nd ed., Norton, 1925; 3rd ed., revised, Norton, 1930, 308pp.).

*The Ways of Behaviorism,* N.Y.: Harper, 1928, 144pp.

# Index

Prepared by Vernelia A. Crawford

*Note:* This index includes titles of chapters listed under the appropriate subject classification. With the exception of these specific page references, which are hyphenated, the numbers in each instance refer to the *first* page of a discussion. A page number followed by a letter (n) in parentheses indicates the number of a footnote reference.